GCSE

MATHEMATICS

Robert Powell

BPP Letts Educational Ltd

First published 1993 by BPP (Letts Educational) Ltd
Aldine House, Aldine Place, London W12 8AW

Reprinted 1994

Editorial team: Emma Touffler, Wayne Davies

Text: © 1993 Robert Powell

Illustrations: Barbara Linton, John Heseltine

Typesetting: Philippa Jarvis, James Stewart, Carla Mans

Design and illustrations © BPP (Letts Educational) Ltd

British Library Cataloguing-in-Publication Data
Powell, Robert
    Maths. – (GCSE/Key Stage 4 Study Guides)
    I. Title II. Series
    510.76

ISBN 1 85758 236 5

Printed and bound in Great Britain by Ashford Colour Press

Acknowledgements
I would like to thank the following people for their help and support in producing this book.
Annette Duckworth and John Sharples for all their help and advice, and John Ingles for his help and advice on the Scottish aspects of this book. I would also like to thank all my colleagues for their support and advice and Linda, without whom this work would never have been finished.
    I am also grateful to the following Examining Groups for permission to use the specimen questions included in this book:
Northern Examinations and Assessment Board (NEAB), Midland Examining Group (MEG), Southern Examining Group (SEG), The University of London Examinations and Assessment Council (ULEAC), Welsh Joint Education Committee (WJEC), Northern Ireland Schools Examinations and Assessment Council (NISEAC), Scottish Examinations Board (SEB). The answers provided are the author's alone, and the Examining Groups can accept no responsibility for them.
    I would also like to thank Ford UK and The National Statistical Office for permission to use extracts from their publications and the controller of Her Majesty's Stationery Office for permission to use extracts from the National Curriculum.

R G Powell, 1993
Head of Mathematics, Burton Borough School, Shropshire

Contents

Contents

Mathematics in the National Curriculum

The National Curriculum deals with the period of compulsory education from age 5 to 16 in four Key Stages At the end of each Key Stage (i.e. at ages 7, 11, 14 and 16) attainments in specified subjects are tested. At the end of Key Stage 4 (KS4), assessment is made through the GCSE.

Attainment Targets

The knowledge, understanding and skills which you are expected to have acquired at the end of each Key Stage are identified under broad areas of study known as Attainment Targets (ATs). In Mathematics there are five ATs:

AT1   Using and Applying Mathematics
AT2   Number
AT3   Algebra
AT4   Shape and Space
AT5   Handling Data

Each of these areas is of equal importance and is divided into 10 levels, Level 1 being the lowest and Level 10 the highest. At Key Stage 4 a pupil should be working between Levels 4 and 10, depending on his or her ability.

A Programme of Study common to every pupil in the country is provided within the National Curriculum and, although teaching methods may differ from school to school, each has an obligation to ensure that the Programme of Study appropriate to each pupil's needs is provided. The Programme of Study forms the basis of this book.

In Northern Ireland the introduction of the National Curriculum is one year later than in England and Wales. There are also some small differences between the curriculums. A sixth Attainment Target, Measure, is included as a separate strand in the Irish National Curriculum. Scotland, too, has its own National Curriculum. Most of the topics covered by this book are being taught in Scottish schools and will be examined at Standard Grade.

GCSE/Key Stage 4

The grades given in your GCSE in Mathematics will reflect the level of the National Curriculum you have achieved.

The relationship between National Curriculum levels and GCSE grades is shown below:

GCSE Grade	NC Level
A★	10
A	9
B	8
C	
	7
D	
	6
E	
F	5
G	4

About this book

This book contains all the Mathematics topics you will need while you work through Key Stage 4 and towards GCSE assessment at age 16. It provides topic-by-topic coverage of the Programme of Study on which your Mathematics syllabus is based. Throughout the book there are worked examples and questions to help you to practise what you have learned.

Letts Check

Before you attempt Key Stage 4 Mathematics, it is a good idea to recap what you have learned at Key Stage 3. The mathematics in the Letts Check section reflects the standard you should have reached before you begin Key Stage 4.

Here you will find questions graded according to Levels 3 to 5 of the Attainment Targets. You should be able to answer the questions here before you begin working through the main text of this book. If you have difficulty with them, it may be a good idea to work through a Key Stage 3 Mathematics text book.

The main text

This book is divided into five main sections which reflect the five Attainment Targets for Mathematics. The first deals with coursework and the remaining four cover Number, Algebra, Shape and Space, and Handling Data.

Coursework

Section 1 offers you guidance on compiling, completing and presenting your coursework. It covers the ways in which mathematics is used and applied. Before you start any coursework, remember to consult your teacher, the expert on the best way to achieve the highest possible grade for any coursework you have to do.

A guide to the coursework requirements for each of the GCSE and SCE examinations is given in the breakdown of examination courses, but you should also check your syllabus.

Sections 2 to 5

Your final examinations will assess your ability in each of these areas: Number, Algebra, Shape and Space, and Handling Data. Sections 2 to 5 cover each of these in turn.

Before you begin to revise for your written papers you should try to find out from your teacher which level of GCSE examination you are likely to be entered for. This is important because not all candidates have to work up to Level 10. Once you have done this, you will be able to find out from the examination breakdown which level you shoud be working to.

In this book, each area is developed from Level 6 to Level 10. At each level the concepts are explained, followed by questions to enable you to practise these skills and ensure that you understand each idea. Check that you have the correct answers before you continue. It is almost impossible to revise mathematics successfully without working through questions, either from this book or from your school text book. The first questions in each section are specific to one idea but by the end you will find that the questions contain a mixture of ideas.

If you have difficulty with an idea, go back through the notes and, if you are still having problems, ask your teacher to explain the idea to you again. Most importantly, don't ignore problem areas because later work may depend on your understanding of this idea.

Once you have completed a level in one of the sections, there are two different ways in which you could work.

❶ You could continue through the same section, working with similar concepts but at higher levels. The advantage of this method is that you are developing ideas which are fresh in your mind. The disadvantage is that if you do not allow yourself sufficient time to revise you may run out of time to revise the later sections thoroughly.

❷ You could go to work at the same level in the next section of the book. The advantages of this method are that you ensure that you cover the whole examination syllabus equally and that you allow yourself time between studying the same concept at higher levels to digest the ideas you have worked on. The disadvantage is that you will have to move around the book. If you do this, make sure you keep a record of the work you have revised.

Whichever way you choose to work, the book contains Hints, Notes and Remember points which will help you when you come to revise.

You will require a calculator for your final examination and for your revision, but remember to show your working out.

Examination questions

The section containing examination questions will familiarise you with the different types of question you will face in the exam. By the time you come to revise, you will already have successfully completed many questions that could have been set on GCSE or SCE papers. The questions in this section assess concepts from the higher levels of study, so don't be worried if you find them difficult – they are!

Hints for revision

At school, your time is planned and organised for you by your teachers. Your homework and coursework have to be done because there are deadlines for completing it. Revising is different: it has to be planned by you, and only you can decide when you have done enough. Remember that it is better to revise than to resit. Remember also that you have to revise for all your subjects. Split your revision time into sessions and allocate enough study time for each subject. Be honest with yourself about what you can achieve in each session, and remember to take breaks from studying so that you don't become over-tired or frustrated.

By allowing yourself a long period of revision, you will improve your chances of achieving a good grade. It is not a good idea to try to cram all your revision into a short period.

Get into the habit of doing some mathematics every day, even if you have exams in other subjects before you take your maths exams.

When you revise, find a quiet room where you won't be disturbed by people, pets, television or music. Study at a desk or table where you have everything you need. The best way of revising mathematics is to practise. Choose a question and attempt it. If you get stuck, refer back to the section which covers the relevant topic, then attempt the question again.

Syllabus tables and paper analysis

There are a number of different examinations available in Mathematics and they are all slightly different. Before you begin to use this study aid you **must** find out from your teacher which examination syllabus you are following.

This is a list of the syllabuses available for examination. You should be doing one of these:

Title	Syllabus code	Examining Group
Mathematics (Options A, B, C1 and C2)	1384	ULEAC
Mathematics (Kent Mathematics project)	1396	ULEAC
Mathematics (without coursework)	1660	MEG
Mathematics (with coursework)	1661	MEG
Mathematics (SMP 11–16)	1663	MEG and ULEAC
Mathematics (MEI)	1665	MEG
Mathematics (SMP graduated assessment)	1666	MEG
Mathematics (National Curriculum syllabus) (Note: There are 5 different versions within this syllabus)	NC 94/51	SEG
Mathematics (with coursework)	Syllabus A	NEAB
Mathematics (without coursework)	Syllabus B	NEAB
Mathematics (modular)	Syllabus C	NEAB
Mathematics (with coursework)	Syllabus A	WJEC
Mathematics (without coursework)	Syllabus B	WJEC
Mathematics		City and Guilds
Mathematics (without coursework)	0580	IGCSE
Mathematics (with coursework)	0581	IGCSE

The next pages give you a guide to what you can expect in each of these examinations. For more details you should ask your teacher for a syllabus or write directly to the appropriate examination group. You need only read the syllabus details for the course you are following.

ULEAC (Options A, B, C1 and C2)

Option A

Attainment Target 1 will be assessed by coursework worth 20% of your marks. Your teacher will determine your level of entry at one of three tiers for the examinations at the end of the course which carry 80% of the marks and assess ATs 2–5.

Tier	Paper	Time	%
Foundation	Paper 1	$1\frac{1}{2}$ hrs	40
	Paper 2	$1\frac{1}{2}$ hrs	40
Intermediate	Paper 3	$1\frac{3}{4}$ hrs	40
	Paper 4	$1\frac{3}{4}$ hrs	40
Highest	Paper 5	2 hrs	40
	Paper 6	2 hrs	40

Coursework activities will be provided to your school by the examination council. These activities will include practical, problem-solving, investigational and computing work. At least one of these must be an extended piece of work. The activities provided will cover Number, Algebra, Shape and Space, and Data Handling.

Option B

In this option the final examination papers are the same as in Option A. It has coursework tasks, provided by your school or centre. The difference appears in the assessment of AT1 (Using and Applying Mathematics), which will be assessed by two final coursework tasks based upon six activities provided by the council. These tasks will be done in your classroom in supervised conditions and marked by your teacher using performance indicators. They will take 2–3 hours each.

Option C1

This option has the same examination structure as Options A and B. The difference in this option is that AT 1 will be assessed by externally set and marked tasks. Your school or centre will be provided with a bank of activities and a set of level-specific criteria called performance indicators. These should help you prepare for your terminal tasks or extension papers. There will be no choice of task. There will be a terminal examination worth 80% of your final marks, and terminal tasks worth the remaining 20%.

Option C2

This is similar to Option C1 but the terminal examination carries 100% of the final marks.

ULEAC
(Kent Mathematics project)

This syllabus has a terminal examination which is made up of two papers. Your entry tier will be determined by your teacher. The papers carry 80% of the marks.

Tier	Papers	Allowable Grades	Time (hours)
Foundation	1, 2	3–6	1 hr
Intermediate	3, 4	4–8	$1\frac{1}{2}$ hrs
Higher	5, 6	6–10	2 hrs

During your course your teacher will have assessed your ability to carry out practical and investigational work, discuss mathematics, carry out mental calculations and undertake short or long tasks. This will probably be done using your normal class and homework. This work will have been collected as evidence of your achievement. You should check with your teacher that you have done all these things. The coursework carries 20% of the final marks. All five attainment targets carry the same marks.

MEG (without coursework)

This examination consists only of terminal papers. You will be entered at one of the tiers by your teacher. The levels given below in brackets indicate higher and lower levels available in exceptional circumstances.

Tier	Paper	Target NC Levels	Time	% of mark
Basic	1	4–6	2 hrs	50%
	4	4–6 (3–7)	2 hrs	50%
Central	2	7–8	$2\frac{1}{2}$ hrs	50%
	5	7–8 (5–9)	$2\frac{1}{2}$ hrs	50%
Further	3	9–10	$2\frac{1}{2}$ hrs	50%
	6	(7–10)	$2\frac{1}{2}$ hrs	50%

The first paper at each tier will consist of short and longer answers. The second paper will consist of structured questions and extended-answer questions.

MEG (with coursework)

This examination consists of two terminal papers worth 80% of the final marks and coursework worth 20%. You will be entered for papers at one of three tiers. The levels given below in brackets indicate higher and lower levels available in exceptional circumstances.

Tier	Paper	Target NC Levels	Time	% of mark
Basic	1	4–6	1 hr 35 mins	40%
	4	4–6 (3–7)	1 hr 35 mins	40%
Central	2	7–8	2 hrs	40%
	5	7–8 (5–9)	2 hrs	40%
Further	3	9–10	2 hrs	40%
	6	(7–10)	2 hrs	40%

The first paper at each tier consists of short and longer answers. The second paper consists of structured questions and extended-answer questions.

Each of the five attainment targets in mathematics carry 20% of the final marks.

Coursework

You must submit two extended tasks which should each have taken you the equivalent of two or three weeks' work.

One of the tasks must be an investigation and the other a piece of practical work and each should reflect the Programme of Study for Attainment Target 1 (Using and Applying Mathematics). Your work will be assessed by your teacher and then externally checked.

MEG and ULEAC (SMP 11–16)

Entry is at one of five tiers. These are called Green (the lowest), Blue, Red, Yellow and Yellow Extension (the highest). Each tier sets two papers which assess Attainment Targets 2 to 5. Each of the examination papers carries 40% of the final marks (10% for each AT). You will have to submit coursework which is worth a maximum of 20% of the final mark.

The papers consist of:

Tier assessed	Paper	Time	Target NC Levels	NC Levels assessed
Green	Paper 1	$1\frac{1}{2}$ hrs	4–5	3–5
	Paper 2	$1\frac{1}{2}$ hrs + 20 min oral		
Blue	Paper 2	$1\frac{1}{2}$ hrs + 20 min oral	5–6	4–6
	Paper 3	$1\frac{1}{2}$ hrs		
Red	Paper 3	$1\frac{1}{2}$ hrs	6–7	5–7
	Paper 4	$1\frac{1}{2}$ h + 20 min oral		
Yellow	Paper 4	$1\frac{1}{2}$ h + 20 min oral	7–8	6–9
	Paper 5	2 hrs		
Yellow Extension	Paper 5	2 hrs	8–10	7–10
	Paper 6	$2\frac{1}{2}$ hrs		

You must attempt all the questions in each of the papers you do. Papers 2 and 4 have a 20 minute oral before you start, so be on time!

AT 1 will be assessed by coursework. This is marked against a set of attributes or process strands. The coursework for this examination is made up of:

- A piece of Practical Mathematics which should take up two weeks of lessons and homework.
- An investigation which should take up two weeks of lessons and homework. For students being examined at the Green or Blue level, a portfolio demonstrating investigative approaches to your work, containing at least 4 pieces of work, is required.

MEG (MEI syllabus)
Mathematics in Education and Industry

This is a modular scheme allowing your performance to be assessed before the end of Key Stage 4.

The assessment is made up of:

Either   Coursework + three examination papers, each $1\frac{1}{4}$ hours long (two papers for Levels 4 and 5);

Or   Problem-solving papers (Levels 8, 9 and 10 only).

The examination papers consists of:

Tier	NC Levels assesssed	Papers
A	3–5	4, 5
B	3–6	4, 5, 6
C	4–7	5, 6, 7
D	5–8	6, 7, 8
E	6–9	7, 8, 9
F	7–10	8, 9, 10

For tiers A–E you also have to do coursework, worth 20% of the final marks. For tier F you can sit a problem-solving paper (Paper 11).

Coursework

This consists of (a) a school task for each level entered, and
                        (b) two extended tasks.

Each school task set by the examination group is level-specific and provides 50% of the assessment at this level.

Level	
4	Shape and Space
5	Mental Calculations (no calculators permitted)
6	Number
7	Mental Calculations (no calculators permitted)
8	Data Handling
9	Data Handling
10	Data Handling

Extended tasks are worth 15% of the total assessment at each level (each should take about two weeks to complete). Between them, the tasks must cover practical work and investigations. Suitable tasks are outlined in Section 1 on coursework.

MEG (SMP 11–16 graduated assessment)

This assessment has three main components.

1 Staged assessments which carry 30% of the final marks. These take place as follows:

- March of Year 10   Stages 1 and 2 Green, Blue and Red Tiers or Stages 2 and 3 for the Yellow Tier;
- November of Year 10   Stages 2 and 3 for Green, Blue and Red Tiers or Stages 2 and 4 for the Yellow Tier;
- May of Year 11   Stages 3 and 4 for Green, Blue and Red Tiers or Stages 4 and 5 for the Yellow Tier.

2 Open-ended coursework (20% of the final marks).

3 Terminal papers (50% of the final marks).

On this course there are five entry tiers:

Tier	Assessment	Attainment Targets	Time	% of final marks
Green	Recaps at four stages and four aural tests. One extended investigation or portfolio of work and one extended practical task. Exam.	2–5	$1\frac{3}{4}$ hrs	50%
Blue	Recaps at four stages and three aural tests. One extended investigation or portfolio of work and one extended practical task. Exam.	2–5	2 hrs	50%
Red	Recaps at four stages and three aural tests. One extended investigation and one extended practical task. Exam.	2–5	2 hrs	50%
Yellow	Recaps at six stages and two aural tests. One extended investigation and one extended practical. Exam.	2–5	2 hrs	50%
Yellow Extension	As for Yellow Tier			

NEAB Syllabus A (with coursework)

This consists of a terminal examination of Attainment Targets 2–5, carrying 80% of the final marks.

Coursework covers AT1 (Using and Applying Mathematics) and carries the remaining 20% of the final marks.

You will be entered for one of three options, according to your ability. The levels given below in brackets indicate higher and lower levels available in exceptional circumstances.

Option	Target Levels	Papers	Time
P	4–6	Paper P1	$1\frac{1}{2}$ hrs
	(3-7)	Paper P2	$1\frac{1}{2}$ hrs
Q	5–8	Paper Q1	2 hrs
	(4-9)	Paper Q2	2 hrs
R	7–10	Paper R1	$2\frac{1}{4}$ hrs
	(6-10)	Paper R2	$2\frac{1}{4}$ hrs

Coursework

Your coursework will be set by your school. You will be expected to achieve a level from 1–10 in each of the three areas of Attainment Target 1 (Application, Mathematical Communications and Reasoning, Logic and Proof). During your course you are expected to build a portfolio containing a minimum of four completed pieces of work to provide evidence of your achievement. The level of the tasks undertaken will be dictated by your teacher.

NEAB Syllabus B (without coursework)

This syllabus is assessed with terminal papers covering all the Attainment Targets (there is no coursework).

You will be entered for one of the following options:

Option	Target NC Levels	Papers	Time	ATs examined
P	4–6	P1	$1\frac{1}{2}$ hrs	2–5
		P2	$1\frac{1}{2}$ hrs	2–5
		P3	1 hr	1
Q	5–8	Q1	2 hrs	2–5
		Q2	2 hrs	2–5
		Q3	$1\frac{1}{2}$ hrs	1
R	7–10	R1	$2\frac{1}{4}$ hrs	2–5
		R2	$2\frac{1}{4}$ hrs	2–5
		R3	$1\frac{1}{2}$ hrs	1

NEAB Syllabus C (modular)

This is a modular scheme of assessment which is made up of:
- One terminal paper worth a maximum of 50% of the final marks;
- Two module papers worth a maximum of 30% of the final marks;
- Coursework worth 20% of the final marks.

The terminal paper will be one of these three:

Paper	Target NC Levels	Time	ATs Examined
P	4–6	$1\frac{1}{2}$ hrs	2–5
Q	5–8	2 hrs	2–5
R	7–10	$2\frac{1}{4}$ hrs	2–5

The two modules which you will have to do are taken from this list:

	Time	Month assessed
Design: Shape and Space	1 hr	January
Patterns and Functions	1 hr	January
Planning Number	1 hr	April
Decision Making/Data Handling	1 hr	April

SEG

There are five versions of assessment within this syllabus. If you are following this syllabus you need to check with your teacher which version you are following.

I A traditional approach to the written papers and coursework designed and marked by your school.

II A traditional approach to the written papers and coursework designed by your school but marked by the examination group.

III A set of papers with coursework marked by your school.

IV A set of papers based on appropriate themes following the Enterprising Mathematics course, with coursework set and worked by your school.

V A traditional set of papers with an externally assessed written paper to assess AT1.

Your entry into an of these examination versions will be at one of the following tiers:

Tiers	Target NC Levels	Allowed levels	Papers	Time	% of marks
F (Foundation)	4–6	3–7	1	1 hr	35%
			2	1 hr	35%
			7	Coursework	20%
			8	Aural test (20 mins)	10%
I (Intermediate)	5–8	4–9	3	$1\frac{1}{2}$ hrs	35%
			4	$1\frac{1}{2}$ hrs	35%
			7	Coursework	20%
			9	Aural test (20 mins)	10%
H (Higher)	7–10	6	5	2 hrs	35%
			6	2 hrs	35%
			7	Coursework	20%
			10	Aural test (20 mins)	10%

An aural test will be set by the examination group to reflect the standard of each tier for whichever version of assessment you are following.

Each of the examination papers will have short questions and longer questions requiring specific and open answers. You must answer all the questions.

WJEC Syllabus A (with coursework)

This course consists of two terminal examination papers, worth 80% of your final marks, assessing Attainment Targets 2 to 5, and coursework worth 20% which assesses Attainment Target 1.

You will be entered for one of three tiers:

Tier	Target Levels	Papers	Assessing ATs	Time
A	7–10	1	AT 2 (Number), AT3 (Algebra)	$2\frac{1}{2}$ hrs
		2	AT 4 (Shape), AT5 (Handling Data)	$2\frac{1}{2}$ hrs
B	5–8	1	AT 2 (Number), AT3 (Algebra)	2 hrs
		2	AT 4 (Shape), AT5 (Handling Data)	2 hrs
C	4–6	1	AT 2 (Number), AT3 (Algebra)	$1\frac{1}{2}$ hrs
		2	AT 4 (Shape), AT5 (Handling Data)	$1\frac{1}{2}$ hrs

Coursework

Your school will be provided with a bank of short and long tasks, by the examination group.

Your coursework will consist of two short tasks each worth a maximum of 11 marks, and one long task worth 22 marks. There are a further six marks available for a continuous assessment of your work.

Short tasks	These will be done in school under supervision and for one of these you will not be allowed to use a calculator.
Long tasks	These have two parts. In the first you have to do some of your work outside school. The second part will be a piece of structured assessment related to the work done over the past two weeks, and has to be done in one hour under supervision.

Tasks in tiers A and B are targeted at Levels 5 and 6, or 7 and 8, or 9 and 10, and in Tier C at Level 4 or Levels 5 and 6.

Continuous Assessment	The marks for this are given for oral and written communication.

WJEC Syllabus B (without coursework)

In this course there is no coursework. You will be entered for one of three tiers and sit three examination papers.

Tier	Target NC Levels	Papers	Assessing ATs	Time
A	7–10	1	AT 2 (Number), AT3 (Algebra)	$2\frac{1}{2}$ hrs
		2	AT 4 (Shape), AT5 (Handling Data)	$2\frac{1}{2}$ hrs
		3	AT 1 (Using and Applying Mathematics)	2 hrs
B	5–8	1	AT 2 (Number) AT3 (Algebra)	2 hrs
		2	AT 4 (Shape), AT5 (Handling Data)	2 hrs
		3	AT 1 (Using and Applying Mathematics)	2 hrs
C	4–6	1	AT 2 (Number) AT3 (Algebra)	$1\frac{1}{2}$ hrs
		2	AT 4 (Shape), AT5 (Handling Data)	$1\frac{1}{2}$ hrs
		3	AT 1 (Using and Applying Mathematics)	2 hrs

City and Guilds

This examination is offered at three levels:

Option P	Two written papers covering levels 4, 5, 6
Option Q	Two written papers covering levels 6, 7, 8
Option R	Two written papers covering levels 8, 9, 10

Coursework with this examination is limited to a maximum of 20% of the final mark.

International General Certificate of Secondary Education (IGCSE)

This syllabus is based on the National Curriculum for England and Wales and is designed to meet the needs of students on an international basis.

There are two options: without coursework (0580), and with coursework (0581). There are two tiers of entry in each option.

Without coursework (0580)

Tier	Target Grades	Papers	%	Time
Core	C–G	1	35%	1 hr
		3	65%	2 hrs
Extended	A–E	2	35%	$1\frac{1}{2}$ hrs
		4	65%	$2\frac{1}{2}$ hrs

With coursework (0581)

Tiers	Target Grades	Papers	%	Time
Core	C–G	1	30%	1 hr
		3	50%	2 hrs
Extended	A–E	2	30%	$1\frac{1}{2}$ hrs
		4	50%	$2\frac{1}{2}$ hrs

Coursework is worth 20% of the final marks. It comprises assignments in the areas of Statistics and/or Probability, Geometry, Investigations and the Practical Applications of Mathematics.

Standard Grade Examinations in Scotland

The National Curriculum for England and Wales does not apply in Scotland. However, the mathematics within the Standard Grade Examination in Scotland is similar to that taught to England and Wales. Where it is different, this will be pointed out for you.

In Scotland all candidates are assessed by a system common to all levels, and grades are given on a seven-point scale, one being the highest. The final certificate also records your level of attainment in each of the following units.

(i) Knowledge and Understanding

This element covers facts, skills and concepts needed to solve mathematical problems. It includes appropriate notation and use of symbols. You can think of this section as the tool kit from which you can use ideas in the other elements of your work.

(ii) Reasoning and Application

This element assesses your understanding and ability to make decisions about your work. You are encouraged to show initiative and present the best possible solutions.

(iii) Investigation

This reflects the use of important mathematical activities like the collection of data and the exploration of patterns, making conjectures and generalising a solution or mathematical model of the results.

External assessment is at two of three levels where you sit papers at either Foundation and General levels or at General and Credit levels. In some cases you may be advised by your teacher to sit only one paper.

Paper	Grades assessed	Element assessed	Time
Foundation	6, 5	Knowledge and Understanding Reasoning and Application	70 mins
General	4, 3	Knowledge and Understanding Reasoning and Application	90 mins
Credit	2, 1	Knowledge and Understanding Reasoning and Application	135 mins

Papers consist of a mixture of short and extended-response questions set in context. At Foundation level you will also have four questions read to you. These questions are not printed on the question paper. To achieve a grade you must gain approximately 55% as your final mark.

The assessment of your investigations must reflect these four activities:
1. The identification and use of real data taken from available sources or a survey.
2. The use of measuring and drawing instruments.
3. The recognition or exploration of pattern, forming conjectures, proof, and generalisation of a problem.
4. The formulation of a mathematical model.

You must write up your findings in the form of a report.

Your final grade in this section of your work will be derived from a set of three dissimilar investigations representing your best work. If you are working at Credit level, it is important that you choose investigations which extend your mathematical thinking rather than concentrating on real-life problems.

Out of 12 marks for each investigation, a possible 4 marks are given for each of the following:
1. Understanding and ordering the task
2. Carrying out the task
3. Communication

Scottish Standard Grade Mathematics

There are a number of mathematical topics within this book which you will not need for Scottish Standard Grade Mathematics.

Not needed: Sampling, probability, tree diagrams, cumulative frequency.

Pupils at all levels **should** understand bar charts, pictograms, pie charts, tabulated results, straight-line graphs, mean of ungrouped data.

Partially needed: Vectors are not included in S-Grade but are required if you decide to do Revised Highers.

You should understand the term 'congruent' but the proofs are not required.

   The examination is at three levels Foundation (F), General (G) and Credit (C). Below is a list of topics included in Standard Grade Mathematics.

❶ If you are doing Foundation Level you only need to cover the topics marked with an (F).

❷ At the General Level you will need to study everything marked (F) and (G).

❸ At Credit Level you will need to be able to do everything in the list.

NB: This is a basic list. You should always get a syllabus for your year of exam entry if you wish to be sure there are no changes to the syllabus.

Contents of S–Grade Mathematics

Number

(F) +, −, ×, ÷ whole numbers and decimals; (G) rounding to decimal places; (C) significant figures.

(F) Reading decimals on scales (hundredths only).

(F) Reading directed numbers on scales; (G) coordinates.

(G) + and − of integers (positive and negative numbers), (C) ×, ÷.

(F) Fractions; (G) +, −, × equivalence and converting fractions to decimals; (C) ÷

(F) Percentage of a quantity; (G) Expressing one quantity as a percentage of another.

(F) Know $\frac{1}{2}$ = 50% and $\frac{1}{4}$ = 25%.

(C) Simplification of square roots, e.g. $\sqrt{ab} = \sqrt{a}\sqrt{b}$, $\sqrt{\frac{a}{b}} = \frac{\sqrt{a}}{\sqrt{b}}$, $\frac{a}{\sqrt{b}} = \frac{a\sqrt{b}}{b}$

(G) Use index notation, e.g. find 2^5.

(G) Scientific notation.

(F) Ratio, e.g. 3:1 or 1:5; (G) splitting a quantity in a given ratio.

(F) Rate, e.g. miles per gallon.

(G) Time, distance, speed. Calculate one of these, given the other two.

Money

(F) Calculate simple interest for a whole year; (G) simple interest part of a year; (C) compound interest.

(F) Calculations involving money in context; (C) depreciation and appreciation.

Measure

(F) Measuring: reasonable accuracy, (G) required accuracy, (C) appropriate accuracy.

(F) Interrelation of metric units.

(F) Telling, recording and calculating time.

Scale drawing

(F) Scales expressed in words; (G) expressed in ratios.

(G) Constructing triangles given two sides and the included angle, one side and two angles, or three sides.

(F) Enlarging or reducing figures by doubling or halving.

Similarity
(F) Similarity of rectangles; (G) right-angled triangles (C) triangles.

Ratios of similar figures areas and volumes.

Coordinates and graphs
(F) Coordinates in the first quadrant; (G) all quadrants.

(G) Plotting the equations of straight lines; (C) from gradient and y intercept.

Three-dimensional shapes
(F) Recognise and name the cube, pyramid, cylinder, cuboid, cone and sphere;
(C) triangular prism.

(F) Recognise familiar shapes from their two-dimensional representation;
(C) pyramid, cylinder, triangular prism.

(F) Nets of cubes and cuboids.

Perimeter
(F) Perimeter of rectilinear figures; (G) circumference of circle; (C) length of arc.

Area and volume
(F) Calculate areas of rectangle, square, right-angled triangle and irregular figures by counting squares.

(G) Calculate areas of any triangle (given base and height), circle, kite, rhombus and shapes made up of these.

(C) Sectors of circles.

(G) Calculate surface areas of cubes, cuboids, cylinders and triangular prisms; (C) solids made up of composites of these.

(F) Calculate volumes of cubes and cuboids and other solids by counting cubes; (C) cylinders and triangular prisms.

(C) Calculate volumes of composite solids.

Angles
(F) Measure and draw angles accurately, know angle facts and angle relationships made by parallel lines.

(F) Know the angle and diagonal properties of a square and angle properties of a triangle.

(C) Know the angle properties of kite, parallelogram, rhombus, isosceles and equilateral triangles, and Pythagoras' theorem.

(G) Use Pythagoras' theorem to find right-angled triangles.

(F) Relationships between radius and diameter; (G) relationships between radius and tangent and angles in a semicircle; (C) tangents from external points and perpendicular bisectors to chords.

(F) Use the above to calculate angles and lengths of figures.

Symmetry
(F) Recognise and draw line symmetry; (G) recognise and draw rotational symmetry.

Trigonometry
(F) Use three-figure bearings and the eight main compass points.

(F) Measure a bearing; (G) plot a point given two bearings.

(G) Solve right-angled triangles using Sine, Cosine and Tangent ratios.

(C) Find the area of a triangle using the formula: Area $= \frac{1}{2}$bc sin A or other methods.

(C) Find the gradient of a slope.

(C) Know the relationship between the Sine, Cosine and Tangent.

(C) Use the Sine and Cosine rules.

NB: The relationships $\sin^2 x° + \cos^2 x° = 1$ is not used or referred to in this book, and $\tan x° = \frac{\sin x°}{\cos x°}$ is mentioned but not used.

(C) Graphs of Sine, Cosine and Tangent functions.

(C) Solving trigonometric functions, e.g. $2 \sin x° = 1$ $(0 \leq x \leq 180)$

Relationships

(F) Extending simple number patterns; (G) generalising simple number patterns.

(G) Collecting like terms.

(G) Multiplying out expressions/expanding brackets; (C) more difficult expressions.

(G) Factorising simple expressions.

(C) Factorising more difficult expressions, including trinomials and using the difference of two squares.

(C) Reducing algebraic fractions to their lowest form.

(C) +, −, ×, ÷ algebraic fractions.

(C) Simplify expressions using the laws of indices.

Formulae

(F) Evaluating formulae expressed in words; (G) Evaluating formulae expressed in symbols.

(F) Constructing formulae with guidance.
(C) Constructing formulae to describe relationships expressed graphically.

(C) Change the subject of a formula.

(C) Describe the effect of changing a variable in an expression.

Proportion and variation

(F) Direct proportion; (G) inverse proportion.

(G) Direct variation including graphs; (C) inverse and joint variation including graphs.

Graphs and tables

(F) Extracting data from pictograms, bar charts, line graphs and pie charts; (G) interpretation.

(C) Understanding why graphs may be misleading.

(F) Simple codes.

(F) Constructing pictograms, bar charts, line graphs and pie charts, given scale and structure; (G) no scale given.

(C) Significance of the point of intersection of two graphs.

(G) Graphs in context, e.g. speed/time.

(C) Determination graphically of the solution to a graph and improvement by iteration.

(F) Trends suggested by graphs.

(C) Communicating information graphically and deciding which graph to use.

(F) Extracting data from tables with two categories; (G) with five categories.

(F) Constructing tables with guidance.

(F) Reading diagrams like flow charts.

Equations

(G) Solving simple equations; (C) solving more complicated equations.

(C) Solving quadratic equations with real roots.

(G) Solving inequalities.

(C) Solving simultaneous equations.

(C) Linear programing of real-life problems.

Functions

(C) Using the f(x) notation.

(C) Quadratic functions.

(C) Exponential functions.

(C) Trigonometric functions.

(C) $f(x) = \frac{a}{x}$

Examinations in Northern Ireland

The National Curriculum in Northern Ireland is different from that used in England and Wales and it does not come into operation until 1995. The mathematics in Northern Ireland's National Curriculum is covered in this book, but there are some small differences in the levels at which the work is placed. The following syllabus will be used to assess pupils in Northern Ireland in 1994. There are three tiers of entry for examinations. There is also an Aural and Computational test to assess your ability to carry out mental calculations.

For the teacher-assessed part of your examination you must submit three assignments.

At least one must be done from each of these two areas. These tasks are set by the examination group.

① Practical geometry/measurement/everyday applications of mathematics/statistical work.

② Pure mathematical investigation.

The oral component of your assessment will be based on your coursework.

The examinations follow this pattern:

Tier	Papers	Levels Target NC	Time	% of marks
Foundation	1	4–6	$1\frac{1}{2}$ hrs	35
	2		$1\frac{1}{2}$ hrs	35
	Aural & Computation test		30 mins	10
	Assignments			15
	Oral response			5
Intermediate	3	5–7	2 hrs	35
	4		2 hrs	35
	Aural & Computation test		30 mins	10
	Assignments			15
	Oral response			5
High	5	6–10	$2\frac{1}{2}$ hrs	35
	6		$2\frac{1}{2}$ hrs	35
	Aural and Computation test		30 mins	10
	Assignments			15
	Oral response			5

Examination groups and addresses

City and Guilds	76 Portland Place London W1N 4AA
MEG	Midland Examining Group 1 Hills Road Cambridge CB1 2EU
NEAB	Northern Examinations and Assessment Board Devas Street Manchester M15 6EX
NISEAC	Northern Ireland Schools Examinations and Assessment Council Beechill House 42 Beechill Road Belfast BT8 4RS
SEB	Scottish Examination Board Ironmills Road Dalkeith Midlothian EH22 1LE
SEG	Southern Examining Group Stag Hill House Guildford GU2 5XJ
ULEAC	University of London Examinations and Assessment Council Stewart House 32 Russell Square London WC1B 5DN
WJEC	Welsh Joint Education Committee 245 Western Avenue Cardiff CF5 2YX

Letts check

The mathematics listed below is part of the National Curriculum for students in England and Wales. It is also required by students studying Standard Grade Mathematics in Scotland and the National Curriculum for Northern Ireland.

The work in this book does not cover all the mathematics that you could be given in your final GCSE or SCE examinations, as it has been assumed that you already understand all the lower level skills.

This section of the book lets you check your understanding of these skills and gives you a list of the mathematics you should be able to do before you start revising from this book. If you have difficulty with these skills you should talk to your teacher or perhaps work through the **Letts Key Stage 3 Maths** book first.

What's in Level 3?

This is a list of the contents of **level 3** of the National Curriculum. You should be able to do all these things before you start this book. After the list there are questions to help you check your knowledge of **level 3**.

Using and applying mathematics
- Selecting the materials and mathematics for a task using alternative approaches to overcome difficulties
- Explaining work and recording findings systematically
- Investigating and testing predictions and general statements
- Checking results are sensible

Number
- Reading, writing and ordering numbers up to 1000
- Learning and using addition and subtraction facts to 20 (including zero)
- Learning and using 2, 5 and 10 times tables and multiplication facts up to 5×5
- Solving problems involving multiplication or division of whole numbers or money, with a calculator where necessary
- Understanding remainders, and rounding up and down
- Making estimates based on familiar units
- Recognising that the first digit is the most important in indicating the size of a number, and approximating to the nearest 10 or 100
- Using decimal notation for money
- Recognising negative whole numbers in familiar contexts
- Using a wider range of metric units of length, capacity and 'weight', and standard units of time
- Choosing and using appropriate units and instruments; interpreting numbers on a range of measuring instruments, with appropriate accuracy

Algebra
- Developing a variety of strategies to perform mental calculations using number patterns and equivalent forms of two-digit numbers
- Explaining number patterns and predicting the next number in a sequence
- Recognising whole numbers divisible by 2, 5 or 10
- Using inverse operations in a simple context

Shape and space

- Sorting 2D and 3D shapes, giving reasons
- Recognising reflective symmetry in a variety of shapes in 2D and 3D
- Using and understanding compass bearings, and the terms 'clockwise' and 'anticlockwise'

Handling data

- Extracting specific pieces of information from tables and lists
- Entering and accessing information in a simple database
- Entering data into a simple computer database and using it to answer simple questions
- Constructing and interpreting bar charts and pictograms
- Placing events in order of 'likelihood' and using appropriate words to identify the chance
- Understanding the idea of 'evens' and saying whether events are more or less likely than this
- Distinguishing between 'fair' and 'unfair'

Level 3 Questions

Number

1 (a) Write the number three hundred and sixty five.
   (b) Write 264 in words.
   (c) Put these numbers in order with the largest first:
       125   675   360   25

2 Work out the following in your head:
   (a) $13 + 7 =$ (b) $16 - 8 =$ (c) $9 + 6 =$ (d) $14 - 9 =$ (e) $17 + 0 =$

3 Work out the following in your head:
   (a) $2 \times 7 =$ (b) $5 \times 9 =$ (c) $10 \times 8 =$ (d) $4 \times 4 =$

4 (a) Work out the cost of 4 tickets which cost £2·56 each.
   (b) There are 24 pupils in a class. If they sit in groups of 4 how may groups will there be?

5 (a) 62 sweets are shared by 10 people. How many sweets does each get and how many are left over?
   (b) The *Letts* rugby team has 15 players. They go to matches in their cars. Each car will tae only 4 players. How many cars will they need and how many people will there be in the car which is not full?

6 (a) Estimate the height of a door in metres (m).
   (b) Estimate the height of your desk in centimetres (cm).

7 (a) What is £17 to the nearest £10?
   (b) What is £452 to the nearest £100?

8 Anne buys a birthday present which costs three pounds twenty four. It costs her one pound thirty six to post it. How much does she spend? (Show your working out.)

9 What temperature is shown on this thermometer?

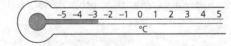

10 Measure the length of this page.

11 Complete the following:
    (a) There are _____ g in a kilogram (kg).
    (b) There are _____ minutes in one hour.
    (c) There are _____ ml in a litre.

(d) There are _____ days in one week.

(e) There are _____ cm in a kilometre (km)

12 Complete the following:

(a) Adrian measured his height in _____.

(b) Susan measured a pint of _____.

(c) Mr Osborne timed the race using a _____.

(d) Tracy ran a mile in 7 _____.

Algebra

13 (a) Use the calculation 24 + 89 = 113 to work out 29 + 84.

(b) Use the calculation 39 – 17 = 22 to work out 59 – 17.

14 (a) What are the next three numbers in this pattern?

3   6   9   12

Explain why in your own words.

(b) Continue the following pattern for three calculations:

9 + 11 = 20

19 + 11 = 30

29 + 11 = 40

15 Without doing any calculations, say which of the following numbers is divisible by
(a) 2, (b) 5 and (c) 10.

32   65   302   35   56   200   18   160   87   470

16 Use the appropriate inverse (opposite) operations to answer the following:

(a) The attendance at the last concert in a tour was double the attendance at the first concert. If 5000 people saw the last concert, how many people saw the first?

(b) In a party game David is blindfolded and given directions across a room avoiding all the furniture. He moves 3 steps forward, 2 steps to the left, 4 steps forward, 6 steps to the right and 1 step back. Direct him back to the start.

Shape and space

17 An eccentric removal company always sorts objects by shape before transporting them to a new house. As a new employee of this company, sort the following objects found in one room, giving each category an appropriate title:

a work-out video, a tennis ball, a set of building blocks, round cushions, a poster, a shoe box, a Frisbee, a CD player, an oval mirror

18 How many lines of symmetry does each of these shapes have?

(a)   (b)   (c)

19 Imagine you are standing in the middle of a large compass looking North.

(a) What is the direction of the flats?

(b) If you face the church and then make a quarter turn anticlockwise which way will you be facing?

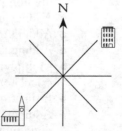

Handling data

20 From this table find the cost of printing a 36 print film 30% bigger.

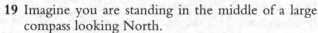

Print Size \ No. of Exp.	UP TO 24 PER FILM	UP TO 36 PER FILM
REGULAR	£2.89	£3.89
30% BIGGER	£3.29	£4.29
100% BIGGER (35mm full frame users only)	£4.99	£5.99

21 Each member of class 2A took a turn picking a counter from a bag containing 5 coloured counters. The results are shown in this table. Draw a bar chart of this information.

Colour	Tally
Blue	＃＃ ＃＃ I
Green	II
Yellow	＃＃ IIII
Black	III
Red	＃＃ II

22 Place these events in order of likelihood:
   (a) It will snow in August this year.
   (b) You were born.
   (c) You will stay on at school.
   (d) It will rain in half an hour.

23 Say which of the following have a better than even chance:
   (a) Your favourite television star will visit your school.
   (b) You will paint in a lesson today.
   (c) You will get more than half of these questions right.

24 Say which of the following is fair:
   (a) You and your friend buy a bag of 20 sweets between you and your friend eats 15 of them.
   (b) Your school football team draws Liverpool in the Cup.
   (c) You play a game in which someone rolls a die and you win if it comes up 1 or 4 or 5, and they win if it comes up 2 or 3 or 6.

What's in Level 4?

This is a list of the contents of **level 4** of the National Curriculum. You should be able to do all these things before you start this book. After the list there are questions to help you check your knowledge of **level 4**.

Using and applying mathematics

- Selecting the materials and mathematics to use for a task when choice is involved; planning work methodically
- Recording findings and presenting them by talking, writing or drawing
- Using examples to test solutions, statements or definitions
- Making generalisations or simple hypotheses

Number

- Reading, writing and ordering whole numbers
- Learning multiplication facts up to 10×10 and using them in multiplication and division problems
- Adding and subtracting mentally two two-digit numbers
- Adding mentally several single-digit numbers
- Adding and subtracting two three-digit numbers, without a calculator
- Multiplying and dividing two-digit numbers by a single-digit number, without a calculator
- Estimating and approximating to check addition and subtraction calculations
- Adding and subtracting numbers with up to 2 decimal places, and multiplying and dividing whole numbers
- Understanding and using the effect of multiplying whole numbers by 10 or 100
- Understanding and using the relationship between place values in whole numbers
- Recognising and understanding simple fractions in everyday use
- Understanding and using decimal notation to 2 decimal places in the context of measurement; appreciating the continuous nature of measurement
- Recognising and understanding simple percentages
- Reading calculator displays to the nearest whole number and knowing how to interpret results which have rounding errors

- Solving addition, subtraction, multiplication and division problems using numbers with up to 2 decimal places
- Making sensible estimates of a range of measures in relation to everyday objects
- Understanding the relationship between units of length, capacity, 'weight' and time

Algebra

- Generalising (mainly in words) patterns which arise in various situations, including symmetry of results, multiples, factors and squares
- Applying strategies such as doubling and halving to explore properties of numbers
- Recognising that multiplication and division are inverse operations and using this to check calculations
- Dealing with inputs to and outputs from simple function machines
- Understanding and using simple formulae or equations expressed in words
- Learning the conventions of the coordinate representation of points; using coordinates in the first quadrant

Shape and space

- Constructing simple 2D and 3D shapes from given information, and knowing associated language
- Reflecting simple shapes in a mirror line
- Understanding the congruence of simple shapes
- Understanding and using language associated with angle
- Specifying location by means of coordinates in the first quadrant and by means of angle and distance
- Recognising rotational symmetry
- Finding perimeters of simple shapes
- Finding areas by counting squares, and volumes by counting cubes

Handling data

- Inserting, interrogating and interpreting data in a computer database
- Specifying an issue for which data are needed
- Collecting, grouping and ordering discrete data using tallying methods and creating a frequency table for grouped data
- Understanding and using the median and mode in everyday contexts
- Constructing and interpreting bar-line and line graphs and frequency diagrams with suitable class intervals for discrete variables
- Creating a decision tree diagram with questions to sort and identify a collection of objects
- Understanding, calculating and using the mean and range of a set of data
- Giving and justifying subjective estimates of probabilities
- Understanding and using the probability scale from 0 to 1
- Listing all the possible outcomes of an event

Level 4 Questions

Number

1 (a) Write 60 254 in words.
  (b) Write in figures the number three million, seven hundred and one thousand, eight hundred and seventy five.
  (c) Write the following numbers in order, largest first:
     8260   3175   42 732   318   43 692   2065   4037   10 515

2   Work out the following in your head:
   (a) 6×8 (b) 7×9 (c) $27 \div 9$ (d) $8\overline{)64}$

3   Work out the following in your head:
   (a) Sam weighs 64 kg and Jason weighs 47 kg. What is their combined weight?
   (b) Sam eats 58 g of chocolate and Jason eats 89 g. How much more chocolate does Jason eat?

4   Answer the following without using a calculator:
   (a) What is $268 + 453$?
   (b) What is the total attendance at a football match if 559 home fans and 274 away fans attend?
   (c) What is $832 - 175$?
   (d) If 984 copies of this book are delivered to a warehouse and then 576 copies are sent out to local book shops, how many copies are left in the warehouse?

5   Answer the following without using a calculator:
   (a) What is 72×8?
   (b) What is the cost of 7 comics which cost 63p each?
   (c) What is $75 \div 3$?
   (d) If 72 eggs are collected on a farm, how many boxes of 6 eggs can be filled?

6   Calculate the following:
   (a) The combined length of two pieces of wood 5·23 m long and 1·69 m long.
   (b) The difference in weight between a parcel weighing 3·07 kg and one weighing 1·85 kg.
   (c) Two sisters are 5 and 18 years old. How many *times* longer has the older sister been alive?

7   Estimate the following by approximating to the nearest 10:
   (a)   22   (b)   58   (c)   93   (d)   88
        +31   +29   −41   −32

8   Answer the following without using a calculator:
   (a) 10×36 (b) 84×10 (c) 100×23 (d) 48×100

9   Shade in the given fraction in each of these shapes:
   (a)   (b)

   $\frac{1}{2}$ $\frac{1}{4}$

   (c) What is $\frac{3}{10}$ of 200?
   (d) What is $\frac{1}{5}$ of 45?

10 What lengths do these measurements show?
   (a)   (b)

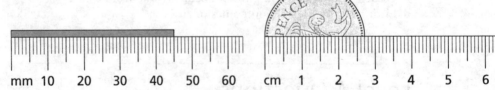

   mm 10   20   30   40   50   60   cm 1   2   3   4   5   6

11 (a) Write 6 out of 12 as a percentage.
   (b) What is 25% of 36?

12 (a) In a record shop 100 LPs take up 857 mm of shelf space. How much space do 239 LPs take up? (Give your answer to the nearest mm.)
   (b) How many packets of 37 balloons are needed to give 286 children in a primary school one balloon each?

13 Five lengths of wire are cut from a single length. The first two pieces are each 2·56 m long and the third piece is 3·18 m long. The fourth piece of wire is one third of the length of the third piece, and the fifth piece is the same length as the other four put together. Calculate:

(a) The length of the fourth piece of wire.

(b) The length of the fifth piece of wire.

(c) The length of wire remaining after all five pieces have been cut from a single piece 25 m long.

Algebra

Answer questions **14–17** without using a calculator.

14 Write down all the factors of the following numbers:
(a) 20   (b) 12

15 Write down the first five multiples of 7.

16 Write down the squares of the following numbers:
(a) 2   (b) 5   (c) 10

17 Write down the square roots of the following numbers:
(a) 25   (b) 81   (c) 49

18 $4 \times 32 = 128$ Use this multiplication pattern to work out the following:
$8 \times 16 = 128$ (a) 32×4 (b) 64×2
$16 \times 8 = 128$

19 (a) If $24 \times 36 = 864$ what is $864 \div 24$?
(b) If $2352 \div 7 = 336$ what is 7×336?

20 Put the following numbers into this simple function machine and write down the answers that would come out.
(a) 4   (b) 6

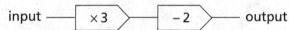

What numbers would you have to input to get the following outputs?
(c) 19   (d) 13

21 I double a number and add one and the answer is 25. What was the number?

22 Write down the coordinates of the points marked A, B, C and D.

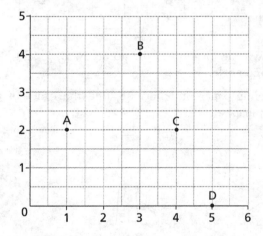

Shape and space

23 Draw a rectangle 3 cm wide and 5 cm long.

24 Draw a circle with a radius of 3 cm.

25 Draw the net of a cube.

26 Decide which of the following words goes with which of the diagrams:
   obtuse, reflex, parallel, acute, vertical, horizontal

(a)   (b) 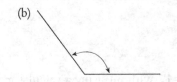   (c)

(d) 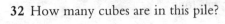   (e)   (f)

27 Copy this shape and draw its reflection in the mirror line.

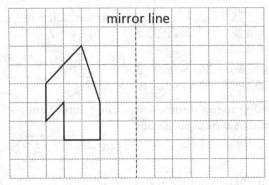

mirror line

28 Which of the following shapes are congruent?

A   B   C   D   E

29 Write down the location of the points A, B, C and D in question 22 in terms of distance and angle.

30 Using tracing paper or otherwise, find the order of rotational symmetry of the following shapes:

(a)   (b)   (c)

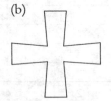 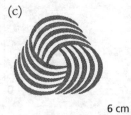

31 (a) Find the perimeter in cm of this rectangle.
   (b) Find the area of the rectangle in centimetre squares (cm²).

6 cm

4 cm

32 How many cubes are in this pile?

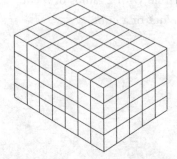

Handling data

33 A bird watcher records the number of a particular type of bird she sees each day for 30 days.

24	35	47	53	42	34	45	35	42	36
28	19	16	32	24	26	29	21	36	30
20	26	42	27	28	31	39	16	27	23

Using class intervals of 10 units, create a grouped frequency table of this information.

34 In a game of backgammon James got the following scores on the dice.

3	7	8	9	7
4	6	5	7	10
2	11	5	12	3

Find the mean, mode, median and range of his scores.

35 This graph shows the conversion rate of dollars to pounds. Use the graph to answer the following questions.

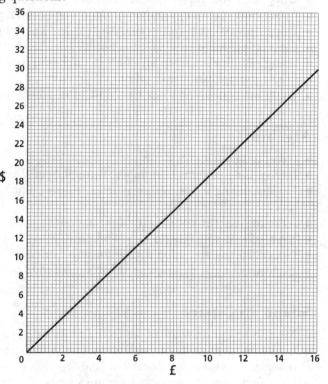

(a) How many dollars would you get for £9?

(b) How much would you get if you changed $25 into pounds?

36 Write down the probability of each of the following events:

(a) You are reading this book.

(b) You are currently performing a parachute jump.

(c) You are currently holding a blue pen. (Give reasons for your answer.)

What's in Level 5?

This is a list of the contents of **level 5** of the National Curriculum. You should be able to do all these things before you start this book. After the list there are questions to help you check your knowledge of **level 5**.

Using and applying mathematics

- Selecting the materials and mathematics for a task, and checking there is sufficient information; working methodically and reviewing progress
  Breaking tasks down into smaller, more manageable tasks
- Interpreting mathematical information presented in oral, written or visual form
- Generalising from a number of particular examples and carrying out simple tests

Number

- Using appropriate non-calculator methods to multiply or divide a three-digit number by a two-digit number
- Multiplying and dividing mentally single-digit multiples of powers of 10 with whole number answers
- Calculating fractions and percentages of quantities, with a calculator where necessary
- Using unitary ratios
- Understanding the idea of scale in maps and drawings
- Using 'trial and improvement' methods
- Approximating, using significant figures or decimal places
- Using Imperial units still in everyday use and knowing their rough metric equivalents
- Converting one metric unit to another
- Using negative numbers in context, including ordering, addition, subtraction and simple multiplication and division
- Using index notation to express powers of whole numbers

Algebra

- Generating sequences
- Recognising patterns in numbers through spatial arrangements
- Understanding and using terms such as 'prime', 'square', 'cube', 'square root' and 'cube root'
- Recognising patterns in equivalent fractions
- Expressing simple functions symbolically
- Understanding and using simple formulae or equations expressed in symbolic form
- Understanding and using coordinates in all four quadrants

Shape and space

- Measuring and drawing angles to the nearest degree
- Explaining and using properties associated with intersecting and parallel lines and triangles, and knowing associated language
- Identifying the symmetries of various shapes
- Using networks to solve problems
- Specifying location by means of coordinates in four quadrants
- Finding areas of plane figures (excluding circles) using appropriate formulae
- Finding volumes of simple solids (excluding cylinders) using appropriate formulae
- Finding the circumference of circles, practically, introducing the ratio π

Handling data

- Inserting and interrogating data in a computer database; drawing conclusions
- Designing and using an observation sheet to collect data; collating and analysing results
- Collecting, ordering and grouping continuous data using equal class intervals and creating frequency tables
- Constructing and interpreting pie charts from a collection of data with a few variables
- Constructing and interpreting conversion graphs
- Constructing and interpreting frequency diagrams and choosing class intervals for continuous variables
- Understanding that different outcomes may result from repeating an experiment
- Recognising situations where estimates of probability can be based on equally likely outcomes, and others where estimates must be based on statistical evidence

- Knowing that if each of n events is assumed to be equally likely then the probability of one occurring is $\frac{1}{n}$

Level 5 Questions

Number

1   Answer the following without using a calculator:
   (a)   345
       × 27
   (b)   478
       × 43
   (c) $12\overline{)216}$
   (d) $15\overline{)525}$

2   Work out the following in your head:
   (a) 500×70
   (b) $800 \div 20$

3   Calculate the following:
   (a) $\frac{3}{8}$ of 32
   (b) $\frac{2}{5}$ of 60
   (c) 7% of £200
   (d) 15% of £320

4   This is a plan of a kitchen drawn to a scale of 1 cm = 1·2 m. How long and how wide is the real kitchen?

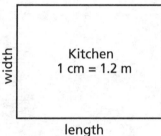

width | Kitchen
1 cm = 1.2 m

length

5   Use 'trial and improvement' methods to find the length of the sides of this square to 1 decimal place.

13 cm²

6   Write the following to the indicated number of decimal places:
   (a) 2·543 (2 d.p.)
   (b) 15·67 (1 d.p.)
   (c) 3·415 (3 d.p.)

7   Write the following to the indicated number of significant figures:
   (a) 2345 to 2 s.f.
   (b) 4789 to 1 s.f.
   (c) 36 425 to 2 s.f.

8   (a) A $\frac{1}{2}$ lb pack weighs approximately how many g?
   (b) A 2 lb bag of sugar weighs approximately how many kg?
   (c) About how many litres are there in 1 gallon?
   (d) About how many km is 15 miles?

9   Convert the following:
   (a) 110 cm to metres   (b) 2·5 kg to grams (c) 3700 mm to metres

10 Put the following temperatures in order, coldest first:
       ⁻2   ⁻5   4   0   3

11 (a) The temperature outside on a cold day is 7°C colder than inside. If the temperature inside is 2°C what is the temperature outside?
   (b) If the temperature outside starts off at 8°C and drops by 2°C six times during the night, what is the temperature in the morning?

12 (a) Write $2 \times 2 \times 2 \times 2 \times 2 \times 2$ as a power of 2.
   (b) Write $3 \times 3 \times 3 \times 3$ as a power of 3.
   (c) Write $4 \times 4 \times 4 \times 4 \times 4$ in the form 4^n.

Algebra

13 Write down the first eight numbers in each of the following sequences.
(a) Starting with 1, 1, each number is the sum of the previous two numbers.
(b) Starting with 1, each number is double the previous number.
(c) Starting with 1, 3, the number you add on increases by 1 each time.

14 Write down which of the following numbers are prime, squares or cubes.
(a) 25   (b) 27   (c) 29   (d) 17   (e) 64

15 It takes Joe 117 seconds to serve a hamburger.
(a) How long does it take him to serve n hamburgers?
(b) How many hamburgers can he serve in m seconds?

16 Use the formula $\frac{1}{2}(b \times h)$ to find the area of this triangle.

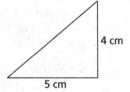

17 Plot the following coordinates on the grid and join up the points.
(a) (2, 2)
(b) (⁻4, 2)
(c) (⁻4, ⁻3)
(d) (2, ⁻3)

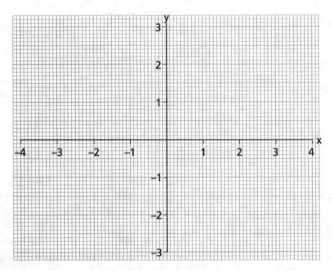

Shape and space

18 Measure the following angles.

(a)   (b)   (c)

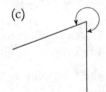

19 (a) Without measuring, write down all the angles which are equal to a. Give reasons for your answers.
(b) Without measuring, what is the sum of angles e and h?

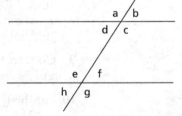

20 Write down the order of rotational symmetry of each of the following solids about the axis shown.

(a)   (b)

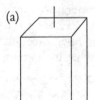
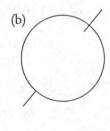

21 A van needs to collect parcels from each of the following depots. The mileage between cities is shown. Starting in any city, which is the shortest route to visit each depot?

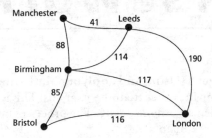

22 Calculate the volume of this cuboid.

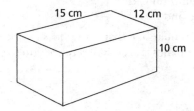

Handling data

23 The heights of 20 pupils are measured to the nearest mm.

142·3   151·7   159·8   139·6   145·3   148·2   153·6   151·8   149·6   155·0
139·1   132·4   158·6   143·7   141·0   139·5   152·9   145·8   149·5   130·7

Create a grouped frequency table of this information.

24 Look at this pie chart.
What % of all pupils come to school by bus?

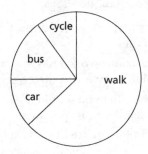

25 Fifty students obtained the following marks out of ten in a test:

5   3   4   4   5   5   7   4   3   4   3   4   5   2   7   5   7   1   7   6
5   8   6   4   5   4   3   6   1   3   6   3   2   6   6   3   5   4   3   5
6   7   8   9   6   4   2   1

Draw a pie chart of these results.

26 (a) Use the fact that 1 kg is equivalent to 2·2 lb to draw a conversion graph for kilograms (kg) to pounds (lb).

(b) Use your graph to convert the following weights to pounds (lb).
(i) 3 kg   (ii) 2500 g   (iii) 4·5 kg

(c) Use your graph to convert the following weights to kilograms (kg).
(i) 9 lb   (ii) 6 lb   (iii) 8 ounces

27 (a) What is the probability of getting a 2 on a fair die?
(b) What is the probability of getting a 2 on a fair die with twenty faces?

Coursework

Attainment Target 1 (Using and applying Mathematics) of the National Curriculum is very different from the other attainment targets. This is because it develops the processes used to solve problems mathematically. The processes involved in mathematical thinking are divided into three main areas:

1 Applications
2 Mathematical communication
3 Reasoning, logic and proof

It is important to remember that any coursework you do or any examination which assesses how Mathematics is used will require you to satisfy certain objectives to allow you to achieve a grade.

Getting started

Your teacher should have explained to you what coursework you will be doing as part of the course you are following.

If this involves short tests (usually about an hour long) your teacher will probably have practised the methods used to solve similar tasks with you.

This section of this book deals with investigations and practical tasks and should help you with this type of coursework.

Longer tasks will be explained by your teacher and you should use the methods covered here to help you as your task develops.

Remember: Your teacher is the expert in what you have to do to achieve the best possible grade.

As you develop your coursework tasks you will have to suggest ways forward. Your teacher will not be able to give you direct help without this affecting your final grade.

However, if you ask whether you should try one approach or another they may be willing to advise you which has the most potential.

When you need to consult your teacher have ideas prepared so that you get the most out of this contact time.

Here are some questions you might want to ask your teacher:

- How long does this piece of work have to be?
- How does this piece of work fit into my examination course?
- When do you want this piece of work to be handed in?

Try to avoid asking what you have to do.

Your work may be marked by more than one person. Make sure you explain everything you have done and make sure that your work can be easily read and understood.

Hint: If you can find an adult not involved in the teaching of Mathematics to read through your work and they can understand what you have done and why without any further explanation from you, then your work is probably clear enough.

Make sure when your work is completed you have done everything that your teacher has suggested you do (or hinted might be a good idea), and that your teacher is happy with your work.

To ensure that their assessment of your work is fair your teacher may wish to question you about what you have done and why.

Here are some questions your teacher might ask you about your work. They may indicate things you need to develop.

- What did you find out before you started? (You may not have written this down in your plan!)

- Why did you do it this way? (There may be other ways or perhaps a much simpler way!)
- Did you think of trying this? (You should have tried this!)
- Have you checked your answers? (You may have an incorrect answer you haven't checked!)
- Do you think this answer is accurate enough? (It could be more accurate!)
- What do these results mean? (You haven't explained clearly enough!)
- Are these the results you expected? (You haven't said what you hoped to find out or your results do not reflect what you said you were going to do!)
- How have you extended your work beyond your original plan? (Do you need to extend your work?)
- Explain this to me? (Your explanation may not be clear enough!)

Remember: Your teacher is there to help you but they are not allowed to give you answers without recording this help and that may reflect in your final marks.

Your teacher's questions will probably be on areas of your work which they believe you could improve. This should suggest to you things you could do to make your work better!

Do's and Don'ts

Here are some hints to help you with your coursework:

1 Do make sure that your coursework includes your best work.
2 Do make sure the work is mathematical!
   (Many students complete pieces of coursework which as pieces of English or Design would be excellent but which are poor as pieces of Mathematics.)
3 Do remember to produce a thorough plan of what you intend doing.
4 Do check with your teacher that your task and plan are suitable.
5 Do try to think up your own ideas and approaches.
6 Do use the consultation time with your teacher to help you develop your work.
7 Do make sure that you explain everything you do, and why you did it, and everything you have found out, no matter how trivial you think it is.
8 Do make sure your answers are sensible.
9 Do check what resources you can use to help you with your work.
10 Do keep a record of how much time you've spent on it.

These are some things you should avoid doing:

1 Don't rush your work, and don't leave it until the last minute to do the work.
2 Don't copy out of books or magazines or from other people.
3 Don't paste in lots of pictures without explaining how they relate to your work.
4 Don't keep changing your task.
5 Don't panic if you get stuck.

What should be in your work

The National Curriculum says you should be able to do the following things. You can use these statements as a checklist as you complete your work.

Level	Application	Mathematical communication	Reasoning, logic and proof
3	Find ways of overcoming difficulties in solving problems	Use or interpret appropriate mathematical terms and mathematical aspects of everyday language in a precise way. Present results in a clear and organised way	Investigate general statements by trying out some examples
4	Identify and obtain information necessary to solve problems	Interpret situations mathematically, using appropriate symbols or diagrams	Give some justification for your solutions to problems. Make generalisations
5	Carry through a task by breaking it down into smaller, more manageable tasks	Interpret information presented in a variety of mathematical forms	Make a generalisation and test it
6	Pose your own questions or design a task in a given context	Examine critically the mathematical presentation of information	Make a generalisation giving some degree of justification
7	Follow new lines of enquiry when investigating within Mathematics itself or when using Mathematics to solve a real-life problem		Examine and comment constructively on generalisations or solutions
8	Give a logical account of your work, with reasons for choices made		Understand the role of counter example in disproving generalisations or hypotheses
9	Co-ordinate a number of features or variables in solving problems		Justify your solutions to problems involving a number of features or variables
10	Explore independently a new area of Mathematics		Handle abstract concepts of proof and definition

Using and applying Mathematics is often assessed by doing short or long **investigations** of what might be described as Pure Mathematics or by investigating different **practical applications** of Mathematics.

Investigations

Whether an investigation is set by the examination board and has to be completed in one hour or whether it represents 20 hours' work the processes you should go through are basically the same.

These are most easily illustrated by example:

In a new building there are one hundred computer terminals. The computer in each room has to be connected to every other computer. How many connections are needed?

Note: In this investigation you are looking for a single solution. That is not usually the case.

The first step is to break the problem down into a simpler problem or problems. (The simpler the better!)

Draw diagrams and tabulate your results in order.

The smallest possible number of computers would be 1.

With 1 computer you don't need any connection.

Computers 1   Lines 0

With 2 computers you will need 1 line between them.

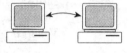

Computers 2   Lines 1

With 3 computers you will need 3 lines between them.

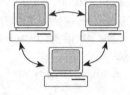

Computers 3   Lines 3

With 4 computers you will need 6 lines between them.

You can now begin to tabulate the results you have just found.

Computers	Lines
1	0
2	1
3	3
4	6

You may be able to see a pattern beginning to develop in the number of lines. If not you could try some more simple examples.

Hint: Look at the gaps between the values in the lines column to see if you can find a pattern.

You may notice that the gaps between the values in the lines column are increasing by 1 each time.

From this you can predict that for 5 computers there will be 10 lines. You can prove this by illustrating the number of lines needed for 5 computers.

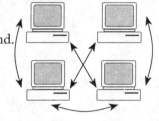

You now have a very crude way of finding the number of lines needed for 100 computers. If you had the time you could extend your list to 100. But there must be a more efficient way.

When you add a computer to the system how many extra lines are added?

If a sixth computer is added there will be 5 new lines (1 to each of the existing computers).

When the seventh is added there will be 6 new lines.

The number of new lines added each time is 1 less than the number of computers.

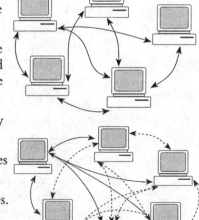

You can now state a general pattern for the number of extra lines each extra computer will create.

When the nth computer is added this will add $(n-1)$ extra lines.

The time before, when the $(n-1)$th computer was added, there would have been 1 less than this or $(n-2)$ extra lines.

The time before that 1 less again, or $(n-3)$.

This will happen n times so the last value will be $(n-n)$ extra lines when the first computer is added.

This gives you a sequence for n computers.

The number of lines for n computers is

$$(n-1) + (n-2) + (n-3) + (n-4) + \ldots + (n-[n-1]) + (n-n)$$

Note: This particular sequence of numbers occurs quite frequently in investigations.
Going back to the original problem:
When $n = 100$ this would give you $99 + 98 + 97 + 96 + \ldots + 3 + 2 + 1 + 0$

This is better but it would still be time-consuming to have to add together 100 numbers. A useful method for adding lists of numbers together would be helpful!

Look at the first and last numbers in the list. They add to 99.
$99 + 0 = 99$

Now look at the next number in from each end of the list. They also add to 99.
$98 + 1 = 99$

This happens all the way along the list. There are 100 numbers in the list so if you add the first 50 to the last 50 in this way then you get 50 lots of 99.

99	98	97	96	....	52	51	50
+	+	+	+		+	+	+
0	1	2	3	....	47	48	49
99	99	99	99	....	99	99	99

Therefore the number of lines for 100 computers will be
$99 \times 50 = 4950$ lines

The general rule for the total of n numbers added together is $\frac{1}{2}n(n-1)$.

Remember: The solution to this problem is less important as an example than the process you have gone through to produce the answer. The problems you have to solve will be very different but the process you use to find their solutions will be similar.

This is the basic process which the majority of all investigational work should follow.

1 Make sure you have read the question thoroughly and understand what you have to do.

2 If you are given questions to answer, do them. (They will have been put there to help you!)

3 If you have the choice of what you have to do simplify the problem as much as possible.

4 Collect evidence by drawing or calculating values in a logical way. (Start with the simplest and only change one thing at a time.)

5 Put your results in a table in order. (You must have at least 4 or 5 values in your table before it is of any value.)

6 Make predictions of what the next values will be.

7 Show that you have checked that your predictions work.

8 Look for patterns and write down in your own words what you see.

   If what you write down is not important you will not lose any marks. But if you leave something out then you might. For example, if you notice that the values in the table are all triangular numbers then say so. By stating this fact you have shown you know what a triangular number is!

9 Try to generalise your solution in your own words or even better in an algebraic form.

10 If you can't find an answer and you have done all the things above don't worry. Sometimes the solutions to investigational problems you have chosen yourself will be very difficult to find.

Remember: You don't always need the answer to get a good grade. It is more important that you have used mathematical processes to complete your work. Here is another example to show you how to apply the processes listed above.

Space Stations - A space station is to be built by fitting together cubic sections.
Investigate the ways in which sections in space can be fitted together.
(They must be fitted face to face with no overlaps.)

This is a complex problem and so before you start you must **plan each stage carefully**. You may change your plan as the work develops if the need arises. (This is both allowed and expected.)

Step 1　Start by simplifying the problem. Choose different aspects or variables which you feel may provide you with information.

Don't worry if you find your ideas don't work. Simply say so and then examine some other aspect of the problem.

In this problem you could investigate the number of faces that can be seen or corners or edges or some other feature.

Step 2　Start with the simplest case you can find.

1.　2.

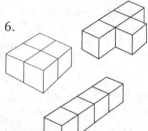

1 cube has 6 faces, 12 edges, 8 corners

There is only one way to put 2 cubes together.

2 cubes have 10 faces, 12 edges, 8 corners

3.

5.
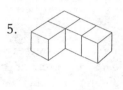

4.

6.
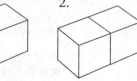

Continue to gather data (in this case by drawing).

With 3 or more cubes there are different ways to put them together.

Once you have sufficient data you can begin to tabulate your results.

Concentrate on the relationships between two variables, for example the number of cubes and the number of faces.

Step 3　Tabulate your results.

Diagram no.	Cubes	Faces
1	1	6
2	2	10
3	3	14
4	3	14
5	4	18
6	4	16

Step 4　Make predictions.

You can make a statement of conjecture or prediction after you have gathered evidence of something you believe to be true.

Be very careful not to make a prediction of the relationship between the values too soon.

Before diagram 6 above you might have predicted a relationship of $f = 4c + 2$ but this is not true for diagram 6.

You may wish to group the results or diagrams to simplify the problem still further.

Step 5　Check your predictions.

When you have made a conjecture or prediction and tried to generalise the problem, expressing it either in your own words or, better still, in algebraic form, you should always check your results, attempting to prove or disprove your conjecture.

This could be done by stating what the next result will be and then drawing it to prove you were correct.

Note: Proof should be recorded carefully and in as much detail as you can. Explain each step you take in full and why you have taken it.

Once you have proved or disproved the conjecture summarise your results concisely.

Once you have completed your examination of these two variables you can extend your work by looking at other combinations of variables.

Here is a summary of the basic process you should follow.

- Always plan your work carefully.
- Simplify the problem if you can.
- Always write down what you have done and why you have done it.
- Always put in all the work you have done even if it fails to lead you to a solution.
- Always check and prove any generalisation you make.

Remember: Always keep a record of the time you spent doing the work.

Your teacher will probably give you some starting points for investigation. Here are a few you might like to think about as alternatives.

Before you begin any investigation in this list check with your teacher that you can include it as part of your examination coursework.

Rebounds A snooker ball is hit so that it rebounds off any cushion it hits at 45° to the cushion. Investigate which pocket the ball falls into.

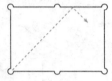

Diagonals If a diagonal cut is made across this rectangle it cuts through 4 squares. Investigate the number of squares cut by the diagonals for different rectangles.

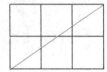

Squares How many squares can you draw on this pattern of dots? Investigate the number of squares you can draw as the number of dots increases.

Dates In any month on a calendar choose any four by four square of dates and investigate number patterns that occur.

e.g. $1 + 4 + 22 + 25 = 52$
$9 + 10 + 16 + 17 = 52$

S	M	T	W	T	F	S
			1	2	3	4
5	6	7	8	9	10	11
12	13	14	15	16	17	18
19	20	21	22	23	24	25
26	27	28	29	30		

Straw towers If you were building a tower with straws you would need the straws and different types of connectors. Investigate any relationships between the number of straws and the different types of connectors you would need to make different towers.

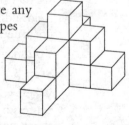

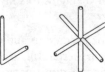

Fibonacci numbers If you count the number of sections in each of the spiral rings in different directions on a pine cone you will find they are Fibonacci numbers!

$$1, \ 1, \ 2, \ 3, \ 5 \ ,...$$

These numbers can also be used to provide a rough comparison between miles and kilometres. Investigate Fibonacci numbers.

Km	1	1	2	3	5	8	13...
	↓	↓	↓	↓	↓	↓	↓
miles	1	1	2	3	5	8	13...

Converting fractions to decimals

Some fractions can be expressed as decimals to one place, some to 2 decimal places, etc.

$$0{\cdot}5 = \tfrac{1}{2} \qquad \tfrac{2}{7} = 0{\cdot}\dot{2}8571\dot{4}$$

Investigate the length of the decimal for different fractions.

Multiplication This method is called the Russian Peasant method.

$$65 \times 27$$
$$130 \times 13$$
$$260 \times 6$$
$$520 \times 3$$
$$1040 \times 1$$

Try a few examples yourself.

Investigate!

Now add up the numbers on the left with odd partners:

$$65 + 130 + 520 + 1040 = 1755$$

Practical applications

Practicals will tend to be longer pieces of work.

They will probably involve doing some research and then explaining your results.

Research can take the form of gathering data or making measurements, sometimes both.

Some students think that this type of coursework is easier than the investigational coursework. It is not. The same high standards will be expected.

As in the investigational work there is a pattern to the form that most practicals will take.

1 You will either be given or choose a practical problem to solve.

2 You will be expected to have a clear plan of how you expect to approach the problem.

3 You will usually need to break the problem down into smaller parts.

4 You will form a conjecture or hypothesis of what the result may be and then gather useful data from a number of sources to check this.

5 From this data you will produce ordered tables which enable you to use your data easily.

6 You will form conclusions or solutions, check them, and relate them back to the original problem.

7 You will form some final hypothesis based on all the relevant data.

8 You will discuss any limitations of your work. You will probably extend your ideas or suggest ways in which they might be extended.

Here is another example to show you how to apply the processes listed above.

Your school is to be opened to the public in the evenings.
It is felt that the parking will be inadequate.
Investigate and if necessary re-design the parking around your school.

The first step is to identify exactly what the problem is and to plan a course of action which will enable you to investigate and formulate an answer.

First, break down the problem. There are two distinct parts to this piece of work.

(i) The need for extra parking.

  Here are some factors that might be worth consideration.

  (a) How much parking is there now?

  (b) How many extra cars is the use of the school's facilities likely to generate?

(ii) Where and how extra parking might be provided.

  (a) What areas could be utilised to provide more parking?

  (b) How much space is needed to park a car?

  (c) How many more cars will the space available allow you to park?

You may of course have other ideas of your own!

Now write this down in a clear plan of what you want to find out and how you expect to do it.

The solution to (i) could involve you measuring the car park and drawing a plan or simply finding a large scale plan of your school with parking already marked.

The solution to (ii) will probably require you to produce a survey. This is likely to involve research into what facilities will be offered and how many people these will involve.

You may wish to compare your school with a community school already being used in the evenings or with a local leisure centre.

Using statistics

When your coursework task requires you to collect and use data this basic procedure might help you. You can look at **section 5** of this book to help you develop these skills.

Start:	Write down what you hope to find out. This is called making a hypothesis.
Design your data collection sheet:	Write down some explanation of how you intend to use this to produce a fair set of results. Note things which may have a negative effect on your survey.
Collect data:	There are a number of ways that you can do this. By a survey, by observation, experiment, from published information.
Tabulate your results:	This can be done by tallying and then using a frequency table or a grouped frequency table.
Illustrate your work:	Bar charts, pictograms, histograms, pie charts, frequency polygons, cumulative frequency curves etc.
Use your results:	Calculate averages (mean, mode, median) and range.
Comment on your results.	

Remember: If you don't know what data you will require from your survey you could waste a great deal of valuable time.

Having established the need for the extra parking spaces (or not!) you will then have to provide possible solutions.

When you are looking at areas that could be utilised for new parking you may wish to carry out a survey on the location of the new area.

There may be many factors which affect people's opinions on this issue.

This could also involve carrying out land surveys and calculations of earth to be moved etc. and you may also want to look at relative costs.

To decide on the parking space needed you should have an idea of how much room a car needs to park and open its doors and also how much room a car needs to manoeuvre in and out of a space. This could be done by measuring a selection of cars or gathering manufacturers' data.

Your work should offer a comprehensive analysis of the problem and offer a range of solutions based on the information you have gathered.

You must also look at the limitations of your work. For example, there may be limitations in the accuracy of the data you have gathered or the costing of the project.

You should also address the question of how you might extend your work. For example, you could produce a scale model.

Here is an example of how to plan a practical task.

Choose two newspapers. Compare their coverage of sport, fashion or their advertisements.
Plan what you are going to do.

What are you going to compare?

How are you going to compare?

Your plan might contain ideas like these:

> I am going to compare the sizes of the fashion sections of the *Sun* and the *Guardian* by counting the total number of words each contains.
>
> I am going to work out what percentage of each paper is devoted to fashion.
>
> I am going to work out which has the highest percentage of fashion pictures.
>
> I am going to do a survey of which fashion section people like best.
>
> I am going to check my results by repeating this for a number of issues.
>
> I am going to use the information I gather to write a report comparing these two papers.

This work is planned in a logical way. It contains surveys to provide statistical data which you are going to compare in different ways. It will contain some calculation of different variables. You have shown that you intend checking your results and extending the results.

Some ideas you might like to develop

Practical Mathematics is everywhere around you. If you have to do a practical task choose one that you find interesting.

Your teacher will probably give you some ideas that you can develop as coursework. Here are a few more.

If you decide you would like to try any of these check with your teacher before you start to make sure that they form an acceptable alternative to those you have already been given.

1 Redesign your bedroom.
2 How heavy is your house?
3 Design a kitchen for an elderly, blind or disabled person.
4 Redesign your garden.
5 Find the cost of running a car for a year.
6 Where is the best place to shop?
7 Redesign the scoring system for a game of your choice.
8 Would a cafeteria system be better in providing food in your school?
9 Where is the best place to save your money?
10 Using public transport how far could you get from your school in 12 hours?
11 Plan a camping holiday for yourself and three friends.
12 Which is the best newspaper for … ?
13 Investigate the cost of getting married.
14 Investigate the cost of having a baby.
15 Redesign the packaging for …
16 How expensive is sport?

Oral component

Not all syllabuses have an oral component. In those which do its value is usually low (about 5%). You should check whether you have to do an oral test as part of your final examination.

Oral tests are spoken by a teacher and you are expected to write your response on a pre-printed examination sheet.

These tests are often given before the start of one of your written papers.

Your teacher will have sample oral tests appropriate to the examination you are doing.

It is difficult to revise the skills needed to complete this type of task but there are some do's and don'ts.

DO   – Listen carefully. (Make sure your teacher knows before the test starts if you have any difficulty in hearing.)

DO   -   Write down all the values you are given. The teacher's instructions will be clear. They will only repeat the question the allowed number of times.

DO   -   If you are allowed a calculator use it. Sometimes when the pressure is on you can make simple errors.

DO   -   Check your work if there is time.

DON'T -   Use a calculator if it is not allowed.

DON'T -   Panic or rush. The question will be read twice and will generally be quite easy!

Sample test

Here are some questions to try. You could get someone to read them out for you. Allow yourself a maximum of 5 minutes.

Cover up the answers at the bottom of the page before you start.

1   What is the total cost of 6 pens costing 40 pence each?

2   At a restaurant 4 people pay £64 for a meal. They share the cost equally. How much does each pay?

3   The distance across a circle is 3 m. What will the approximate distance around the circle be?

4   How many 32p stamps can you buy for £5?

5   At midday the temperature was 8°C. Overnight it fell by 11°C. What was the new temperature?

6   A mechanic is paid £7·50 an hour. How much will he be paid for 3 hours' work?

7   The bus fare is 70p. It is increased by 10%. What is the new bus fare?

8   The next train is at 8:42 am. It is now 7:53 am. How long do I have to wait?

9   You buy a magazine which costs £2·75 and a book which costs £3·50. How much change will you get from £10?

10   How many sides has an octagon?

11   What do the angles of a triangle add up to?

12   If today is the 20th of April what will the date be in 4 weeks' time?

Answers

1	£2·40	2	£16	3	between 9 and 10 metres
4	15	5	⁻3°C	6	£22·50
7	77p	8	49 minutes	9	£3·75
10	8	11	180°	12	18th of May

2.6a   Ordering decimals and appreciating place values

Ordering decimals

When you have to put a list of decimals in order it is easier if they are all expressed to the same number of places.

E.g. Write the following numbers in order, largest first:

     0·2   0·21   0·021   0·202   0·1002   0·0201

Since adding zeros after the last digit on the right hand side of the decimal point has no effect on the number you can add extra zeros at the end to make the numbers the same length.

    0·2000   0·2100   0·0210   0·2020   0·1002   0·0201

You should now find it much easier to put them in order:

    0·2100   0·2020   0·2000   0·1002   0·0210   0·0201

Putting them back into their original form:

    0·21   0·202   0·2   0·1002   0·021   0·0201

?

1 Put the following numbers in order, smallest first:

    0·1   0·106   0·16   0·016   0·1006

Remember: Put zeros after each number to make them the same length.

Place value

Each of the places after the decimal point has its own value.

E.g.

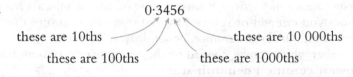

              0·3456

these are 10ths   these are 10 000ths

    these are 100ths   these are 1000ths

$$0\cdot3 = \tfrac{3}{10} \quad 0\cdot04 = \tfrac{4}{100} \quad 0\cdot005 = \tfrac{5}{1000} \quad 0\cdot0006 = \tfrac{6}{10000}$$

?

2 Write the value of the underlined digit in each of the following numbers in words and as a fraction.

(a) 5·4<u>6</u>   (b) 7·8<u>2</u>9   (c) 0·35<u>7</u>   (d) 6·5<u>8</u>2   (e) <u>7</u>·304

2.6b   Equivalent fractions and ratios, decimals and percentages

Equivalent fractions

Two fractions are equivalent or equal if both the top and bottom numbers (the numerator and the denominator) in the first fraction can be multiplied or divided by the same value to give the second fraction.

E.g.

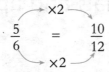

$$\frac{5}{6} = \frac{10}{12} \qquad \frac{15}{20} = \frac{3}{4}$$

Note: To check that the fractions are equivalent find the multiplier between the numbers on the top and check that the multiplier on the bottom is the same.

> **1** Say which of the following pairs of fractions are equivalent:
>
> (a) $\frac{5}{8}, \frac{15}{24}$ (b) $\frac{6}{8}, \frac{3}{4}$ (c) $\frac{3}{2}, \frac{15}{20}$ (d) $\frac{3}{8}, \frac{15}{40}$

Mixed numbers

A mixed number is one which is made up of a whole number and a fraction. You often need to convert mixed numbers into equivalent improper or top heavy fractions before you can use them in calculations. An improper fraction has a numerator which is larger than the denominator.

E.g. (a) Express $2\frac{2}{3}$ as an improper fraction.

$$\frac{3}{3} + \frac{3}{3} + \frac{2}{3} = \frac{8}{3}$$

(b) Express $\frac{14}{5}$ in its lowest form.

$$\frac{5+5+4}{5} = 2\frac{4}{5}$$

> **2** (a) Write $4\frac{2}{3}$ as an improper fraction.
>
> (b) Express $\frac{9}{2}$ in its lowest form.

Using equivalent fractions

The equivalence of fractions is used when you add or subtract fractions.

Before you can add or subtract fractions you must ensure that they have the same denominator, called the common denominator. To do this you first decide what is the first number which can be divided by the denominators of both fractions. This is called the **lowest common denominator**.

You then convert each fraction into an equivalent fraction with the common denominator on the bottom. The number you multiply the denominator by to get the common denominator also multiplies the numerator of your fraction.

E.g. $\frac{2}{3} + \frac{4}{5}$

The smallest number divisible by both 3 *and* 5 is $3 \times 5 = 15$
so the lowest common denominator is 15.
3 goes into 15 five times so you multiply the top and bottom of $\frac{2}{3}$ by 5:

$$\frac{2}{3} = \frac{10}{15}$$

5 goes into 15 three times so you multiply the top and bottom of $\frac{4}{5}$ by 3:

$$\frac{4}{5} = \frac{12}{15}$$

So $\frac{2}{3} + \frac{4}{5} = \frac{10}{15} + \frac{12}{15} = \frac{22}{15} = \frac{15+7}{15} = 1\frac{7}{15}$

The same method is used when you are subtracting.

E.g. $\frac{5}{6} - \frac{1}{4}$

The lowest common denominator is 12.
6 goes into 12 twice so

$$\frac{5}{6} = \frac{10}{12}$$

4 goes into 12 three times so $\frac{1}{4} = \frac{3}{12}$

So $\frac{5}{6} - \frac{1}{4} = \frac{10}{12} - \frac{3}{12} = \frac{7}{12}$

3 Complete the following calculations:

(a) $\frac{3}{4} + \frac{1}{3} = \frac{}{12} + \frac{}{12} = 1\frac{}{12}$

(b) $\frac{2}{5} - \frac{1}{4} =$

(c) $\frac{5}{8} + \frac{1}{4} =$

(d) $\frac{3}{4} - \frac{1}{2} =$

Remember: When you are working with fractions you should always simplify your answer.

Equivalent ratios

Ratio is a comparison between similar quantities. It can be expressed as a ratio A to B or $A : B$ or as a fraction $\frac{A}{B}$. A and B can be multiplied or divided by the same number without changing their ratio.

E.g. Two people receive money. A receives £250 and B receives £150. What is the ratio of $A : B$ expressed in its lowest form?
The ratio $A : B$ is 250 : 150.
Each of these numbers can be divided by 50 giving:
The lowest ratio of $A : B$ is 5 : 3.

Note: Ratios should usually be expressed as whole numbers e.g. 1 : 1·5 will normally be written as 2 : 3.

4 Reduce the following ratios to their lowest form:

(a) 12 : 8   (b) 15 : 20   (c) 60 : 40   (d) 54 : 36

Using equivalent ratios

If you know the ratio between numbers and you know one of the numbers, then you can calculate the other number.

E.g. Two lengths are in the ratio 3 : 5. If the first length is 120 m what is the second length?
Multiplying both sides of the ratio by 40 gives 120 : 200.
This is equivalent to the ratio 3 : 5.

$$\frac{3}{5} = \frac{120}{l}$$

$\times 40$ $\times 40$

So if the ratio of the lengths is 3 : 5 then the ratio of the lengths is 120 : 200.
So the second length is 200 m.

5 The length and width of a room are in the ratio 4 : 3.
(a) What is the width of the room if the length is 3·2 m?
(b) What is the length of the room if the width is 3·6 m?

Remember: Find an equivalent ratio which includes the number given in the question.

Equivalent fractions, decimals and percentages

You should be able to relate a fraction to its decimal and percentage equivalents.

Percent means *out of 100*. Therefore 1% is the same as one hundredth (100th).

$$1\% = \tfrac{1}{100} = 0 \cdot 01$$

By making the denominator into a power of 10 you can relate a fraction to a decimal. By making the denominator into 100 you can relate a fraction to a percentage.

E.g. $\frac{1}{2}$ is equivalent to $\frac{5}{10}$ (multiplying top and bottom by 5)

so $\frac{1}{2}$ is the same as 5 tenths or 0·5

$\frac{1}{2}$ is equivalent to $\frac{50}{100}$ (multiplying top and bottom by 50)

so $\frac{1}{2}$ is the same as 50%

?

> **6** By finding equivalent fractions write the following as a decimal and as a percentage:
>
> (a) $\frac{1}{4}$ (b) $\frac{1}{5}$ (c) $\frac{2}{5}$ (d) $\frac{1}{10}$

2.6c   Fractions, decimals and percentages

To convert a fraction into a decimal you divide the numerator by the denominator (the top number by the bottom number).

E.g. Express $\frac{5}{6}$ as a decimal.

$$\boxed{5} \div \boxed{6} = \boxed{0.8333333}$$

Note: When some fractions are converted into decimals the digits repeat or recur. These decimals are called **recurring decimals**. (If the last digit in the display is different it may be because the calculator has rounded the displayed number.)

Recurring decimals can be written using a dot over the first and last digits in the recurring sequence.

E.g. $\frac{5}{6} = 0 \cdot 8333333 \ldots = 0 \cdot 8\dot{3}$

$\frac{4}{7} = 0 \cdot 57142857142857 \ldots = 0 \cdot \dot{5}7142\dot{8}$

Remember: All the numbers between the dots repeat (recur).

?

> **1** Use your calculator to convert the following fractions into decimals:
>
> (a) $\frac{7}{20}$ (b) $\frac{5}{8}$ (c) $\frac{13}{16}$ (d) $\frac{19}{33}$ (e) $\frac{1}{7}$

Once a fraction has been converted into a decimal it can easily be converted into a percentage. To change a decimal into a percentage you multiply by 100.

E.g. Express 0·125 as a percentage.

0·125 × 100 = 12·5%

?

> **2** Express each of the following decimals as a percentage:
>
> (a) 0·5   (b) 0·75   (c) 0·375   (d) 0·06   (e) 0·60   (f) 0·175

To express one number as a percentage of another you can use the methods used above.
E.g. In a class of 25 pupils 13 are girls. Express this as a percentage.

Step 1   Write the problem as a fraction
$\frac{13}{25}$ are girls

Step 2   Convert this into a decimal by dividing 13 by 25

Step 3   Change into a percentage by multiplying by 100
          $0.52 \times 100 = 52\%$
So 52% of the class are girls.

> **3** Express the following first as a fraction, then as a decimal and then as a percentage:
> (a) In a survey of 50 new cars 9 were red.
> (b) In a packet of 60 seeds 12 failed to germinate.
> (c) In a standard attainment test Linda got 20 marks out of 24.

Remember: Always write a fraction in its lowest form.

2.6d   Fractional and percentage changes

When numbers are increased or decreased the change can be expressed as a fraction or percentage.

Note: When you work the following sections you should use the method you have been taught at school.

Increasing or decreasing by a given fraction

E.g. Increase £96 by a quarter.

Method 1 First, calculate $\frac{1}{4}$ of £96.
This is written $\frac{1}{4} \times 96$ or $0.25 \times 96 = 24$
Adding this to the original amount gives $96 + 24 = 120$
so the answer is £120.

Method 2 Increasing 96 by a quarter is the same as multiplying it by $1+\frac{1}{4}$.
$1\frac{1}{4} \times 96 = \frac{5}{4} \times 96 = £120$

Decreases can be calculated in a similar way by taking the decrease from the original value.

> **1** Calculate the following:
> (a) an increase of $\frac{1}{4}$ on £56   (b) an increase of $\frac{1}{3}$ on £75
> (c) a decrease of $\frac{1}{5}$ on £60   (d) a decrease of $\frac{1}{4}$ on £24

Increasing or decreasing by a given percentage

E.g. Calculate an 8% increase on the price of a television costing £450.

Method 1 First, calculate 8% of £450.
$8\% = \frac{8}{100} = 0.08$ so 8% of £450 is $0.08 \times 450 = £36$
This gives a total new cost of £450 + £36 = £486.

Method 2 An 8% increase can also be calculated by adding the 8% to the original 100% of the cost.
$100\% + 8\% = 108\%$ which can be written as $\frac{108}{100}$ or 1.08.
So an 8% increase is $1.08 \times £450 = £486$.

> **2** Calculate the values of the following after the % increases:
> (a) £250 after an increase of 12%

(b) a 16% increase on 80 m
(c) a 25% increase on an attendance of 6500
(d) a 9% increase on sales of £2400
(e) the cost of a £1500 computer after VAT at 17·5% is added

There are two similar methods which can be used to calculate % decreases.

E.g. In a sale prices have been reduced by 15%. Calculate the sale price of a coat that originally cost £80.

Method 1 Calculate 15% of £80 and take this away from £80.
15% = $\frac{15}{100}$ = 0·15 so 15% of £80 is 0·15 × 80 = £12

This gives a sale price for the coat of £80 − £12 = £68.

Method 2 Take the 15% from the original 100% leaving 85%.
85% = $\frac{85}{100}$ = 0·85 giving 0·85 × £80 = £68

3 Calculate the values of the following after the % decreases:
(a) £150 after a decrease of 8%
(b) a decrease of 12% on £250
(c) the price of an £11 500 car after a discount of 15%
(d) a 6% drop in an attendance of 850

Calculating increases and decreases as a fraction or percentage

You may be given the original value and the new value and asked to calculate the change (increase or decrease) as a fraction or percentage.

E.g. The cost of a computer game goes up from £40 to £45.
The increase in cost is £45 − £40 = £5.
The original cost is £40.
Dividing the increase by the original cost gives $\frac{5}{40} = \frac{1}{8}$
So the change in price is an increase of $\frac{1}{8}$.
Converting to a percentage:
$\frac{1}{8}$ = 0·125, 0·125 × 100 = 12·5%

So the percentage increase in the price is 12·5%.

Percentage decreases are calculated in the same way.

Hint: The original value often appears in the question after the word 'from'.

4 (a) Calculate the percentage increase if a concert ticket goes up from £25 to £27.
(b) Calculate the percentage change if the cost of a CD increases from £10 to £10·40.
(c) Calculate the percentage decrease if a camera is reduced from £160 to £148·80.

Remember: Always divide the change by the original value **not** the value after the change has taken place.

2.6e Calculating with ratios

It is very important that when you are writing two numbers as a ratio they must first be expressed in the same units.

E.g. Express 15p to £3 in its lowest form.
This becomes 15p : 300p and dividing both sides by 15 gives 1 : 20.

1 Express the following ratios in their lowest form:
   (a) 450 g : 1·35 kg   (1 kg = 1000 g)
   (b) 3 feet : 4 inches   (there are 12 inches in a foot)

Remember: Make sure your units are the same.

Sharing out a quantity in a given ratio

E.g. Mr Sharp and Mrs West share an inheritance of £64 000 in the ratio 5 : 3. How much will each get?
You add the numbers in the ratio to get the total number of shares or parts.
5 + 3 = 8 so there are 8 parts in all.

Method 1 Work out how much each part is worth.
64 000 ÷ 8 = 8000
Mr Sharp receives 5 of the 8 parts or 5 shares at £8000 each.
5 × 8000 = 40 000
So Mr Sharp's share of the inheritance is £40 000.

Method 2 Mrs West receives 3 of the 8 parts or $\frac{3}{8}$
$\frac{3}{8}$ × 64 000 = 24 000
So Mrs West's share of the inheritance is £24 000.

Hint: You can check the answer by adding the two results. They should add up to the total value.

2 You can make concrete by mixing gravel, sand and cement in the ratio 3 : 2 : 1 by volume.
   (a) How much gravel will be needed to make 12 cubic metres of concrete?
   (b) How much cement is needed to make 30 cubic meters of concrete?
   (c) If you have 2 cubic metres of sand how much concrete can you make?

Remember: As the units are the same they can be ignored in the calculation but must be put in the answer.

Increasing or decreasing by a given ratio

E.g. A cook book gives the following recipe for apple pie. This quantity is enough for 4 people. How much of each ingredient would you need to make an apple pie for 6 people?

500 g cooking apples
Granulated sugar to taste
200 g plain flour
2·5 ml salt
50 g lard
50 g margarine
Cold water to mix

The ratio of the amount required to the amount in the recipe is 6 : 4 which can be simplified to 3 : 2.
   To calculate the amount of each ingredient needed you could divide by 2 (because the amount in the recipe represents 2 parts) and then multiply by 3.
The quantity of apples you would now need is
          (500 g ÷ 2) × 3 = 250 g × 3 = 750 g
   An alternative is to convert the ratio to a fraction or a decimal and then use it to increase each of the values in the recipe.
To convert the ratio, divide the size you want by the size you have:
          $\frac{6}{4} = \frac{3}{2} = 1·5$
This gives you the multiplier you can then use to increase each of the values in the recipe.

If you multiply the 500 g of apples by 1·5 you get 500 g × 1·5 = 750 g. The two methods have the same result.

?

3 The recipe below for beef, tomato and mushroom stew makes enough for 4 people. Calculate the ingredients necessary to feed 10 people, using whichever method you find easier.

800 g stewing steak
30 g plain flour
Salt and pepper to taste
1 medium sized onion
3 medium sized leeks
100 g button mushrooms
50 g lard
400 g tinned tomatoes

4 Using the recipe in the example above, calculate the amount of apples and flour required to make apple pie for 3 people.

Remember: To get the multiplier, divide the size you want by the size you have.

You can use this method for any list of quantities. For example, if you want to enlarge a design the measurements of the design are like the ingredients in a recipe.

2.6f   Checking your answers

Whenever you do a calculation, either with or without a calculator, you should always check that your answer is sensible by doing an approximate calculation.

Multiplication problems

E.g. What is the cost of 28 cans of cat food which costs 39p a can?
You can estimate the answer by thinking:
"28 cans is about 30 cans and 39p is near enough 40p so the answer is about 30 × 40p = 1200p = £12"
Doing the calculation gives 28 × 39p = 1092p = £10·92 which is near enough to the estimate for you to know that the answer is sensible.

So you can work out a rough estimate by expressing each number to 1 significant figure.

?

1 Calculate the approximate answers to the following:
(a) Calculate the cost of 9 train tickets at £12·86 each.
(b) Calculate the cost of 17 wooden posts at £4·80 each.
(c) A line of 316 coins is laid down for charity. Calculate the length in metres of the line if the approximate diameter of each coin is 26 mm.
(d) Calculate the cost of 19 m of material at £9·99 a metre.

2 Now work out the exact answers.

Division problems

To estimate the answer to a division problem you can use the same method as for multiplication or you can try to spot connections between numbers to make it easier.

E.g. What is 285 ÷ 7?
You could approximate 285 to 300 (to 1 s.f.) and then work out 300 ÷ 7 by calculator or on paper.

However, since you know your 7 times table (and your 4 times table) you can work out $280 \div 7$ in your head because $7 \times 4 = 28$.

$285 \div 7$ is about $280 \div 7$ which you know is 40

so you can say the answer to $285 \div 7$ is about 40.

When you're estimating the answer to a division problem you want to cancel numbers as much as possible so you don't have to do any hard working out.

E.g. (a) What is the approximate answer to $\dfrac{28 \times 63}{17}$?

28 to 1 significant figure is 30
63 to 1 significant figure is 60
17 to 1 significant figure is 20

Rough estimate: $\dfrac{30 \times \overset{3}{60}}{\underset{1}{20}} = 30 \times 3 = 90$

You can say that $\dfrac{28 \times 63}{17}$ is *approximately equal to* $\dfrac{30 \times 60}{20}$

The signs $\approx$ and $\triangleq$ mean approximately equal to.

So $\dfrac{28 \times 63}{17} \approx 90$

(b) What is the approximate answer to $\dfrac{12 \times 372}{6}$?

You can cancel the 12 and the 6 to give $\dfrac{\overset{2}{12} \times 372}{\underset{1}{6}} = 2 \times 372$

Now using the method for multiplication problems,

$2 \times 372 \approx 2 \times 400$

So $\dfrac{12 \times 372}{6} \approx 800$

3 Work out the approximate answers to the following:

(a) $\dfrac{15 \times 89}{5}$ (b) $\dfrac{42 \times 71}{39}$ (c) $\dfrac{930}{32 \times 11}$ (d) $\dfrac{25 \times 57}{12 \times 18}$

Remember: 25 rounds up!

4 Now work out the accurate answers.

2.7a Multiplying and dividing powers of 10 in your head

Multiplying by numbers bigger than 1

Multiply the digits and then count up the 0's and put them on the end.

E.g. Multiply 600 by 700.
Multiplying the digits $6 \times 7 = 42$
There are four zeros which go after the 42.
This gives you $600 \times 700 = 420\,000$.

1 Work out the following in your head:

(a) 20×30 (b) 40×80 (c) 60×90 (d) 50×40

(e) 20×400 (f) 600×30 (g) 700×300 (h) 6000×40

Dividing by numbers bigger than 1

When you have to divide, you can use a similar method. This time you divide the digits and then divide the tens. Alternatively, cancel the zeros until you get a single digit on the bottom and then divide as normal.

E.g. Divide 8000 by 200.
$8000 \div 200$ becomes $(8 \div 2) \times (1000 \div 100) = 4 \times 10 = 40$
Alternatively, cancelling gives:
$$\frac{80\cancel{0}\cancel{0}}{2\cancel{0}\cancel{0}} = \frac{80}{2} = 40$$

2 Work out the following in your head:

(a) $900 \div 30$ (b) $2000 \div 40$ (c) $3000 \div 60$

(d) $6000 \div 300$ (e) $50\,000 \div 2000$

Multiplying by numbers less than 1

The method used to multiply numbers less than 1 is the same as for numbers bigger than 1 but the effect is different.
Look carefully at the following calculations.

$$30 \times 200 = 6000$$
$$30 \times 20 = 600$$
$$30 \times 2 = 60$$

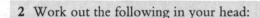

$$30 \times 0{\cdot}2 = 6$$
$$30 \times 0{\cdot}02 = 0{\cdot}6$$

Note: Multiplying by a number less than 1 has a decreasing effect.

To multiply by a number less than 1 in your head, first ignore the decimal point and do the calculation. Then look at the number of decimal places and adjust your answer to make it smaller.

E.g. (a) Multiply 40 by 0·2.

Step 1   Ignore the decimal point and carry out the calculation
           $40 \times 2 = 80$
Step 2   0·2 has **1** decimal place so move the decimal point **1** place to the **left**.
           $40 \times 0{\cdot}2 = 8{\cdot}0 = 8$

(b) Multiply 70×0.02.

Step 1 $70 \times 2 = 140$
Step 2   There are **2** decimal places so move the decimal point **2** places to the **left**.
          $70 \times 0.02 = 1.4$

Dividing by numbers less than 1

Dividing by a number less than 1 gives you the opposite effect to multiplying by a number less than 1.

E.g. $40 \div 0.2 = 200$

Note: Dividing by a number less than 1 has an increasing effect.

The easiest way to deal with this type of problem is to multiply both numbers by a power of ten so that the decimal becomes a whole number.

E.g. (a) $40 \div 0.2 = (40 \times 10) \div (0.2 \times 10) = 400 \div 2 = 200$

(b) $30 \div 0.05 = (30 \times 100) \div (0.05 \times 100) = 3000 \div 5 = 600$

Alternatively, you can ignore the decimal point, do the calculation and then adjust the number of decimal places.

E.g. (a) Divide 40 by 0.2.

Step 1 $40 \div 2 = 20$
Step 2   There is **1** decimal place so add **1** zero.
          $40 \div 0.2 = 200$

(b) Divide 30 by 0.05.

Step 1 $30 \div 5 = 6$
Step 2   There are **2** decimal places so add **2** zeros.
          $30 \div 0.05 = 600$

?

3 Work out the following in your head:

(a) 2×0.6	(b) 300×0.5	(c) 60×0.4
(d) 50×0.2	(e) $200 \div 0.5$	(f) $80 \div 0.4$
(g) $700 \div 0.07$	(h) $20 \div 0.05$	(i) $30 \div 0.06$

Remember: Multiplying by a number less than 1 decreases. Dividing by a number less than 1 increases.

2.7b   Solving problems with numbers of any size

You need to be able to use your calculator effectively to solve problems. The most common mistake made with this kind of work is that people divide when they should have multiplied and multiply when they should have divided. Always check that your answer is sensible.

E.g. Calculate the number of seconds in a year.

1 year = 365 days
1 day = 24 hours
1 hour = 60 minutes
1 minute = 60 seconds

Therefore there are 31 536 000 seconds in a year.

?

1 (a) Calculate the number of cm² in one square foot. (1 inch = 2·538 cm)

Hint: Calculate the number of cm² in 1 square inch and multiply by the number of square inches in a square foot.

(b) Calculate the number of inches in 1878 mm. (Give your answer to the nearest inch.)

Hint: Convert the distance to cm and then divide by the number of cm in 1 inch.

Often problems will involve multiplication and division.

E.g. Scales give Anjit's weight as 62 kg. Calculate his weight in stones and pounds. (1 lb = 0·454 kg)

First change his weight to pounds

To convert to stones, divide by 14

and then multiply the decimal part by 14 to convert it back to pounds

This rounds up so Anjit weighs 9 stone 11 (to the nearest lb).

Hint: You can use the same method to calculate answers given in hours and minutes.

?

2 (a) Michael travels 36 miles in 45 minutes. Calculate his average speed in miles per hour.
(b) If he continues at this average speed how long will it take him to travel another 52 miles? Give your answer in hours and minutes.

3 Driving in town Helen's car will do 48 miles to the gallon. If the tank of her car holds 52 litres of petrol how far can Helen travel in town on a full tank? (1 gallon = 4·546 litres)

4 Calculate the number of square yards of wall that can be painted with a 5 litre tin of paint if 1 litre covers 12 m². (0·8361 m² = 1 square yard)

2.7c Using memory and brackets on your calculator

Memory

Most calculators have a series of **memory** keys which give you the chance to store information or calculations you have already done. The memory facility is most useful when you have to do calculations which keep using the same number. You should always familiarise yourself with the way that your calculator works. Try not to use a new calculator that you are not sure of in an examination.

Remember: Different calculators have different memory keys. If you are not sure how your calculator works, ASK YOUR TEACHER.

These instructions may help you.

(a) To put a number into the memory of your calculator, for example 5, you might press these keys

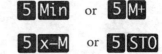

(b) To recall the number you might press

MR or RM or

MRC or RCL or SUM

(c) To add a value to the number already in the memory (e.g. 7)

7 M+

To subtract a value from the number already in the memory (e.g. 8)

8 M-

Then the appropriate command from (b) to show you the result.

(d) To multiply the memory by a number (e.g. 6)

6 × MR =

See (b) for the different memory recall commands.

Dividing a number by the memory is similar.

(e) To clear the memory on a scientific calculator you might press

CE x-M or AC Min

This should make the M disappear.

1 Use the memory facility on your calculator to work out the cost of these amounts after VAT (value-added tax) at 17·5% is added on.

(a) £25   (b) £36   (c) £250   (d) £178·56

Hint: 17·5% can be written 0·175. The amount plus VAT can be calculated by using 1·175. Try using this value in the memory of your calculator.

2 Use the memory facility on your calculator to work through the sequence on the right.

Enter 0·5 into the memory.

Let $x = 100$.

Write down each value of the sequence.

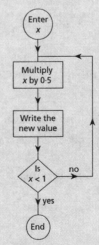

Brackets

There are two main types of calculator which are used in schools.

❶ **LTR calculators** which work left to right as you enter data.
❷ **Scientific calculators** which place an order of importance on the data you put into the calculator and carry out operations only when a bracket is closed or the = key is struck.

The scientific calculators have **brackets** to allow you to carry out calculations efficiently.

Most have several levels of brackets (also called parenthesis).

Look for the keys marked $\boxed{(...}$ or $\boxed{(}$ to open or start the bracket

$\boxed{...)}$ or $\boxed{)}$ to close or finish the bracket

Note: To do all the following work and in your exams you will need a scientific calculator.

3 Do the following calculations on your calculator:
  (a) $3 \times 4 + 2$ (b) $3 \times (4 + 2)$ (c) $8 + (4 \div 2)$ (d) $(8 + 4) \div 2$

Note: The inclusion of the brackets changes the meaning of the question.

When you enter a string of commands into a scientific calculator it will perform them in the following order ('BIDMAS'):

1 Brackets
2 Indices (powers or roots)
3 Division or multiplication
4 Addition or subtraction

When you are doing calculations it is important to remember that the calculator works in this way.

E.g. $\dfrac{8 + 12}{2} = 10$

But if you do this calculation on a scientific calculator

$\boxed{8}\ \boxed{+}\ \boxed{12}\ \boxed{\div}\ \boxed{2}\ \boxed{=}$

You will get the answer $\boxed{\qquad 14}$

This is because the calculator divides before adding.
$(12 \div 2 = 6) + 8 = 14$

To get the required result it is necessary to put brackets around the $(8 + 12)$. The calculator will deal with brackets first.

Remember: The horizontal bar used to show division acts like a bracket. If a part of the calculation appears either above or below the line it should be put into a bracket. This will help you avoid mistakes.

E.g. (a) $\dfrac{165 + 333}{13}$ becomes $(165 + 333) \div 13$

(b) $\dfrac{2717}{24 \times 19}$ becomes $2717 \div (24 \times 19)$

4 Use your calculator to evaluate the following. Round your answers to 1 d.p.
  (a) $15 \cdot 5 - \dfrac{16 \cdot 4}{2 \cdot 6}$ (b) $\dfrac{48 \cdot 2}{4 \cdot 2 \times 1 \cdot 6}$ (c) $\dfrac{15 \cdot 2 + 23 \cdot 4}{4 \cdot 8}$ (d) $\dfrac{13 \cdot 2 + 24 \cdot 7}{21 \cdot 3 - 17 \cdot 2}$

(e) The formula $V = \pi h(R^2 - r^2)$ gives the volume of material in this tube.

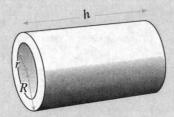

Calculate the volume of the tube when: $R = 10$ mm, $r = 8$ mm, $h = 300$ mm.

Hint: Write down the formula and then replace R, r and h with the values given. You will need to use the bracket facility on your calculator.

5 Calculate the value of the y coordinate using $y = x^2(4 - x)$ for values of x from $^-2$ to 2.

Remember: You should always try to use your calculator as efficiently as possible. Practise using the memory and bracket facilities as you work through the other sections of this book.

2.7d Choosing the appropriate degree of accuracy

Taking measurements

When you are measuring things it is important to realise that you are only working to a reasonable degree of accuracy. What is reasonable depends on the context.

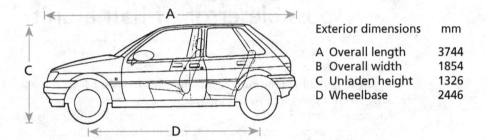

Exterior dimensions	mm
A Overall length	3744
B Overall width	1854
C Unladen height	1326
D Wheelbase	2446

The length of a car may be measured in millimetres but the degree of accuracy required is not that strict: a few mm longer or shorter doesn't matter.

The car's cylinders may also be measured in millimetres but here the degree of accuracy is *to the nearest mm*. If the cylinder is cut 1 mm too large or too small then the engine won't work.

The accuracy that can be achieved depends on the instrument you measure with.

1 Describe an appropriate instrument for measuring each of the following. Say what degree of accuracy you would expect in each case.
   (a) An angle in a maths lesson.
   (b) The time for the 100 metre sprint in the Olympics.
   (c) The distance between London and Manchester on a map.
   (d) The distance between London and Manchester in a car.
   (e) The speed of a car.
   (f) A patient's temperature.
   (g) Your weight.
   (h) The ingredients for a recipe.

The required degree of accuracy is often given in a question by indicating the number of decimal places or significant figures required in the solution.

When the degree of accuracy is not given

If the degree of accuracy is not indicated in a question you normally work to one more significant figure or decimal place than has been used in the question.
Or the degree of accuracy may be common sense, as in question **1** above.

E.g. The length of this page is 297 mm (to the nearest mm). If you divided it into seven equal bands, how wide would each band be?

$$2\ 9\ 7 \div 7 = 42.428571$$

This is accurate to a millionth of a millimetre. But you can't measure paper to this degree of accuracy. It would be enough to give your answer to 1 d.p., which is probably as accurate as you could draw with a sharp pencil.
So the answer is 42·4 mm (to 1 d.p.)

Remember: State the degree of accuracy in your answer.

?

> **2** Give your answers to the following questions to the appropriate degree of accuracy.
> (a) A book has 150 pages and is 11 mm thick. How thick is chapter 1, which has 29 pages?
> (b) The total weight of 11 people in a lift is 801·7 kg. What is their average weight?

2.7e Recognising that a measurement is in possible error of half a unit

You know that all measurements are approximations. Measurements cannot be given exactly so they are given to the nearest practical units.

Measuring a value to the nearest unit means deciding that it is nearer to one mark than another, in other words it is within half a unit of that mark.

Anything within the shaded area is 5 to the nearest unit.

If David's age is 14 to the nearest year that means he is actually between $13\frac{1}{2}$ and $14\frac{1}{2}$.

E.g. In a class survey the following information was recorded.

David Carter	
Height	158 cm
Weight	48 kg
Waist	67 cm
Neck	32 cm
Leg	70 cm

David's height is given as 158 cm. Since this has been measured to the nearest cm David's height could be anywhere within 0·5 cm either side of 158 cm.

The *smallest* he could be is 157·5 cm because this is the smallest measurement which rounds up to 158 cm.
What is the tallest David could be?

He must be less than 158·5 cm because this rounds up to 159 cm. But anything under 158·5 cm would be 158·49999… cm so it would round down to 158 cm.
The possible range of heights (*h*) for David is 157·5 cm ≤ *h* < 158·5 cm.

Note: At the upper end a less than sign is used. Although *h* can come very close to 158·5 cm it will never equal it.

?

1 Complete the following table for David's measurements.

	Minimum possible measurement	Maximum possible measurement	Range
Height			
Weight			
Waist			
Neck			
Leg			

2.7f   Compound measures

Speed is an example of a compound measure. It is a combination of two other measures: distance and time. Speed can be measured in miles per hour (mph), metres per second (m/s) or any other combination of a unit of distance divided by a unit of time. Units of compound measures often include the word 'per', which tells you to divide.

The formula for speed is

$$\text{average speed} = \frac{\text{distance travelled}}{\text{time taken}}$$

E.g.   Calculate the average speed (s) of a car travelling 80 miles (d) in 2 hours (t).

$$s = \frac{d}{t} = \frac{80}{20} = 40$$

The units are miles ÷ hours
therefore s = 40 miles per hour (mph)

The formula for finding speed can be rearranged to enable you to calculate distance travelled or time taken.

$$\text{distance travelled} = \text{average speed} \times \text{time taken} \quad \text{or} \quad \text{time taken} = \frac{\text{distance travelled}}{\text{average speed}}$$

?

1 (a) David's car travels 120 miles in 3 hours. Calculate his average speed.
(b) Amajit jogs at a steady 6 miles per hour for half an hour. How far does she travel?
(c) How long will it take a launch cruising at a speed of 8 km/h to travel 40 km?

Another example of a compound measure is **density**.

$$\text{density} = \frac{\text{mass}}{\text{volume}}$$

Density may be measured in kilograms per litre or g/cm³ or any other combination of a unit of weight divided by a unit of volume.

This formula can also be rearranged:

$$\text{mass} = \text{density} \times \text{volume} \quad \text{or} \quad \text{volume} = \frac{\text{mass}}{\text{density}}$$

2 (a) Gold has a density of 19·3 g/cm³. Calculate the mass of a bar of gold with a volume of 20 cm³.
(b) The density of aluminium is 2·7 g/cm³. What is the volume of a block of aluminium with a mass of 810 grams?
(c) Calculate the density of a 3 cm³ block of copper with a mass of 26·7 g.

An everyday example of a compound measure is **value for money**. We use this to compare the value of products which come in different sized packs.

E.g. Which of these two boxes of washing powder is better value?

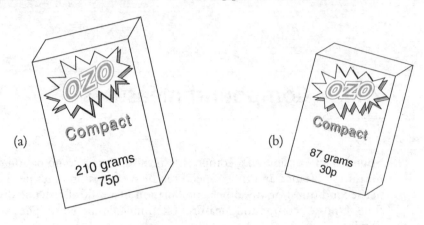

To find out which is better value you divide the quantity by the cost to get the number of grams per penny in each box.

(a) $\dfrac{210g}{75p} = 2\cdot8$ g/p   (b) $\dfrac{87g}{30p} = 2\cdot9$ g/p

So pack (b) gives you more for your money.

3 Which of the following are better value?

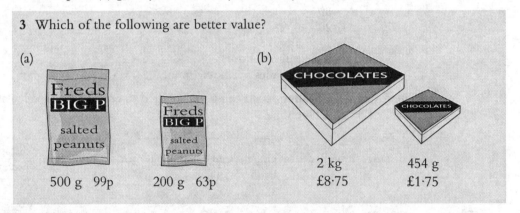

2.7g Positive integers as a product of primes

A **prime** number is a number with only two factors, 1 and the number itself. (1 is not a prime number.)

1 Make a list of the first ten prime numbers.

Apart from prime numbers themselves, all positive integers (counting numbers) can be expressed as the product of two or more prime numbers. You may be asked to find the prime factors of a number, or to express a number as the product of its prime factors. To do this you can use a factor tree.

E.g. Express 40 as a product of primes.

First find the prime factors of 40. This can be done in a number of ways, depending which factors of 40 you think of first:

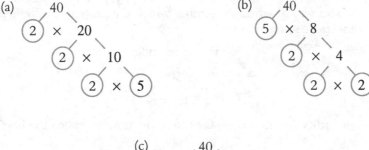

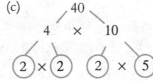

Each diagram goes on until each line (or branch) ends in a prime number.
The prime factors of 40 are 2 and 5.
In each case the factor tree gives the same result: 2, 2, 2 and 5.
40 as a product of primes is: $40 = 2 \times 2 \times 2 \times 5$ or $2^3 \times 5$

?

2 Use factor trees to find the prime factors of the following numbers:

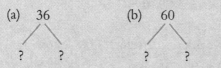

(a) 36   (b) 60   (c) 65

3 Express the following numbers as the product of prime factors. (Use the factor tree method as in the example.)

(a) 42   (b) 64   (c) 95   (d) 144   (e) 343

(f) The year you were born.

To show that a number is prime you have to show that it is not divisible by any number between 1 and itself. But you don't have to try dividing it by every number in between! You can immediately discount all the even numbers (except 2) and all the multiples of 5 (except 5 itself). To check for divisibility by 3 add all the digits and if the total is divisible by 3 then so is the number itself e.g. 87 becomes $8 + 7 = 15 = 3 \times 5$ so 87 is divisible by 3.

After checking 2, 3 and 5 you only need to check for prime factors less than $n/5$. (If n had a factor of $n/5$ or bigger it would have to go into n either 2, 3, 4 or 5 times but you've already checked that n is not divisible by these numbers.) Use your tables to check for divisibility.

?

4 Investigate which numbers up to 100 are prime.

2.8a Using index notation for powers and roots

Powers

You already know that $2 \times 2 \times 2 \times 2 \times 2 \times 2$ can be written as 2^6. We say *2 to the power 6*. This way of writing a number which is repeatedly multiplied by itself is called **index notation** or index form.

In the expression

— this is the index

2^6

— this is the base

the **index** tells us how many times the number (called the base) has been multiplied by itself.

?

1 Write the following in index form:

(a) $5 \times 5 \times 5 \times 5$

(b) $3 \times 3 \times 3 \times 3 \times 3 \times 3 \times 3$

(c) $\frac{1}{2} \times \frac{1}{2} \times \frac{1}{2}$

(d) 6

(e) $\frac{1}{7 \times 7 \times 7 \times 7}$

(f) $0 \cdot 21 \times 0 \cdot 21$

Look for the key marked $\boxed{x^y}$ or $\boxed{y^x}$

E.g. Calculate the value of 2^{16}

$$\boxed{2}\,\boxed{x^y}\,\boxed{1}\,\boxed{6}\,\boxed{=}\,\boxed{\qquad 65536}$$

?

2 Use your calculator to work out the value of the following:

(a) $3 \cdot 5^5$

(b) $4 \cdot 15$ to the power 4

(c) $\left(\frac{1}{2}\right)^6$

3 The number of germs on a slide doubles every minute. If you begin with just one germ calculate the number of germs after 24 minutes.

Negative powers

Look at this list of numbers.
Can you say what is happening
from one number in the sequence
to the next?

$2^4 = 16$
$2^3 = 8$
$2^2 = 4$
$2^1 = 2$

You can extend the sequence to find values for 2^0, 2^{-1}, 2^{-2}, 2^{-3} etc.

If you continue to apply the same rule
(divide by 2) you get these results.

$2^0 = 1$
$2^{-1} = \frac{1}{2}$
$2^{-2} = \frac{1}{4}$
$2^{-3} = \frac{1}{8}$

If you compare positive and negative powers (indices) you should notice that a relationship exists between them.

Positive index   Negative index

$2^3 = 8$ $2^{-3} = \dfrac{1}{2^3} = \dfrac{1}{8}$ ← Inverse or reciprocal of number

Number

4 Write each of the following as a fraction:
(a) 3^{-2} (b) 4^{-2} (c) 2^{-5} (d) 5^{-2}

You can use the $\boxed{x^y}$ key on your calculator for negative powers too.

E.g. Calculate the value of 3^{-4}

$$\boxed{3}\,\boxed{x^y}\,\boxed{4}\,\boxed{+/-}\,\boxed{=}\quad \boxed{0.0123456}$$

5 Calculate the values of each of the numbers in the following sequences:

(a) $3^3,\ 3^2,\ 3^1,\ 3^0,\ 3^{-1},\ 3^{-2},\ 3^{-3}$

(b) $5^3,\ 5^2,\ 5^1,\ 5^0,\ 5^{-1},\ 5^{-2},\ 5^{-3}$

(c) $4^3,\ 4^2,\ 4^1,\ 4^0,\ 4^{-1},\ 4^{-2},\ 4^{-3}$

6 You should already have noticed something about 2^0, 3^0, 4^0 and 5^0.
Use your calculator to work out the value of the following:
(a) 23^0 (b) 15^0 (c) 1000^0 (d) $\left(\frac{1}{2}\right)^0$ (e) 0.23^0

Remember: Any number to the power 0 is 1.

Calculating with index numbers

E.g. Calculate the value of $2^3 + 3^2$
$$2^3 + 3^2 = (2 \times 2 \times 2) + (3 \times 3) = 8 + 9 = 17$$
$$\boxed{2}\,\boxed{x^y}\,\boxed{3}\,\boxed{+}\,\boxed{3}\,\boxed{x^y}\,\boxed{2}\,\boxed{=}\quad\boxed{17}$$

7 Calculate the value of the following:
(a) $3^3 - 2^2$ (b) $2^3 \times 3$ (c) $4^3 \times 2^{-2}$ (d) $16^9 \div 4^{17}$ (e) $2.5^{-3} - 5^{-2}$

Roots

Imagine you could multiply a number a by itself $\frac{1}{2}$ a time. You would write this $a^{\frac{1}{2}}$.

Multiplying $a^{\frac{1}{2}}$ by $a^{\frac{1}{2}}$ would be the same as multiplying a by itself one whole time so
$$a^{\frac{1}{2}} \times a^{\frac{1}{2}} = a$$
$$\left(a^{\frac{1}{2}}\right)^2 = a$$

So $a^{\frac{1}{2}}$ must be the square root of a.
$$a^{\frac{1}{2}} = \sqrt{a}$$

In the same way that the index $\frac{1}{2}$ represents the square root, other roots can also be represented by fractions.
$$a^{\frac{1}{3}} = \sqrt[3]{a}$$
$$a^{\frac{1}{4}} = \sqrt[4]{a} \text{ etc.}$$

The nth root is represented by the index $\frac{1}{n}$.

8 Write the following in index form:

(a) $\sqrt{9}$ (b) $\sqrt[3]{64}$ (c) the 5th root of 10   (d) $\sqrt[16]{487.49}$

To calculate a root on your calculator you can use the inverse of the key used to calculate powers.

Above the $\boxed{x^y}$ key you should see $x^{\frac{1}{y}}$ (the yth root of x).

E.g. Calculate the value of $2{\cdot}48832^{\frac{1}{5}}$ (the 5th root of $2{\cdot}48832$)

$$\boxed{2}\ \boxed{\cdot}\ \boxed{4}\ \boxed{8}\ \boxed{8}\ \boxed{3}\ \boxed{2}\ \boxed{\text{INV}}\ \boxed{x^y}\ \boxed{5}\ \boxed{=}\qquad\boxed{1.2}$$

9 Use your calculator to work out the value of the following:

   (a) $\sqrt[3]{4913}$ (b) $6{\cdot}25^{\frac{1}{2}}$ (c) $1\ 679\ 616^{\frac{1}{4}}$ (d) $32^{\frac{1}{5}}$

2.8b   Standard index form

Standard index form (SI form) or scientific notation is used to enable us to write very large or very small numbers more easily. Instead of having to write in all the zeros in numbers like 2 000 000 (two million) or 0·000002 (two millionths), we can express them as powers of 10.

E.g. 2 000 000 (two million) $= 2 \times 10 \times 10 \times 10 \times 10 \times 10 \times 10$
      Hence 2 000 000 can be written as 2×10^6.

Remember: 10^2 is one hundred
                    10^3 is one thousand
                    10^4 is ten thousand
                    10^5 is one hundred thousand
                    10^6 is one million

To change a number to standard form, put a decimal point after the first digit and then count how many places the decimal point has moved. This gives you the power of 10.

E.g. Change 3 567 000 to standard index form.

$$3{\cdot}576\ 000{\cdot}$$

The point has moved 6 places so multiply by 10^6.
3 567 000 $= 3{\cdot}567 \times 10^6$

Remember: In standard form only one digit must be used before the decimal point.

The number is written as $a \times 10^n$ where $1 \le a < 10$ (a is between 1 and 10) and n is a whole number.

E.g. 35 000 is $3{\cdot}5 \times 10^4$
      26 is $2{\cdot}6 \times 10^1$

1 Write the following numbers in standard index form:
   (a) The radius of Mercury is 2 420 000 m.
   (b) The radius of Venus is 6 085 000 m.
   (c) The radius of Jupiter is 71 400 000 m.

2 Write the following numbers in ordinary form:
   (a) The radius of Pluto is 3×10^6 m.
   (b) The distance of the earth from the sun is $1{\cdot}496 \times 10^{11}$ m.

Numbers less than 1 can also be written in standard index form.

E.g. Write 0·000002 in standard form.

      0·000002 is 2 millionths or $\frac{2}{1\,000\,000}$

which can be written as $\frac{2}{10^6}$ or $2 \times \frac{1}{10^6}$

The general rule is that $\frac{1}{10^n}$ is written as 10^{-n}

so $0 \cdot 000002 = 2 \times 10^{-6}$

Remember: 10^{-1} is one 10th
10^{-2} is one 100th
10^{-3} is one 1000th
10^{-4} is one 10 000th
10^{-5} is one 100 000th
10^{-6} is one 1 000 000th

To change a number less than 1 to standard form, put a decimal point after the first digit and then count how many places the decimal point has moved to the right. The power of 10 is minus the number of places the point has moved.

?

3 Write each of the following numbers in standard index form:

(a) $0 \cdot 003$ (b) $0 \cdot 052$ (c) $0 \cdot 00000861$ (d) $0 \cdot 00703$

4 Write each of the following numbers in ordinary notation:

(a) 5×10^{-5} (b) 8×10^{-1} (c) $9 \cdot 3 \times 10^{-4}$ (d) $6 \cdot 32 \times 10^{-2}$

Look for the key marked **EXP** or **E** or **EE**
This is called the exponent key.

To enter $5 \cdot 38 \times 10^4$ press

5 **.** **3** **8** **EXP** **4**

Display: [5.38 04] or [5.38 E 04] or [5.38 04]

Calculations in standard index form

If you're working without a calculator start by grouping the numbers and the powers of 10. Do the calculation and then put the answer in standard form.

E.g. (a) Multiply 4×10^3 by 6×10^5

$(4 \times 10^3) \times (6 \times 10^5) = (4 \times 6) \times (10^3 \times 10^5)$
$= 24 \times (10 \times 10 \times 10) \times (10 \times 10 \times 10 \times 10 \times 10)$
$= 24 \times 10^8$

which is $2 \cdot 4 \times 10^9$ in standard form

4 **EXP** **3** **×** **6** **EXP** **5** **=** [2.4 09]

Remember: You must write $2 \cdot 4 \times 10^9$. 2·4 09 is not an acceptable way to write $2 \cdot 4 \times 10^9$.

(b) Divide 8×10^5 by 2×10^3

$(8 \times 10^5) \div (2 \times 10^3) = (8 \div 2) \times (10^5 \div 10^3)$
$= 4 \times \dfrac{10 \times 10 \times 10 \times 10 \times 10}{10 \times 10 \times 10}$
$= 4 \times 10^2$

(c) Multiply 2×10^3 by 3×10^{-5}

$(2 \times 10^3) \times (3 \times 10^{-5}) = (2 \times 3) \times \dfrac{10 \times 10 \times 10}{10 \times 10 \times 10 \times 10 \times 10}$
$= \dfrac{6}{10^2}$
$= 6 \times 10^{-2}$

When you answer the following questions, give your answer in standard index form. (You may use a calculator.)

5 (a) $(7 \times 10^4) \times (5 \times 10^7)$ (b) $(8 \times 10^6) \div (2 \times 10^2)$

   (c) $(4 \cdot 3 \times 10^5) \times (7 \cdot 8 \times 10^9)$ (d) $(2 \cdot 7 \times 10^{20}) \div (9 \cdot 5 \times 10^{14})$

6 A light year is approximately $9 \cdot 46 \times 10^{15}$ m. Calculate in metres the distance to the star Rigel in Orion's belt which is $5 \cdot 4 \times 10^2$ light years from the earth.

7 The volume of the earth is approximately $1 \cdot 4 \times 10^{27}$ m³.
   The mass of the earth is approximately 2×10^{30} kg.
   Calculate the density of the earth in kg/m³ $\left(\text{density} = \dfrac{\text{mass}}{\text{volume}} \right)$.

8 Calculate $(4 \cdot 8 \times 10^3) \div (1 \cdot 6 \times 10^{-2})$.

9 The common cold virus is 5×10^{-7} m long.
   (a) How long would a chain of 12 000 viruses be?
   (b) How many viruses would fit into 1 mm?

Addition and subtraction

If you're adding or subtracting numbers in standard form without using a calculator it is important to take care over the powers of 10.
To add or subtract numbers with the same power of 10 you add or subtract the digits then multiply by the power of 10 and convert your answer to standard form.

E.g. $(5 \times 10^3) + (6 \times 10^3) = (5 + 6) \times 10^3$
$$= 11 \times 10^3$$
$$= 1 \cdot 1 \times 10^4$$

If you have to add or subtract numbers with different powers of 10 it is often easiest if you convert them back to normal notation first.

E.g. (a) $(2 \times 10^3) + (3 \times 10^5) = 2000 + 300\,000 = 302\,000$

     which is $3 \cdot 02 \times 10^5$ in standard form.

    (b) $(2 \times 10^6) - (3 \times 10^5) = 2\,000\,000 - 300\,000 = 1\,700\,000$ which is $1 \cdot 7 \times 10^6$

An alternative method is to convert one number so that both numbers have the same power of 10.

E.g. $3 \times 10^5 = 300\,000 = 300 \times 10^3$
    so $(2 \times 10^3) + (3 \times 10^5) = (2 \times 10^3) + (300 \times 10^3)$
$$= 302 \times 10^3$$
$$= 3 \cdot 02 \times 10^5$$

2.8c   Substituting negative numbers into formulae

Replacing a letter in a formula by a number is called **substitution**.

E.g. x, y and z are connected by the formula $x = 3y - 2z$.
    Calculate the value of x when $y = {}^-2$ and $z = {}^-5$.
    Substituting these values into the formula you get
$$x = 3y - 2z$$
$$= (3 \times {}^-2) - (2 \times {}^-5)$$
$$= {}^-6 - ({}^-10)$$
$$= {}^-6 + 10$$
$$= 4$$

The key ±⁄ changes a + number to a − and a − number to a +.

$3 \times 2\text{±} - 2 \times 5\text{±} = \boxed{ 4}$

> **1** Calculate the value of the following. (Remember to set them out correctly.)
> (a) If $r = p - 2q$ work out r when $p = 7$ and $q = \text{}^-3$.
> (b) If $a = 2b + 3c$ work out a when $b = \text{}^-5$ and $c = \text{}^-4$.
> (c) If $t = 4r - s$ work out t when $r = \text{}^-\frac{1}{2}$ and $s = \text{}^-5$.

The same methods are used for formulae involving multiplication and division.

E.g. a, b and c are connected by the formula $a = \dfrac{4bc}{b - 2c}$.

Calculate the value of a when $b = \text{}^-2$ and $c = \text{}^-3$.

$$a = \frac{4 \times {}^-2 \times {}^-3}{{}^-2 - \left({}2 \times {}^-3\right)} = \frac{24}{{}^-2 - {}^-6} = \frac{24}{{}^-2 + 6} = \frac{24}{4} = 6$$

> **2** (a) If $x = 3yz$ work out x when $y = \text{}^-4$ and $z = \text{}^-2$.
> (b) If $a = 5bc - c$ work out a when $b = \text{}^-3$ and $c = \text{}^-2$.
> (c) If $t = w(v + u)$ work out t when $w = \text{}^-2$, $v = \text{}^-4\cdot5$ and $u = \text{}^-1\cdot5$.
> (d) If $p = \dfrac{r}{s} - t$ work out p when $r = 12$, $s = \text{}^-3$ and $t = \text{}^-2$.
> (e) If $a = \dfrac{b^2 + c^2}{d}$ work out a when $b = \text{}^-3$, $c = \text{}^-4$ and $d = 5$.

> **3** (a) Find the value of $\dfrac{5a + 9b + 8c}{a + b + c}$ when $a = \text{}^-2$, $b = 3$ and $c = 5$.
> (b) Find the value of $s = ut + \frac{1}{2}at^2$ when $t = 0\cdot5$, $a = \text{}^-3$ and $u = 6$.
> (c) Calculate $\dfrac{-b + \sqrt{b^2 - 4ac}}{2a}$ when $a = \text{}^-2$, $b = \text{}^-3$ and $c = 2$.

2.8d Calculating with fractions

Addition of mixed numbers

To add mixed numbers together you can either add the whole numbers then add the fractions or convert the mixed numbers into improper (top heavy) fractions and then add them.

E.g. $2\frac{3}{4} + 1\frac{1}{8} = \frac{11}{4} + \frac{9}{8} = \frac{22}{8} + \frac{9}{8} = \frac{31}{8} = 3\frac{7}{8}$

Subtraction of mixed numbers

If the fractional part of the number you are taking away is smaller than the fractional part of the first number then you can subtract the whole numbers and subtract the fractions separately.

E.g. $2\frac{3}{4} - 1\frac{1}{8}$
First the whole numbers: $2 - 1 = 1$
and then the fractions: $\frac{3}{4} - \frac{1}{8} = \frac{6}{8} - \frac{1}{8} = \frac{5}{8}$
Giving a total answer of $1\frac{5}{8}$

If the fractional part of the number you are taking away is larger then you convert both mixed numbers into improper fractions.

E.g. $2\frac{1}{8} - 1\frac{3}{4} = \frac{17}{8} - \frac{7}{4} = \frac{17}{8} - \frac{14}{8} = \frac{3}{8}$

1 (a) $3\frac{1}{4} + 2\frac{1}{2}$　　(b) $2\frac{1}{2} - 1\frac{1}{8}$　　(c) $3\frac{1}{4} + 1\frac{3}{8}$　　(d) $4\frac{3}{7} - 2\frac{8}{9}$

Multiplication

When you multiply fractions together you multiply the numerators (top numbers) together and you multiply the denominators (bottom numbers) together.

E.g. $\frac{3}{4} \times \frac{1}{2} = \frac{3}{8}$

We can illustrate this like this:

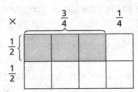

2 (a) $\frac{1}{3} \times \frac{1}{2}$　　(b) $\frac{2}{3} \times \frac{1}{2}$　　(c) $\frac{3}{5} \times \frac{3}{4}$　　(d) $\frac{7}{8} \times \frac{2}{5}$

Note: On some calculators you can do fractions.

To multiply mixed numbers, the first step is to change both of the mixed numbers into improper or top heavy fractions. Then multiply as above. Convert your answer back into a mixed number.

E.g. $1\frac{3}{4} \times 1\frac{1}{2} = \frac{7}{4} \times \frac{3}{2} = \frac{21}{8} = 2\frac{5}{8}$

3 (a) $2\frac{1}{2} \times 1\frac{1}{2}$　　(b) $3\frac{3}{8} \times 2\frac{3}{4}$　　(c) $1\frac{3}{13} \times 2\frac{1}{2}$

Remember: Some questions that involve the multiplication of fractions can be simplified by cancelling.

E.g. $1\frac{3}{5} \times 1\frac{2}{3}$

Without cancelling $1\frac{3}{5} \times 1\frac{2}{3} = \frac{8}{5} \times \frac{5}{3} = \frac{40}{15} = 2\frac{10}{15} = 2\frac{2}{3}$

With cancelling　$1\frac{3}{5} \times 1\frac{2}{3} = \frac{8}{{}_1\cancel{5}} \times \frac{\cancel{5}^1}{3} = \frac{8}{3} = 2\frac{2}{3}$

4 (a) $2\frac{1}{2} \times 1\frac{3}{5}$　　(b) $3\frac{3}{4} \times 2\frac{2}{5}$

Division

Dividing by a number means finding out how many times it goes into something.
For example, $6 \div \frac{1}{2}$ means how many halves are there in 6.
There are 2 halves in 1 so there are 12 halves in 6 (6×2).
$6 \div \frac{1}{2}$ is the same as $6 \times$ (the number of times $\frac{1}{2}$ goes into 1) or $6 \times (1 \div \frac{1}{2})$.

$1 \div \frac{1}{2}$ is called the inverse (or reciprocal) of $\frac{1}{2}$. (The inverse of $\frac{1}{2}$ is 2.)

So to divide by a fraction you multiply by its inverse.
To divide by a general fraction $\frac{a}{b}$ you multiply by $1 \div \frac{a}{b}$.

$$1 = \frac{b}{a} \times \frac{a}{b}$$

Dividing both sides by $\frac{a}{b}$ gives $1 \div \frac{a}{b} = \frac{b}{a}$

So to divide by a fraction you turn it upside down and then multiply.

E.g. $\frac{3}{4} \div \frac{1}{2}$

$\frac{3}{4} \div \frac{1}{2} = \frac{3}{{}_2\cancel{4}} \times \frac{\cancel{2}^1}{1} = \frac{3}{2} = 1\frac{1}{2}$

?   5   (a) $\frac{3}{4} \div \frac{1}{8}$ (b) $\frac{2}{5} \div \frac{1}{2}$ (c) $1\frac{3}{4} \div \frac{1}{2}$

Remember: When you are doing any calculations which involve fractions you should always simplify your answer.

2.8e   Checking your answers

When you are doing any calculation you should check whether your answer is about right (of the right order of magnitude).

Note: This is particularly important in exams.

The following steps should help you work out an approximate answer.

Step 1   Look for any decimals which represent familiar fractions, such as 0·25 and 0·5.
Step 2   If the calculation involves division, cancel any numbers which are approximately equal to a multiple of each other.
Step 3   Round the numbers you have left to 1 or 2 significant figures.

E.g.   (a) Work out the approximate value of $\dfrac{0\cdot25 \times 82\cdot8}{5\cdot6}$.

     Step 1 $0\cdot25 = \frac{1}{4}$
     Step 3   82·8 is about 80
                    so the top line is equal to about $\frac{1}{4} \times 80 = 20$

Dividing this by 5·6 will give you about 3 or 4.

  (b) Work out the approximate value of $\dfrac{1\cdot6 \times 450}{3}$.

     Step 2   1·6 is about 1·5, which is half of 3

     Cancelling gives $\dfrac{1\cdot6 \times 450}{3} \approx \dfrac{1 \times 450}{2} = 225$

  (c) Work out the approximate area of a room 3·65 m wide and 4·35 m long.

     Step 3   3·65 m ≈ 4 m and 4·35 m ≈ 4 m

This gives you an approximation of 4 × 4 = 16 square metres.

?

1   Work out the approximate value of the following:
   (a) $\dfrac{0\cdot75 \times 41}{3}$ (b) $\dfrac{2\cdot6 \times 17}{5}$ (c) $3\cdot142 \times 10\cdot2 \times 10\cdot2 \times 50$

2   (a) Calculate the actual area of the room in the example above.
   (b) If this room is carpeted with carpet which costs £15·99 a square metre what is the approximate cost? (Use the estimate of the floor area obtained in the example.)
   (c) Calculate the actual cost of the carpet.

3   Estimate the value of the following. (**DO NOT** use a calculator.)
   (a) $\dfrac{3736}{24 \times 19}$ (b) $\dfrac{178 + 466}{13}$ (c) $\dfrac{293 - 127}{141}$ (d) $124 \times (381 - 178)$

4   Compare the approximations you have worked out to the accurate answers to these questions.

2.9a   Rational and irrational numbers

Rational numbers

Most of the numbers we use in everyday life are rational numbers.

A **rational** number is any number that can be expressed as a vulgar fraction, i.e. written in the form $\frac{a}{b}$, where a and b are whole numbers.

All integers (positive and negative whole numbers) are rational because they can be written as $\frac{a}{1}$.

All vulgar fractions are rational because they are already in the form $\frac{a}{b}$.

All terminating decimals (decimals which stop after a number of places) are rational because they can be written in the form $\frac{a}{10^n}$.

E.g.   0·375 stops after 3 decimal places so it can be written as $\frac{375}{1000}$.

All recurring decimals (decimals which repeat after a number of places) are rational. (Remember dots are used to indicate the first and last number in any repeating pattern.)

E.g. $0 \cdot \dot{5} \dot{4} = 0 \cdot 545454\ldots$ repeats after two decimal places.

Multiplying by 100 gives 54·54545…

54·5454545…   this is 100 × the value

− 0·5454545…   this is 1 × the value

54·0000000…   this is 99 × the value

so $0 \cdot \dot{5} \dot{4} \times 99 = 54$

$0 \cdot \dot{5} \dot{4} = \frac{54}{99} = \frac{6}{11}$

This can be done for any recurring decimal but you are not required to learn it.

?

1 Investigate using your calculator which vulgar fractions less than 1 recur when written as decimals.

Some of your answers will have had obvious repeats. Others may have appeared not to repeat at all. Some have a recurring pattern which is too long to show up on your calculator.

E.g. $\frac{9}{19} = 0 \cdot \dot{4}7368421052631578\dot{9}$

This decimal repeats after 18 digits!

If your calculator does not have sufficient display to show you the solution, you can use pen and paper methods or write a simple programme to carry out the process for you.

?

2 Without using your calculator, write the following fractions as decimals:

   (a) $\frac{1}{7}$ (b) $\frac{2}{13}$ (c) $\frac{4}{21}$

Irrational numbers

An **irrational** number is one which is **not** rational. An irrational number cannot be expressed as $\frac{a}{b}$ with a and b both whole numbers. If you expressed an irrational number as a decimal it would go on for ever (to infinity) without repeating.

There are many more irrational numbers than rational numbers but you will mainly use rational numbers. However, there are two irrational numbers you will use often. These are π (pi) and $\sqrt{2}$ (the square root of 2).

If you look at each of these values on your calculator you will see that they do not repeat.

At a higher level you could use an iterative method to show that $\sqrt{2}$ never ends and never repeats within the limits of your ability to calculate it.

2.9b   Upper and lower bounds

You have seen that a measurement to the nearest unit really refers to an interval of one unit centred on that measurement. Now you need to be able to find the possible values of a number expressed to any degree of accuracy, not just to the nearest unit.

If you think of the range of possible values, the bottom end of the range is called the **lower bound** (lower limit), and the top end of the range is called the **upper bound** (upper limit). When you are asked to give the upper and lower bounds of a number you need to know whether the quantity you are dealing with is discrete or continuous. Money is an example of a **discrete** quantity because you have to count it in whole numbers of pence. You either have one value or the next.

E.g.   A salesman's salary is £16 000 to the nearest £1000. What are the possible values of his actual salary?

$$£15\ 500 \leq £16\ 000 \leq £16\ 499\text{·}99 \quad \text{NOT} \quad £15\ 999\text{·}50 \leq £16\ 000 \leq £16\ 000\text{·}50$$

Measurement is **continuous** so although there is an upper bound there is no maximum value.

E.g. $15\text{·}5 \text{ m} \leq 16 \text{ m} < 16\text{·}5 \text{ m}$

Note: Although the value can be close to 16·5, it is always less than 16.5.

By convention we round 5 up so the lower limit is included.

1 Give the upper and lower bounds for the following amounts:

(a) £12 (to the nearest £)   (b) £60 (to the nearest £10)

(c) £750 (to the nearest £50)   (d) £8·90 (to the nearest 10p)

2 Give the upper and lower bounds for the following measurements:

(a) 638 kg (to the nearest kg)   (b) 1700 g (to the nearest 100 g)

(c) 10 m (to the nearest m)   (d) 495 cm (to the nearest 5 cm)

If the degree of accuracy is not given in a question it may be implied by the way the number is written.
If a measurement is given as 4·6 m the possible range of values is $4\text{·}55 \leq 4\text{·}6 < 4\text{·}65$.
If the measurement is given as 4·60 m then the range becomes $4\text{·}595 \leq 4\text{·}60 < 4\text{·}605$.

Remember: 4·6 and 4·60 do not imply the same accuracy.

3 Give the upper and lower bounds for the following:
(a) A room is 3·7 m long.
(b) A newspaper report indicates that the attendance at a football match was 11 000.

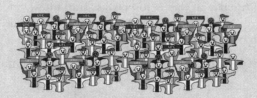

(c) An object is weighed on two different sets of scales, one of which is more accurate than the other. The scales show the following amounts:
   (i) 2·61 kg   (ii) 2·610 kg

2.10a Upper and lower bounds in calculations

Addition

E.g. Find the upper bound for the perimeter of a rectangular building plot which has sides of 40 m and 18 m measured to the nearest metre.

The upper bounds of the plot's measurements are 40·5 m and 18·5 m. The upper bound of the perimeter is therefore
$$2(l + w) = 2(40·5 + 18·5) = 118 \text{ m}$$

1 Calculate the lower bound length for the perimeter of the building plot.

2 Calculate the upper and lower bounds for the perimeters of the following rectangles:

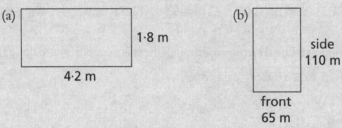

(a) 1·8 m   4·2 m

(b) side 110 m   front 65 m

Subtraction

There are two types of subtraction problem involving upper and lower bounds. In the first type, you have to subtract numbers which are both approximations.

E.g. The plot of land represented by the rectangle in question 2(b) above is to be fenced all round apart from a distance of about 50 m, where there is already a wall. Calculate the maximum and minimum lengths of fence needed.

Length of fencing = perimeter − length of wall
The minimum length of fencing is required when the perimeter is at its minimum value and the wall is at its maximum value.
So minimum fencing = 348 − 50·5 = 297·5 m
Similarly, maximum fencing = upper bound perimeter − minimum wall
Maximum fencing = 352 − 49·5 = 302·5 m

3 If a space is to be left in the fencing for gates measuring 2·3 m, calculate the new upper and lower bounds for the amount of fencing needed.

4 If $a = b − 2c$ find the upper and lower bounds for a when $b = 4·8$ (to 1 d.p.) and $c = 1·7$ (to 1 d.p.).

The second type of subtraction question involves subtracting from a fixed total.

E.g. On the day of the St Joseph's school photograph about 30 of the 927 pupils were absent. Find the upper and lower bounds for the number of pupils in the photograph.

First find the upper and lower bounds for the number of pupils who were away:
$$25 \leq 30 \leq 34$$

Now subtract these from the total:
$$927 − 25 = 902$$
$$927 − 34 = 893$$

Note: Subtracting the minimum number of absent pupils gives the maximum number in the photograph and vice versa.

5 (a) Of the 927 pupils at St Joseph's about 500 are boys. Calculate the maximum number of girls.

(b) To the nearest 50, 750 pupils are under 16. Calculate the minimum number of pupils who are 16 or over.

Multiplication

Multiplying approximations together means the errors are also multiplied.

E.g. A square has sides of 3 m. Find the possible values for its area.

$2{\cdot}5$ m $\leq$ side length $< 3{\cdot}5$ m
$2{\cdot}5^2$ m^2 $\leq$ area $< 3{\cdot}5^2$ m^2
$6{\cdot}25$ m^2 $\leq$ area $< 12{\cdot}25$ m^2

So there is 1 m between the upper and lower bounds for the sides of the square but the difference between the upper and lower bounds for the area is 6 m^2.

6 A lawn is 15 m long and 8 m wide to the nearest metre.
(a) Calculate the upper bound area of the lawn.
(b) Calculate the lower bound area.
(c) The lawn is to be seeded at a rate of 30 grams per square metre. Calculate the maximum amount of seed required.

Division

E.g. The ceiling of the room shown is to be painted. The instructions on the paint state that 1 litre of paint will cover 13 m^2. Calculate the upper and lower bounds of the amount of paint needed.

First you need to know the upper and lower bounds for the area of the ceiling.

Upper bound $= 5{\cdot}25 \times 6{\cdot}65$
$\qquad\qquad = 34{\cdot}9125$ m^2
Lower bound $= 5{\cdot}15 \times 6{\cdot}55$
$\qquad\qquad = 33{\cdot}7325$ m^2

The upper and lower bounds for the area covered by 1 litre of paint are 13·5 m^2 and 12·5 m^2.
To calculate the amount of paint needed you must divide the area of the ceiling by the amount that 1 litre will cover.
To calculate the *maximum* amount needed you assume the worst: maximum ceiling area and minimum paint coverage.

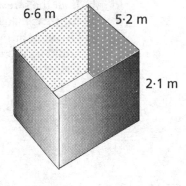

6·6 m   5·2 m

2·1 m

$$\frac{\text{maximum area of ceiling}}{\text{minimum coverage}} = \frac{34 \cdot 9125}{12 \cdot 5}$$

$$= 2{\cdot}793 \text{ litres}$$

7 (a) Which measurements would you need to use to find the minimum amount of paint needed?
(b) Assuming the room has no doors or windows, calculate the minimum number of 1 litre tins needed to paint the walls.
(c) Again ignoring any doors or windows, what is the maximum number of 1 litre tins needed to paint the walls?

2.10b The effects of error on calculations involving measurement

You have seen that the difference between the upper and lower bounds of a measurement can give you different results.

These may not be significant for one item but you should be aware that the greater the number of items collected together the greater the possible error.

1 Imagine from research you find out that people's average weight is 160 lbs.

How many of these average people can you safely put into this lift?

Maximum weight 2000 lbs

If the research is incorrect, putting the same number of people in the lift could have very serious consequences.

Imagine the possible result of putting the same number of people in the lift if their average weight was 190 lbs! The safety limit would be exceeded by 280 lbs.

Often the possible effects of errors in measurements are most pronounced in industrial use.

2 A firm manufactures screws with a weight of 16 grams (to the nearest gram). The manufacturers wish to produce 1 000 000 (1 million) screws.

(a) What are the upper and lower bounds of the weight of the screws?
(b) If all the screws are exactly 16 g how many kilograms of steel will be needed for their manufacture?
(c) Use your answer to part (a) to calculate the maximum amount of steel that could be required.
(d) Calculate the minimum amount of steel that could be required.

Remember: Small errors in measurement are magnified when you are dealing with multiple items.

3.6a　Rules for generating sequences

A sequence is a list of numbers arranged according to a rule.

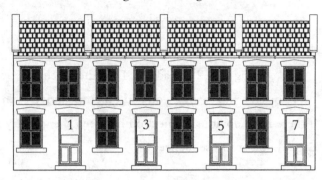

The rule here is + 2 starting at 1.

?

> **1** Write the first five numbers in the sequences generated by these rules:
> (a) Rule + 3　starting at 1
> (b)　　− 2　starting at 20
> (c)　　× 5　starting at 1
> (d)　　− 2　starting at 1

Sequences can also be generated by a combination of rules.

?

> **2** Write down the first five numbers generated by the following rules:
> (a)　　× 3　+ 2　starting at 1
> (b)　　× 2　− 2　starting at 1
> (c)　　− 2　× 3　starting at 10

Describing sequences

Some sequences are easier to describe in words.

E.g.　Describe the sequence 2, 5, 10, 17, 26, ...

> "In this sequence you start with 2 then add on 3 and then 5 and then 7 and so on."

> or "Starting with 2 you add on 3 and then each time you add on 2 more than you added on the last time."

> or "Start with 2 and add on consecutive odd numbers beginning with 3."

?

> **3** Explain in words how these sequences are generated:
> (a) 1, 3, 6, 10, 15, 21, ...
> (b) The Fibonacci sequence 1, 1, 2, 3, 5, 8, ...

Using the difference method to find the rule

Looking at a sequence of numbers you should be able to find the rule which generated the sequence. First look at the **difference** between the numbers in the sequence.

E.g.　Look at this sequence:

$$3 \quad 5 \quad 7 \quad 9 \quad 11 \quad ...$$

$$+2 \quad +2 \quad +2 \quad +2$$

The gap here is always 2 so the rule is + 2 starting with 3.

Sometimes you will need to use the difference method twice to find the rule.

E.g. Look at this sequence:

$$2 \quad 6 \quad 12 \quad 20 \quad 30 \quad \ldots$$

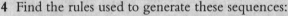

The *gap* increases by 2 each time.

"Starting with 2 you add on 4 and then each time add on 2 more than the last time."

or "Starting with 2 you add on consecutive even numbers beginning with 4."

If there is no obvious connection between the gaps try looking for a **multiplier**.

E.g. Look at this sequence:

$$1 \quad 5 \quad 21 \quad 85 \quad 341 \quad \ldots$$

You multiply by 4 every time so the rule must include × 4.
Look at the original sequence. If you multiply 1 by 4 you get 1 less than you want so you need to multiply by 4 **and then add 1**.
Check next term: $(5 \times 4) + 1 = 21$.
So the rule is × 4 + 1 starting at 1.

?

> **4** Find the rules used to generate these sequences:
> (a) 3, 4, 5, 6, 7, ...
> (b) 3, 6, 9, 12, 15, ...
> (c) 1, 3, 7, 15, 31, ...
> (d) 1, 3, 11, 43, 171, ...
>
> **Remember:** They may have more than one part.

3.6b Solving linear equations

An equation is a statement including the = sign which tells you that two things are equal to each other. A **linear** equation has no squares or higher powers.

$x - 3 = 8$ and $y = 2x + 1$ are linear equations

To **solve** an equation you have to find the value or values of the unknown which make the statement true. We say these values **satisfy** the equation.

To solve a linear equation you want to get the unknown value by itself on one side of the equation. Then the answer will appear on the other side of the equation.

E.g. Solve $x - 3 = 8$
Add 3 to both sides to remove the − 3:
$$x - 3 + 3 = 8 + 3$$
$$x = 11$$

The result is that the x is left equalling the answer.

This process is called **balancing the equation**.

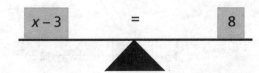

The balance will be maintained if you:

❶ add the same value to both sides of the equation.
❷ subtract the same value from both sides.
❸ multiply each side by the same amount.
❹ divide each side by the same amount.

To help you get the unknown quantity on its own, look at what has been done to it and do the opposite. If 4 has been added then subtract 4. If x is multiplied by 3 then divide by 3.

Remember: Always do the same to both sides of the equation.

?

> **1** Solve the following linear equations:
> (a) $x + 3 = 6$ (b) $a - 4 = 6$ (c) $2x = 6$ (d) $\dfrac{b}{5} = 3$

When the equations get more difficult you should break them down into stages and deal with each operation $(+, -, \times, \div)$ in turn.
Anything added to or subtracted from the unknown quantity is dealt with first.
Next you deal with any values which multiply or divide the unknown.

E.g. Solve $3a - 4 = 5$

$$3a - 4 + 4 = 5 + 4 \qquad \text{First add 4 to both sides to remove the } -4.$$
$$3a = 9$$
$$\frac{3a}{3} = \frac{9}{3} \qquad \text{Next divide both sides by 3 to remove the } \times 3.$$

Hence $a = 3$ Check: $3 \times 3 - 4 = 9 - 4 = 5$

Note: Always substitute your answer back into the equation to check it.

If there are brackets or an expression involving division you need to apply these steps twice.

E.g. (a) Solve $2(x + 1) - 5 = 3$

First deal with what's outside the bracket.

$$2(x + 1) - 5 + 5 = 3 + 5 \qquad \text{Add 5 to remove the } -5.$$
$$2(x + 1) = 8$$
$$\frac{2(x+1)}{2} = \frac{8}{2} \qquad \text{Divide by 2 to remove the } \times 2.$$
$$(x + 1) = 4$$

Now deal with what's in the bracket.
$$x + 1 - 1 = 4 - 1$$
$$x = 3 \qquad \text{Check: } 2(3 + 1) - 5 = 8 - 5 = 3$$

(b) Solve $\dfrac{x + 3}{2} = 7$

$$\frac{2(x + 3)}{2} = 2 \times 7 \qquad \text{Multiply both sides by 2 to remove the } \div \text{ by 2.}$$
$$x + 3 = 14$$
$$x + 3 - 3 = 14 - 3 \qquad \text{Now subtract 3 from each side to remove the } + 3.$$
$$x = 11 \qquad \text{Check: } \frac{11 + 3}{2} = 7$$

?

> **2** Solve the following equations:
> (a) $2x + 3 = 9$ (b) $5a - 4 = 6$ (c) $\dfrac{b}{5} + 2 = 3$
> (d) $\dfrac{x + 1}{2} = 4$ (e) $3(x - 2) = 12$ (f) $\frac{1}{2}(3x - 1) - 7 = 0$

Sometimes the unknown appears on both sides of an equation. To solve this type of equation you first need to get all the letter terms on one side of the equation.

E.g. Solve $3x + 7 = 15 - x$

Group the letters on the side of the equation where they will be positive.
Adding x to both sides will remove the $-x$ from the right hand side (RHS).

$3x + x + 7 = 15 - x + x$

$4x + 7 = 15$

Now you can continue as before.

$4x + 7 - 7 = 15 - 7$

$4x = 8$

$\dfrac{4x}{4} = \dfrac{8}{4}$

$x = 2$ Check: LHS $= 3 \times 2 + 7 = 13$

RHS $= 15 - 2 = 13$

? **3** Solve the following equations:

(a) $2x + 3 = 9 - x$ (b) $2 - 2x = 8x + 12$

Forming equations

You will often be given information in written form or on a diagram and asked to find an unknown quantity. You need to form your own equation and then solve it to find the answer.

E.g. (a) When x is doubled and 8 is added the result is 26. Find the value of x.

Express the statement algebraically:

$2x + 8 = 26$

Now solve it:

$2x = 18$

$x = 9$

(b) Trebling a number and then taking away 5 gives the same result as doubling it and adding 2. What is the number?

Call the number x (or any other letter).

$3x - 5 = 2x + 2$

Collect like terms:

$3x - 2x = 5 + 2$

$x = 7$

Remember: Always check your answer by substituting it back into the equation.

Check: LHS $= (3 \times 7) - 5 = 21 - 5 = 16$

RHS $= (2 \times 7) + 2 = 14 + 2 = 16$

? **4** Express the following statement algebraically and hence find the number:
If you subtract 6 from a number and then multiply the answer by 5 you get the same result as subtracting 4 and then multiplying by 3.

E.g. Jane, Gurjit and Richard have been collecting money for charity. Gurjit has collected 3 times as much as Jane and Richard has collected £6 more than Jane. Altogether they have collected £41. How much did each collect?

If you let Jane's money $= £x$, then Gurjit's will be $£3x$, and Richard's will be $£(x + 6)$.

Since this adds up to £41 you can write the equation as:

$x + 3x + (x + 6) = 41$

Simplifying gives $5x + 6 = 41$

$5x = 35$

$x = 7$

So Jane collected £7, Gurjit £21 and Richard £13.

Check: $7 + 21 + 13 = 41$

5 Martin is 3 years older than Sandra and Abdul is two years younger than Sandra. Together Martin's, Sandra's and Abdul's ages add up to 43 years. Find their individual ages.

6 A bag contains white, grey and black counters. There are 14 more grey counters than white, and 6 fewer black counters than white. There are 44 counters altogether.
(a) Write this as an algebraic equation.
(b) Use this equation to find the number of white counters.

You may also be asked to find missing angles. You can use the properties you know (such as the angles of a triangle add to 180°) to form an equation.

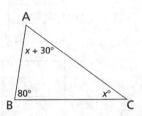

E.g. Angles in a triangle = 180°
$$80° + (x + 30°) + x = 180°$$
$$2x + 30° = 100°$$
$$2x = 70°$$
$$x = 35°$$
Check: $\angle A = 65°$, $\angle B = 80°$
and $\angle C = 35°$ which add to 180°.

7 Find the value of x in the following diagrams:

(a) (b)

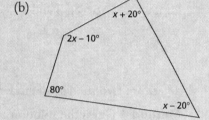

Hint: The angles in a quadrilateral add to 360°.

You can apply the same technique in work on length or area.

E.g. Find the value of x in this diagram if the perimeter of this shape is 38 m.

First find the lengths of the sides which are not marked.
Since the sides are parallel both unmarked sides must be 4 m.
Perimeter = total length of all sides
$$9 + (2x + 4) + 5 + 4 + 4 + 2x = 38$$
$$26 + 4x = 38$$
$$4x = 12$$
$$x = 3$$

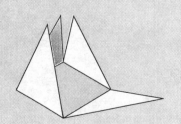

8 Four identical triangles and a square are to be used to construct a pyramid. The base of each triangle is 5cm wide and its height is $(4x - 3)$ cm.

If the total surface area including the base is 115 cm² find the value of x.

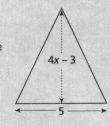

3.6c Solving simple polynomials

If you have an equation like $x^2 = 13$ you can find the value of x using a method called a **search**.

E.g. Find the value of x to 2 decimal places if $x^2 = 13$. (In other words, find the square root of 13.)
The square root gives you the sides of the square with an area of 13.

The answer is not going to be a whole number because a square with sides of length 3 has an area of $3 \times 3 = 9$ (this is the closest whole number **below** the answer) and a square with sides of 4 units has an area of $4 \times 4 = 16$ (this is the closest whole number **above** the answer).

The solution must be somewhere between 3 and 4.

There are two similar methods you can use to find the answer.

Method 1 Guess the solution to 1 decimal place and then improve your guess until you get an answer to the required degree of accuracy.

Guess: 3·4 $3·4 \times 3·4 = 11·56$ which is too small
 $3·5 \times 3·5 = 12·25$ still too small
 $3·6 \times 3·6 = 12·96$ close but still too small

Guess: 3·62 $3·62 \times 3·62 = 13·1044$ too big
 $3·61 \times 3·61 = 13·0321$ better but still a little too big

So $\sqrt{13}$ must be between 3·6 and 3·61. To 2 decimal places the answer must be either 3·60 or 3·61. To check whether the answer is nearer 3·60 or 3·61, find the square of 3·605.

$$3·605 \times 3·605 = 12·996025 \text{ which is too small}$$

so the answer must be bigger than 3·605 so round up.

$$\sqrt{13} = 3·61 \text{ (to 2 d.p.)}$$

1 Use a decimal search to find the square root of 17 to 2 decimal places.

2 Cleano Ultra is going to be sold in boxes which are cubes. The box must have a capacity of 800 cm³. Use a decimal search to calculate the length of each side of the box to 2 decimal places.

Hint: Start with $10 \times 10 \times 10 = 1000$ which is too big.

Method 2 You know $\sqrt{13}$ must be between 3 and 4.

Use 3·5 (the point half way in between) as a first estimate.

If the square of 3·5 is too low, then you know $\sqrt{13}$ must be between 3·5 and 4. If the square is too high then $\sqrt{13}$ must be between 3 and 3·5. $3·5 \times 3·5 = 12·25$ which is too low

So the answer must be between 3·5 and 4.
Again you have an upper limit and a lower limit so you can repeat the process.

The next step is to find the mid-point (mean value) of 3·5 and 4. To do this you add them and divide by 2.

$$\frac{3·5 + 4}{2} = \frac{7·5}{2} = 3·75$$

This will be your new estimate.

You then continue to replace either the upper or lower value until you have a solution.

Lower value	Upper value	Estimate (mean value)	(Estimate)^2	Outcome
3	4	3·5	12·25	Low so replace lower value
3·5	4	3·75	14·0625	High so replace higher value
3·5	3·75	3·625	13·140625	High
3·5	3·625	3·5625	12·691406	Low
3·5625	3·625	3·59375	12·915039	Low
3·59375	3·625	3·609375	13·027588	High
3·59375	3·609375	3·6015625	12·971252	Low
3·6015625	3·609375	3·6054688	12·999405	Low
3·6054688	3·609375	3·6074219	13·013493	

Since the upper and lower values in the last line both round to 3·61 to the required accuracy of 2 d.p. you can stop.

Note: This process is very long-winded and repetitive. In practical situations where this type of search is necessary a computer would probably be used.

> 3 Use this method to find $\sqrt{17}$ to 2 d.p.
> You might like to try writing a simple program to do the hard work for you.

3.6d Drawing and interpreting simple mappings

A *relation* is any connection between two sets. For example, 'is a member of' is a relation which connects football players and football teams.

A **mapping** is a special type of relation where every element of the first set is only connected to *one* element of the second set. This is like saying no player can be a member of more than one team.

You can show a mapping using a **mapping diagram** like this.

The left hand side of a mapping diagram is called the **domain** and the right hand side is called the **co-domain**, **range** or **image set**. In this mapping, the **image** of 0 is 0, the image of 1 is 2 etc.

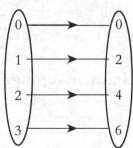

This mapping can be written as $x \to 2x$. (We say 'x maps into $2x$' or 'x goes to $2x$'.) This can also be written in the form of a function $f\!: x \to 2x$.

> **1** Work out the values of the following mappings for values of x from 1 to 4:
> (a) $x \to 3x$ (b) $x \to 2x + 1$ (c) $x \to 2 - x$
>
> Write them in the form
>
> | 1 | $\to$ | |
> |---|-------|--|
> | 2 | $\to$ | |
> | 3 | $\to$ | |
> | 4 | $\to$ | |

Plotting graphs of mappings

You can put values of x together with their images under a mapping to get pairs of coordinates. You can then plot these coordinates on a pair of Cartesian axes to get a **graph** of the mapping.

E.g. Draw a graph of the mapping $x \to x + 2$.

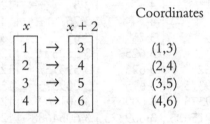

x		$x + 2$	Coordinates
1	$\to$	3	(1,3)
2	$\to$	4	(2,4)
3	$\to$	5	(3,5)
4	$\to$	6	(4,6)

Plot the points and join them to form a straight line.

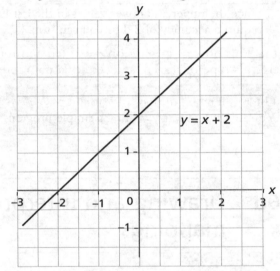

$y = x + 2$

Instead of writing $x \to x + 2$ you can write $y = x + 2$. This is called the *equation* of the line.

> **2** (a) Write this mapping in the form $x \to$
> (b) Plot the points given by the mapping.
> (c) Join the points to produce a line.
> (d) What is the equation of this line?
>
> | 1 | $\to$ | 2 |
> |---|-------|---|
> | 2 | $\to$ | 3 |
> | 3 | $\to$ | 4 |
> | 4 | $\to$ | 5 |

Linear mappings

A linear mapping is one which gives a straight line graph. You can always recognise a linear mapping because it does not have any powers of x other than x^1 (which is usually written as just x).

To draw the graph of a linear mapping or linear equation you need to plot 3 points. Two are enough to give you a line but you should always plot a third point as a check.

You are interested in the points at which the line of the graph crosses the axes. If you are not told what values of x to use then choose three easy ones, such as $^-1$, 0 and 1. Or you can try putting $y = 0$ into the equation to find where the line crosses the x-axis.

E.g. Draw the graph of $y = 2x + 3$.

x		y
-1	→	1
0	→	3
1	→	5

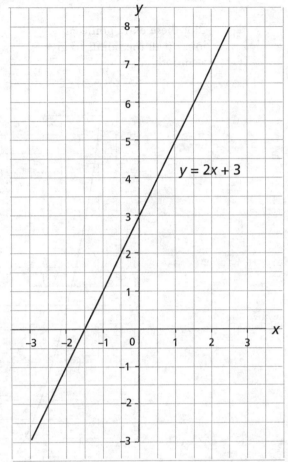

$y = 2x + 3$

3 Draw the graphs of the following, using values of x from $^-1$ to 1.
(a) $x \rightarrow 2x - 1$ (b) $y = 3x$ (c) $y = 5 - 2x$ (d) $x \rightarrow \frac{1}{2}x$ (e) $x \rightarrow 4$

Non-linear mappings

A mapping which includes x to any power other than 1 will give you a curve. When you are drawing a graph which is not a straight line you need to plot more points to be able to see the shape of it. Using consecutive values of x will help you to see the pattern.

Plot extra points to check the shape of the graph near its turning points (where it changes direction) and anywhere the shape is not clear from the points you've already plotted.

Remember: Always use negative values of x as well as positive values.

E.g. Draw the graph of the mapping $x \rightarrow x^2$.

First try using values of x from $^-3$ to 3.

$x \longrightarrow x^2$	
-3	9
-2	4
-1	1
0	0
1	1
2	4
3	9

Plot the points with coordinates (x, x^2).

To check the shape near the
origin $(0, 0)$ use the extra
values $x = \frac{1}{2}$ and $x = -\frac{1}{2}$.

Plot these extra points and
join up all the points to give
a smooth curve.

$x \longrightarrow x^2$	
$-\frac{1}{2}$	$\frac{1}{4}$
$\frac{1}{2}$	$\frac{1}{4}$

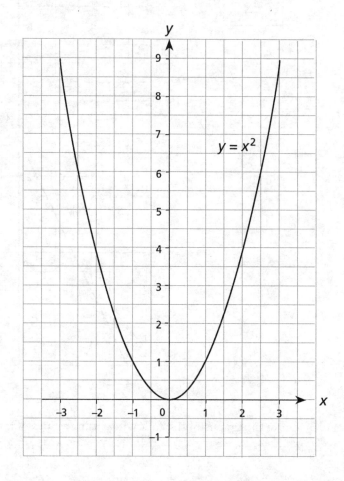

4 Using values of x from -3 to 3 draw the graphs of the following. (Plot any extra
points you need to be sure of the shape.)
(a) $x \rightarrow x^2 + 1$
(b) $y = x^3$

3.7a   Sequences in symbolic notation

Consider the sequence 4, 7, 10, 13, 16, ... The rule for this sequence is + 3 starting with 4. But this rule only tells you how to find a term if you know the term which comes before it. What if you wanted to find the hundredth term? Or the millionth term? You need to be able to generalise this statement by writing it *algebraically* so you can work out a term just from the number (position) of the term, without having to work out all the terms before it.

To do this you number the terms. The first term is called u_1, the second is called u_2 and so on. Everything you need to know about the sequence is given by the **general term** or **nth term**, u_n.

E.g.   Write down the first eight terms of the sequence with general term $u_n = 3n - 3$.

$u_1 = 3(1) - 3 = 0$
$u_2 = 3(2) - 3 = 3$
$u_3 = 3(3) - 3 = 6$
$u_4 = 3(4) - 3 = 9$
$u_5 = 3(5) - 3 = 12$
$u_6 = 3(6) - 3 = 15$
$u_7 = 3(7) - 3 = 18$
$u_8 = 3(8) - 3 = 21$

n	1	2	3	4	5	6	7	8
$3n - 3$	0	3	6	9	12	15	18	21

?

1   Write down the first five terms of the sequences with the following general terms:
(a) $3n^2$ (b) $4n - 1$ (c) $\frac{1}{2}n^2$ (d) $\frac{2}{3}n$

2   If $u_n = 5 \times 2^{n-1}$ calculate:
(a) the third term   (b) the sixth term   (c) u_{10}

Arithmetic sequences

Sequences which are generated by adding or subtracting the same number each time are called **arithmetic** sequences.

E.g.   Look at this sequence:

Term number   1   2   3   4   5   ... n ...

Term   4   7   10   13   16   ... u_n ...

$+3$ $+3$ $+3$ $+3$

The gap between consecutive terms is always 3. **Multiplying** the term number **by 3** gives this sequence:

3   6   9   12   15   ...

This is one less than you want each time. To correct this you **add 1**.

This gives the sequence you want:

4   7   10   13   16   ... $3n + 1$ ...

So this is the sequence $u_n = 3n + 1$ or simply $[3n + 1]$.

Remember: If the gap between terms is constant (always the same) it gives you the multiplier of n and you then adjust by adding or subtracting.

3 Write down the nth term in each of these sequences:
   (a) 1, 4, 7, 10, 13, ...
   (b) 3, 5, 7, 9, 11, ...
   (c) 4, 9, 14, 19, 24, ...

4 Investigate the number of hidden faces when bricks are laid along the ground. Try making some sketches, tabulate your results and look for a sequence in them. Try to express the sequence algebraically.

5 In the first year of his new job Joe is paid a salary of £8500. Each year his salary is increased by £900. What is his salary
   (a) in his fifth year at work?
   (b) in his eighth year in this job?
   (c) after 12 years?
   (d) if he works in the same place for 30 years?

   Hint: First write down Joe's salary for his nth year at work.

Geometric sequences

Sequences which are generated by multiplying or dividing by the same number each time are called **geometric** sequences.

E.g. Look at this sequence:

Term number	1	2	3	4	5	...	n	...
Term	1	4	16	64	256	...	u_n	...

$\times 4 \quad \times 4 \quad \times 4 \quad \times 4$

In this sequence you multiply by 4 an extra time for each new term.
Multiplying 4 by itself the same number of times as the term number gives this sequence:

Term number	1	2	3	4	5	...	n	...
Term	4	16	64	256	1024	...	4^n	...

You have multiplied 4 by itself one too many times so **divide by 4**.

Term number	1	2	3	4	5	...	n	...
Term	1	4	16	64	256	...	4^{n-1}	...

This gives the sequence you want. So the general term is $u_n = 4^{n-1}$

Remember: If the multiplier between terms is constant then the general term has this number raised to a power and you adjust by multiplying or dividing.

6 Write down the nth term for each of the following sequences:
   (a) 1, 3, 9, 27, 81, ...
   (b) 5, 25, 125, 625, 3125, ...
   (c) 4, 20, 100, 500, 2500, ...
   (d) 7, 21, 63, 189, 567, ...
   (e) $1, \frac{1}{3}, \frac{1}{9}, \frac{1}{27}, \frac{1}{81}, \ldots$

7 Consider the sequence 2, 4, 8, 16, 32, ...
   (a) Write down the general term, u_n.
   (b) Use your answer to part (a) to find the general term for this sequence:
       6, 12, 24, 48, 96, ...

Other sequences

If the gaps between the terms are not constant and the multipliers between terms are not constant then we need to look for some other kind of pattern.

When this happens it is likely that the nth term will involve a power of n, with or without some addition, subtraction, multiplication or division to correct it.

E.g. Look at this sequence:

2   5   10   17   26   ...

+3   +5   +7   +9

You cannot use the examples above to write the general term of this sequence. Try comparing it with this sequence:

1   4   9   16   25   ... n^2 ...

This gives you one less than you want each time so add 1.

The general term is $n^2 + 1$.

?

8 By comparing them with the sequence $[n^2]$, write the nth term for each of the following sequences:
(a) 0, 3, 8, 15, ...
(b) 4, 9, 16, 25, ...
(c) 2, 8, 18, 32, ...

Fractions

If you have a sequence involving fractions treat it as two separate sequences: the sequence of numerators (top numbers) and the sequence of denominators (bottom numbers).

E.g. Express $\frac{1}{2}, \frac{2}{3}, \frac{3}{4}, \frac{4}{5}$, ... in general terms.

First consider the sequence of numerators:

1   2   3   4   ...

The general term for this sequence is clearly n.

Now consider the sequence of denominators:

2   3   4   5   ...

The general term for this sequence is $n + 1$.

Putting them together gives the general expression $\dfrac{n}{n+1}$.

?

9 Write the general expression for each of the following sequences:
(a) $\frac{1}{2}, \frac{2}{5}, \frac{3}{8}, \frac{4}{11}$, ...
(b) $\frac{2}{3}, \frac{4}{5}, \frac{8}{7}, \frac{16}{9}$, ...

3.7b   The rules of indices

You know that 2 to the power 6 means 2 multiplied by itself 6 times.

$2 \times 2 \times 2 \times 2 \times 2 \times 2 = 2^6$

The power is also called the **index**.

Using indices (powers) allows you to shorten expressions in algebra.

$a \times a \times a \times a$ can be shortened to a^4

$y \times y \times y \times x \times x$ can be shortened to $y^3 x^2$

Adding and subtracting

When you have numbers raised to a power you can always add or subtract them by first writing them as ordinary numbers (or using your calculator).

E.g. $3^4 + 2^3 = 3 \times 3 \times 3 \times 3 + 2 \times 2 \times 2 = 81 + 8 = 89$
$4^3 - 2^4 = 4 \times 4 \times 4 - 2 \times 2 \times 2 \times 2 = 64 - 16 = 48$

Expressions with **different** indices cannot be added $\cancel{a^3 + a^2}$ or subtracted $\cancel{a^5 - a^2}$

Only terms with the same letter and the same power can be added or subtracted.

E.g. $x^2 + x^2 = 2x^2$
$3a^4 - a^4 = 2a^4$

When terms can be added or subtracted a question may ask you to *collect like terms* or to *simplify* the expressions.

1 Simplify the following expressions where possible:

(a) $3a^2 + 5a^2$ (b) $4x^3 + 4x^2$ (c) $2x^3 + 4y^2 + x^3 + 3y^2$ (d) $5b^5 - b^5$

Multiplying

When you multiply expressions with indices together this is what happens:

$$a^3 \times a^2 = (a \times a \times a) \times (a \times a)$$
$$= a \times a \times a \times a \times a$$
$$= a^5$$
$$= a^{(3 + 2)}$$

Remember: When you multiply expressions involving indices the indices are added.

E.g. $2n^4 \times 5n^3 = (2 \times 5) \times n^4 \times n^3$
$= 10 \times n^{(4 + 3)}$
$= 10n^7$

You can use this rule to simplify expressions which contain more than one unknown. First collect the letters together.

E.g. Simplify $a^2b^3 \times ab^2c$
$a^2b^3 \times ab^2c = (a^2 \times a) \times (b^3 \times b^2) \times c$
$= a^{(2 + 1)} \times b^{(3 + 2)} \times c$
$= a^3b^5c$

2 Simplify the following:

(a) $2x^2 \times 4x^5$ (b) $3a^5 \times 6a^4$ (c) $5y^4 \times 8y^7$ (d) $x^2y \times 3xy^4$

3 Work out the following, leaving your answer as a power:

(a) $10^{27} \times 10^4$ (b) $7^2 \times 7^{12}$ (c) $(3 \times 5^4) \times (2 \times 5^{11})$

Dividing

When you divide expressions involving indices this happens:

$$a^8 \div a^2 = \frac{a^8}{a^2}$$
$$= \frac{a \times a \times a \times a \times a \times a \times \cancel{a} \times \cancel{a}}{\cancel{a} \times \cancel{a}}$$
$$= a^6$$
$$= a^{(8 - 2)}$$

Remember: When you divide expressions involving indices the indices are subtracted.

E.g. $10n^6 \div 2n^4 = \frac{10}{2} \times (n^6 \div n^4)$

$$= 5 \times n^{(6 - 4)}$$
$$= 5n^2$$

4 Simplify the following:
  (a) $a^6 \div a^2$ (b) $3x^5 \div 2x^2$ (c) $4x^5 \div x^2$ (d) $4a^3b \div 2a^2$

5 Work out the following, leaving your answer as a power:

  (a) $7^4 \div 7^2$ (b) $9^5 \div 9^2$ (c) $\dfrac{5^2 \times 2^5}{2^3}$ (d) $10^{17} \div 10^4$

Powers of powers

If you take an expression involving a power and raise it to another power this is what happens:

$$(a^3)^2 = a^3 \times a^3$$
$$= (a \times a \times a) \times (a \times a \times a)$$
$$= a^6$$
$$= a^{(2 \times 3)}$$

Remember: When you raise a power to another power you multiply the indices (powers).

In an expression like $5ab^2$ only the b is to the power 2. If a whole expression is to the power then **brackets** are used.

E.g. Simplify $(3y^2)^3$
       That means the 3 is cubed **and** the y^2 term is cubed.
       $(3y^2)^3 = 3^3 \times (y^2)^3$
       $= 27 \times y^{(2 \times 3)}$
       $= 27y^6$

6 Simplify the following expressions:

  (a) $(a^2)^4$ (b) $(3x^3)^2$ (c) $(4n^3)^4$ (d) $(a^2b^3c)^4$

7 Simplify the following expressions:

  (a) $(a^2b \times a^3)^2$ (b) $(xy)^3 \times x^2y$ (c) $\left(\dfrac{4a^7b^2}{a^2b}\right)^3$

3.7c   Reciprocals

To understand the idea of a reciprocal it helps if you first think of the number which you can multiply by which leaves other numbers unchanged. This number is of course 1.
1 is called the **identity** for multiplication.
The **reciprocal** of a number (except 0) is 1 divided by the number.

E.g. The reciprocal of 2 is $\frac{1}{2}$ or 0·5.

       The reciprocal of 100 is $\frac{1}{100}$ or 0·01.

Note: The reciprocal of the reciprocal of a number is the number itself.

E.g. The reciprocal of $\frac{1}{2}$ is 2.
       The reciprocal of $\frac{1}{100}$ is 100.

       The reciprocal of 37 is

       `1 ÷ 3 7 =` `0.027027`

       To calculate the reciprocal of the reciprocal of 37

       `0.027027` `Min` `1 ÷` `MR` `=` `37`

If you multiply a number by its reciprocal you get 1.

$$p \times \frac{1}{p} = \frac{p}{p} = 1 \quad (p \neq 0)$$

So if you multiply by a number and then multiply by its reciprocal you get back to where you started.

$$(q \times p) \times \frac{1}{p} = q \times \left(p \times \frac{1}{p}\right) = q \times 1 = q \quad (p \neq 0)$$

So the reciprocal of a number is the **inverse** (opposite) of the number when it comes to multiplication. The reciprocal undoes the effect of the number.

The reciprocal is also the inverse for division.

$$(q \div p) \div \frac{1}{p} = \frac{q}{p} \times \frac{p}{1} = \frac{qp}{p} = q \quad (p \neq 0)$$

?

1 Without using your calculator, write down the reciprocals of the following numbers:
   (a) 10   (b) 7   (c) 3   (d) ‾3   (e) ‾$\frac{1}{4}$ (f) $\frac{1}{1000}$ (g) 1

Look for the key marked $\frac{1}{x}$

To find the reciprocal of a number (e.g. 5) press 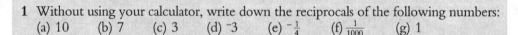 5 $\frac{1}{x}$

Display: $\boxed{0.2}$

If you press the key twice you get back the number you started with.

5 $\frac{1}{x}$ $\frac{1}{x}$ $\boxed{5}$

?

2 Write down the reciprocals of the following numbers:
   (a) 49   (b) 703   (c) 0·42   (d) 0·00071

3 Investigate reciprocals as numbers get close to 0 and as they get large, both positive and negative.

Dividing by a number is the same as multiplying by its reciprocal.

$$q \div p = \frac{q}{p} = q \times \frac{1}{p} \quad (p \neq 0)$$

E.g.   Calculate 520 ÷ 13

$520 \div 13 = 520 \times \frac{1}{13}$

5 2 0 × 1 3 $\frac{1}{x}$ = $\boxed{40}$

This can be extremely useful if you already have a value in your calculator and you need to divide something by it.

Remember: The reciprocal of a number is the value that when multiplied by that number gives you 1.

3.7d   Solving simple inequalities

You are familiar with the symbol = which means that two things are the same. An **inequality** is a statement which tells you that two things are not the same.

   $x < 5$ means that x is less than 5 $x > 5$ means that x is greater than 5

Note: $x < 5$ is the same as $5 > x$.

Sometimes the inequality includes the value at the limit (end). Then the symbols become

$\leq$ less than or equal to   and $\geq$ greater than or equal to

If $x > 5$ there are infinitely many values of x which make this true. But if you have two inequalities involving x then you can find a finite number of whole number solutions.

E.g. Find the possible values of n if n is a whole number and $^-3 < n \leq 5$.
This means n is greater than $^-3$ and less than or equal to 5.

$n = ^-2, ^-1, 0, 1, 2, 3, 4$ or 5 **Note:** $^-3$ is not included but 5 is.

?

> **1** If n is a whole number, find the values of n which satisfy the following inequalities:
> (a) $^-3 \leq n \leq 3$ (b) $9 > n > 3$

3.7e   Solving more polynomials

You have solved simple polynomial equations such as $x^2 = 17$ using 'trial and improvement' (search) methods. More complicated polynomials can be solved in the same way: by making an estimate of the solution and then improving it until you get the required degree of accuracy.

E.g. Solve the equation $x^2 + x = 8$ to 2 d.p. using a search.

First look for the nearest whole numbers to the solution.
$2^2 + 2 = 6$ which is too small
$3^2 + 3 = 12$ which is too big

So x must be between 2 and 3.

Try $x = 2 \cdot 2$ which   gives $2 \cdot 2^2 + 2 \cdot 2 = 7 \cdot 04$ which is too small
       $x = 2 \cdot 4$ gives $2 \cdot 4^2 + 2 \cdot 4 = 8 \cdot 16$ which is too big

It looks like the answer is going to be closer to $2 \cdot 4$ than $2 \cdot 2$.

Try $x = 2 \cdot 35$ gives $2 \cdot 35^2 + 2 \cdot 35 = 7 \cdot 8725$ (this is too small)
       $x = 2 \cdot 37$ gives $2 \cdot 37^2 + 2 \cdot 37 = 7 \cdot 9869$ (this is just too small)
       $x = 2 \cdot 38$ gives $2 \cdot 38^2 + 2 \cdot 38 = 8 \cdot 0444$ (just too big)

The value you are looking for is between $2 \cdot 37$ and $2 \cdot 38$. To be correct to 2 d.p. you need to check whether to round up or down.

$x = 2 \cdot 375$ gives $2 \cdot 375^2 + 2 \cdot 375 = 8 \cdot 015625$ (too big)

The solution must be less than $2 \cdot 375$ so round down.

$x = 2 \cdot 37$ (to 2 d.p.)

?

> **1** Solve the following equations to 2 d.p. using this method:
> (a) $x^2 - x = 10$ (b) $x^3 + x = 12$

3.7f   Simultaneous equations

You know how to solve a linear equation involving one unknown. When you have more than one unknown you need to have more than one equation in order to get a solution. To get a solution when you have **two** unknowns you need to have **two** equations.

You need to find a value of x and a value of y which make both equations true *at the same time*. Another way of saying 'at the same time' is 'simultaneously' so these equations are called **simultaneous equations**.

You can find a solution either algebraically or by drawing the line given by each equation and finding the point where they cross.

Solving simultaneous equations algebraically

There are two algebraic methods which can be used to solve simultaneous equations. In either case the main thing to remember is that you have to eliminate (get rid of) one of the variables as a first step.

Method 1 This method involves multiplying one or both of the equations so that one of the variables appears the same number of times in both equations. You then add or subtract the equations so that this variable is removed.

E.g. Solve $2x + y = 7$ (A)

$3x + 2y = 11$ (B)   Label the equations (A) and (B)

By multiplying (A) by 2 you get $2y$ in both equations.

2×(A) $4x + 2y = 14$
(B) $3x + 2y = 11$

Take equation (B) from 2(A).

2(A) − (B) $4x - 3x = 14 - 11$
$x = 3$

You now know $x = 3$. Put this back into one of the equations.
Putting $x = 3$ into (A):
$(2 \times 3) + y = 7$
$y = 1$
Therefore $x = 3$ and $y = 1$
Check your answers by substituting them back into the other equation, (B):
$(3 \times 3) + (2 \times 1) = 11$

Remember: Always check your answers by substituting them into the equation you did not use to find the second unknown.

1 Solve the following pairs of simultaneous equations:
(a) $a + 2b = 9$ (b) $7x + 3y = 27$
$3a + b = 7$ $2x + y = 8$

Sometimes you have to multiply both equations to make one of the variables appear the same number of times.

E.g. Solve $3x + 2y = 7$ (A)
$2x + 5y = 12$ (B)

You could make either the x or y coefficients (this means the numbers in front of x and y) the same size.
By multiplying equation (A) by 2 and equation (B) by 3 the x coefficients become the same.

2(A) $6x + 4y = 14$
3(B) $6x + 15y = 36$

3(B) − 2(A) $15y - 4y = 36 - 14$
$11y = 22$
$y = 2$

Put this into one of the equations to find the value of x.
Putting $y = 2$ into (A):
$3x + (2 \times 2) = 7$
$3x + 4 = 7$
$3x = 3$
$x = 1$

Therefore $y = 2$ and $x = 1$

Check by substituting into (B): $(2 \times 1) + (5 \times 2) = 12$

> **2** Solve the following pairs of simultaneous equations. Remember to check your answers by substituting them back into the equations.
>
> (a) $2m + 3n = 27$ (b) $2a + 5b = 13$
> $3m + 2n = 28$ $5a + 3b = 23$

If one of the variables has a negative coefficient then you can make the coefficients the same size (but one negative and one positive) and then add the equations.

E.g. Solve $2x + y = 40$ (A)

            $3x - 2y = 4$ (B)

     2(A) $4x + 2y = 80$

     (B) $3x - 2y = 4$

     2(A) + (B) $7x = 84$

                 $x = 12$

Substituting $x = 12$ into (A):

     $(2 \times 12) + y = 40$

           $24 + y = 40$

               $y = 16$

Therefore $x = 12$ and $y = 16$

Check these values satisfy (B): $(3 \times 12) - (2 \times 16) = 4$

> **3** Solve each of the following pairs of simultaneous equations:
>
> (a) $2a + 3b = 16$ (b) $7p + 3q = 61$ (c) $4m + 3n = 93$
> $3a - b = 13$ $4p - 2q = 20$ $3m - 4n = 1$

Method 2 An alternative method is to rearrange one of the equations so that one variable is expressed in terms of the other and then substitute this into the second equation.

E.g. Solve the pair of equations (A) $2x + 3y = 14$ and (B) $3x - y = 10$.

(B) can easily be rewritten as $y = 3x - 10$

You now have a value of y which can be substituted into equation (A) which you can now solve because there is only one unknown.

Substituting you get $2x + 3(3x - 10) = 14$

                     $2x + 9x - 30 = 14$

                          $11x = 44$

                            $x = 4$

You can now substitute $x = 4$ back into one of the equations to find the value of y.

Substituting into (B):

$(3 \times 4) - y = 10$

         $y = 2$

Check by substituting both answers back into (A): $(2 \times 4) + (3 \times 2) = 14$

> **4** Use this method to solve the following: $2r - 3s = 19$
> $3r - s = 11$

> **5** Emma buys 4 ham rolls and 1 cheese roll and pays £7·35.
> Wayne buys 3 ham rolls and 2 cheese rolls and pays £7·20.
> (a) Write down an equation for Emma's rolls and one for Wayne's.
> (b) Solve the equations simultaneously to find the cost of each type of roll. (Use whichever method you prefer.)

> **6** The Taylors and the Hannons have booked the same holiday. The Taylor family have to pay £1880 for two adults and three children. The Hannon family will pay £2110 for three adults and two children.
> (a) Write down the equation for each family.
> (b) Work out the cost of the holiday for each adult and each child.

Using graphs to solve simultaneous equations

You can solve simultaneous equations by drawing a graph of the two equations. The x and y coordinates of the point where the two lines cross give you the solution to the equations.

E.g. Solve the following pair of simultaneous equations by drawing a graph.
(A) $y - x = 2$
(B) $2x - y = 2$

The first step is to rearrange each equation in the form $y = mx + c$.
(A) $y = x + 2$
(B) $y = 2x - 2$

Next substitute x values into each equation to calculate some coordinates.

Remember: Three points for a line.

Here are two of the ways to set this out

x	$x + 2$
0	2
1	3
2	4

x	0	1	2
$2x$	0	2	4
-2	-2	-2	-2
y	-2	0	2

Plot the points for equation (A) and join them to form a line.

Then do the same for equation (B).

The point of intersection is (4, 6).

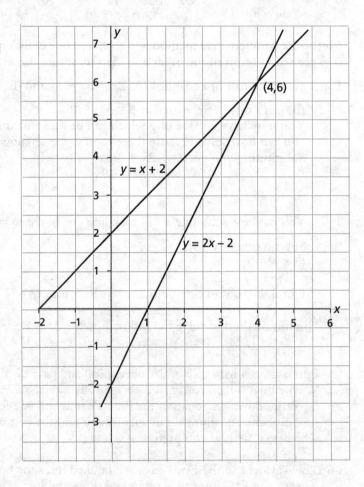

Check that this solution is correct by putting these values back into the equations.

Substituting $x = 4$ and $y = 6$ into (A): $6 - 4 = 2$
Check that (B) also works.

?

7 The following pairs of equations have been drawn for you. What are their solutions?

(a) $y = 7 - x$
$y = x + 1$

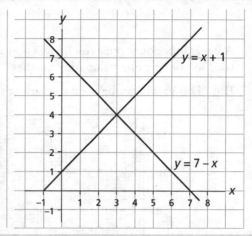

(b) $y = 2x + 1$
$y = \frac{1}{2}x + 4$

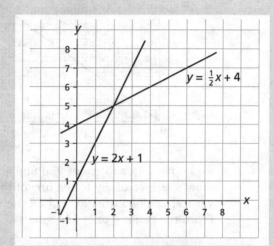

8 Solve these pairs of simultaneous equations by graphical methods.

(a) $y = x - 1$
$y = 7 - x$

(b) $3x - y = 2$
$x - 2y = {}^-6$

9 The milk lady in Dickens Road has worked out the bills for two houses for a week.

Address	Skimmed Milk	Gold Top Milk	Total Cost
36 Dickens Road	18	2	610p
38 Dickens Road	25	5	925p

(a) Using S = Skimmed milk and G = Gold top write down an equation for the cost of the milk at each house.

(b) Rewrite the equations in the form $G = mS + c$.

(c) Draw the graphs of both equations on the same pair of axes.
   Hint: The solutions must be positive so you only need positive axes. (G on the vertical axis goes to 350 and S goes to 40.)

(d) Use your graph to work out the cost of each type of milk.

Remember: Always check your solutions by substituting them back into the equations.

3.7g Graphs of linear functions

A linear function is one which gives you a straight line graph. This type of graph is often used to convert one value into another.

E.g. This graph can be used to convert ounces to grams and grams to ounces.

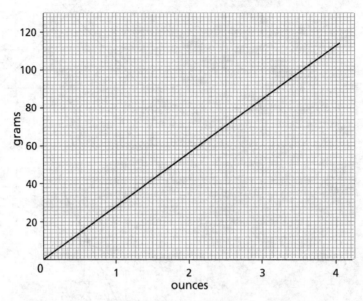

To convert 4 oz to grams you find 4 oz on the horizontal axis (ounces) and draw a line vertically to the line of the graph and then horizontally to the vertical axis (grams) and read off the value.
From the graph 4 oz = 113 grams

1 Use the graph to convert the following weights into grams:
  (a) 3 oz   (b) 1 oz   (c) $2\frac{1}{2}$ oz

2 Use the graph to convert the following weights into ounces:
  (a) 40 g   (b) 800 g   (c) 400 g

Hint: The last 2 values are not on the graph but 100 g is.

Given the rate of conversion between two quantities you need to be able to draw your own graph.

E.g. Given the fact that 0°C = 32°F and 100°C = 212°F you can draw a straight line graph to enable you to convert temperatures.

Choosing a suitable scale, plot the points (0, 32) and (100, 212) and join them with a straight line.

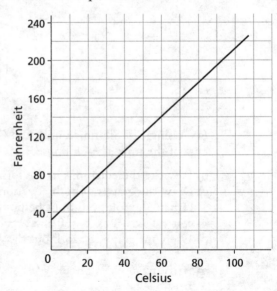

3 The exchange rate between the pound and the French franc is about £1 to 12F.

(a) Draw a conversion graph to show the exchange rate between the two currencies.

Hint: Zero is the same in any currency!

(b) Use your graph to find the following:
(i) 20F in £   (ii) 35F in £   (iii) £3·50 in F   (iv) £35 in F

(c) The exchange rate changes to £1 = 11·5F. Draw the new line representing this change on your graph.

3.7h   Graphs on a computer or calculator

You can use a computer to generate more complicated graphs for you.

There are a number of programmes which will do this. Your school will probably have database programmes such as GRASS or QUEST.

Once you have produced a graph you should be able to interpret it. You may wish to discuss the largest and smallest results, the range of results or perhaps the gradient and y intercept of a straight line and the implications of this.

3.7i   Flow charts

A flow diagram or flow chart is a simple way of listing a set of instructions. Each type of instruction has its own shape.

    ◯   first and last instruction

    ▢   single instruction

    ◇   question with yes or no answer

    ⬭   print or write down the value

Flow charts without loops

A flow chart without a loop follows through a single process very much like a simple number machine.
You input a value and follow the steps in the flow chart to get an output.

Given values of x, the flow chart on the right can be used to find values of y for the equation
$y = x^2 + 2x - 15$.

The flow chart helps you calculate each part of the equation and then put the three parts together to give the value of y.

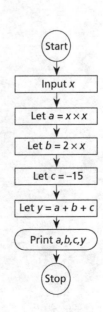

?

1 Use the flow chart to help you complete the following table.

x	a	b	c	y
⁻3	9	⁻6	⁻15	⁻12
⁻2				
⁻1				
0				
1				
2				
3				

Flow charts with loops

A flow chart with a loop is a much more efficient way of repeating a process. The next value you wish to input can be done automatically within the flow chart by using a loop. You can then put in an instruction so that the process stops when a certain value is reached.

Alternatively you can put a counter into the flow chart to count how many times a process has been repeated and stop the process after the required number of calculations.

A computer programme developed from a flow chart with a loop in it will keep calculating values until it reaches an instruction to stop (or you switch it off!).

E.g. If you follow the instructions in this flow chart you should get these results.

1
4
9
16
25
36
49
64
81
100

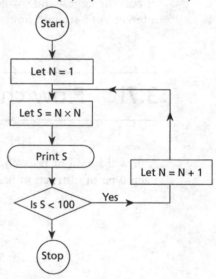

2 Work through this flow chart.

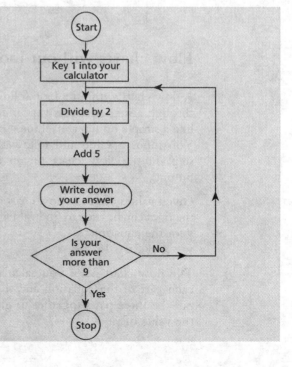

3 Write a flow chart to work out the areas of circles with radius 1 m , 2 m, up to 10 m.

A flow chart with a loop in it does not always produce more than one answer. If the instruction to print the answer is outside the loop then only one answer is produced. A flow chart like this can be used to find a solution to a problem.

E.g. Find the sides of the largest cube with whole number sides which can be made out of 250 cm^3 of material.

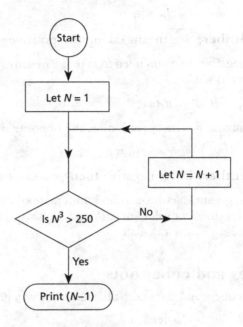

This flow chart gives the result 6.

3.8a   Relating powers and roots

Squares and square roots

Squaring and taking the square root are inverse (opposite) operations so if you square n and then take the square root you get

$$\sqrt{n^2} = n \ \ (n \geq 0)$$

Remember: $\sqrt{}$ means taking the positive square root.

If n is negative then you need to take the negative square root to get back to the number you started with.

$$\overline{\sqrt{(^-n)^2}} = {}^-n \ \ (n \geq 0)$$

You can also do the operations in the opposite order to get the same result:

$$\left(\sqrt{n}\right)^2 = \sqrt{n} \times \sqrt{n} = n$$

Remember: If n is negative then you can't take the square root.

Try using your calculator to find the square of the square root or the square root of the square for different values of n. (You won't always get back the original number because of rounding by the calculator.)

Cubes and cube roots

If you cube n and then take the cube root you get

$$\sqrt[3]{n^3} = \sqrt[3]{n \times n \times n}$$

The cube root is the number you have to multiply by itself 3 times to get n^3 so

$$\sqrt[3]{n^3} = n$$

If you cube the cubed root you get

$$\left(\sqrt[3]{n}\right)^3 = \sqrt[3]{n} \times \sqrt[3]{n} \times \sqrt[3]{n}$$

By definition, $\sqrt[3]{n}$ is the number you multiply by itself 3 times to get n so

$$\left(\sqrt[3]{n}\right)^3 = n$$

So cubing and taking the cube root are inverse operations. Each one undoes the effect of the other.

Higher powers

All powers follow the same pattern.

If n is an odd number, raising to the power n and taking the nth root are inverse operations.

$$\sqrt[n]{x^n} = x$$

If n is even then

$$\pm \sqrt[n]{x^n} = x$$

1 Simplify the following expressions:

(a) $\left(\sqrt{xy}\right)^2$ (b) $\sqrt[5]{a^5}$ (c) $\sqrt[7]{(3y)^7}$ (d) $\sqrt[3]{8a^3}$ (e) $\sqrt[3]{b^6}$ (f) $\sqrt{a^4 b^2}$

2 Write x as a power or root of y in each of the following cases:

(a) $y = x^6$ (b) $y = \sqrt[5]{x}$ (c) $y = \sqrt[3]{x^2}$

Hint: First write x^2 as a power of y.

3.8b   Manipulating algebraic expressions

Brackets

Brackets are used to group like terms together.
$(x + 3) + (x + 3) = 2(x + 3)$

The bracket means that an operation applies to more than one term.
$2(x + 3)$ means $2 \times x$ **and** 2×3
$ab^2 = a \times b \times b$ but $(ab)^2 = a \times a \times b \times b$

You can remove the brackets from an expression by multiplying out (expanding) the contents.

E.g.   (a) $4(x + 2) = 4 \times x + 4 \times 2$
$= 4x + 8$

(b) $2y(x - 3) = 2y \times x - 2y \times 3$
$= 2xy - 6y$

Remember: If the value multiplying the bracket is negative it will change the sign of each term inside the bracket.

(c) $^-3(2x - 5) = {}^-3 \times 2x - {}^-3 \times 5$
$= {}^-6x + 15$

Sometimes an expression has brackets within brackets.

E.g.   Simplify $3a[(a + 3b) - 5(2b - a)]$

Deal with the inside brackets first:	$3a[(a + 3b - 10b + 5a)]$
Collect like terms:	$3a[a + 5a + 3b - 10b]$
Simplify:	$3a[6a - 7b]$
Multiply out:	$18a^2 - 21ab$

?

> 1 Expand (multiply out) the following expressions:
> (a) $3(x + 5)$ (b) $^-2(x + 5)$
> (c) $^-3x(x - 4)$ (d) $x\,[4(3x + 2) - 3(2x - 4)]$

Multiplying two brackets

$(a + b)(c + d)$ means $(a + b) \times (c + d)$

Each term in the first bracket is multiplied by each term in the second bracket:

$(a + b)(c + d) = a(c + d) + b(c + d)$
$= ac + ad + bc + bd$

Remember: Be careful with the signs: $+ \times +$ and $- \times -$ are $+$
and $+ \times -$ and $- \times +$ are $-$

E.g.   Expand $(x + 3)(x + 4)$

Step 1	$(x+3)(x+4)$	giving	$x \times x$
Step 2	$(x+3)(x+4)$	giving	$x \times 4$
Step 3	$(x+3)(x+4)$	giving	$3 \times x$
Step 4	$(x+3)(x+4)$	giving	3×4

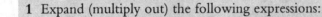

You then add the results together which gives

$$(x + 3)(x + 4) = [x \times x] + [x \times 4] + [3 \times x] + [3 \times 4]$$
$$= x^2 + 4x + 3x + 12$$

Collecting like terms $= x^2 + 7x + 12$

Note: This result is typical of what happens when you multiply out two brackets of this form. Try to remember this pattern.
$$(x + a)(x + b) = x^2 + (a + b)x + ab$$

2 Multiply out the following:
(a) $(x + 2)(x + 3)$ (b) $(x - 2)(x + 3)$ (c) $(x - 4)(x - 2)$

3 Multiply out the following expressions. These are some common types of quadratics that you will probably have seen before.
(a) $(a + b)(a - b)$ (This is called the difference of two squares.)
(b) $(a + b)^2$
(c) $(a - b)^2$

4 Expand the following:
(a) $(x + 5)^2$ (b) $(x - 2)^2$ (c) $(x - y)(x + y)$
(d) $(2x + 3)(x + 2)$ (e) $(5x + 4)(3x + 7)$ (f) $(ax + b)(cx + d)$

Factorising

When the terms or parts of an expression have a common factor you can simplify the expression by **factorisation**. This is the reverse of the process you have just been using.

E.g. Factorise $ab + ac$

The terms ab and ac have a common factor a so you can take out the a.
$ab + ac = a(b + c)$

So the factors of $ab + ac$ are a and $(b + c)$.

Check: $a(b + c) = ab + ac$

Always make sure that you have used the highest possible common factor. Also make sure that you have not changed any signs.

Remember: Always check your answers by multiplying out or expanding the expression.

E.g. Factorise $3a + 4bx - 3b - 4ax$

Hint: Do this in simple steps!

Write down each step so you can easily find any mistakes and so an examiner can see what you have done.

Step 1   Collect together similar terms
$3a - 3b + 4bx - 4ax$

Step 2   Take out the common factors
$3(a - b) + 4x(b - a)$

It would help to have $(a - b)$ and $(b - a)$ the same way round. Try again but this time put the letters in the same order.

Step 1 $3a - 3b - 4ax + 4bx$

Step 2 $3(a - b) - 4x(a - b)$

Now the brackets are the same. This is what you should always aim to do. Now simplify further by taking out the common factor $(a - b)$

$$3(a - b) - 4x(a - b) = (3 - 4x)(a - b)$$

5 Factorise the following expressions:
(a) $2a + 4b$ (b) $2a^2 - 4a$ (c) $^-4a - 6b$
(d) $5y^3 + 10y^2 - 25y$ (e) $ax + 2a + 2bx + 4b$

Factorising quadratics

A **quadratic** is a polynomial in which the highest power is 2. A quadratic in one variable is an expression of the form $ax^2 + bx + c$ with $a \neq 0$.

You have seen above that when expressions of the form $(x + p)$ and $(x + q)$ are multiplied together the result is a quadratic.

$$(x + p)(x + q) = x^2 + (p + q)x + pq$$

Turning this around tells you that quadratics can be factorised into a pair of brackets.

$$x^2 + (p + q)x + pq = (x + p)(x + q)$$

E.g. Factorise $x^2 + 7x + 10$

Suppose $x^2 + 7x + 10 = (x + p)(x + q)$
$x^2 + 7x + 10 = x^2 + (p + q)x + pq$

So you need to find values for p and q such that $p + q = 7$ and $pq = 10$.
In other words, look for two factors of 10 which add to give 7.
2 and 5 fit these conditions.

So $x^2 + 7x + 10 = (x + 2)(x + 5)$

Check: $(x + 2)(x + 5) = x^2 + 5x + 2x + 10 = x^2 + 7x + 10$

The following steps will help you to factorise quadratics.
Factorise $x^2 + bx + c$

Step 1   First deal with the x^2 term.
$(x \quad)(x \quad)$

Step 2   Sort out the signs in the brackets.
(a) If c is positive then the signs in the brackets will both be the same. The signs will be
$+$ if b is positive and $-$ if b is negative.
$(x + \quad)(x + \quad)$ or $(x - \quad)(x - \quad)$
(b) If c is negative then the signs in the brackets will be different.
$(x + \quad)(x - \quad)$

Step 3   Now look for the numbers to go in the brackets.
The two numbers must multiply to give c (c is the *product* of the two numbers) and they must add or subtract to give b (b is the *sum* or *difference*).

Remember: If the signs are the **same** look at the **sum**.
If the signs are **different** look at the **difference**.

(a) In the quadratic $x^2 + 5x + 6$ you are looking for two numbers which multiply together to give 6 and add up to 5.

(b) In the quadratic $x^2 + x - 6$ the c term is negative so the signs in the brackets will be different. You are looking for two numbers whose product is 6 and whose **difference** is 1.

E.g. Factorise $x^2 - 5x + 6$

Step 1 $(x \quad)(x \quad)$ x^2 factorises into x in each bracket.

Step 2 $(x - \quad)(x - \quad)$ The sign in front of the c value is $+$ so both signs are the same. The sign in front of the b value is $-$ so both signs in the brackets must be $-$.

Step 3 $(x - 2)(x - 3)$ The numerical values in the brackets must multiply together to give 6 and add up to give 5. So the values must be 2 and 3.

Check: $(x - 2)(x - 3) = x^2 - 3x - 2x + 6 = x^2 - 5x + 6$

If you have a quadratic with a number a in front of the x^2 term then factorising is a bit more difficult but the steps above are still applied.

Step 1 The factors of a go in front of the xs in each bracket.

Step 2 As above.

Step 3 The factors of c are now multiplied by the factors of a to give b.

E.g. Factorise $5x^2 + 13x + 6$

Step 1 The factors of 5 are 1 and 5.
$(5x \quad)(x \quad)$
Step 2 The signs are both $+$.
$(5x + \quad)(x + \quad)$
Step 3 The possible factors of 6 are 1 and 6 or 2 and 3.
$(\quad + 1)(\quad + 6)$ or $(\quad + 2)(\quad + 3)$
The signs are the same so you are looking for a **sum** to equal 13.

Possibilities: $1 \times 1 + 5 \times 6 = 31$
$\qquad\qquad 1 \times 6 + 5 \times 1 = 11$
$\qquad\qquad 1 \times 2 + 5 \times 3 = 17$
$\qquad\qquad 1 \times 3 + 5 \times 2 = 13 \qquad$ which gives the desired result.

So $5x^2 + 13x + 6 = (5x + 3)(x + 2)$

Check: $(5x + 3)(x + 2) = 5x^2 + 10x + 3x + 6 = 5x^2 + 13x + 6$

6 Factorise each of the following:
(a) $x^2 + 6x + 8$ (b) $x^2 + 6x - 7$ (c) $x^2 + 8x + 15$
(d) $x^2 - 9x + 20$ (e) $2x^2 + 7x + 3$ (f) $5x^2 + 9x - 2$

The difference of two squares

A quadratic in the form $a^2 - b^2$ represents a difference of two squares.
In question 3 above you saw that $(a + b)(a - b) = a^2 - b^2$.
Turning this around shows you how to factorise the difference of two squares:
$$a^2 - b^2 = (a + b)(a - b)$$

E.g. Factorise $4x^2 - 25$

$$4x^2 - 25 = (2x)^2 - 5^2$$
$$= (2x + 5)(2x - 5)$$

Check: $(2x + 5)(2x - 5) = 4x^2 - 10x + 10x - 25 = 4x^2 - 25$

7 Factorise each of the following:
(a) $x^2 - 4$ (b) $9x^2 - 1$

Factorising expressions involving roots

You already know how powers and roots are related and how to use the rules of indices.
You can use this knowledge to simplify individual expressions involving roots.

E.g. Simplify the following expressions:

(a) $\sqrt{a^6} = \sqrt{a^{(3 \times 2)}}$
$\qquad = \sqrt{(a^3)^2}$

The square and the square root cancel each other out so
$\sqrt{a^6} = a^3$

(b) $\sqrt{a^5} = \sqrt{(a^4 \times a)}$
$\qquad = \left(\sqrt{a^4}\right) \times \left(\sqrt{a}\right)$
$\qquad = \left(\sqrt{(a^2)^2}\right) \times \left(\sqrt{a}\right)$
$\qquad = a^2 \times \left(\sqrt{a}\right)$
$\qquad = a^2\sqrt{a}$

When terms involving roots are added or subtracted you can simplify each term and then take out common factors.

E.g. Factorise $\sqrt{a^3} + \sqrt{a}$

$$\sqrt{a^3} = \sqrt{a^2 \times a}$$
$$= \sqrt{a^2} \times \sqrt{a}$$
$$= a\sqrt{a}$$

So $\sqrt{a^3} + \sqrt{a} = a\sqrt{a} + \sqrt{a}$
$$= \sqrt{a}\,(a+1)$$

8 Factorise each of the following:

(a) $\sqrt{a^3} + \sqrt{a^2}$ (b) $\sqrt{a^9} + \sqrt{a^7}$ (c) $\sqrt{a^5} + \sqrt{a^4}$ (d) $\sqrt{8a^3} + \sqrt{2a}$

Transforming formulae

Transforming a formula or equation means rearranging to change the subject of the formula or equation.

E.g. $A = l \times w$ (Area = length × width)

A stands alone on one side of the equation so the **subject** of this formula is A.
You can make either l or w the subject of the formula:

$$l = \frac{A}{w} \text{ or } w = \frac{A}{l}$$

To change the subject of the formula we use **inverse operations**.
Suppose you want to make w the subject of the formula. You can see that w is multiplied by l.
To get w on its own you need to do the opposite (inverse) of multiplying by l.
The inverse of multiplication is division so you divide both sides by l.
This has the effect of leaving the w on one side of the equation and the other parts of the expression on the other.

$$A = l \times w$$

Dividing both sides by l you get $\dfrac{A}{l} = \dfrac{l \times w}{l}$

Since l divided by l is 1 you get $\dfrac{A}{l} = 1 \times w$ or $\dfrac{A}{l} = w$

You need to know the inverse of each operation to be able to transform an equation or formula.

Operation	Inverse operation
+	−
−	+
×	÷
÷	×
x^n (x to the power n)	$\sqrt[n]{x}$ (the nth root of x)
$\sqrt[n]{x}$ (the nth root of x)	x^n (x to the power n)

Remember: Take care over + and − signs when you are taking roots.

These operations must be carried out in the correct order.

Suppose you want to make x the subject of a formula.

Step 1 If the x term is contained in a bracket or root sign, deal with anything outside the bracket or root sign. (Remember that an expression like $\dfrac{x+2}{3}$ is another way of writing $\frac{1}{3}(x+2)$, so think of this as having a bracket.)
First remove any terms added to or subtracted from the bracket, and then deal with any multiplier or divisor.

E.g. $y = 2\sqrt{x+1} - 7$

Add 7 to both sides

$y + 7 = 2\sqrt{x+1}$

Then divide by 2

$\dfrac{y+7}{2} = \sqrt{x+1}$

Step 2 Deal with the root sign or the power (if the bracket is raised to a power).

Remember you can think of an expression like $\dfrac{1}{x+7}$ as $(x+7)^{-1}$ so this counts as a power.

Step 3 Now remove any terms added to or subtracted from the term involving x.

Step 4 Deal with any value multiplying or dividing the x term.

Step 5 Deal with any powers or roots.

Here is an example to show you all the steps. You won't usually have to use all of them.

E.g. $y = \sqrt{2x^2 + 3} - 1$

Step 1	$y + 1 = \sqrt{2x^2 + 3}$
Step 2	$(y+1)^2 = 2x^2 + 3$
Step 3	$(y+1)^2 - 3 = 2x^2$
Step 4	$\dfrac{(y+1)^2 - 3}{2} = x^2$
Step 5	$\sqrt{\dfrac{(y+1)^2 - 3}{2}} = x$

9 Make the highlighted letter the subject in each of the following equations:

(a) $y = a - bx$

(b) $w = \dfrac{u-v}{x}$

(c) $s = ut + \frac{1}{2}at^2$

(d) $z = \dfrac{ax}{by}$

(e) $m = 4n^2 - p$

(f) $y = \sqrt{\dfrac{3}{x+2}}$

3.8c Functions and formulae

There are a wide range of formulae and functions which you may be expected to understand and use. In this unit you will work with some of them, using what you have learned about transforming formulae.

Temperatures

The formula used to change temperatures given in degrees Celsius (Centigrade) into temperatures in degrees Fahrenheit is:

$$f = 1{\cdot}8c + 32$$

This formula can be transformed (rearranged) to give you temperatures in degrees Celsius:

$$f - 32 = 1{\cdot}8c$$

$$\dfrac{f - 32}{1{\cdot}8} = c$$

E.g. If the temperature is 46°F what is it in degrees C?

Substituting $f = 46$ into the formula gives

$$c = \frac{46 - 32}{1 \cdot 8} = \frac{14}{1 \cdot 8} = 7 \cdot 777\,°C$$

so the temperature is $7 \cdot 8\,°C$ (to 1 d.p.).

> **1** Convert the following temperature into degrees Celsius:
>   (a) 80 °F   (b) 110 °F   (c) 20 °F

Simple interest

Simple interest (I) is calculated by multiplying the amount invested (the principle, P) by the length of time the money is invested (T) and the rate of interest ($R\%$) converted to a fraction.

$$I = \frac{P \times R \times T}{100} \qquad \text{or} \qquad I = \frac{PRT}{100}$$

E.g. Calculate the simple interest if £5000 is invested at 7% for 4 years.

$$I = \frac{PRT}{100} \quad \text{therefore} \quad I = \frac{5000 \times 7 \times 4}{100} \quad \text{so } I = £1400$$

You can also use the formula to calculate the principle, rate or time.

E.g. Calculate the rate at which £3000 must be invested if you receive £900 interest after 5 years.

First transform the formula to make R the subject.

$$\frac{PRT}{100} = I$$

$$PRT = 100\,I$$

$$R = \frac{100\,I}{PT}$$

Substituting in the given values you get

$$R = \frac{100 \times 900}{3000 \times 5} = 6$$

The rate of interest is 6%.

> **2** (a) Calculate the simple interest if £2000 is invested at 6% for 10 years.
>   (b) Calculate the amount which must be invested (principle) to produce £300
>   interest if it is invested at 5% for 6 years.
>   (c) Calculate the time it would take to earn £1600 interest if you invested £20 000 at 8%.
>   (d) Calculate the rate at which £50 000 is invested if after 10 years the interest is
>   £37 500.

This type of manipulation of formulae to allow you to solve a problem is an important skill.

> **3** The equation $y = mx + c$ is the equation
>   of a straight line.
>
>   (a) Rearrange the formula to make x
>   the subject.
>
>   (b) If the gradient $m = 3$ and the value
>   of the y intercept $c = 2$,
>   calculate the values of x given
>   the following values of y:
>   (i) $y = 8$ (ii) $y = {}^{-}1$

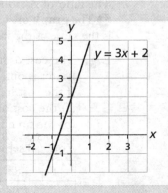

?

4 Average speed is given by the equation $s = \dfrac{d}{t}$ (speed = distance ÷ time).
How long would it take a car travelling at an average speed of 42 mph to travel 147 miles?

Hint: You want to know the time taken so rearrange the formula to make *t* the subject of the equation.

5 An engineer wants to construct a cylinder with a capacity (volume) of 499 cm³ and a height (*h*) of 9 cm. What should the radius (*r*) of the cylinder be?
(The volume of a cylinder is given by $V = \pi r^2 h$.)

6 When you are dealing with electricity you may use the relationship $P = VI$, where *P* is the power (measured in watts), *V* is the voltage (measured in volts) and *I* is the current (measured in amps).
The mains electricity supply is 240V. What is the minimum size fuse you can use for a 3 kW (3000 watts) heater?

Hint: Fuses are measured in amps. The size of the fuse must be at least as big as the current.

3.8d   Direct and inverse proportions

Direct proportion

If *A* and *B* are in **direct proportion**, then as one grows bigger the other also grows bigger by the same proportion e.g. if *B* doubles then *A* also doubles.
We write
$$A \propto B$$
E.g. Imagine you buy some bulbs.

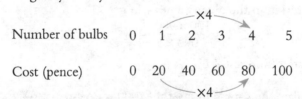

For every extra bulb you buy the cost goes up by the same amount (20p). So the cost of the bulbs will be proportional to the number you buy.
Number of bulbs ∝ cost

If $A \propto B$ then there are three things which are true.

❶ **The multiplier rule**
If *A* is multiplied by a value then *B* must be multiplied by the same value.
❷ **The constant ratio rule**
The ratio of *A* : *B* is the same for every pair of values *A* and *B*.
❸ The **graph** of *A* against *B* is a straight line through (0, 0) and the gradient of the graph is the same as the ratio of *A* : *B*.

E.g. The cost of heating a greenhouse is directly proportional to the time that the heater is on.
If the cost in pence, *c* = 17·6 when the time in hours, *t* = 8 calculate
(a) the cost of heating the greenhouse for 15 hours.
(b) the time if the cost is 41·8p.

You can set out this information like this:

t	8	15	*b*
c	17·6	*a*	41·8

You can use either the multiplier rule or the constant ratio rule for both parts of the question. Here is one example of each.

The multiplier rule	The constant ratio rule

t 8 → 15 t ⟨ 8 b ⟩

c 17·6 a c ↘17·6   41·8 ↙

The multiplier from 8 to 15 is $\frac{15}{8} = 1\cdot875$

The ratio $t : c = 8 : 17\cdot6 = b : 41\cdot8$

So $\frac{b}{41\cdot8} = \frac{8}{17\cdot6}$

Multiplying 17·6 by 1·875 gives $a = 33$

$b = \frac{41\cdot8 \times 8}{17\cdot6}$

$b = 19$

So the answer to part (a) is 33p.

So the answer to part (b) is 19 hours.

1 In an electroplating process the mass (m) of the metal deposited on a surface is proportional to the time (t) that the process is applied for.
If $m = 27\cdot5$ when $t = 5\cdot5$ calculate to 1 d.p. the values of
(a) m when $t = 9$.
(b) t when $m = 43$.

2 On holiday you change £150 into 26 100 Pesetas. If the exchange rate remains the same, find out the number of Pesetas you would get for
(a) £250.
(b) £60.
(c) What is the cost in £ of a gift which costs 10 092 Pesetas?

Inverse proportion

If A is **inversely proportional** to B, then if B gets bigger A gets smaller by the same factor e.g. if B increases by a factor of 2 (B doubles) then A decreases by a factor of 2 (A is halved). We write

$$A \propto \frac{1}{B}$$

When the variables are inversely proportional, as one is multiplied by a number the second is divided by the same number.

E.g. Imagine a group of people want to hire a minibus. The hire charge is £60 a day. If only 1 person uses the minibus it will cost them £60, for 2 people the cost will be £30 each and for 3 people the cost will be £20 each.
We can complete a table and graph showing number of people and cost.

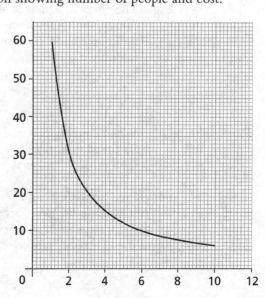

People	Cost (£)
1	60
2	30
3	20
4	15
5	12
6	10
8	7·50
10	6

×3   ÷3

Look carefully at the shape of the graph. It is typical of an inversely proportional relationship.

E.g. Boyle's law states that the volume of a gas at a constant temperature is inversely proportional to its pressure.
V represents the volume in litres and P the pressure in millibars.
$V = 45$ when $P = 600$
Calculate V when $P = 1050$.

The multiplier from 600 to 1050 is $\dfrac{1050}{600} = 1 \cdot 75$

$$\begin{array}{ccc} & \overset{\times 1 \cdot 75}{\longrightarrow} & \\ P & 600 & 1050 \\ \\ V & 45 & x \\ & \underset{\div 1 \cdot 75}{\longrightarrow} & \end{array}$$

The multiplier for pressure becomes the divisor for volume.
Volume at 1050 millibars is $45 \div 1 \cdot 75 = 25 \cdot 7$ litres (to 1 d.p.)

---

3 The length of a string and the frequency of the note it produces are inversely porportional. A string of length 65 cm is tuned to D which has a frequency of 147 Hz (Hertz).
Calculate the lengths of the strings which would produce the following frequencies:
(a) 110 Hz (A)
(b) 196 Hz (G)

Note: Use the memory or brackets facility on your calculator.

Inverse square law

This law occurs naturally in physics and other areas of science. It states that one quantity varies inversely as the square of another.
We write

$$A \propto \frac{1}{B^2}$$

If B increases, then A decreases by the **square** of the same factor e.g. if B doubles then A is divided by 4.

Newton's law of gravity follows this rule. The force of attraction between two objects weighing m_1 and m_2 in kg separated by a distance s in metres is given by

$F = \dfrac{G m_1 m_2}{s^2}$ (where G is the gravitational constant $6 \cdot 670 \times 10^{-11}$ Nm²/kg²)

So $F \propto \dfrac{1}{s^2}$

E.g. The effect of a light source on a point varies inversely as the square of the distance between them. Readings are taken of the illumination 1 m away from the source and 3 m away from the source. By how much does the light intensity change?
Let I be the illumination and d the distance from the source.

$$I \propto \frac{1}{d^2}$$

When d increases $\times 3$, I decreases by a factor of $3^2 = 9$.
So the illumination of a surface 3 m away from the light source will be $\frac{1}{9}$ of the illumination 1 m away.

---

4 Using Newton's law the force of attraction between two objects is found to be 40 N.
(a) Calculate the new force if the distance between the objects is doubled.
(b) Calculate the new force if the distance between the objects is decreased to $\frac{1}{5}$ of the original distance.

3.8e   y = mx + c

Any equation which gives a straight-line graph can be expressed in the form $y = mx + c$. By understanding the simple properties of an equation written in this form you can draw straight line graphs without needing to calculate values first. This can save you a lot of time and effort.

You already know how to draw the graphs of simple expressions by substituting values of x into the equation.

?

> **1** Draw the graphs of the following equations:
>   (a) $y = 3x - 1$ (b) $y = x + 3$ (c) $y = 4x - 2$
>
>   **Remember:** Substitute in 3 easy values of x for a line.

Now look at the **gradient** (or steepness) of the graph of $y = 3x - 1$ in question 1(a). The line goes up 3 squares for every 1 across. This means the gradient is 3.
The line crosses the y-axis at $y = ^-1$.
Compare the gradient and the point of intersection with the equation of the graph.

In the equation of a straight line expressed in the form $y = mx + c$, the m value gives you the gradient and the c value the point of intersection on the y-axis.
Now look back at your answers to 1(b) and 1(c) to check that this is true.

Remember: When an equation is written in the form:

$$y = mx + c$$

This value gives the gradient of the line

This value and its associated sign give the point of intersection on the y-axis

E.g. In the equation $y = 3x - 2$

The gradient of this line will be 3 (3 up for each 1 across)

The point of intersection on the y-axis will be −2

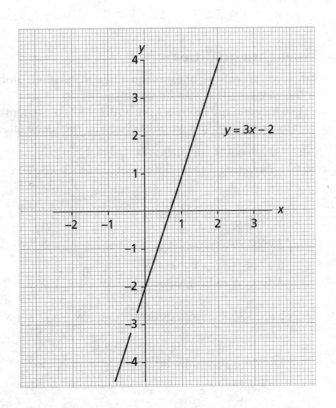

$y = 3x - 2$

2 Sketch the graphs of the following equations:
(a) $y = 2x - 2$
(b) $y = 4x + 1$
(c) $y = x$ **Hint:** $c = 0$
(d) $y = {}^-2x$ **Hint:** The gradient is negative so the graph goes down.
(e) $y = x + 3$
(f) $y = {}^-2x + 3$

Equations are not always given to you in the form $y = mx + c$. You may have to do some rearranging to get the equation into this form.

E.g.   Sketch the graph of $2x + 3y = 5$.

First rewrite the equation in the form $y = mx + c$.
$$2x + 3y = 5$$
$$3y = {}^-2x + 5$$
$$y = \tfrac{1}{3}({}^-2x + 5)$$
$$y = \tfrac{{}^-2}{3}x + \tfrac{5}{3}$$

So the gradient is $\tfrac{{}^-2}{3}$ and the y intercept is $\tfrac{5}{3}$.

3 Sketch the graphs of the following equations:
(a) $2x + 3y = 12$ (b) $5x + y = 5$ (c) $4x + 3y = 15$
(d) $3x - 5y = 15$ (e) $2x - 3y = 12$

Remember: This method of sketching a graph is a quick and useful way of checking any graph you have drawn.

3.8f   Solving inequalities

You have already solved very simple inequalities of the form ${}^-3 \le n < 5$, which told you that an unknown was greater than or less than a given number.

An inequality may also involve algebraic expressions. Inequalities of this type are called inequations.

$$x + 2 \le 4 \qquad 3x - 7 > 8 \qquad 3(x - 1) > 13 - x \qquad x^2 - 3x + 17 \le 0$$

Linear inequalities

When you are solving linear inequalities (inequations) you deal with them in a similar way to the way you deal with linear equations.

You may add and subtract from both sides of the statement and multiply and divide both sides by positive values without changing the inequality.

E.g.   (a) Solve the inequality $2x + 3 < 11$.

Subtracting 3 from both sides $2x + 3 - 3 < 11 - 3$
$$2x < 8$$

Dividing both sides by 2 $\dfrac{2x}{2} < \dfrac{8}{2}$

Therefore $x < 4$

(b) Solve $3x - 1 > x + 9$

Adding 1 to both sides $3x - 1 + 1 > x + 9 + 1$
$$3x > x + 10$$
Subtracting x from both sides $3x - x > x - x + 10$
$$2x > 10$$

Dividing both sides by 2 $\dfrac{2x}{2} > \dfrac{10}{2}$

Therefore $x > 5$

1 Solve the following inequalities:

(a) $6x + 3 < 33$ (b) $4(3x + 5) < 32$

(c) $3x + 6 < x + 2$ (d) $\dfrac{x+9}{2} > 3$

When multiplying or dividing both sides of the statement by a negative value it is very important that you remember that the inequality reverses.
Think of what happens with numbers.

$$7 > 3$$

Multiplying both sides by $^-1$ gives $^-7 < ^-3$

There are two ways of dealing with this.

E.g. Solve the inequality $7 - 3x < 13$.

Method 1

$$7 - 3x < 13$$
$$7 - 3x + 3x < 13 + 3x$$
$$7 < 13 + 3x$$
$$7 - 13 < 13 - 13 + 3x$$
$$^-6 < 3x$$

This method is longer but avoids dividing by $^-3$ and the change of sign.

$$\frac{^-6}{3} < \frac{3x}{3}$$
$$^-2 < x$$

Method 2

$$7 - 3x < 13$$
$$7 - 7 - 3x < 13 - 7$$
$$^-3x < 6$$

Dividing by $^-3$ $\dfrac{^-3x}{^-3} > \dfrac{6}{^-3}$ **Remember:** Reverse the inequality sign.

$$x > ^-2$$

Remember: $^-2 < x$ and $x > ^-2$ mean the same. The arrow always points to the smaller quantity.

2 Solve the following inequalities:

(a) $12 - x > 8$ (b) $15 - 3x < 2(x - 5)$

Non-linear inequalities

Inequalities may also involve higher powers of x.

E.g. Solve the inequality $x^2 + 3 < 12$.

Subtracting 3 from both sides $x^2 + 3 - 3 < 12 - 3$
$$x^2 < 9$$

Since $^-x \times ^-x = x^2$ and $x \times x = x^2$ you obtain two inequalities.

$$(x)^2 < 9 \qquad \text{and} \qquad (^-x)^2 < 9$$
$$\text{gives } x < 3 \qquad \text{gives} \qquad ^-x < 3$$

So $x < 3$ and $x > ^-3$
This is usually written $^-3 < x < 3$.

Solve the inequality using the positive root of x^2 and then remember that in the negative root the inequality changes direction.

E.g. Solve the inequality $x^2 + 1 > 50$.

$$x^2 + 1 - 1 > 50 - 1$$
$$x^2 > 49$$
$$x > 7$$

Changing the sign and reversing the inequality gives $x < ^-7$.
So the solutions are given by $x > 7$ or $x < ^-7$.

3 Solve the following inequalities:

(a) $2x^2 - 1 > 1$ (b) $x(x - 2) < 2(2 - x)$

3.8g   Graphs of linear inequalities

> **1** Draw the graphs of the following equations. (Draw the lines very lightly. You
> will see why later.)
> (a) $y = x$ (b) $y = 2x$ (c) $y = 3$
> (d) $x = 2$ (e) $y = {}^-x$ (f) $y = 2x - 3$

Look at the graph of $y = x$ in question 1(a). On one side of the line, $y < x$ and on the other side, $y > x$.

So we can use a region or area of the graph to illustrate $y < x$ or $y > x$. The region includes all the points which make the inequality true.

With < and > the points on the line are not included in the region so the line is dotted to show that it's not part of the region.

With ≤ (less than or equal to) or ≥ (greater than or equal to) the line is drawn solid to show that it's included in the region.

E.g.   Draw a graph to illustrate the region $x < 2$.

First draw the graph of $x = 2$. Then on one side of the line you will have $x < 2$. Make the line dotted because it's not part of the region.

Shade the side you do **not** want. (This is called shading the complement.) This leaves the side you do want clean and easier to use.

This side is the answer.

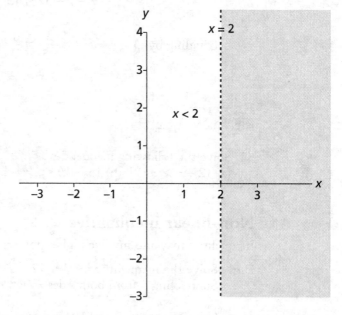

Note: Some people shade the area they do want. Make it clear in your diagram which you have shaded.

When the line is vertical or horizontal deciding which side to shade is relatively easy. If the line is diagonal you can decide which side to shade by choosing an easy point on one side of the line and seeing whether it satisfies the inequality (makes the inequality true).

> **2** Illustrate the following inequalities using the graphs you drew in question 1.
> (a) $y > x$ (b) $y ≤ 2x$ (c) $y > 3$
> (d) $x ≥ 2$ (e) $y < {}^-x$ (f) $y > 2x - 3$

Remember: Shade the area you do not want.

In each of these cases the region which satisfies the inequality only has one boundary (edge). In every other direction it goes on forever.

By using three or more inequalities you can locate a region which is bounded on every side.

E.g. Illustrate $x < 2$, $y > ^-x - 1$ and $y < 2$ on the same pair of axes.

This means that all the points (x, y) which satisfy all three inequalities are contained in the unshaded region.

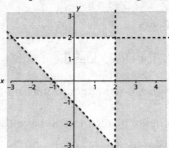

?

3 Illustrate the regions given by the following inequalities:
(a) $x < 2$, $y > ^-1$ and $y < 2x + 2$
(b) $y > ^-3$, $y < x - 1$ and $y < ^-x$

3.8h Recognising graphs of simple functions

Quadratics

You should recognise that these are all quadratic expressions:
$$2x^2 + 5x - 3, \qquad x + x^2 - 6, \qquad 2x^2 - 7, \qquad y^2 + 4$$

Remember: You can recognise a quadratic expression because the highest power is 2.

What shape is the graph of a quadratic?

E.g. Draw the graph of $y = x^2$.

Remember: For a curve use at least 5 values, including negative ones, and then use extra values where you need to check the shape.

x	x^2
3	9
2	4
1	1
$\frac{1}{2}$	$\frac{1}{4}$
0	0
$^-\frac{1}{2}$	$^-\frac{1}{4}$
$^-1$	1
$^-2$	4
$^-3$	9

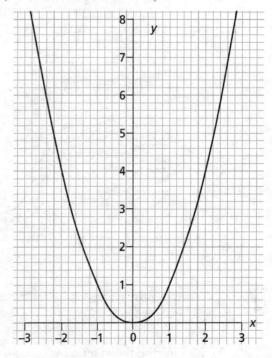

Now you can see that the y-axis needs to go from 0 to 9. Plot these points and join them with a smooth curve.

This curve is called a **parabola**.

?

1 Using a single pair of axes plot the graphs of the following quadratic expressions:
   (a) $x^2 - 1$ (b) $x^2 + 1$ (c) $x^2 + 2$
   (d) $x^2 + 3$ (e) $^-x^2$ (f) $^-x^2 + 2$

2 (a) What effect does the number added to or subtracted from the x^2 term have on the graph?
   (b) What is the effect of making the x^2 term negative?

More complex quadratics still have the same shape.

E.g. Draw the graph of $y = x^2 - 2x - 3$.

x	4	3	2	1	0	$^-1$	$^-2$	$^-3$	$^-4$
x^2	16	9	4	1	0	1			
$-2x$	-8	-6	-4	-2	0	2			
-3	-3	-3	-3	-3	-3	-3			
y	5	0	$^-3$	$^-4$	$^-3$	0			

Note: You should notice that each row has a distinct pattern.
Complete the table yourself.

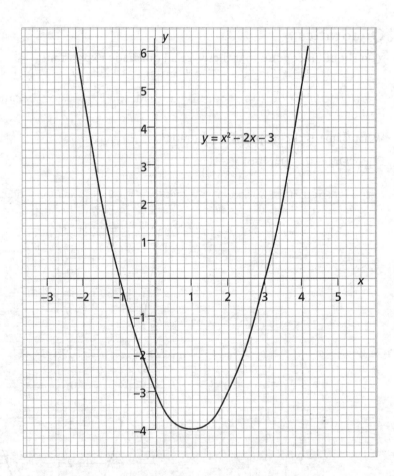

?

3 Draw the graphs of the following quadratics:
   (a) $y = 5 - x^2$ (b) $y = 2x^2 - 3x - 2$ (c) $y = x^2 + 5x + 6$

Multiplying the x^2 term by 2 in question 3(b) makes the parabola thinner.

So you have seen that the graph of a quadratic equation is always a parabola.

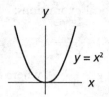

If the x^2 term is negative then the parabola is inverted (upside down).

Cubics

In a **cubic** expression the highest power is 3.

E.g. Draw the graph of $y = x^3$ (the simplest cubic function).

First calculate some values of y.

x	y
2	8
1	1
0	0
-1	-1
-2	-8

Plot these points.

These don't give you enough idea of the shape so calculate some more values to check the shape when $-1 \le x \le 1$.

x	y
$\frac{3}{4}$	0·42
$\frac{1}{2}$	0·13
$\frac{1}{4}$	0·02
$-\frac{1}{4}$	-0·02
$-\frac{1}{2}$	-0·13
$-\frac{3}{4}$	-0·42

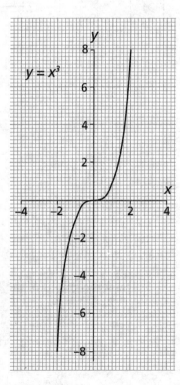

You can't plot these points exactly but they give you a guide for the shape near (0, 0). Now join the points with a smooth curve.

Note: The graph of x^3 is **not** the typical shape produced by a cubic. The graph of a cubic can have 1, 2 or 3 turning points.

4 Starting with values of x from -2 to 2 draw the graphs of the following cubics:
   (a) $\frac{1}{2}x^3$ (b) $2 - x^3$ (c) $x^3 - 4x^2 + 3x$

Note: Adding a number to the expression or making the x^3 term negative has the same effect as with a quadratic.

Reciprocals

Here are some examples of reciprocal expressions:

$$\frac{1}{x}, \quad \frac{5}{x}, \quad \frac{1}{x+12}, \quad \frac{3}{x+a}$$

A reciprocal function has the form $y = \dfrac{a}{x+b}$, where a and b are any number (positive or negative).

E.g. Draw the graph of $y = \dfrac{1}{x}$.

This looks like x and y are inversely proportional. So y gets bigger as x gets smaller and y gets smaller as x gets bigger.
Let x be from $^-3$ to 3 ($^-3 \le x \le 3$).

x	$\dfrac{1}{x}$	y
3	$\frac{1}{3}$	0·3
2	$\frac{1}{2}$	0·5
1	1	1
$\frac{1}{2}$	2	2
$\frac{1}{4}$	4	4
$^-\frac{1}{4}$	$^-4$	$^-4$
$^-\frac{1}{2}$	$^-2$	$^-2$
$^-1$	$^-1$	$^-1$
$^-2$	$^-\frac{1}{2}$	$^-0·5$
$^-3$	$^-\frac{1}{3}$	$^-0·3$

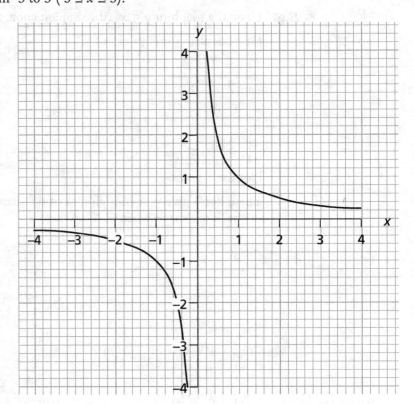

Note: When x is very small (either positive or negative), y gets very large, and as x gets very close to 0, y becomes infinite. So the graph never touches the y-axis. As x gets very large (either positive or negative), y gets very small but never reaches 0. So the graph never touches the x-axis.

?

5 Draw the graphs of the following reciprocal functions:

(a) $\dfrac{2}{x}$ (b) $\dfrac{1}{x+2}$ (c) $\dfrac{1}{x-2}$ (d) $\dfrac{^-4}{x}$

Remember: These are the shapes of the most common types of curve:

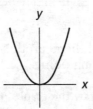 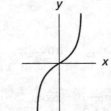 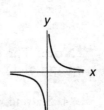

Making any of these expressions negative will reflect the curve in the x-axis.
Adding or subtracting a constant will move the curve up or down the y-axis.

E.g. Choose the right equation from the following list for each of the graphs below.

(a) $y = 2x^2$ Positive parabola through (0, 0), steeper than x^2.
(b) $y = x^3$ Positive cubic which crosses x-axis at 0 only.
(c) $y = x^2 + 2$ Positive parabola which crosses y-axis at 2.
(d) $y = 4 - x^2$ Negative parabola which crosses y-axis at 4.
(e) $xy = 1$ Reciprocal. Look for 2 separate parts to the graph.
(f) $y = 2x^3 + x^2 - 3x$ Positive cubic with 2 or 3 turning points.

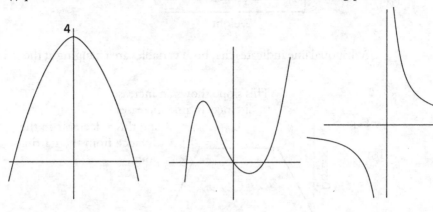

This is an inverted parabola so its equation must be equation (d).

This is the graph of a cubic. It has 3 turning points so it must be (f).

This is the graph of a reciprocal so the equation must be (e).

3.8i   Graphs of real-life situations

Graphs can be used to display many different types of information. But there are some things all graphs have in common.

    Graphs in two dimensions have two axes which enable you to compare two variables.

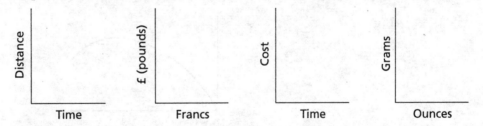

The line of the graph shows you the relationship between the two variables.

A horizontal or vertical line shows that one of the variables remains constant (unchanged) as the other variable changes.

E.g.

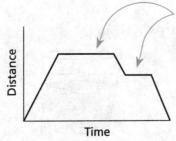

The horizontal parts of the line show periods when the time changes but the distance from the start does not. (The subject being graphed is therefore stationary.)

A vertical break in the line represents a sudden jump in values.

E.g.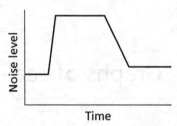

The gaps indicate that when a parcel reaches a certain weight the cost to post it jumps (instantly) to the next value.

A diagonal line indicates that both variables are changing at the same time, at a steady rate.

E.g.

This slope shows an increase in distance as time increases and this a decrease in the distance from the starting point.

This graph shows a rapid increase in noise level when my favourite record comes on.

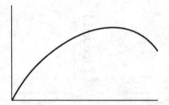

A curved graph means that the rate of change of one variable with respect to the other keeps varying.

E.g.

This curve shows the height of a ball being thrown up in the air, plotted against time. The ball starts off gaining height very rapidly so the curve starts off nearly vertical. As it travels the ball slows down so it gains height less and less quickly. This is shown by the gradient of the curve decreasing. Eventually the ball stops and begins to fall back down.

Graphing relationships

This flask is being filled with water.

The graph of the diameter of the water's surface against the depth of water in the flask looks like this.

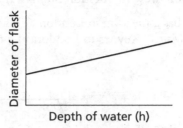

1 These flasks are also being filled with water.

Match these graphs to the flasks above.

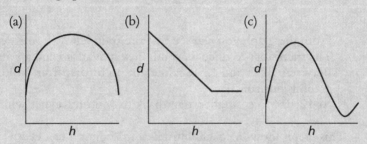

2 Look at these graphs which show William riding his bike.

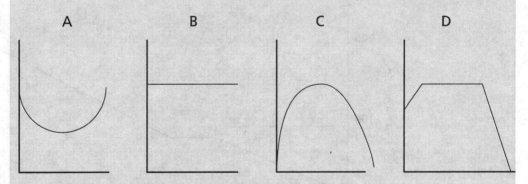

(a) Which of the graphs shows William travelling at a constant speed?

(b) Which shows William starting from a set of traffic lights when they go green and then stopping at the next red light?

(c) Which graph shows William accelerating, travelling at a constant speed and then quickly stopping?

3 Draw a graph to describe the following:

(a) I turned on the hot tap to fill the bath. When it was half full I turned on the cold tap as well. Then I turned both taps off.

(b) The exchange rate between the pound and the dollar was steady but now it's falling.

(c) I left home and walked slowly to the bus stop. I waited a short while for the bus and then travelled to town. The bus stopped twice on the way.

Travel graphs

The graph you drew in question 3(c) is a travel graph.

E.g. Mike has a meeting in London. This travel graph shows his journey by train from Milton Keynes to London, the time he spends in London and the return journey.

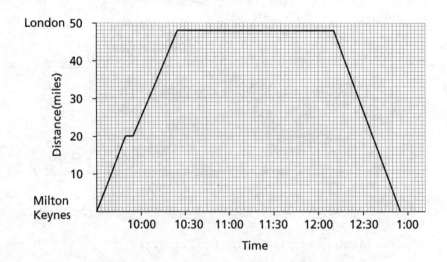

From the graph you can see that the train left Milton Keynes at 9:30 am.
The train stopped once for 5 minutes at Watford and arrived in London at 10:25.
Between 10:25 and 12:10 Mike got no further from Milton Keynes so the graph is horizontal.
At 12:10 Mike caught a train back to Milton Keynes which did not stop.

?

4 This graph shows a coach journey from London to Leeds (195 miles). The coach stops at a motor way service station on the way.
(The graph does not return to the bottom line because the journey is one-way.)

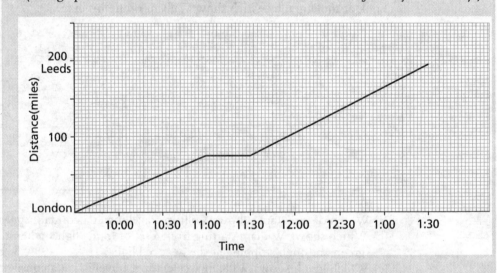

(a) How long does the journey from London to Leeds take?
(b) How far is the service station from London?
(c) How long does the coach stop at the service station?

A travel graph can be used to find the average speed for the journey or part of a journey.

The formula used is average speed $= \dfrac{\text{distance travelled}}{\text{time taken}}$

Remember: The time taken must be in hours.

E.g. Looking at the travel graph of Mike's journey from Milton Keynes to London you can see that the return journey took 45 minutes and the distance travelled was 48 miles.
First convert the time taken to hours.
45 minutes = 0·75 hours

$$\text{average speed} = \frac{\text{distance travelled}}{\text{time taken}} = \frac{48}{0·75} = 64 \text{ mph}$$

5 Using the graph in question 4 calculate the speed of the coach
(a) before it stopped at the service station.
(b) after it stopped at the service station.

Remember: The time taken must be in hours.

Curved graphs

A curve is produced when the rate at which the variables change is no longer steady.

E.g. Linda's heart rate is monitored while she is doing aerobics. This graph shows the results.
From this graph it is possible to find Linda's pulse rate at various times through the exercise and to say what is happening.

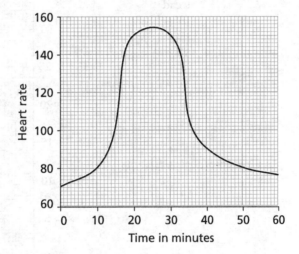

The aerobics begin with a warm up session.
The exercise gets harder during the middle period.
As the exercise continues Linda's pulse remains above its starting point and then in the last part of the session it drops back towards its normal rate.

6 Use the graph to answer the following questions.
(a) What was Linda's heart rate at the start of the exercise session?
(b) About how long did the warm up last?
(c) For how long was Linda's heart beat over 120?

3.9a Expressing general laws in symbolic form

You may be given a set of data or a graph and asked to express the relationships displayed in an algebraic form.

If you are given a set of data you may be able to see a constant relationship between the two variables but it is often far easier if you graph the relationship.

E.g. This table shows the cost of gas for cooking and heating.

Therms used	10	20	30	40	50
Cost (£)	17.00	21.50	26.00	30.50	35.00

Try to find a connecting rule between the cost and the number of therms used.

$$\text{Gradient} = \frac{\text{rise}}{\text{tread}}$$
$$= \frac{(35-17)}{(50-10)}$$
$$= \frac{18}{40}$$
$$= \pounds0{\cdot}45 \text{ per therm}$$

Cost intercept = £12·50

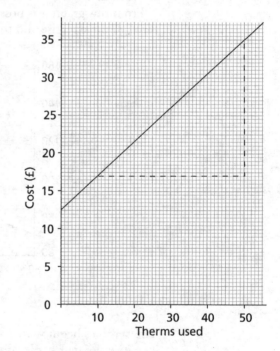

Since this is a straight-line graph the gradient will give you a rate per therm.

And the intercept on the cost axis will give you a standing charge.

Therefore the connecting formula is

Cost = 0·45 × therms used + 12·50

1 A printer is producing a circular. The following is a table of charges.

Charges (£)	130	180	230	280	330
Number of copies	1000	2000	3000	4000	5000

By drawing a graph or otherwise, work out an equation to give you the cost of any number of circulars.

The same basic principles can be used to tackle more difficult examples. It is always better to get a straight-line graph if possible. Then you can be sure of the shape so your answers will be more accurate. And a straight line is much easier to draw!

E.g. Rita and Gurbash have recorded the following results for an experiment in science.

Area (A)	1	4	9	16	25	36
Result (R)	20	30	40	50	60	70

The results go up in equal steps but the areas don't, so plotting area against the results would not give a straight line.
Looking at the table they can see that all the areas are squares. So they try constructing a table of width ($\sqrt{A}$) and results.

Width (w)	1	2	3	4	5	6
Result (R)	20	30	40	50	60	70

Now the results go up in equal steps **and** the widths go up in equal steps which means a linear relationship between width and the results obtained.

By graphing this relationship they obtain the graph on the right.

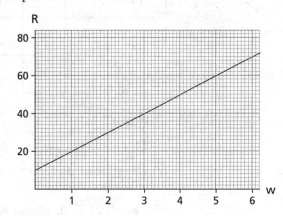

Since this relationship gives a straight line they know they can express it in the form
$$R = mw + c$$
From the graph, the gradient $m = 10$ and the R intercept $c = 10$.
This gives them $R = 10w + 10$

Substituting in $w = \sqrt{A}$ gives

$$R = 10\sqrt{A} + 10$$

Note: By putting $w = \sqrt{A}$ you get a straight line instead of a curve.

Some questions involve more complicated relationships. But the graphs involved should be graphs you are familiar with. This type of question usually has several parts to lead you through to the result.

E.g. Isobel is trying to work out a rule to help her calculate stopping distances. She has this data from the highway code.

Speed in miles per hour	0	30	50	70
Stopping distance in feet	0	75	175	315

(a) Plot the information on a graph with distance (*d*) on the vertical axis and speed (*s*) on the horizontal axis.

(b) Join the points with a smooth curve. This is the black curve.

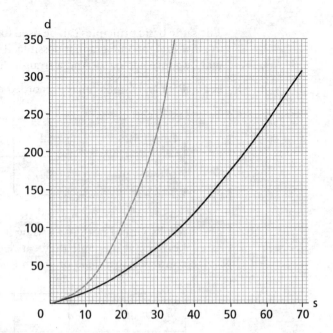

Note: This curve looks like a quadratic with a fractional coefficient of s^2.

(c) Complete this table.

Speed (*s*)	0	10	20	30	40	50	60	70
s^2	0	100	400	900				
$\dfrac{s^2}{4}$	0	25	100	225				

(d) Plot the values of $\dfrac{s^2}{4}$ on your graph and join them with a smooth curve. This has been done in green on the original graph above.

(e) Use your graph to help you find an approximate equation linking speed and stopping distances.

The graph of $\dfrac{s^2}{4}$ is similar to the graph of speed against stopping distance. By dividing s^2 by numbers larger than 4 the values of $\dfrac{s^2}{n}$ become closer to the original graph.

The graph $d = \dfrac{s^2}{15}$ is very close to the graph of speed against stopping distance. So an approximate relationship is $d = \dfrac{s^2}{15}$.

?

2 A paper rocket is fired into the air.

The following heights are recorded over the rocket's flight.

Paper rocket

Height (m)	2	6	8	8	6	2
Time (s)	0	1	2	3	4	5

(a) Draw the graph of the rocket's flight. (Put time on the horizontal axis.)
(b) What is the maximum height reached by the rocket?
(c) Plot the graph of $h = {}^-(t - 2 \cdot 5)^2$ on the same axes.
(d) Use this to help you work out an equation for the rocket's flight.

3.9b The rules of indices for negative and fractional indices

Negative indices

You have used the rules of indices for positive whole number indices. These same rules can be extended to negative indices.

Remember: A negative index gives the inverse (reciprocal) of the positive index.

$$x^{-n} = \frac{1}{x^n}$$

E.g. $2x^{-2} \times 3x^{-3} = \frac{2}{x^2} \times \frac{3}{x^3}$

$$= \frac{2 \times 3}{x^2 \times x^3}$$

When you multiply you add the indices:

$$= \frac{6}{x^{(2+3)}}$$

$$= \frac{6}{x^5}$$

$$= 6x^{-5}$$

$$= 6x^{(-2 + -3)}$$

So the same rule applies for negative indices: when you multiply expressions you add the indices.

?

> **1** Simplify the following:
>   (a) $x^{-4} \times x^{-3}$ (b) $3x^{-2} \times 2x^{-4}$ (c) $2x^{-1} \times 2x^{-2}$
>
>   (d) $3a^{-6} \times 2a^{-4}$ (e) $5b^7 \times 12b^{-4}$ (f) $x^{-3}y^2 \times 7x^{-2}y^{-4}$

Dividing expressions involving negative indices takes a bit more care.

E.g. (a) $x^{-5} \div x^{-3} = \frac{1}{x^5} \div \frac{1}{x^3}$

To divide by a fraction you multiply by its inverse:

$$= \frac{1}{x^5} \times \frac{x^3}{1}$$

$$= x^3 \div x^5$$

When you divide you subtract the indices:

$$= x^{(3-5)}$$

$$= x^{-2}$$

$$= x^{(-5 - -3)}$$

(b) $6x^{-4} \div 3x^{-1} = (6 \div 3) \times (x^{-4} \div x^{-1})$

$$= 2x^{(-4 - -1)}$$

$$= 2x^{(-4 + 1)}$$

$$= 2x^{-3}$$

?

> **2** Simplify the following:
>   (a) $x^{-6} \div x^{-2}$ (b) $8x^{-6} \div 2x^{-2}$ (c) $7x^{-5} \div x$ (d) $5x^3 \div x^{-4}$
>
>   (e) $21a^{-3}b^{-1}c \div 3a^2b^{-4}c^{-8}$

You also need to take care with the + and − signs when you raise a power to a negative power.

E.g. $(z^{-2})^{-3} = (\frac{1}{z^2})^{-3}$

$$= (\frac{z^2}{1})^3$$

When you raise a power to a power you multiply:

$$= z^{(2 \times 3)}$$
$$= z^6$$
$$= z^{(-2 \times -3)}$$

3 Simplify the following expressions:

(a) $(a^{-3})^7$ (b) $(2b^4)^{-1}$ (c) $(4n^{-3})^{-4}$ (d) $(x^2y^{-3}z^{-1})^{-5}$

Fractional indices

The rules for indices can also be extended to fractional indices.

Remember: A fractional index represents a root.

$$x^{\frac{1}{n}} = \sqrt[n]{x}$$

Where the index is of the form $\frac{a}{b}$ with $a \neq 1$ it gives the bth root of x^a which can also be written $\sqrt[b]{x^a}$.

4 Express the following in the form $\sqrt[b]{x^a}$:

(a) $x^{\frac{2}{5}}$ (b) $x^{\frac{3}{7}}$ (c) the cube root of x^2 (d) the square root of x cubed

E.g. $x^{\frac{1}{2}} \times x^{\frac{1}{4}} = x^{\frac{2}{4}} \times x^{\frac{1}{4}}$

$$= \sqrt[4]{x^2} \times \sqrt[4]{x}$$
$$= \sqrt[4]{x^2 \times x}$$
$$= \sqrt[4]{x^3}$$
$$= x^{\frac{3}{4}}$$
$$= x^{\left(\frac{1}{2}+\frac{1}{4}\right)}$$

So the rules of indices apply to fractional values in exactly the same way.

5 Simplify the following:

(a) $x^{\frac{1}{3}} \times x^{\frac{1}{2}}$ (b) $x^{\frac{2}{3}} \times x$ (c) $x^{\frac{2}{7}} \times x^{\frac{3}{4}}$

E.g. $x^{\frac{1}{2}} \div x^{\frac{1}{6}} = x^{\left(\frac{1}{2}-\frac{1}{6}\right)}$

$$= x^{\left(\frac{3}{6}-\frac{1}{6}\right)}$$
$$= x^{\frac{1}{3}}$$

6 Simplify the following:

(a) $x^{\frac{3}{5}} \div x^{\frac{1}{5}}$ (b) $a^{\frac{4}{3}} \times a^{\frac{1}{6}}$

E.g. (a) $\left(x^{\frac{1}{5}}\right)^2 = x^{\frac{1}{5}} \times x^{\frac{1}{5}}$

$$= x^{\left(\frac{1}{5}+\frac{1}{5}\right)}$$
$$= x^{\frac{2}{5}}$$
$$= x^{\left(2 \times \frac{1}{5}\right)}$$

(b) $\left(x^{\frac{1}{7}}\right)^{\frac{1}{2}} = x^{\left(\frac{1}{7} \times \frac{1}{2}\right)}$

$$= x^{\frac{1}{14}}$$

7 Simplify the following:

(a) $\left(a^{\frac{2}{3}}\right)^3$ (b) $\left(x^{\frac{1}{2}}\right)^7$ (c) $\left(x^2y\right)^{\frac{1}{5}}$

3.9c   Solving equations using graphs

Quadratics

A quadratic equation is an equation of the form $ax^2 + bx + c = 0$, with $a \neq 0$.

You can solve an equation of this form by plotting the graph of $y = ax^2 + bx + c$ and finding the value of x when $y = 0$. This means finding the values of x where the graph crosses the x-axis.

E.g.   Solve the equation $x^2 - x - 2 = 0$ by drawing the graph of $y = x^2 - x - 2$.

First produce a table of results.

x	$^-3$	$^-2$	$^-1$	0	1	2	3
x^2	9	4	1	0	1	4	9
$-x$	3	2	1	0	$^-1$	$^-2$	$^-3$
-2	$^-2$	$^-2$	$^-2$	$^-2$	$^-2$	$^-2$	$^-2$
y	10	4	0	$^-2$	$^-2$	0	4

Plot the points and join them with a smooth curve.

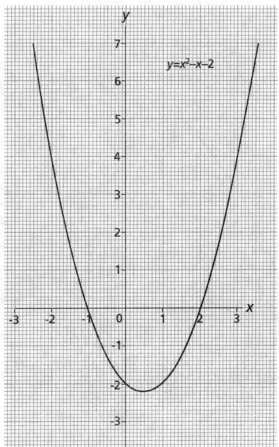

The solution of the equation is given by the points at which the curve crosses the x-axis.
$x^2 - x - 2 = 0$ when
$x = {}^-1$ and when $x = 2$

Remember: Always check your results by substituting your solutions back into the equation.
Check: $2^2 - 2 - 2 = 0$ $(^-1)^2 - (^-1) - 2 = 0$

?

1 Where you can, solve the following equations by drawing their graphs. (One of the equations has no solution.)
   (a) $x^2 - 5x + 4 = 0$ $(0 \le x \le 5)$
   (b) $x^2 - 3x + 2 = 0$ $(^-1 \le x \le 4)$
   (c) $2 + x - x^2 = 0$ $(^-2 \le x \le 3)$
   (d) $x^2 - 4x + 4 = 0$ $(^-1 \le x \le 4)$
   (e) $x^2 + 3 = 0$ $(^-2 \le x \le 2)$

A quadratic equation has two solutions if the curve crosses the x-axis, it has one solution if the curve just touches the x-axis and it has no solution if the curve does not cross or touch the x-axis.

Another way to find the solutions of a quadratic equation is by drawing a curve and a straight line. The solutions are given by the points where the line crosses the curve.

E.g. A gardener wants to build a flower bed in her garden. She has 10 m of edging to construct a rectangular bed.
   (a) Find the maximum area of flower bed she can make with this edging.
   (b) If the gardener wants the area of the flower bed to be 4·5 m² what should the length be?

Draw a graph of area against length for the flower bed.

Copy and complete this table of values:

Length	0	0·5	1	1·5	2	2·5	3	3·5	4	4·5	5
Width	5	4·5	4	3·5	3						
Area	0	2·25	4	5·25	6						

Copy and complete the graph.

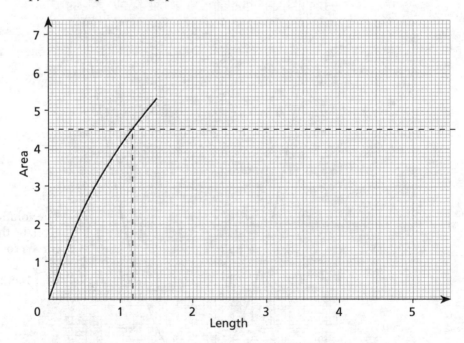

Let length $= l$ and width $= w$.
We know $2(l + w) = 10$
$l + w = 5$
$w = 5 - l$

Let the area of the bed = A.

$$A = lw$$
$$= l(5 - l)$$
$$= 5l - l^2$$

So the equation of the curve is $A = 5l - l^2$.

(a) From the graph, the maximum area is 6·25 m².

(b) Draw a horizontal line across the graph with the equation $A = 4.5$.
This line crosses the curve at two points. At these points you draw a vertical line to the l-axis.
This gives you two possible lengths for the flower bed.
To 1 decimal place, the length is 1·2 m or 3·8 m.

These points are the solutions of the equation $5l - l^2 = 4.5$.

Remember: Always check your answers.

If length = 1·2 then width = 3·8 and area = 1·2 × 3·8 = 4·56m².
Similarly if length = 3·8 (with width and length swapped over).
4·56m² is near enough 4·5m² so the answers are correct to 1 d.p.

Note: The accuracy of the answers depends on how carefully the graph is drawn.

?

2 Draw the graph of $y = x^2$ ($^-3 \leq x \leq 3$) and then use it to solve the following equations.
(a) $x^2 = 4$
(b) $x^2 = 2x + 3$ (Draw the line given by the equation $y = 2x + 3$ and find where it crosses the curve.)
(c) $x^2 = {}^-x$

3 Draw the graphs of $y = x^2 + 2x - 4$ ($^-4 \leq x \leq 3$) and $y = x + 2$ on the same pair of axes. Use the graph to solve the equation $x^2 + 2x - 4 = x + 2$.

Cubics

A cubic equation is one in which the highest power is 3.
One way to solve a cubic equation is to draw the graph of the equation and then find the points of intersection with the x-axis (where $y = 0$).

E.g. Solve the equation $x^3 - 3x^2 - x + 3 = 0$ by drawing its graph. ($^-2 \leq x \leq 4$)

Let $x^3 - 3x^2 - x + 3 = y$

x	4	3	2	1	0	$^-1$	$^-2$
x^3	64	27	8	1	0	$^-1$	$^-8$
$-3x^2$	$^-48$	$^-27$	$^-12$	$^-3$	0	$^-3$	$^-12$
$-x$	$^-4$	$^-3$	$^-2$	$^-1$	0	1	2
$+3$	3	3	3	3	3	3	3
y	15	0	$^-3$	0	3	0	$^-15$

Plot these points and join them with a smooth curve.

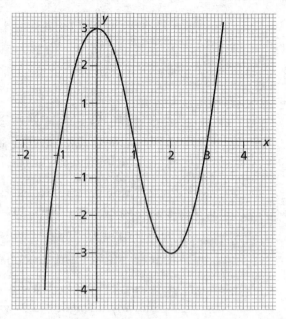

The solutions to the equation
$x^3 - 3x^2 - x + 3 = 0$
are given by the points where the graph crosses the x-axis.
These points are
$x = {}^-1$, $x = 1$ and $x = 3$.

A cubic equation can always be written in the form $x^3 = ax^2 + bx + c$.

You can then solve the equation by plotting the curves $y = x^3$ and $y = ax^2 + bx + c$ and finding their points of intersection.

E.g. Solve the equation $x^3 = 3x^2 - 2x$ by drawing a graph of $y = x^3$ and $y = 3x^2 - 2x$.

x	$^-1$	0	1	2
x^3	$^-1$	0	1	8

x	$^-1$	0	1	2
$3x^2$	3	0	3	12
$-2x$	2	0	$^-2$	$^-4$
y	5	0	1	8

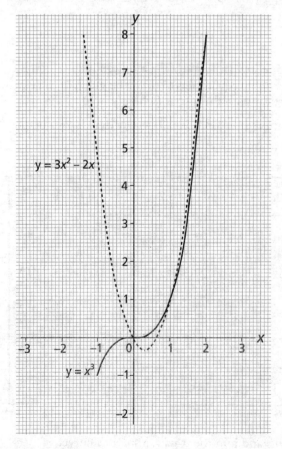

You can see from the graph that $y = x^3$ and $y = 3x^2 - 2x$ cross at the points $(0, 0)$, $(1, 1)$ and $(2, 8)$.
So the x values which satisfy the equation $x^3 = 3x^2 - 2x$ are $x = 0$, $x = 1$ and $x = 2$.

4 Draw the graphs of the following cubics and find their solutions.
  (a) $x^3 + 1 = 0$ ($^-2 \leq x \leq 1$)
  (b) $x^3 - 6x^2 + 9x = 0$ ($^-1 \leq x \leq 4$)

5 Draw the graph of $y = x^3$ ($^-2 \leq x \leq 2$) and use it to solve the following equations.
  (a) $x^3 = 0$
  (b) $x^3 = x^2 - x + 1$
  (c) $x^3 = 2x - 4$
  (d) $x^3 + x = 0$
  (e) $x^3 - x^2 - 2x = 0$

A cubic equation may have 1, 2 or 3 solutions. It must always have at least 1 solution.

3.9d Growth and decay rates

Growth and decay rates can be constant or varying. A **constant** rate of growth occurs when a fixed amount is regularly added to the starting value.
This kind of growth gives a straight-line graph with the gradient equal to the growth rate.

E.g. A factory produces 20 cars every week.

Week	0	1	2	3	4
Cars	0	20	40	60	80

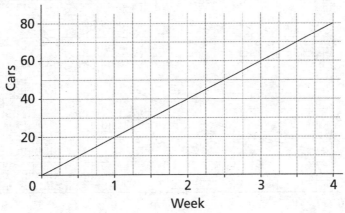

The total number of cars produced grows at a constant rate of 20 per week.

Exponential growth

A quantity which grows by being multiplied by the same value at regular intervals is described as growing **exponentially**.

E.g. A young tree grows 20% in height each year.
If the tree is 1 m tall when it is planted how tall will it be after 10 years?
Draw a graph to show its growth over these 10 years.

The height increases by 20% so height at end of year = 1·20 × height at start of year.
The height is given by repeatedly multiplying by 1·2.
After n years the height is $1 \times 1 \cdot 2^n$ m.

If your calculator has a constant key **K** you can do this:

1 . 2 × K = = = =

As each = sign is keyed in the next value appears on the calculator.

Alternatively you can use the **Xʸ** key.

The results given to 2 d.p. are:

Year	0	1	2	3	4	5	6	7	8	9	10
Size (m)	1.00	1.20	1.44	1.73	2.07	2.49	2.99	3.58	4.30	5.16	6.19

× 1.2   × 1.2

After 10 years the tree will be 6·19 m tall (to 2 d.p.).

The graph of this data looks like this.

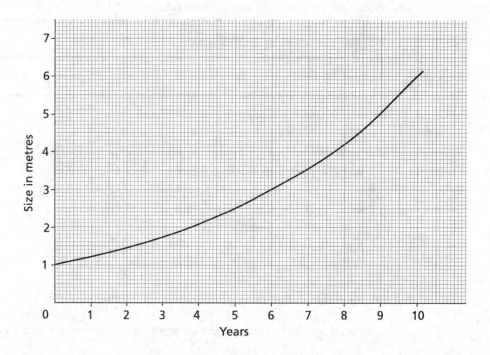

Note: The curve gets progressively steeper.

?

1 A microscopic organism reproduces itself by splitting into two at the end of each minute. Assuming that you start with only one organism complete a table of the number of micro-organisms at the end of each minute over a period of 15 minutes.

2 When a child was born her grandparents invested £100 in an account that guaranteed to pay a fixed rate of 12% per annum (per year). She is to be given the contents of the account when she is 18.
(a) Draw a table of the results to show how the account grows over the 18 years.
(b) Draw a graph to illustrate these results.

Exponential decay

Exponential decay works in the same way as exponential growth but with a multiplier of less than 1.

E.g. Suppose a population of birds decreases by 10% every year.
This means the population at the end of a year will be 90% or 0·9 of what it was at the start of the year.
If the population in 1994 is 1000 calculate the decline in the number of birds over the next 10 years.

You calculate the values of the decay in the same way that you calculated growth.

Year	1994	1995	1996	1997	1998	1999	2000	2001	2002	2003	2004
Birds	1000	900	810	729	656	590	531	478	430	387	349

The graph of this data looks like this.

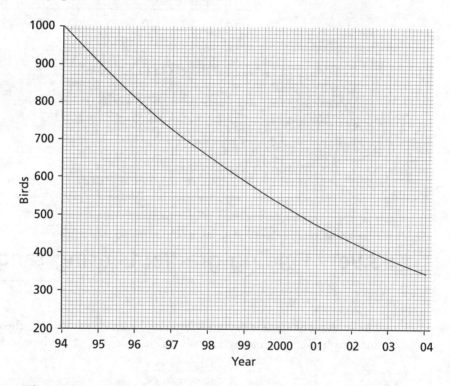

Note: The curve gets progressively less steep.

3 One litre of a salt solution contains 25 grams of salt. 30% of the solution is tipped away and replaced with water. This process is repeated several times.
   (a) Draw a table to show the amount of salt (to 2 d.p.) left in the solution as the process is repeated 10 times.
   (b) Draw a graph of your results.

4 The following results show how a radioactive element decays over a number of seconds.

Time (seconds)	0	40	80	120	160	200	240	280
Radioactivity (counts in seconds)	660	437	300	195	130	87	58	40

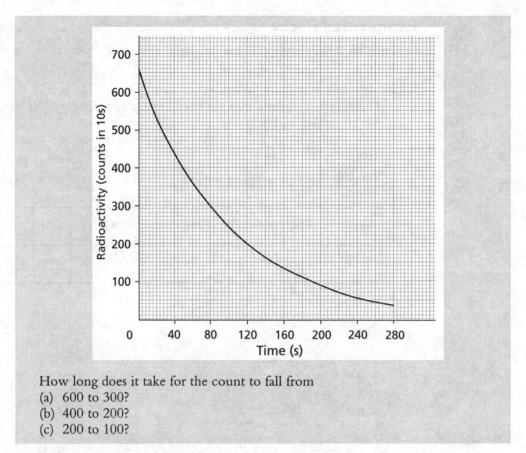

How long does it take for the count to fall from
(a) 600 to 300?
(b) 400 to 200?
(c) 200 to 100?

Remember: Exponential growth or decay occurs when the original value is repeatedly multiplied by the same number. Growth occurs when this multiplier is greater than 1. A multiplier less than 1 gives decay.

3.9e   Finding gradients using tangents

The gradient of a line is the same for every point on the line. So the gradient of a straight line-graph can be found by choosing a suitable part of the line and calculating

$$\frac{\text{increase in } y}{\text{increase in } x}.$$

The gradient of a curve varies from point to point along the curve so you can only find the gradient at a point.

An approximate value for the gradient of a curve at a particular point is given by the gradient of the **tangent** to the curve at that point.

A **tangent** to a curve at a particular point is a straight line through the point following the direction of the curve at that point.

So to find the gradient of this curve at point P you construct a tangent at P and then find the gradient of the tangent AB by drawing in the horizontal line AC and the vertical line BC and calculating $\frac{\text{BC}}{\text{AC}}$.

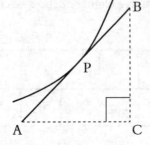

It is important to remember that this method only gives you an approximation of the gradient of the curve at the point P. To make your answer as accurate as possible draw a long tangent and use large values of AC and BC.

?

1 Copy and complete the following table of values and use it to draw a graph of $y = x^2$ with as large a scale as possible.

x	0	0.4	0.5	0.7	0.9	1	1.1	1.5	2
y	0								

By drawing tangents to your graph find the gradients when x has the following values:

(a) $x = 0.5$ (b) $x = 1$

E.g. This graph shows the speed of a car accelerating over a period of 10 seconds. Use the graph to find the acceleration of the car after 5 seconds.

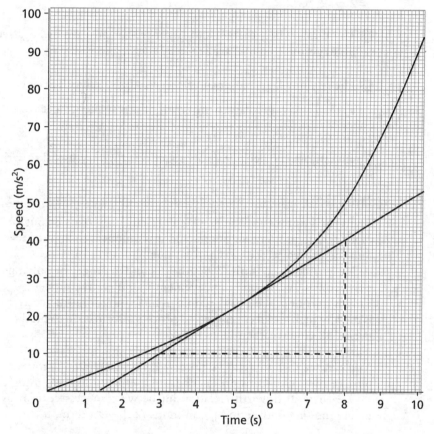

Acceleration is rate of change of speed so the acceleration is given by the tangent of the curve at 5 seconds.

$$\text{Gradient} = \frac{\text{rise}}{\text{tread}}$$
$$= \frac{40 - 10}{8 - 3}$$
$$= 6$$

The units of the gradient are given by $\frac{\text{units on the vertical axis}}{\text{units on the horizontal axis}}$.

The units are $\frac{\text{m/s}}{\text{s}} = \text{m/s}^2$

So the acceleration after 5 seconds is 6 m/s² (to 2 d.p.).

?

2 Use the graph to calculate the acceleration of the car after the following times:
(a) 3 seconds
(b) 7 seconds
(c) 9 seconds

Remember: Make your tangents as long as possible.

3.10a Convergence and divergence

An infinite sequence of numbers (a sequence which goes on forever) will do one of the following things:

❶ The terms will have no pattern e.g. the digits of π written as a decimal: 3, 1, 4, 1, 5, 9, 2, 7, ...

❷ The terms will form a regular pattern e.g. the sequence $u_n = \sin n$, which repeats every 360 terms.

❸ The terms will oscillate (go back and forth) between two values e.g. the sequence 5, 2, 5, 2, 5, ...

❹ The terms will get larger and larger (either positive or negative). This is called **divergence**. E.g. the sequence $u_n = n^2$.

❺ The terms will get closer and closer to a fixed value. This is called **convergence**. E.g. $u_n = \dfrac{1}{n^2}$. As n gets larger the terms of this sequence get closer and closer to 0.

To investigate the behaviour of sequences it is very useful to write them iteratively.

Iteration

An **iterative** process is one in which a calculation is carried out on input data to produce an output and this output is then put back into the process as the next input value.

For example, in **unit 3.6c** the second method of solving polynomials by trial and improvement is an iterative process.

This type of process has become of increasing importance as it is used by high speed computers to process information to predict events like the weather.

You can see that an iterative process always generates a sequence of numbers and each term in the sequence is produced from the previous term using the same process.

We can write down this relationship between successive terms as an **iterative formula** giving the $(n + 1)$th term, u_{n+1} in terms of the nth term, u_n.

E.g. You have already met this way of expressing a sequence using rules such as "you add on 3 every time". This sequence has the iterative formula
$$u_{n+1} = u_n + 3$$

For a sequence to be defined by iteration you also need to know the first term, u_1. Then the iterative formula can be used to generate all the other terms of the sequence.

1 The iterative formula of a sequence is $u_{n+1} = 2 \cdot 5 u_n$.
   If $u_1 = 10$ write down the values of u_2, u_3, u_4, u_5.

2 Write down the first five terms of the sequences generated by the following iterative formulae:

   (a) $u_{n+1} = 3(u_n + 1)$ $u_1 = 5$

   (b) $u_{n+1} = \dfrac{u_n}{5} + 4$ $u_1 = 10$

Investigating convergence

If a sequence converges then the terms of the sequence get closer and closer to a fixed value so the gaps between successive terms must get smaller and smaller.

The easiest way to see whether a sequence converges or not is to calculate the first few terms using a calculator or computer.

To make your investigation as accurate and efficient as possible, do not re-key in values but use the brackets facility or the reciprocal key on your calculator, as necessary.

E.g. (a) Investigate the sequence generated by $u_{n+1} = \dfrac{12}{u_n + 1}$, $u_1 = 2$.

The answers have been written down here rounded to 3 d.p. but the full limit of the calculator's accuracy has been used to calculate each successive term.

Each difference is less than the last. Therefore the sequence converges.

$$\begin{array}{ccccc} u_1 & u_2 & u_3 & u_4 & u_5 \\ 2 & 4 & 2{\cdot}4 & 3{\cdot}5294 & 2{\cdot}6494 \end{array}$$

Difference 2 1·6 1·1294 0·88

Note: If the gaps don't get smaller after a couple of substitutions you can stop.

(b) Investigate the sequence generated by $u_{n+1} = \dfrac{u_n^2 - 5}{2}$, $u_1 = 2$.

This sequence is not converging after five terms. Therefore it is fairly safe to assume it will not converge.

$$\begin{array}{ccccc} u_1 & u_2 & u_3 & u_4 & u_5 \\ 2 & {}^{-}0{\cdot}5 & {}^{-}2{\cdot}375 & 0{\cdot}3203 & {}^{-}2{\cdot}4487 \end{array}$$

Difference 2·5 1·875 2·6953 2·769

Fixed points

The sequence in question 2(b) converges to 5. This value is called the **limit** of the sequence.

If a sequence converges to a limit then that point is fixed for the iteration. That means that if that value is put into the formula the same number will come out.

To find the fixed point put $u_{n+1} = u_n = x$ into the formula.

E.g. The iterative formula $u_{n+1} = \dfrac{u_n}{5} + 4$

becomes $x = \dfrac{x}{5} + 4$

$$5x = x + 20$$
$$4x = 20$$
$$x = 5$$

?

3   Find the fixed points of the following iterations:

(a) $u_{n+1} = 3u_n - 5$ (b) $u_{n+1} = \dfrac{15}{u_n + 2}$

Some iterative formulae converge so strongly that you can start with a value of u_1 which is a very long way from the fixed point and still get a converging sequence.

However, there are some sequences whose iterative formulae have fixed points but which do not converge at all.

> **4**   Investigate whether the following sequences based on the iterative formulae in question 3 converge or diverge:
>
> (a) $u_{n+1} = 3u_n - 5$, $u_1 = 2 \cdot 49$ (b) $u_{n+1} = \dfrac{15}{u_n + 2}$, $u_1 = 100$

Remember: Finding a fixed point is not enough to show convergence.

3.10b   Quadratic equations

You have already seen how to solve quadratic equations by drawing graphs and finding points of intersection. This unit covers various algebraic methods for solving quadratic equations.

Factorisation

You already know how to factorise quadratic expressions into two brackets of the form $(ax + b)(cx + d)$.

So given a quadratic equation you can write it in the form
$$(ax + b)(cx + d) = 0$$
When two numbers multiply together to give zero then at least one of the numbers must itself equal zero.

Therefore $(ax + b) = 0$ or $(cx + d) = 0$ or both.

If $(ax + b) = 0$ then $x = -\dfrac{b}{a}$ and if $(cx + d) = 0$ then $x = -\dfrac{d}{c}$

so the solutions (roots) of the quadratic equation are $x = -\dfrac{b}{a}$ and $x = -\dfrac{d}{c}$.

E.g.   Solve the equation $6x^2 + 5x - 6 = 0$ by factorising.

First factorise $6x^2 + 5x - 6$.
You need to find two factors of 6 which combine with another two factors of 6 to give 5. Because the number term is negative you are looking for the **difference** to equal 5.

Hint: Start by trying the factors which are closest together.

The closest factors of 6 are 2 and 3. Try the factor pairs (2, 3) and (2, 3).
$3 \times 3 - 2 \times 2 = 5$ which gives the result you want.

One factor pair gives the coefficients of x so start with
      $(2x \quad)(3x \quad)$
The other factor pair goes at the ends of the brackets. To get 5 you need to multiply the 3's together and the 2's together so this tells you which bracket to put each number in.
      $(2x \quad 3)(3x \quad 2)$
Because the number term in the original expression is negative the signs in the brackets will be different. To get 5 you subtracted the 2×2 so the $-$ goes in front of the 2.
      $(2x + 3)(3x - 2)$

Check: $(2x + 3)(3x - 2) = 6x^2 - 4x + 9x - 6 = 6x^2 + 5x - 6$

So $6x^2 + 5x - 6 = (2x + 3)(3x - 2)$
Putting $(2x + 3)(3x - 2) = 0$
gives $(2x + 3) = 0$ or $(3x - 2) = 0$
So the solutions are $x = -\frac{3}{2}$ and $x = \frac{2}{3}$.

Remember: Always check your answer by multiplying the brackets.

?

1   Solve the following quadratics by factorising:
(a) $8x^2 + 16x + 6 = 0$ (b) $9x^2 + 27x + 20 = 0$ (c) $6x^2 - 40x - 14 = 0$

Not all quadratics can be factorised into brackets with integer (whole number) coefficients (e.g. $x^2 - 7$) so we need an alternative method.

Hint: If a question asks you to solve a quadratic to a given number of decimal places then you can't do it by factorising!

Completing the square

One method which works for all quadratic equations (unless they don't have any solutions – see below) is completing the square. This is a way of getting x to appear only once in the equation so that you can then simply rearrange it to find the values of x.

E.g. (a) Solve the quadratic $x^2 - 7x - 12 = 0$ to 2 decimal places.

First get the terms involving x on one side and the number on the other.

$$x^2 - 7x = 12$$

Then write the expression on the left hand side (LHS) in the form of a square. To do this you divide the coefficient of x (the number in front of x) by 2.

$$(x - \tfrac{7}{2})^2$$

Expanding this bracket gives $x^2 - 7x + \frac{49}{4}$ or $x^2 - 7x + 12 \cdot 25$

So by adding $12 \cdot 25$ to the LHS you can complete the square. To preseve the equation you must also add $12 \cdot 25$ to the RHS.

$$x^2 - 7x = 12$$
$$x^2 - 7x + 12 \cdot 25 = 12 + 12 \cdot 25$$
$$(x - 3 \cdot 5)^2 = 24 \cdot 25$$

Taking square roots,

$$x - 3 \cdot 5 = \pm\sqrt{24 \cdot 25}$$
$$x = 3 \cdot 5 \pm \sqrt{24 \cdot 25}$$

To 2 decimal places the solutions are $x = 8 \cdot 42$ and $x = {}^-1 \cdot 42$.

(b) Solve the quadratic $3x^2 + 2x - 4 = 0$ to 2 decimal places.

First get all the terms involving x on the left hand side (LHS).

$$3x^2 + 2x = 4$$

Then divide through by the coefficient of x^2.

$$x^2 + \tfrac{2}{3}x = \tfrac{4}{3}$$

Divide the coefficient of x by 2 then square it and add to both sides.

$$x^2 + \tfrac{2}{3}x + \tfrac{1}{9} = \tfrac{4}{3} + \tfrac{1}{9}$$

This can now be factorised.

$$\left(x + \tfrac{1}{3}\right)^2 = \tfrac{13}{9}$$

Taking the square root of both sides

$$x + \tfrac{1}{3} = \sqrt[\pm]{\tfrac{13}{9}}$$

To 2 decimal places the solutions are $x = 0 \cdot 87$ and $x = {}^-1 \cdot 54$.

2 Solve the following equations to 2 decimal places by completing the square:

(a) $x^2 + 3x - 5 = 0$ (b) $x^2 - 2x - 34 = 0$

The formula

You can apply the same process of completing the square to the equation $ax^2 + bx + c = 0$. (Try doing this yourself.)

This gives the following formula for the solutions of a quadratic equation:

$$x = \frac{-b \pm \sqrt{b^2 - 4ac}}{2a}$$

E.g. Solve the quadratic $3x^2 + 2x - 4 = 0$ to 2 decimal places.

Comparing with $ax^2 + bx + c = 0$ you have $a = 3$, $b = 2$ and $c = {}^-4$. Substituting into the formula

$$x = \frac{{}^-2 \pm \sqrt{2^2 - 4 \times 3 \times {}^-4}}{2 \times 3}$$

$$= \frac{{}^-2 \pm \sqrt{4 + 48}}{6}$$

$$= \frac{{}^-2 \pm \sqrt{52}}{6}$$

To 2 decimal places the roots are $x = 0 \cdot 87$ and $x = {}^-1 \cdot 54$.

3 Solve the following quadratics to 2 decimal places using the formula:
(a) $2x^2 - 3x - 7 = 0$ (b) $3x^2 - 5x - 1 = 0$

Note: You will usually be given the formula in an exam.

Iteration

You have seen how a sequence can be defined iteratively by writing u_{n+1} in terms of u_n. By rearranging a quadratic equation in the form

      $x =$ an expression involving x

you can use iteration to generate a sequence of values for x.

If this sequence converges to a fixed point then this fixed point is a solution of the quadratic.

E.g. Rearrange the equation $x^2 + 3x - 5 = 0$ to give an iterative formula.

Note: There are a number of different ways to do this.

(i)   Start by getting $3x$ by itself $3x = 5 - x^2$

      Divide both sides by 3 $x = \dfrac{5 - x^2}{3}$

      This gives the iterative formula $u_{n+1} = \dfrac{5 - u_n^2}{3}$

(ii) Get the number by itself $x^2 + 3x = 5$

      Factorise $x(x + 3) = 5$

      Divide both sides by $(x + 3)$ $x = \dfrac{5}{x + 3}$

      This gives the iterative formula $u_{n+1} = \dfrac{5}{u_n + 3}$

This example illustrates one of the problems with using iteration to solve equations: there are different ways to rewrite an equation.

Often it is necessary to use a different iterative formula to find each solution. It helps if you estimate the solutions (one way to do this is by sketching the graph) and then use your estimates as a value for u_1. By calculating a few more terms in the sequence you should be able to see whether it converges or not.

Remember: Not all iterative formulae produce converging sequences.

If your sequence begins to diverge then stop and try a different iterative formula.

E.g. Solve the equation $x^2 + x - 5 = 0$ to 2 decimal places using iteration.

There are several different ways to rearrange the equation. You could write $x = x^2 - 5$ but it is usually more helpful to have a formula with x on the bottom.

$$\text{Add 5 to both sides} \qquad x^2 + x = 5$$
$$\text{Factorise} \qquad x(x + 1) = 5$$

You can now produce two different iterative formulae by dividing by x or $(x + 1)$.

$$u_{n+1} = \frac{5}{u_n + 1} \qquad \text{or} \qquad u_{n+1} = \frac{5}{u_n} - 1$$

By sketching the graph of $y = x^2 + x - 5$ you can see that the equation $x^2 + x - 5 = 0$ has one solution near $1\cdot8$ and another near $^-2\cdot8$.

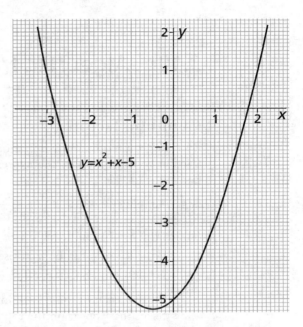

$y = x^2 + x - 5$

Try substituting $1\cdot8$ into each of the iteration formulae. (You can use the reciprocal key on your calculator to help you calculate successive terms without having to re-key in numbers.)

The answers have been written down here rounded to 3 d.p. but the full limit of the calculator's accuracy has been used to calculate each successive term.

You can see from the table that the sequence given by the first iteration formula is tending towards a solution.

	u_1	u_2	u_3	u_4	u_5	u_6
$u_{n+1} = \dfrac{5}{u_n + 1}$	$1\cdot8$	$1\cdot786$	$1\cdot795$	$1\cdot789$	$1\cdot793$	$1\cdot790$
$u_{n+1} = \dfrac{5}{u_n} - 1$	$1\cdot8$	$1\cdot778$	$1\cdot813$	$1\cdot759$	$1\cdot843$	$1\cdot713$

To 2 decimal places the solution is $x = 1\cdot79$.

The second formula does not seem to be converging.

4 Substitute ⁻2·8 into each of the iteration formulae above to find the other solution to 2 decimal places.

5 (a) By sketching the graph of the equation $x^2 + 2x - 5 = 0$ find its approximate solutions.

   (b) Use iteration formulae to solve the equation to 2 decimal places.

Quadratics with no real solutions

You have already seen that if the graph of a quadratic equation does not cross the x-axis then the equation has no real solutions. (If you go on to do Maths at a higher level you will find that 'imaginary' solutions exist.)

By looking at the formula you can see that there will be no real solutions of the equation $ax^2 + bx + c = 0$ if

$$b^2 - 4ac < 0$$

Note: If you are asked to solve a quadratic it will have a solution.

3.10c Algebraic fractions

Common factors

By taking out common factors from the numerator and denominator of an algebraic fraction you can simplify the expression in the same way you would with an ordinary fraction.

E.g. Simplify $\dfrac{(x^2 - x - 6)(x^2 + 4x + 3)}{(x^2 - 9)(x + 1)}$

$(x^2 - x - 6)$ can be factorised to give $(x - 3)(x + 2)$

$(x^2 + 4x + 3)$ can be factorised to give $(x + 3)(x + 1)$

$(x^2 - 9)$ can be factorised to give $(x + 3)(x - 3)$

Putting each of these back into the original expression you can then cancel like terms that appear on the top and bottom.

$$\frac{\cancel{(x-3)}(x+2)\cancel{(x+3)}\cancel{(x+1)}}{\cancel{(x-3)}\cancel{(x+3)}\cancel{(x+1)}} = (x+2)$$

1 Simplify $\dfrac{(x^2 - 2x - 8)(x^2 + 5x + 4)}{(x^2 - 16)(x + 2)}$

Adding and subtracting

To add or subtract any fractions you first have to find a common denominator.
With algebraic fractions the common denominator is usually found by multiplying the denominators together.

E.g. Simplify $\dfrac{1}{x} - \dfrac{2}{x + 2}$

$\dfrac{1}{x} - \dfrac{2}{x+2}$ becomes $\dfrac{(x+2)}{x(x+2)} - \dfrac{2x}{x(x+2)}$

$\dfrac{x+2-2x}{x(x+2)} = \dfrac{2-x}{x^2 + 2x}$

?

2   Simplify the following:

(a) $\dfrac{1}{x+1} - \dfrac{1}{x-1}$ (b) $\dfrac{3}{3x} - \dfrac{2}{3x}$ (c) $\dfrac{3}{x^2-x} - \dfrac{5}{x^2-1}$

Equations

E.g.   Solve the equation $\dfrac{2x+1}{x-1} = \dfrac{6x+1}{3x-2}$

The first step is to multiply both sides of the equation by both denominators.

$$\frac{(3x-2)(x-1)(2x+1)}{(x-1)} = \frac{(6x+1)(3x-2)(x-1)}{(3x-2)}$$

Cancelling gives $(3x-2)(2x+1) = (6x+1)(x-1)$

$$6x^2 - 4x + 3x - 2 = 6x^2 + x - 6x - 1$$

$$^{-}x - 2 = {}^{-}5x - 1$$

Hence $4x = 1$
giving $x = \tfrac{1}{4}$

Remember: Always substitute this value back into the equation to check it works.

?

3   Solve the following equations:

(a) $\dfrac{2}{x} = \dfrac{3}{x+1}$ (b) $\dfrac{x}{3} - \dfrac{x}{4} = 1$ (c) $\dfrac{1}{x-1} + \dfrac{2}{x+1} = \dfrac{3}{x}$

3.10d Finding the area under a curve

There are various methods that can be used to calculate the approximate area under a curve. One way is by approximating the area to a series of rectangles.

E.g.   To calculate its insurance premiums a firm needs to calculate the volume of a warehouse with a curved roof. To calculate the volume they first need to find the area of the end wall.

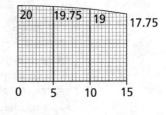

The end wall is 15 m wide and the curve of the roof is given by the equation $y = 20 - 0{\cdot}01x^2$.

First divide the area of the wall into vertical strips of equal width.
Use the equation $y = 20 - 0{\cdot}01x^2$ to calculate the height of the roof at the edge of each strip.

You can now approximate each strip to a rectangle.

x	0	5	10	15
y	20	19·75	19	17·75

Method 1 Using the longer edge for each strip, draw a step-graph above the curve. You can work out the area under the step-graph since you know the height and width of each column.

The area under the step-graph is given by:
(5 × 20) + (5 × 19·75) + (5 × 19)

$$= 5 \times 58 \cdot 75$$
$$= 293 \cdot 75 \ m^2$$

Since the step-graph is always above the curve this gives an **upper bound** for the area under the curve.

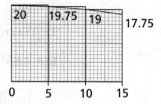

Area of the wall ≤ 293·75 m²

So 293·75 m² is an approximate value for the area but you know it's too big.

Method 2 Using the shorter edge of each strip, draw a step-graph under the curve.
The area of this step-graph is given by:

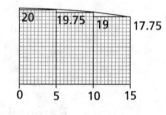

$$(5 \times 19 \cdot 75) + (5 \times 19) + (5 \times 17 \cdot 75)$$
$$= 5 \times 56 \cdot 5$$
$$= 282 \cdot 5 \ m^2$$

This gives a **lower bound** for the area under the curve.

So the area of the warehouse wall is between 282·5 m² and 293·75 m².

Since the roof curves outwards, the area under the curve will be closer to the upper bound than to the lower bound, so a first approximation to the area is 293·75 m².

To get a more accurate approximation for the area under a curve you can take the average of the upper and lower bounds.

$$\frac{293 \cdot 75 + 282 \cdot 5}{2} = 288 \cdot 125$$

So the area of the wall is approximately 288 m².

?

1 (a) Calculate the upper and lower bounds for the area under this curve.
   (b) Which value is a better approximation?
   (c) Calculate the average of the upper and lower bounds.

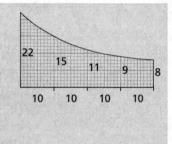

2 Calculate the approximate area under the graph of $y = x^2(4 - x)$ between $x = 0$ and $x = 4$ by drawing a step-graph above the curve with steps of 0·5.

This method of approximating using rectangles becomes more accurate if the width of the strips is reduced. The disadvantage is that when you have a large number of strips to calculate it becomes very long-winded. However, a computer can make an approximation very quickly.

E.g. Calculate the approximate area under the curve $y = 3 + 0 \cdot 1 \ x^2$ between $x = 0$ and $x = 2$.

This simple program in BASIC can be used to calculate the lower bound. The width of each strip in this case is 0·05.

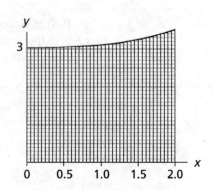

```
10 Let W = 0·05
20 For X = 0 to 2 − W step W
30 Let Y = 3 + 0·1 * X * X
40 Let A = W * Y
50 Let S = S + A
60 Next X
70 Print S
```

For the upper bound replace line 20 with
20 For X = W to 2 step W

Finding the upper and lower bounds and then taking the average means doing two calculations. By approximating each strip to a trapezium you can average out the upper and lower bounds in one single calculation.

The trapezium rule

Divide the area under the curve into strips in the same way but this time join up the points where the edges of the strips meet the curve. Now each strip is a trapezium (or a triangle if the value at one end is 0).

The area of each strip is $\frac{1}{2}h(a + b)$, where a and b are the heights at the edge of the strip and h is the width.

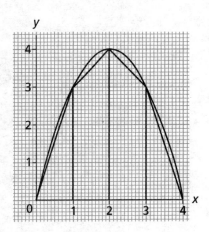

If you divide the area under a curve into n strips of width h and the values of y at the edges of the strips are y_0, y_1, y_2, ..., y_n then

Area of $T_1 = \frac{1}{2}h(y_0 + y_1)$

Area of $T_2 = \frac{1}{2}h(y_1 + y_2)$

Area of $T_3 = \frac{1}{2}h(y_2 + y_3)$

   .
   .
   .

Area of $T_{n-1} = \frac{1}{2}h(y_{n-2} + y_{n-1})$

Area of $T_n = \frac{1}{2}h(y_{n-1} + y_n)$

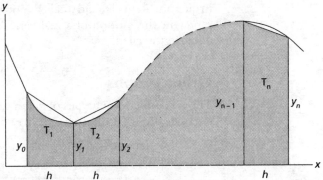

Adding the areas together gives
$\frac{1}{2}h(y_0 + 2y_1 + 2y_2 + ... + 2y_{n-1} + y_n)$

Note: Each height is added in twice apart from those at the ends.

So the trapezium rule says that the approximate area under the curve is

$\frac{1}{2}h[y_0 + y_n + 2(y_1 + y_2 + ... + y_{n-1})]$ or $h[\frac{1}{2}(y_0 + y_n) + y_1 + y_2 + ... + y_{n-1}]$

> **3** Use the trapezium rule to approximate the area under the curve with equation $y = 10 - x^2$ between $x = ^-3$ and $x = 3$ using strips of width 1.

Area under a speed/time graph

If you draw a graph of speed against time then the area under the graph gives the distance travelled.
This is easiest to see when the speed is constant.

E.g. This graph shows a car travelling at a constant speed of 5 m/s for 6 seconds.

Distance travelled
    = average speed × time taken
    = 5 × 6
    = 30 m

Area under the graph
    = 5 × 6
    = 30

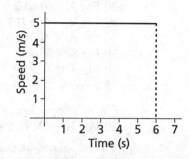

?

4 The graph below shows an imaginary car travelling at 1 m/s for 1 second then 1·5 m/s for the next second, 2 m/s in the third second ... up to 6 seconds. Calculate the distance travelled by the car.

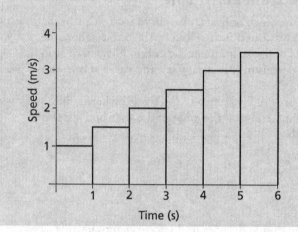

To see what would happen for a curved graph, imagine making the widths of the steps in question 4 smaller and smaller. You would eventually get a smooth curve, which would represent the motion of a real car. The area under the curve would still give you the distance travelled.

Other graphs

The area under other types of graph can also represent a particular quantity. Multiplying together the units on each axis may help you to decide what that quantity is.

E.g. The rate of water flowing through a hosepipe over a 20 second period is shown below.

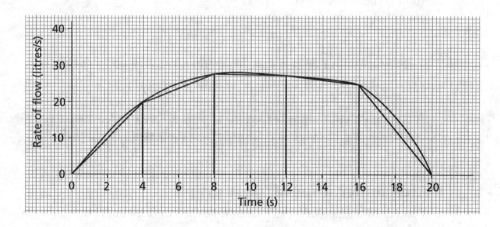

The area under the curve represents the volume of water which flowed through the pipe.

Check: Multiplying units gives litres/seconds × seconds = litres

Use the trapezium method with strips of width 4 seconds to calculate the total volume of water which flowed through the hosepipe.

Area under curve $\approx 4\left(\frac{1}{2}(0 + 0) + 20 + 28 + 27 + 25\right)$
$\qquad\qquad\qquad \approx 4 \times 100$
$\qquad\qquad\qquad \approx 400$

So the volume of water which flowed through the hosepipe in 20 seconds was approximately 400 litres.

5 A lorry is travelling at 25 m/s when the driver applies the brakes. t seconds after applying the brakes the lorry's speed is given by the equation $25 - 0.25\,t^2$. The speed/time graph looks like this.

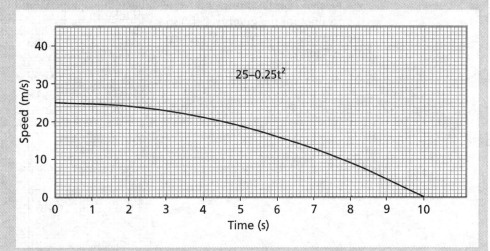

Calculate the speed at 2 second intervals and use the trapezium rule to calculate the distance travelled by the lorry before it stops.

3.10e Sketching the graphs of functions derived from other functions

You are already familiar with the graphs of common functions. Looking at the function $f(x) = x - x^2$ you can say that the shape will be a parabola because the function is a quadratic, and that the parabola will be upside down because the coefficient of x^2 is negative.

This is the graph of the function $f(x) = x - x^2$.

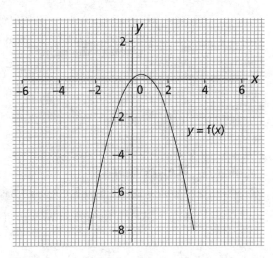

155

It is very useful to be able to sketch the graph of a function by relating it to a function whose graph you already know.

To do this you need to understand what effect changes to a function will have on the shape of the graph.

Translations in the *y*-direction

Adding a number to or subtracting a number from a function has the effect of moving the curve up or down the *y*-axis.

E.g. Sketch the graph of $y = f(x) - 8$, where $f(x) = x - x^2$.

We can call this new function $f'(x) = f(x) - 8$.

To calculate values of y for the graph $y = f'(x)$ you simply subtract 8 from the y values for the graph $y = f(x)$ so the curve moves down the Cartesian plane 8 places.

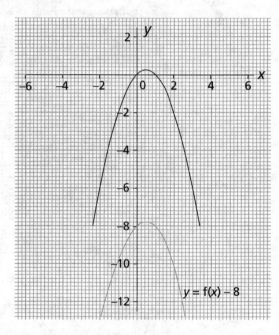

Translations in the *x*-direction

Adding a number to or subtracting a number from x before you substitute it into the function has the effect of moving the curve to the left or right.

E.g. Sketch the graph of $y = f(x - 3)$, where $f(x) = x - x^2$.

Call the new function $f'(x) = f(x - 3)$.

You have to look 3 places to the left on the curve $y = f(x)$ to find the value of $f'(x)$.

$f'(0) = f(-3)$ etc.

Therefore plotting $y = f'(x)$ has the effect of moving the graph 3 places to the right.

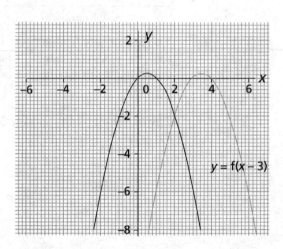

Reflections

Making the function negative has the effect of reflecting the graph in the *x*-axis.

E.g. Sketch the graph of $y = -f(x)$, where $f(x) = x - x^2$.

x	-2	-1	0	1	2
$f(x)$	-6	-2	0	0	-2
$^-f(x)$	6	2	0	0	2

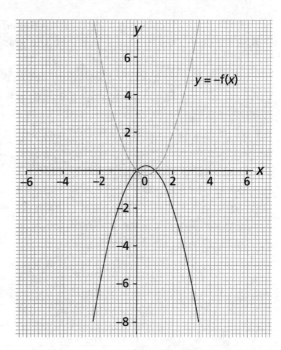

Replacing x with ^-x has the effect of reflecting the graph in the y-axis.

E.g. Sketch the graph of $y = f(^-x)$, where $f(x) = x - x^2$.

x	$^-2$	$^-1$	0	1	2
$f(x)$	$^-6$	$^-2$	0	0	$^-2$
$f(^-x)$	$^-2$	0	0	$^-2$	$^-6$

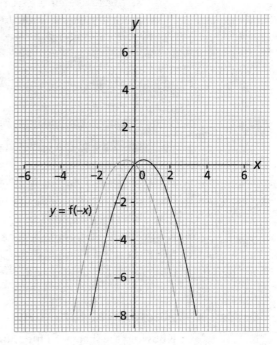

Stretches

Multiplying a function by a constant has the effect of stretching the graph parallel to the y-axis.

E.g. Sketch the graph of $y = 4f(x)$, where $f(x) = x - x^2$.

Every y value is multiplied by 4 so this has the effect of stretching the graph parallel to the y-axis by a factor of 4.

Note: Points on the x-axis are fixed.

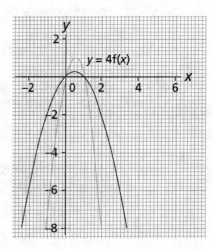

Replacing x with kx has the effect of a stretch parallel to the x-axis but the stretch factor is $1/k$ so if $k > 1$ then the graph gets thinner.

You could describe this is as telescoping $f(x)$ by a factor of k in the x-direction.

E.g. Sketch the graph of $y = f(4x)$, where $f(x) = x - x^2$.

$f(x)$ has roots 0 and 1.

$f(4x) = 4x(1 - 4x)$ has roots 0 and ¼.

The graph of $f(4x)$ is $\frac{1}{4}$ of the width of $f(x)$.

Note: Points on the y-axis are fixed.

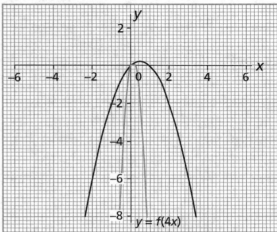

1 Draw the graph of the function $f(x) = x^2 - x - 2$ for $^-3 \le x \le 3$.

Use this to sketch the graphs of the following, and describe how the graph has been transformed in each case.

2 (a) $y = f(x) + 3$ 3 (a) $y = f(x + 3)$
   (b) $y = x^2 - x - 3$ (b) $y = (x - 2)^2 - (x - 2) - 2$

4 (a) $y = f(^-x)$ 5 (a) $y = 2f(x)$
   (b) $y = ^-f(x)$ (b) $y = 4x^2 - 2x - 2$

You can use a combination of these ideas to sketch the graphs of different functions.

6 Sketch the graph of $y = f(x + 1) + 2$.

Remember: $f(x) + a$ moves the graph a places up (down if a is negative).
$f(x + a)$ moves the graph a places to the left (right if a is negative).
$^-f(x)$ reflects the graph in the x-axis.
$f(^-x)$ reflects the graph in the y-axis.
$kf(x)$ stretches the graph by a factor of k parallel to the y-axis.
$f(kx)$ telescopes the graph by a factor of k parallel to the x-axis.

Reciprocal functions

Knowing the shape of a function $f(x)$ does not tell you the exact shape of the graph of the reciprocal function $\frac{1}{f(x)}$ but it does tell you certain characteristics of the graph of $\frac{1}{f(x)}$.

Where $f(x)$ is large $\frac{1}{f(x)}$ will be small and where $f(x)$ is small $\frac{1}{f(x)}$ will be large.

7 (a) Draw the graphs of $y = x$ and $y = \frac{1}{x}$ on the same pair of axes.

(b) Draw the graphs of $y = x^2$ and $y = \frac{1}{x^2}$ on the same pair of axes.

8 By investigating the graphs of various functions and their reciprocals, answer the following questions:

(a) What do you notice about the graph of $\frac{1}{x^a}$ when a is even and when a is odd?

(b) What happens to the graph of $\dfrac{1}{f(x)}$ at points where $f(x) = 1$?

(c) What happens to the graph of $\dfrac{1}{f(x)}$ at points where $f(x) = 0$?

3.10f Sketching graphs of quadratics

You know exactly what the graph of the function $f(x) = x^2$ looks like.

You can apply what you know from **unit 3.10e** to sketch the graph of any quadratic function, using $f(x) = x^2$ as a starting point.

Any quadratic equation can be written in the form $y = ax^2 + bx + c$.

Taking out the coefficient of x^2 gives $y = a(x^2 + \dfrac{b}{a}x) + c$

Completing the square gives $\quad y = a(x + \dfrac{b}{2a})^2 - \dfrac{b^2}{4a} + c$

$$y = af(x + \dfrac{b}{2a}) + c - \dfrac{b^2}{4a}$$

Relating this back to the work in **unit 3.10e** you can see that the graph of $ax^2 + bx + c$ can be obtained from the graph of x^2 by:

(i) stretching the graph by a factor of a in the y-direction.

(ii) translating the graph $\dfrac{b}{2a}$ places to the left. (Remember this means that it moves to the right if $\dfrac{b}{2a}$ is negative.)

(iii) translating the graph $c - \dfrac{b^2}{4a}$ places up (down if this value is negative) with c as the y-intercept.

So a gives you the stretch factor, a and b give the translation in the x-direction and c tells you where the graph crosses the y-axis.

E.g. Express $y = x^2 - 4x + 3$ in the form $y = k(x + p)^2 + q$ and hence sketch the graph of the equation.

$x^2 - 4x + 3 = (x - 2)^2 - 1$

$- 2$ has the effect of moving the graph to the right two places $\qquad (x–2)^2–1 \qquad$ $- 1$ moves the graph down 1 place

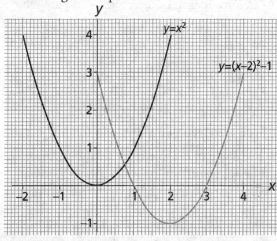

1 Rewrite the following in the completed square form and hence sketch the graphs of the equations. (a) $y = x^2 + 8x + 11$ (b) $y = x^2 - 6x + 13$

4.6a   2D representations of 3D objects

This is an **isometric** drawing of a solid object:

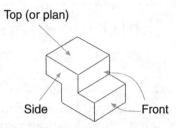

Solid objects can also be drawn using the three views given above: **plan**, **front** and **side** views. The technical name for this type of representation is orthographic projection. The technical name for a view is a **projection** or **elevation**. So the front view can be called the front projection. But the view from above is always called the plan. In this type of representation edges you can see are shown as solid lines and edges which are hidden are represented by dotted lines.

E.g.   This is an orthographic projection of the object shown above.

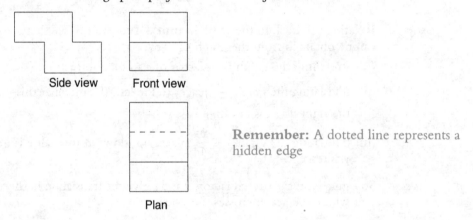

Remember: A dotted line represents a hidden edge

Note: Projections are drawn to scale which means that all the edges are in the same proportions as in the original solid. Each view is drawn to the same scale.

You should be able to recognise a simple object from different views of it.

?

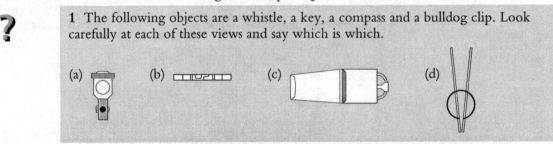

1 The following objects are a whistle, a key, a compass and a bulldog clip. Look carefully at each of these views and say which is which.

(a)   (b)   (c)   (d)

If you are given two views of a solid object then you can draw the third view.

?

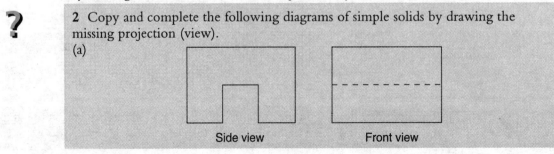

2 Copy and complete the following diagrams of simple solids by drawing the missing projection (view).

(a)

Side view   Front view

(b) Draw the view from the left hand side.

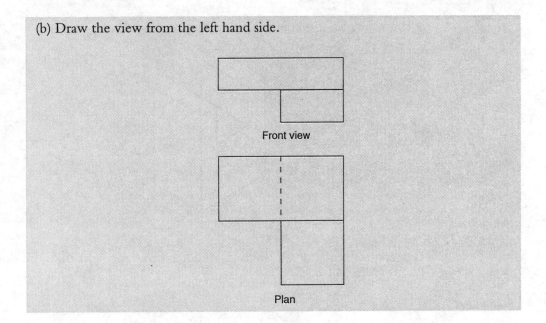

Front view

Plan

If you are given the plan, side and front views (elevations) of a solid shape then you can make an isometric drawing of it.

E.g.

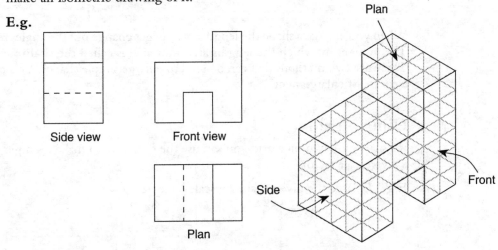

Side view

Front view

Plan

Plan

Side

Front

?

3 Make an isometric drawing of the solid illustrated below.

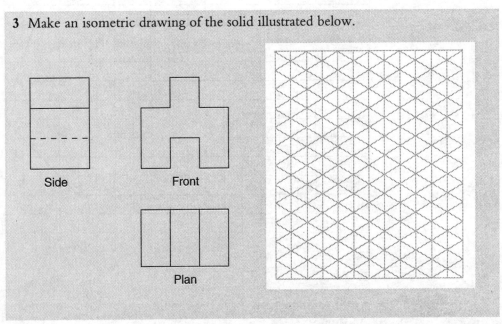

Side

Front

Plan

When you draw a projection of a solid you draw the side you are looking at. This is called first hand projection.

4 Draw the plan, front and side elevations of this solid.

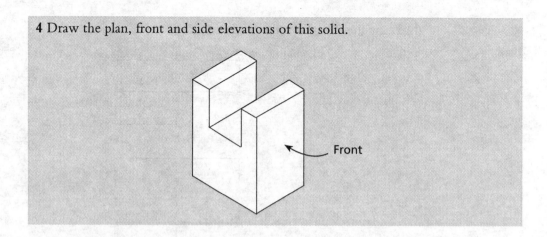

Front

Remember: Include all the hidden edges and represent them by dotted lines.

4.6b   Enlargement

When you enlarge a shape the lengths of its edges change but the angles remain the same.
The number by which the lengths are multiplied is called the **scale factor**.
There are two methods that can be used to enlarge simple shapes. You can use a grid or
a centre of enlargement.

Using a grid

If a shape is drawn on a grid you can use the grid lines to make a simple enlargement by
a given scale factor.

E.g.   Enlarge the given shape by scale factor 2.

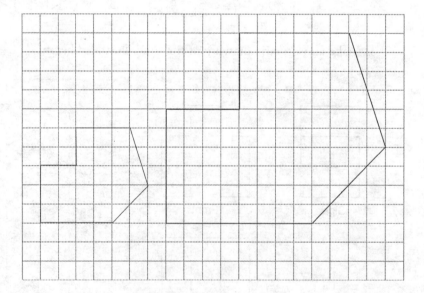

Note: All the lengths have been multiplied by 2 but the angles have remained
the same.

1 Make an enlargement of this figure by scale factor 2.

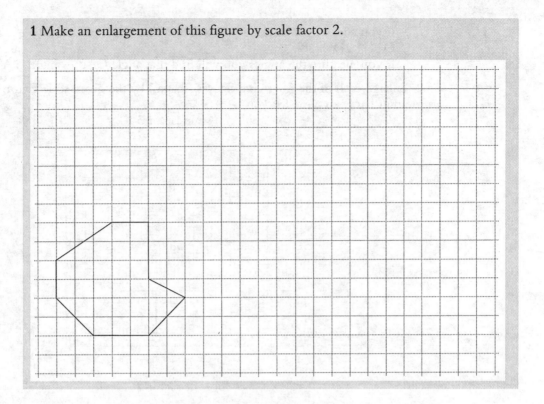

Using a centre of enlargement

To enlarge a shape using this method you draw lines from a point called the **centre of enlargement** through each significant point on the shape. You then measure the distance from the centre of enlargement to a point on your shape. You multiply this distance by the scale factor to get the distance to the corresponding point on the enlarged shape, which will be on the same line. The centre of enlargement is usually labelled O. The original shape is called the **object** and the enlarged shape is called the **image**.

E.g. Enlarge the figure ABC by a scale factor of 2.

Note: This means the distance OA′ (from O to A′) is 2 × the distance OA.

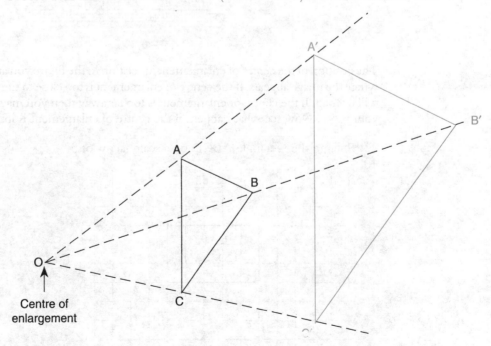

A, B and C represent the vertices (corners) of the object (original shape) and A′, B′ and C′ are the corresponding vertices of the image after enlarging the shape by scale factor 2.

If you check by measuring you will find that OA′ = 2OA, OB′ = 2OB and OC′ = 2OC.

If you measure the angles you will find that angle CAB = angle C′A′B′ etc.

2 Enlarge each of the following figures (shapes) by the given scale factor. The first point has been done for you.

(a) scale factor 3

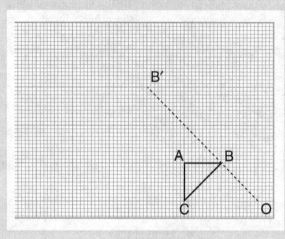

(b) scale factor 2

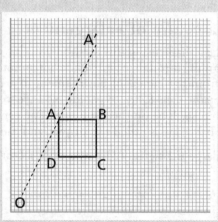

The position of the centre of enlargement in relation to the figure you are enlarging will affect where the image appears. If the centre of enlargement is too close to the object then the image will overlap. If the centre of enlargement is too far away then you may not get the image on your paper. Now see what happens if the centre of enlargement is inside the object.

3 Enlarge the rectangle ABCD by a scale factor of 3.

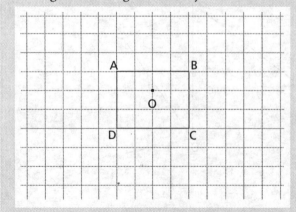

Remember: The position of the centre of enlargement is very important. Be careful if you have to choose your own centre of enlargement that it is in a reasonable position.

Enlargement by a negative scale factor

When you are using a negative scale factor you measure the distance to the point on the original shape in the same way but to find the image point you measure in the opposite direction. So the image will be on the other side of the centre of enlargement.

E.g. Enlarge the following figure by a scale factor of ⁻3.

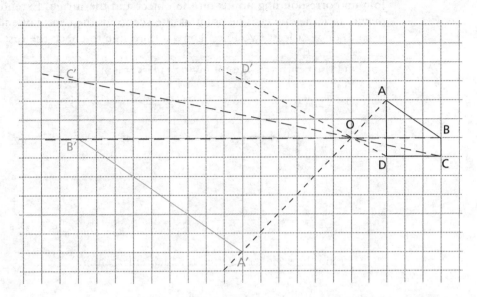

You should notice that the figure has been inverted. It is upside down and back to front. It looks like it has been rotated about the centre of enlargement.

?

4 Enlarge the triangle XYZ by a factor of ⁻2.

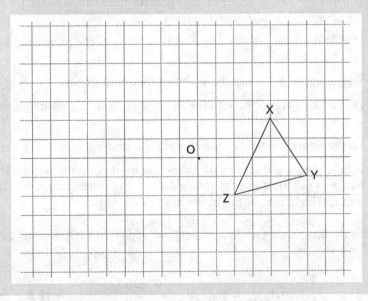

Finding a scale factor

If a shape has been enlarged you can find the scale factor by dividing a length on the image (enlarged shape) by the corresponding length on the object (original shape).

$$\text{Scale factor} = \frac{A'B'}{AB}$$

If a centre of enlargement has been used then the scale factor is also given by

$$\text{Scale factor} = \frac{OA'}{OA}$$

Remember: If the object and the image are on opposite sides of the centre of enlargement then the scale factor is negative.

Finding a centre of enlargement

Join up corresponding points on the object and the image. Extend the lines you have drawn until they meet. The point of intersection is the centre of enlargement. You will need to draw at least two lines. Draw a third line to check the first two are right.

?

5 Find the centres of the following enlargements:

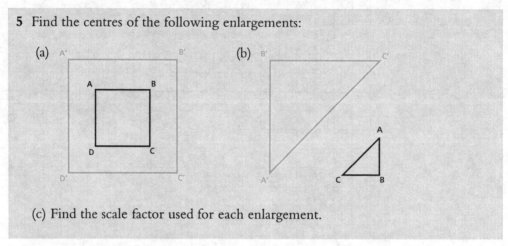

(a)   (b)

(c) Find the scale factor used for each enlargement.

You may be asked to enlarge a shape to fit into a given space.

E.g.   Julie wants to enlarge a photograph so that it will fit into a larger frame.
The photograph is 6 cm wide and 10 cm high.
The frame is 42 cm wide and 60 cm high.

What is the largest factor of enlargement Julie can use if she wants the shape of the photograph to remain the same?

Divide the width of the frame by the width of the photograph.
    42 ÷ 6 = 7

So the frame is 7 times the width of the photograph.

Divide the height of the frame by the height of the photograph.
    60 ÷ 10 = 6

So the frame is 6 times the height of the photograph.

If Julie used a scale factor of 7 then the photograph would be too tall for the frame so she must use the smaller of the two scale factors, 6. The photograph will fill the height of the frame but not its width.

?

6 Find the scale factor of enlargement needed to fit each of these photographs into their new frames.

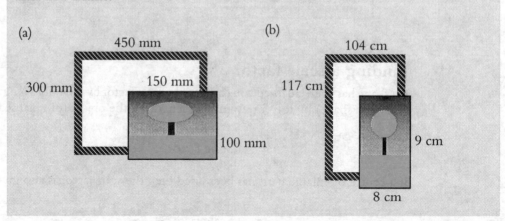

(a)   (b)

4.6c   Quadrilaterals

A quadrilateral is a plane shape with four sides and four angles which always add up to 360°.

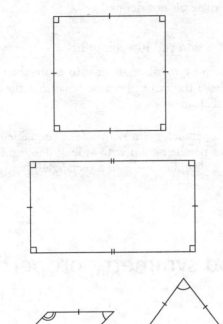

Square

4 equal sides
4 right angles (90°)
equal diagonals which bisect (cut in half) each other at 90°

Rectangle

opposite sides equal
4 right angles (90°)
equal diagonals which bisect each other

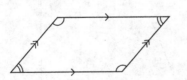

Rhombus

A rhombus is like a pushed over square.

4 equal sides
opposite angles equal
diagonals which bisect each other at 90°

Parallelogram

A parallelogram is like a pushed over rectangle.

opposite sides parallel and therefore equal
opposite angles equal
diagonals which bisect each other

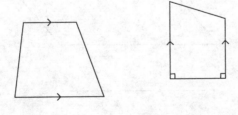

Trapezium

1 pair of parallel sides

Kite

2 pairs of equal sides
1 pair of opposite equal angles
diagonals are perpendicular to each other (at 90°)

1 On this pattern of nine dots it is possible to draw squares in six different positions by joining the dots.

(a) Draw the six squares.
(b) How many different rectangles can you draw?
(c) How many parallelograms can you draw?
(d) How many trapezia can you draw?
(e) How many kites can you draw?
(f) How many other quadrilaterals not defined above can you draw?

Hint: Use the ideas of reflection and rotation to help.

You may have realised that some quadrilaterals fit into more than one category. For example, a parallelogram is also a trapezium because it satisfies the requirements for a trapezium: it has a pair of parallel sides.

2 (a) Which quadrilateral is a parallelogram with sides of equal length?
(b) Which quadrilateral is a parallelogram with at least one right angle?
(c) Which quadrilateral is a rhombus and also a rectangle?

4.6d   Angle and symmetry properties

Quadrilaterals

You are already familiar with the two different types of symmetry: reflection and rotational symmetry.

1 Mark the lines of symmetry for each of the following quadrilaterals:

(a) kite

(b) trapezium

(c) parallelogram

(d) rectangle

(e) rhombus

(f) square

2 Write down the order of rotational symmetry for each of the quadrilaterals in question **1**.

Regular polygons

A regular polygon is a geometrical shape with all its sides and all its angles equal.
Here is a list of the first ten regular polygons. You should know the names of the ones which are most frequently used. These have been highlighted for you.

No. of sides Name

3   equilateral triangle
4   square
5   pentagon
6   hexagon
7   heptagon
8   octagon
9   nonagon
10   decagon
11   undecagon
12   dodecagon

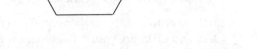

Hexagon

?

3 Mark the lines of symmetry for each of the following regular polygons

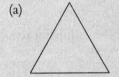

(a)

(b)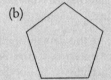

(c)

(d)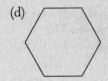

4 Write down the order of rotational symmetry for each of the polygons in question **3**.

Remember: A regular polygon with *n* sides has *n* lines of symmetry and rotational symmetry order *n*.

To draw a regular polygon the first thing you need to do is to work out the size of each angle at the centre of the polygon.

E.g. Draw a regular octagon (8 sides).
Divide 360° by the number of sides: 360° ÷ 8 = 45°
Mark off each 45° around the circle using a protractor or angle measurer. Join up the points you have marked.

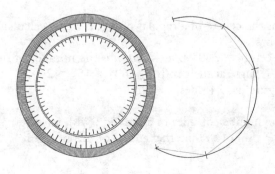

There are three types of angle in a regular polygon.

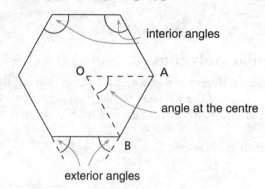

interior angles

angle at the centre

exterior angles

The **angle at the centre** is found by dividing 360° by the number of sides.
The **interior** or **internal angle** is 180° minus the angle at the centre.
The **exterior** or **external angle** is supplementary to the interior angle (they add to 180°) and equal to the angle at the centre.

Looking at the hexagon above you can see that OAB is an isosceles triangle so the angles OAB and OBA are equal. Together they add to 180° minus the angle at the centre (angle sum of a triangle is 180°). But each of these angles is half of an internal angle so internal angle = 180° – angle at the centre.
You can see from the diagram that the exterior and interior angles add up to 180° because they are on a straight line.

?

> **5** Calculate the angle at the centre of each of the following regular polygons and hence work out the exterior and interior angles.
> (a) hexagon   (b) pentagon

There is another way to find the internal angle: by first finding the sum (total) of all the internal angles.
Divide the polygon into the smallest number of triangles possible. For a polygon with n sides this gives $n - 2$ triangles. The sum of the angles in each triangle is 180°. So the sum of the internal angles is given by $180°(n - 2)$.

E.g.

In this case there are 4 triangles. Hence the sum of the internal angles is 4 × 180° = 720°
Alternatively, using the formula $S = 180°(n - 2)$ for the sum of the internal angles,
$S = 180°(6 - 2) = 180° × 4 = 720°$
Dividing by 6 internal angles gives you 120° for each internal angle.

You can use these angle properties to work out how many sides a polygon has given one of its angles.

E.g. If the angle at the centre of a regular polygon is 15° calculate how many sides the polygon has.
Angle at the centre = 360° ÷ n, where n is the number of sides.
So n = 360° ÷ angle at the centre = 360° ÷ 15° = 24
Hence the figure has 24 sides.

?

> **6** (a) Calculate the number of sides of a polygon with an external angle of 18°.
> (b) Calculate the sum of the internal angles of this polygon.

Tesselating

Tesselation means the complete covering of an area by repeating a single shape or combination of shapes without leaving any gaps. It often helps to rotate shapes to tesselate them.

For a single regular shape to be able to tesselate its interior angle must be a factor of 360°.

7 Apart from the hexagon, which two other regular polygons tesselate by themselves?

Note: All triangles and all quadrilaterals can be made to tesselate (if you're careful) because the sum of their interior angles is 180° or 360°.

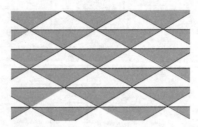

Some polygons will tesselate if they are used in pairs.

E.g. An octagon and a square with the same length sides will tesselate.

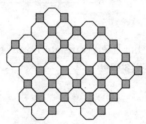

8 Tesselate the following shapes:

(a)   (b)   (c)

4.6e   Transformations

Translation

A translation moves an object from one place to another. A translation maintains orientation (direction), size and shape. Angles, lengths and areas remain unchanged.

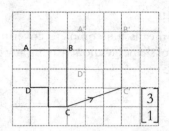

ABCD is translated onto A'B'C'D' by moving it 3 places across and 1 up.

Enlargement

Enlargement increases or decreases size but maintains shape. Angles are unchanged. The ratios between the sides remain constant.

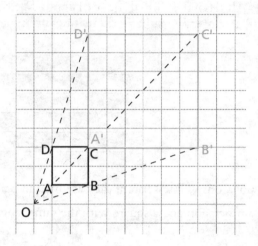

Figure ABCD has been translated onto figure A'B'C'D' by an enlargement factor 3 from a centre of enlargement O.

Rotation

Rotation conserves angles, lengths and areas but alters orientation and position. To define a rotation you must have 3 pieces of information: the centre of rotation, the direction of the rotation and the angle of the rotation (this is called its magnitude).

Note: A positive rotation is anticlockwise.

The figure OABC has been rotated about O in a clockwise direction through an angle of 90° to give O'A'B'C'.

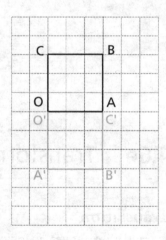

Note: Since O is the centre of rotation it has not moved.

To help you see the effect of simple rotations you can use tracing paper. Trace the figure and then fix the centre of rotation with a pencil and rotate the figure through the angle required.

1 Carry out the following rotations on the rectangle OXYZ:

(a) 90° anticlockwise about O
(b) 90° clockwise about X
(c) ⁻90° about O
(d) 120° clockwise about O
(e) 180° about Y (Say why no direction has been given.)

because 180 clockwise & anti cw is the same thing

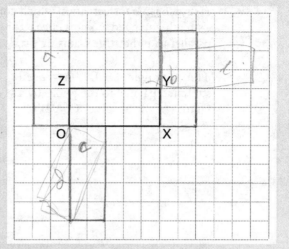

Reflection

Reflection conserves angles, lengths and areas but reverses the object. To define a reflection you need to know the position of the line in which the figure is to be reflected. Corresponding points on the original shape and the reflected shape are the same distance from the line of reflection. The line joining a point to its image is perpendicular (at 90°) to the line of reflection.

The figure OABC has been reflected in the *y*-axis to give O′A′B′C′.

Note: This is sometimes described as a reflection in the line $x = 0$.

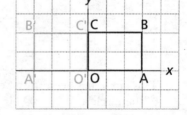

The figure OXYZ has been reflected in the line $y = ⁻x$ to give O′X′Y′Z′.

You can reflect a figure by tracing the figure and the line in which it is to be reflected, then turning the tracing paper over and placing the reflection line back on top of itself.

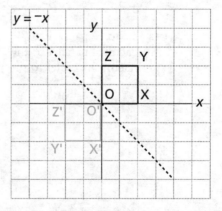

2 Reflect the rectangle OABC in each of the following lines:

(a) the *x*-axis ($y = 0$)
(b) the line $x = 4$
(c) the line $y = x$
(d) the line $y = ⁻x$

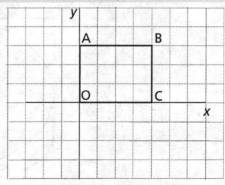

Stretches

A stretch is a transformation which conserves angles but alters lengths and areas. To define a stretch you need to know the factor of the stretch and the direction. Stretches are usually parallel to either the *x*-axis or *y*-axis or both.

The rectangle OABC has been stretched parallel to the *y*-axis by a factor of 2 to give O′A′B′C′.

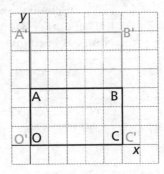

Note: Only the *y* values have changed. The area has doubled.

A stretch often produces a different shape. Stretching a circle can turn it into an ellipse.

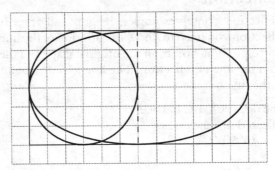

This circle has been stretched by a factor of 2 so the area of the ellipse is twice the area of the circle.

?

3 Stretch the rectangle OPQR by the following factors:

(a) factor 3 parallel to the *x*-axis
(b) factor 2 parallel to the *x*-axis and factor 3 parallel to the *y*-axis

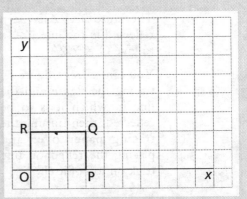

4 If the area of this circle is 6 cm² use this diagram to calculate the area of the ellipse.

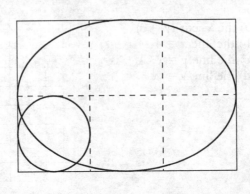

Shears

A shear is a transformation in which one line is fixed and all other points move parallel to the fixed line. The distance a point moves is found by multiplying the factor of the shear by the point's distance from the fixed line. A shear does not conserve angles and may also change lengths.

This is a shear parallel to the *x*-axis by a factor of 1.

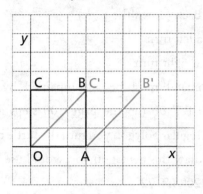

This is a shear parallel to the *y*-axis by a factor of $\frac{4}{3}$.

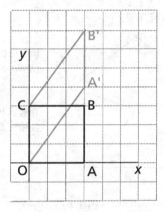

?

5 Shear the rectangle OPQR by a factor of 3 parallel to the *x*-axis.

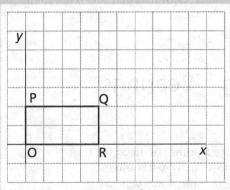

4.6f Using computers to generate and transform 2D shapes

LOGO can be used to produce a range of shapes and paths, from simple shapes like squares and triangles to more complex shapes. There are many different versions of LOGO on the market and the instructions below may not be the same as the ones you have used before.

When LOGO is entered into the computer the cursor, which is usually called the **turtle**, should appear in the middle of the screen. Commands can then be entered which will move the turtle:

FD for forward (up the page)

BK for back (down the page)

LT for a left turn

RT for a right turn

Each command must be accompanied by a distance or an angle, for example:

FD 100 RT 90 (up the page 100 steps and then turn through 90° to the right)

To draw a regular polygon you turn the turtle through the external angles of the polygon.

E.g. To draw this pentagon you would use the following instructions:

FD 200 LT 72
FD 200 LT 72
FD 200 LT 72
FD 200 LT 72
FD 200 LT 72

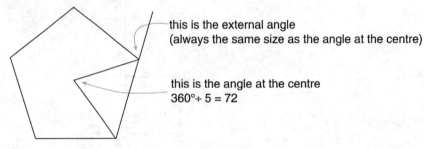

this is the external angle
(always the same size as the angle at the centre)

this is the angle at the centre
360° ÷ 5 = 72

You can use the copy key to avoid making mistakes. This could be written
Repeat 5 [FD 200 LT 72]

?

1 Devise a set of instructions to draw a hexagon.

4.6g   Bearings

To locate a point you need to know how far away it is and in what direction. One way to express direction is using **bearings**. The bearing tells you the angle of the line of direction. Bearings are always measured **clockwise** from North. They should always be given using three figures, e.g. 065° not 65°.

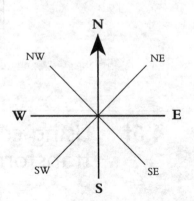

Note: On a page North (N) is usually at the top. Its bearing is 000°.

1 Write the bearing from O for each of the points marked X.

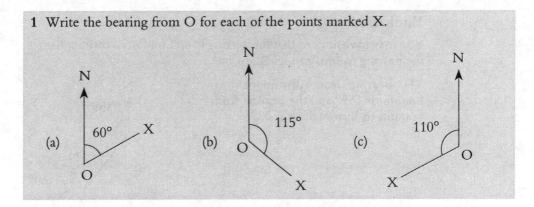

To measure a bearing you can use:

a conventional protractor	or	an angle measurer

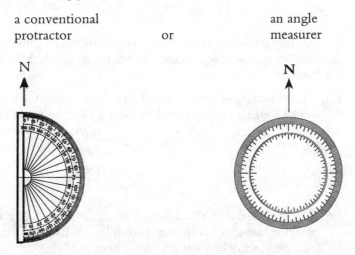

If you're using an angle measurer the 0° line should always be lined up with North. If you're using a protractor to measure a bearing up to 180° the 0° line should be lined up with North. For bearings over 180° the 0° line should be lined up with South and you need to add 180° to the angle on the protractor.

2 Use your angle measurer or protractor to measure the following bearings on this map.

(a) The bearing of
Birmingham from London.

(b) The bearing of
Bristol from Manchester.

(c) The bearing of
Sheffield from Bristol.

(d) The bearing of
Glasgow from Belfast.

(e) The bearing of
London from Birmingham.

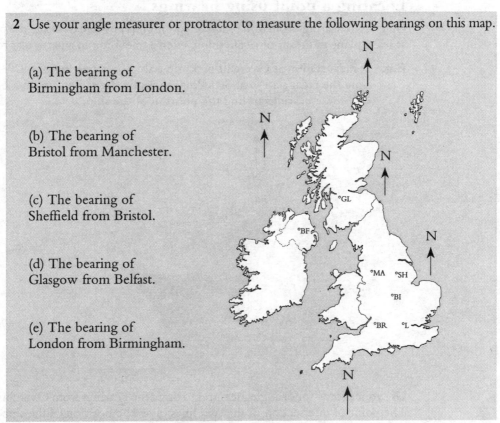

Back bearings

You may have noticed that the bearing from London to Birmingham is 180° greater than the bearing from Birmingham to London.

The bearing from Birmingham to London is 159° and the bearing from London to Birmingham is 339°.

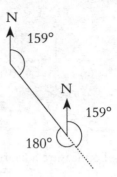

You can find the bearing back along the original bearing line by adding or subtracting 180° from the original bearing. All you need to remember is that your answer must be between 000° and 360°.

E.g. If the bearing of Madrid from Rome is 266°, find the bearing of Rome from Madrid. The bearing back is found by taking 180° from the original bearing.

$$\begin{array}{r} 266° \\ -180° \\ \hline 086° \\ \hline \end{array}$$

?

3 Give the bearing in the opposite direction in each of the following cases:
(a) The bearing of Berlin from Paris is 60°. What is the bearing of Paris from Berlin?
(b) The bearing of Vienna from Athens is 337°.
(c) The bearing from Belgrade to Rome is 248°.

Hint: Drawing a diagram may help.

Locating a point using bearings

Given two bearings from different fixed points it is possible to locate the position of a ship at sea, a plane in the air or of anything, even a television in a particular room in a house.

E.g. A radar station at Overcliff picks up a ship on a bearing of 097°. At the same time the radar station at Star Point picks up the same ship on a bearing of 030°. Use these bearings to find the position of the ship.

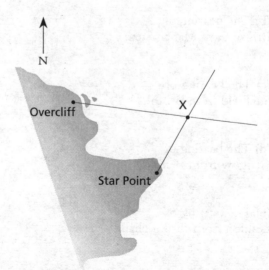

Use your protractor or angle measurer to draw the bearings from Overcliff and Star Point. The point of intersection of the two lines gives the position of the ship, marked X.

4 Use the map in the previous example to answer the following.

(a) The coast guard receives a distress signal from a yacht. Its bearing from the radar station at Overcliff is 085° and from Star Point it is 060°. Mark the position of the yacht on the map with a Y.

(b) A second ship is detected on a bearing of 110° from Overcliff and 100° from Star Point. Mark the position of this ship with a Z.

(c) Calculate the bearing along which each ship will have to sail to reach the yacht.

(d) Calculate the direction which each ship will come from as seen from the yacht.

Remember: All bearings are measured from North (000°) in a clockwise direction and are given using three figures.

4.6h   Circumferences and areas of circles

There are three main circle formulae you need to know:

The diameter of a circle is twice the radius.

$$d = 2r$$
$$\text{Circumference of a circle} = \pi d$$
$$= 2\pi r$$
$$\text{Area of a circle} = \pi r^2$$

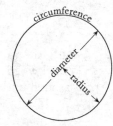

Note: You should learn these formulae.

In a question you will sometimes be given the value of π. It is usually given as 3·14 or 3·142. As a fraction π is $3\frac{1}{7}$ or $\frac{22}{7}$.

If you are not told what value of π to use then use the value on your calculator.

E.g.   Calculate to 2 decimal places the circumference and area of a circle with a radius of 3 m. ($\pi = 3\cdot142$)

Radius = 3 m   Diameter = 6 m

$$
\begin{aligned}
\text{Circumference} &= \pi d & \text{Area} &= \pi r^2 \\
&= 3\cdot142 \times 6 & &= 3\cdot142 \times 3 \times 3 \\
&= 18\cdot852 & &= 28\cdot278 \\
&= 18\cdot85 \text{ m} & &= 28\cdot28 \text{ m}^2
\end{aligned}
$$

3 m

Hint: Always write down the radius and the diameter at the start of your answer. This will help you to avoid using the wrong value in your exam.

1 A clock has a circular face with a radius of 8 cm. Calculate the following to 2 decimal places:

(a) The area of the face of the clock.

(b) The circumference of the face.

2 Milk bottle tops with a diameter of 3·5 cm are cut from a roll of silver foil of the same width which is 20 m long. Calculate:

(a) The area of one milk bottle top.

(b) The number of milk bottle tops you can get from one roll.

Hint: Roll length ÷ diameter of top

(c) The area of silver foil in each roll that is wasted.

Hint: Calculate the area of the roll and take away the area of the number of tops you can get from a roll.

3 A penny farthing has a front wheel with a diameter of 1·2 m and a rear wheel with a diameter of 25 cm.

(a) Calculate how far the bicycle will travel when the front wheel goes around once.
($\pi = 3\cdot142$)

(b) Calculate how far the bicycle will travel when the rear wheel goes around once.
($\pi = 3\cdot142$)

4 A builder has to calculate the number of rectangular paving bricks needed to make a large paved circle with a radius of 2·5 m. Each brick is 7 cm wide and 23 cm long.

(a) Calculate the area of the circle to the nearest square cm.

(b) Calculate the minimum number of bricks needed.

Remember: You must learn the formulae for the area and the circumference of a circle.

4.7a Locating position in 3D

A point in two dimensions, like on a page, can be located by using a pair of Cartesian axes: the *x*-axis (the horizontal axis) and the *y*-axis (the vertical axis).

When you need to locate a point in three-dimensional (3D) space a third axis is used. This is the *z*-axis.

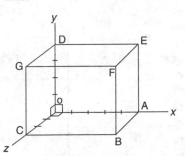

The *z*-axis is perpendicular (at 90°) to both the *x*-axis and the *y*-axis. If you imagine the *x*-axis and the *y*-axis drawn on a page then the *z*-axis is coming out of the page towards you. The coordinates of a point are written in the form (x, y, z).

The coordinates of F are (5, 4, 3).

1 Write down the coordinates of the other vertices (corners) of the cuboid.

2 A small cuboid PQRSTUVW is placed in one corner of a much larger box. The position of the vertex R is given by the coordinates (7, 5, 4).

If the cuboid is placed in the box in a different way but with U retaining its present position at the origin (0, 0, 0), give the possible sets of coordinates for the point R.

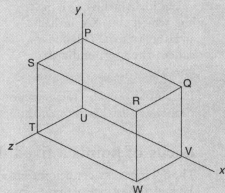

3 A cube has sides of length 3 units. One vertex is fixed at (2, 1, 0).
  (a) How many different positions could the cube be placed in?
  (b) Write down the possible coordinates of the opposite vertex of the cube.

Remember: The coordinates of a point in 3D space are *x*, *y* and *z* in that order.

4.7b Loci

A **locus** is the path traced out as an object moves according to a rule. Another way to describe a locus is as the set of points which satisfy the rule. The points are all the different positions of the object as it moves. The plural of locus is **loci**.

Locus of points a fixed distance from a fixed point

1 Mark a point O on a piece of paper. Mark in points that are 2 cm from O. The more points you draw the clearer the locus will become.

The locus in this case is a circle with its centre at O and a radius of 2 cm.

Remember: The locus of points a fixed distance from a single fixed point is a circle.

Another way to say this is that an object moving at a constant (fixed) distance from a fixed point will always follow a circular path.

Locus of points equidistant from two fixed points

The easiest way to draw the locus of points which are an equal distance from 2 fixed points is by using a pair of compasses. Set the compasses and draw an arc from X and an arc from Y so that the arcs intersect. The point of intersection is the same distance from X and Y. Change the radius of the compasses and repeat the operation to find more points until you are sure of the shape of the locus.

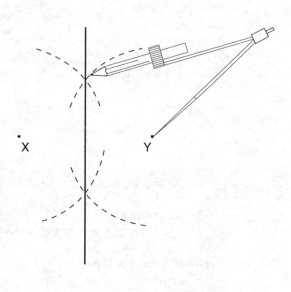

The locus in this case is the line which cuts XY in half and is at 90° to it. This line is called the perpendicular bisector.

Remember: The locus of points equidistant from two fixed points is the perpendicular bisector of the line joining the two points.

Locus of points a fixed distance from a line

The distance between a point and a line is defined as the shortest distance between them. To find the distance of a point from a line you measure the distance *at right angles to the line*.

If you have a line with end points X and Y, then where XY is a straight line the locus will form two parallel lines, on each side of XY.

The ends of the line act like fixed points. You have seen that the locus of points at a fixed distance from a fixed point is a circle. So at the ends the locus will form semicircles around the points X and Y.

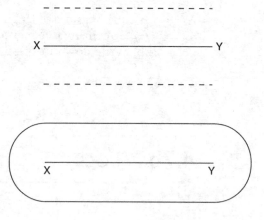

Remember: The locus of points a fixed distance from a line is two parallel lines, one on either side.

Locus of points equidistant from two intersecting lines

To draw the locus of points equally distant from two intersecting lines you can use a pair of compasses.

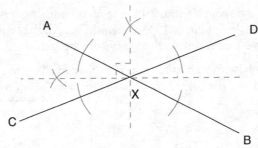

Use your compasses to mark points on AB and CD which are equally distant from X. Then draw intersecting arcs by putting the point of the compasses on each of these points in turn. The points where the arcs intersect are the same distance from both lines. Repeat this process until you have enough points to describe the locus.

This locus forms two lines perpendicular to each other which bisect (cut in half) each of the angles between AB and CD.

Remember: The locus of points equidistant from two intersecting lines is the bisectors of the angles between the lines.

Locus of points whose total distance from two fixed points is fixed

You can draw this locus using a pin board (or a thick newspaper on a flat surface), two pins and a loop of string.

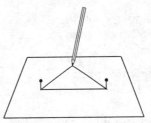

Put some paper on the board and place the pins in the board at a distance apart which is shorter than the loop. Now place your pencil in the loop and pull it tight. Keeping the string tight, draw a line all the way around the two pins. Try changing the distance between the pins and repeating the process.

You can also draw this locus using a pair of compasses. First you need to calculate some distances.

Distance from A	$5\frac{1}{2}$	5	4	3	2	1	$\frac{1}{2}$
Distance from B	$\frac{1}{2}$	1	2	3	4	5	$5\frac{1}{2}$
Total	6	6	6	6	6	6	6

You can now set your compasses and plot the points.

2 Draw the locus of points with a total distance from two points A and B of 10 cm. Start with A and B 7cm apart.

Remember: The locus of an object moving so that the sum of its distances from two fixed points is constant is an ellipse.

3 Two radio stations 70 km apart broadcast over distances of 45 km and 55 km. Using a scale of 1 cm to 10 km draw the loci of the limits of their broadcasting ranges. Shade the area where both stations can be heard.

4 A large rectangular crate is to be moved by rotating it about one edge. This diagram shows the side view of the crate which will rotate about corner C.

Draw the locus of the corner A as the crate is rotated. Clearly label the vertices (corners) once the crate has been rotated. Mark the new position of A as A′, B as B′ etc.
Hint: If you find this difficult to picture then trace the shape, marking A, B, C and D, put a pen in point C and rotate the tracing paper.

5 This diagram shows a garden drawn to scale. In the garden there are already two trees marked A and B and the gardener wishes to plant a third. There are a number of rules he wishes to apply.

(a) The new tree must be an equal distance from both trees A and B.

(b) The new tree must be at least 4 m from the edge of the garden.

(c) The new tree must not be within 14 m of tree B.

Draw the locus given by each of these rules clearly on the diagram and show the possible planting sites for the new tree.

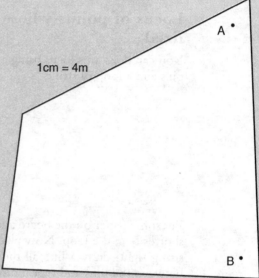

1cm = 4m

4.7c   Pythagoras' theorem

Pythagoras' theorem states that if a square is drawn on the longest side of a right-angled triangle (the **hypotenuse**), its area will be equal to the sum or total areas of the squares drawn on the other two sides.

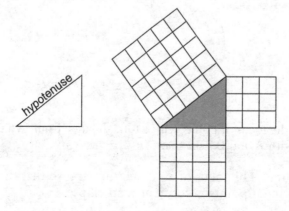

Remember: The square on the hypotenuse is equal to the sum of the squares on the other two sides.

If you call the hypotenuse h and the other sides a and b Pythagoras' theorem can be expressed as

$$h^2 = a^2 + b^2$$

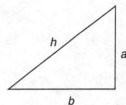

There are two ways in which this information can be used:
❶ Given any two sides of a right-angled triangle you can use the rule to find the third.
❷ Given all three sides of a triangle you can check whether it is right-angled.

E.g. Find the missing side in the following right-angled triangle.

$h^2 = a^2 + b^2$
$h^2 = 3^2 + 4^2$
$h^2 = 9 + 16 = 25$
$h = \sqrt{25}$
$h = 5$ m

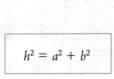

Note: This is a very special triangle.

The (3, 4, 5) triangle is the smallest right-angled triangle with whole number sides. Any triangle with sides in the ratio 3 : 4 : 5 is called a (3, 4, 5) triangle e.g. (6, 8, 10) and (15, 20, 25). Any set of whole numbers which gives the sides of a right-angled triangle is called a **Pythagorean triple**. (5, 12, 13) and (8, 15, 17) are two other examples.

When you are calculating one of the shorter sides and not the hypotenuse the formula needs to be rearranged.

E.g. Find the length of side a in this triangle.

Rearranging the formula gives
$a^2 = h^2 - b^2$

Putting in the values of h and b gives
$a^2 = 7^2 - 5^2$
$a^2 = 49 - 25 = 24$
$a = \sqrt{24}$
$a = 4.90$ (to 2 d.p.)

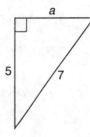

1 Calculate the length of the missing side in each of these triangles:

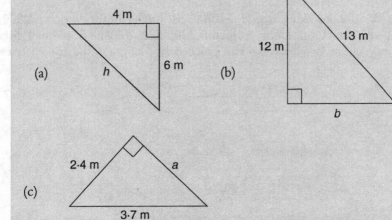

(a)

(b)

(c)

2 Look carefully at the following diagram. How many triangles in the 3, 4, 5 family can you find?

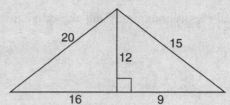

3 A ladder 5 m long is placed against a vertical wall. The foot of the ladder is 2·5 m horizontally from the bottom of the wall. How high up the wall will the ladder reach?

Hint: Diagrams often help.

4 Use Pythagoras' theorem to find out which of the following triangles are right-angled. (They have not been accurately drawn.)

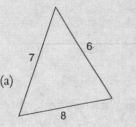 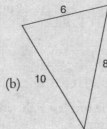 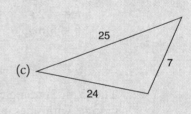

Applying Pythagoras' theorem

Pythagoras' theorem can be used to calculate the length of a vector or the distance between two points expressed as coordinates.

E.g. Calculate the distance between the points (2, 3) and (7, 6).

Hint: Draw a sketch or diagram if it helps.

> The distance between the x values is $7 - 2 = 5$ and the distance between the y values is $6 - 3 = 3$.
> Using Pythagoras, $h^2 = x^2 + y^2$
> $h^2 = 5^2 + 3^2$
> $h^2 = 25 + 9 = 34$
> $h = \sqrt{34}$
> $h = 5·83$ (to 2 d.p.)

5 Calculate the distance of the point (6, 8) from the origin (0, 0).

6 A ski lift takes skiers from the top of Mount Windsor, which is 2500 m high, to the top of Mount Henry, which is 3200 m high. The horizontal distance between the two peaks is 4 km. Calculate the length of the cable between the peaks.

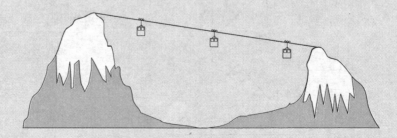

4.7d Areas of plane shapes and volumes of prisms

You already know how to find the area of rectangles, triangles and circles.

Note: You must learn these formulae since they will not be given on formula lists.

Parallelogram

A parallelogram is a quadrilateral with opposite sides parallel.

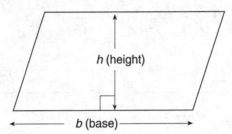

The area of a parallelogram is base × height = bh

This is because you can cut off a triangle at one end and move it to the other to get a rectangle.

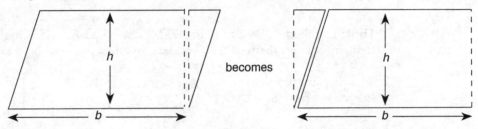

becomes

Rhombus

A rhombus is a quadrilateral with all its sides equal.
   The area of a rhombus can be calculated using the same method as for a parallelogram or by multiplying the diagonals together.

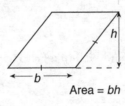

Area = bh

Area = $\frac{1}{2} ab$

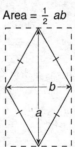

Trapezium

A trapezium is a quadrilateral with one pair of parallel sides.

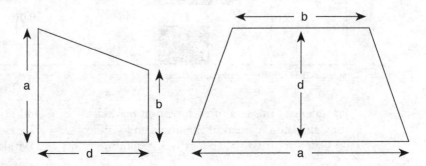

The area of a trapezium is $\frac{1}{2} \times$ (sum of parallel sides) $\times$ height $= \frac{1}{2}(a + b)h$

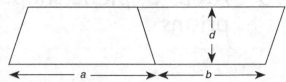

This is because you can take a second trapezium congruent to (the same shape and size as) the first and fit them together to make a parallelogram with sides of length $a + b$. The area of one trapezium will be half the area of the parallelogram.

?

1 This is the plan of a plot of building land drawn to a scale of 1 cm to 10 m. Calculate its area. Give your answer to the nearest square metre.

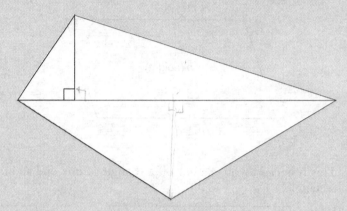

Hint: Divide the plot into triangles. Measure the base and height of each triangle, convert them to their real lengths and work out the area of each triangle.

2 This diagram shows the side view of a staircase.

(a) Calculate the area under the stairs.

(b) Calculate the area of the banisters.

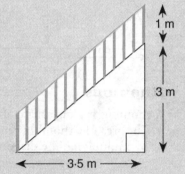

3 This is a drawing of the end wall of a factory.

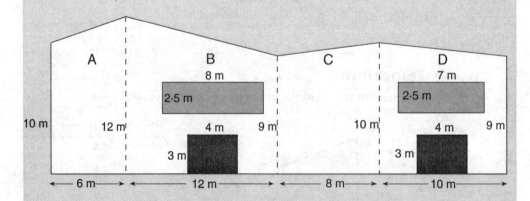

(a) Calculate the area of each section marked A, B, C and D.
(b) Calculate the areas of the doors and windows.
(c) Calculate the total area of wall excluding doors and windows.

Calculating volumes

If a solid has a uniform cross-section (the area is the same throughout its length) then the volume is given by

Volume = cross-sectional area × length

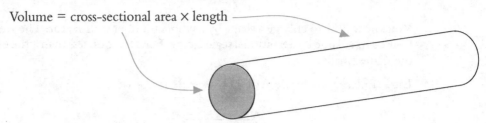

Such a solid is sometimes called a **prism**.

E.g. Calculate the volume of water in this swimming pool.

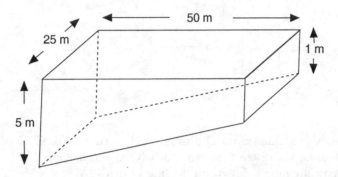

The cross-section of the swimming pool is a trapezium with $h = 50$ m, $a = 1$ m and $b = 5$ m.

Area of cross-section $= \frac{1}{2}(a + b)h$
$= \frac{1}{2}(1 + 5) \times 50$
$= 150$ m²

Multiplying the cross-section by the length gives
$150 \times 25 = 3750$

Therefore the pool holds 3750 m³ of water.

Remember: Volume is in cubic units.

?

4 The track for a new high speed train is to be in a cutting for its entire length to reduce environmental impact. This diagram shows the cross-section of the cutting.

(a) Calculate the area of the cross-section of the cutting.

(b) Use your answer to (a) to calculate the volume of material to be removed for each kilometre of cutting.

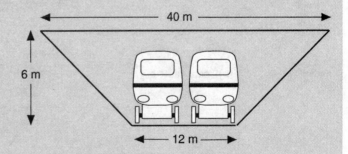

5 A syringe is to be used to draw a sample of blood from a patient in hospital. If the radius of the syringe is 3·5 mm and the length is 25 mm calculate the volume of blood in the syringe when it is full.

6 A manufacturer needs to produce rectangular based boxes with a volume of 1200 cm³. The boxes must pack neatly into crates 50 cm wide, 60 cm long and 50 cm high.
(a) How many boxes will fit into each crate?
(b) Investigate some possible dimensions for the box.

4.7e   Enlarging by a fraction

You know how to enlarge a shape by a whole number scale factor. The same method can be used to enlarge by a fractional scale factor. For a fraction less than 1 the effect is to make the shape smaller.

E.g.   Enlarge the figure ABCD by a scale factor of $\frac{1}{2}$.

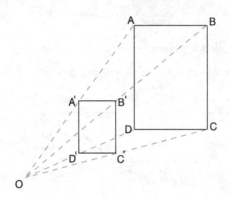

Draw guidelines from O through each corner A, B, C, D of the rectangle.
Measure the distance from O to A (OA) and halve it.
Mark the new point A′ on the line so that OA′ is $\frac{1}{2}$ OA.
Repeat this process for each corner. This gives the figure A′B′C′D′.

?

1   Enlarge each of the following shapes by the given scale factor using the centre of enlargement which has been marked for you.

(a) scale factor $\frac{1}{2}$

(b) scale factor $\frac{1}{3}$

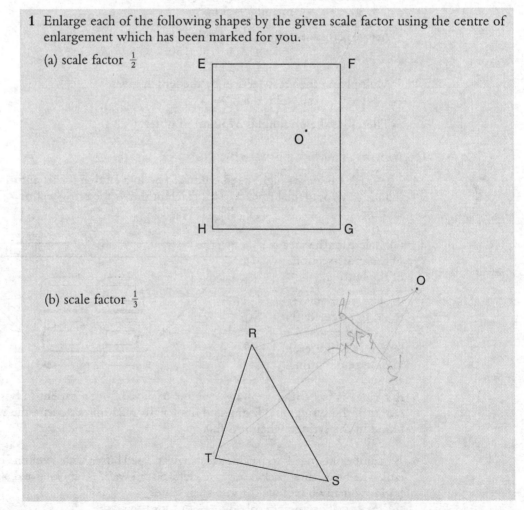

Remember: A scale factor less than 1 will make your figure smaller.

4.8a Similar figures

Two figures are **mathematically similar** if corresponding (matching) angles are all equal and corresponding sides are in the same ratio. One figure may be a scaled up, scaled down, rotated or reflected version of the other.

1 Using a pair of compasses and a ruler construct a triangle that has sides 3 cm, 4 cm and 5 cm long. Use the same method to construct a triangle with sides twice as long. Measure the angles in each of the triangles.

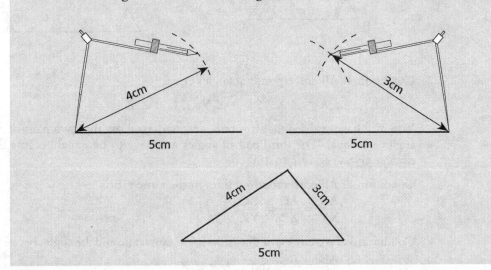

You should have found that, although the sides of the second triangle are twice as long as the first, the angles are the same.

2 Try constructing a triangle with sides half as long as the first triangle. What can you say about the angles?

The triangles you have drawn are mathematically similar.

When you are checking for similarity look for the points which correspond to (match) each other and then label them in the same order on each figure to make it easier to see which angles and sides are corresponding.

E.g. Show that the following quadrilaterals are similar.

A corresponds to W

B corresponds to X

C corresponds to Y

D corresponds to Z

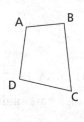

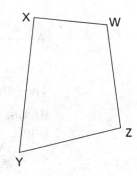

To prove that two quadrilaterals are similar it is enough to show that corresponding angles are equal. Then the sides must be in the same ratio.

Measure the angle at A and the corresponding angle at W. They are the same. The angles at B and X are also equal, and so are the angles at C and Y. The angles of a quadrilateral add to 360° so the remaining angles must be equal. So ABCD and WXYZ are similar.

Check: Measure the lengths of the sides.
WX = 2 AB, XY = 2 BC, YZ = 2 CD, WZ = 2 AD
Corresponding sides are in the same ratio (1 : 2).

Similar triangles

To prove that triangles are similar you don't have to check all the angles and all the sides. If two triangles satisfy *one* of the following conditions then they are similar.

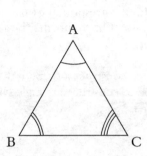 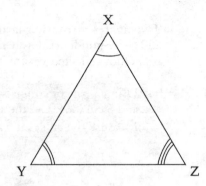

Condition 1: All corresponding angles equal.

$$\angle A = \angle X, \angle B = \angle Y, \angle C = \angle Z$$

You may have realised that it is only necessary to show that two pairs of corresponding angles are equal. The third pair of angles will have to be equal because the angles of a triangle always add up to 180°.

Condition 2: All corresponding sides in the same ratio.

$$\frac{AB}{XY} = \frac{AC}{XZ} = \frac{BC}{YZ}$$

Condition 3: Two corresponding sides in the same ratio and the angles between them equal.

$$\frac{AB}{XY} = \frac{AC}{XZ} \text{ and } \angle A = \angle X$$

Finding missing sides and angles

If you know that two shapes are similar then you can use this to find missing sides or angles.

E.g. Triangles AXY and ABC are similar. Calculate the length of the sides AB and AC.

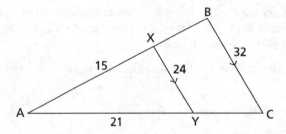

The ratio of BC to XY is $\frac{32}{24} = \frac{4}{3}$

Because the triangles are similar, AB and AX, and AC and AY, are in the same ratio.

$$\frac{AB}{AX} = \frac{4}{3} = \frac{AC}{AY}$$

$$\frac{AB}{15} = \frac{4}{3} = \frac{AC}{21}$$

Using equivalent ratios (or fractions),
AB = 20 and AC = 28

Note: If you have not been told that shapes are similar you must prove it before you can use the properties of similar shapes.

3 (a) Show that the triangles ABC and CDE are similar.

Use the similarity of the triangles to calculate the length of the following sides:

(b) DE   (c) BC

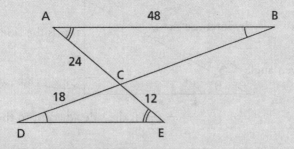

4 (a) Show that the triangles ABC and ADE are similar.

(b) Calculate the length of BC.

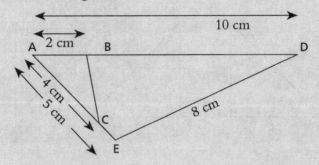

5 Which of the following quadrilaterals is not similar to the other three?

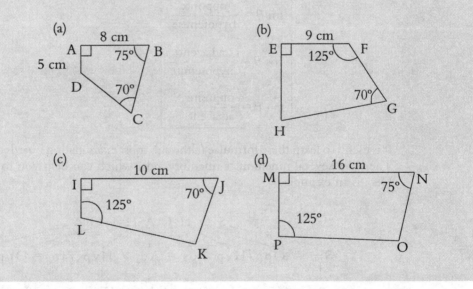

Remember: In similar figures corresponding angles are equal and corresponding sides are in the same ratio.

4.8b   Sin, cos and tan

In a right-angled triangle the sides and angles are related by three trigonometrical (trig) ratios: **sine** (which is usually shortened to **sin**), **cosine** (which is usually shortened to **cos**) and **tangent** (which is usually shortened to **tan**).

To use these ratios you first need to be able to identify which side of a triangle is the **hypotenuse** (always the longest side), which side is **opposite** to a given angle and which side is **adjacent** to (next to) a given angle.

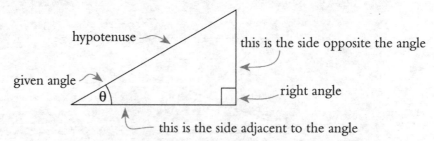

1 Write down the hypotenuse, opposite and adjacent sides to the angle θ (theta) in each of the following triangles:

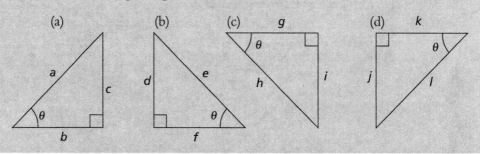

The trig ratios relate an angle θ to the hypotenuse, opposite and adjacent sides in the following ways:

$$\sin \theta = \frac{\text{opposite}}{\text{hypotenuse}}$$

$$\cos \theta = \frac{\text{adjacent}}{\text{hypotenuse}}$$

$$\tan \theta = \frac{\text{opposite}}{\text{adjacent}}$$

It is useful to learn these formulae (although most examination boards give them to you). There are several mnemonics (memory aids) which can help you to remember them. Here is an example:

S O H C A H T O A

Sin = Opp/Hyp   Cos = Adj / Hyp   Tan = Opp/Adj

Some Officers Have Curly Auburn Hair To Offer Attraction

You may have been taught the ratios in the following form:

hypotenuse × sin θ = opposite side   (hyp × sin θ = opp)
hypotenuse × cos θ = adjacent side   (hyp × cos θ = adj)
adjacent × tan θ = opposite side   (adj × tan θ = opp)

Learn the method you have been taught or the one you find easiest to remember.

By cancelling the hypotenuse we get the following relationship:

$$\tan \theta = \frac{\sin \theta}{\cos \theta}$$

Key in the angle and then press `sin` `cos` or `tan`

E.g. (a) Calculate sin 70°.

`7` `0` `sin`

Display: `0.9396926`

(b) Calculate tan 52°.

`5` `2` `tan`

Display: `1.2799416`

Investigate some values of sin, cos and tan for angles between 0° and 90°. You should notice that sin and cos are always less than 1. (This is because the hypotenuse is the longest side.)

The trig ratios can be used to find missing sides and angles in right-angles triangles. Given one side and an angle (other than the right angle) you can find the other sides or given two sides you can find the angles.

Finding missing sides

First you need to decide which ratio to use. Look at which two sides are involved in the question.

E.g. Find the length to 2 d.p. of side x in this triangle.

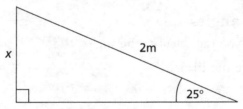

You have been given an angle and the *hypotenuse* and asked to find the side *opposite* the angle. The ratio which links angle, hypotenuse and opposite is *sin*.

$$\sin = \frac{\text{opposite}}{\text{hypotenuse}}$$

Rearranging the formula, opposite = hypotenuse × sin

$$\begin{aligned} x &= 2 \times \sin 25° \\ &= 2 \times 0.4226 \\ &= 0.8452 \\ x &= 0.85 \text{ m (to 2 d.p.)} \end{aligned}$$

`2` `×` `2` `5` `sin` `=` `0.8452365`

Remember: Even when you use your calculator always show all your working out.

2 Use sin, cos or tan to find the missing side x in each of the following triangles. (Give your answer to 2 d.p.)

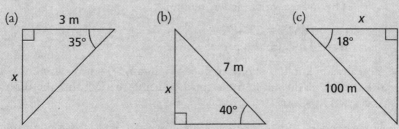

Sometimes you will be asked to find the side which appears on the bottom of a formula. Then you have to rearrange the formula.

?

3 Find the side marked *x* in each of the following triangles. (Give your answer to 2 d.p.)

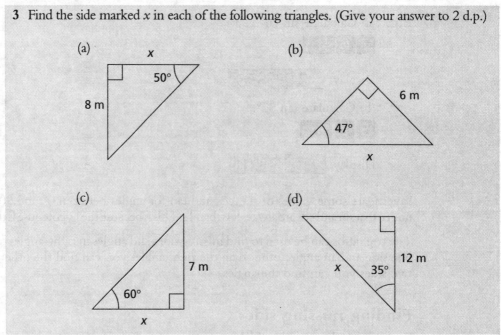

Remember: If you know two sides you can use Pythagoras' theorem to find the third side.

Finding missing angles

Given two of the sides you can calculate the angles.

E.g. Find the angle θ in this triangle.

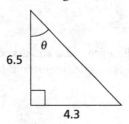

You have been given the *opposite* side and the *adjacent* side to θ so this must be a *tan* problem.

$$\tan \theta = \frac{\text{opposite}}{\text{adjacent}}$$

$$\tan \theta = \frac{4 \cdot 3}{6 \cdot 5} = 0 \cdot 6615$$

To find the angle you have to use the INV (inverse) or 2nd function key on your scientific calculator:

The inverse of tan is written $\tan^{-1}$.

$\tan^{-1} 0 \cdot 6615 = 33 \cdot 486°$
$\theta = 33 \cdot 49°$ (to 2 d.p.)

You already know that one angle is a right angle so now you know two of the angles in the triangle. You can find the third by using the fact that the three angles of a triangle always add to 180°.

Remember: Once you have found the angle θ the remaining angle is $90° - \theta$.

4 Find the angle θ in each of the following triangles. (Give your answer to 2 d.p.)

(a)

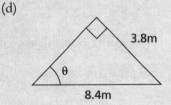

(b)

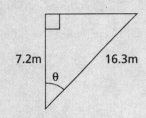

(c)

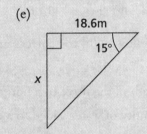

(d)

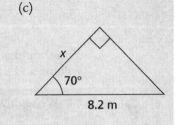

5 These questions are a mixture of the different types covered in this section. Find the side marked *x* or the angle θ in each case. (Give your answer to 2 d.p.)

(a)

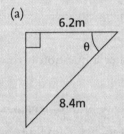

(b)

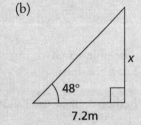

(c)

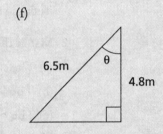

(d)

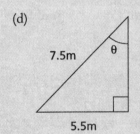

(e)

(f)

6 A glider flies from X to Y to Z. The journey from X to Y is 16·5 km on a bearing of 040° and the journey from Y to Z is 9·8 km on a bearing of 085°. Answer the following to 2 d.p.

(a) Calculate how far C is north of X.

(b) How far east of C is Y?

(c) How far north of Y is Z?

(d) How far east of Y is Z?

(e) Calculate the distance of the glider from its starting point.

(f) Calculate the bearing from X to Z to the nearest degree.

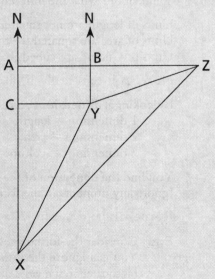

7 Calculate the area of this triangle.

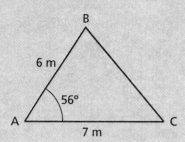

Hint: First calculate its height by dropping a perpendicular from B to AC.

Remember: Some Officers Have Curly Auburn Hair To Offer Attraction!

4.8c Distinguishing between formulae by considering dimensions

You should already be able to work out whether a question involves length, area or volume and use the correct units.

1 Write down whether each of the following are units of length, area or volume:

    (a) cm^2 (b) yards   (c) mm   (d) inches   (e) litres

    (f) cubic feet   (g) cm   (h) m^3 (i) km   (j) sq feet

2 Match the following to the correct units:

    (a) The size of a carpet.

    (b) The length of the drive to a house.

    (c) The quantity of water added to a recipe.

    (d) The distance from Cardiff to London.

    (e) The luggage space in a new car.

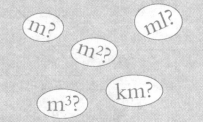

Think about what the different units have in common.

Units of length are not squared or cubed. Length is **1**-dimensional.
Units of area are squared (to the power **2**). Area is **2**-dimensional.
Units of volume are cubed (to the power **3**). Volume is **3**-dimensional.

Note: A litre is really 1000 cm^3.

By looking at **dimensions** you can distinguish between formulae for length, area and volume.
        1 dimension = length
        2 dimensions = area
        3 dimensions = volume

You find the dimension of the formula by counting up the total number of unknowns. Ignore any numbers in the formula.

Remember: r^2 means $r \times r$ and r^3 means $r \times r \times r$.

E.g. Consider the formula $\frac{1}{3}\pi r^2 h$.
      You can ignore the numbers $\frac{1}{3}$ and π.
      r is squared so it gives 2 dimensions + 1 dimension for h gives a total of 3 dimensions.
      Therefore it must be a formula for volume.

3 Write down whether the following formulae are for length, area or volume:
(a) $\frac{4}{3}\pi r^3$ (b) $\pi r^2 l$ (c) $2d$ (d) bh (e) $2(l + w)$

4.8d   Vector notation and translations

A **vector** is a quantity which has both *magnitude* (size) and *direction*. Some examples of vectors are displacement, velocity, force, momentum and acceleration.

In a diagram a vector can be represented in two ways:

❶ By using capital letters at each end and an arrow showing the direction.

This is the vector $\overrightarrow{AB}$. The arrow above the letters tells you the direction.

The magnitude of the vector is written as $|\overrightarrow{AB}|$ (sometimes called the modulus or mod of AB) or AB (the length of the line).

❷ By using a small letter and an arrow showing the direction.

This is the vector **a**.
In handwriting this is written as $\underline{a}$ or $\underset{\sim}{a}$.

The magnitude (length) of the vector is written as $|\mathbf{a}|$ or $|\underline{a}|$ or a.

A vector with magnitude 0 is called the zero vector, written **0**. A vector with magnitude 1 is called a unit vector. Vectors are equal or equivalent if they have the same magnitude and the same direction.

$\mathbf{a} = \mathbf{b}$

Using vectors to describe movement

A vector can be used to represent a move from one place to another or to describe a translation. The move represented by the vector **a** can be written as a **column vector**

$\mathbf{a} = \begin{bmatrix} x \\ y \end{bmatrix}$ or $\begin{pmatrix} x \\ y \end{pmatrix}$

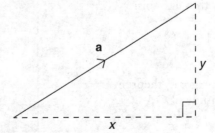

x and y are called the **components** of **a**. The x component gives you the horizontal move and the y component gives you the vertical move.

Imagine a pair of axes with their origin at the start of the vector. The horizontal component is + to the right and − to the left. The vertical component is + up and − down.

1 A knight on a chess board moves either 1 space horizontally and 2 spaces vertically or 2 spaces horizontally and 1 vertically. Write the following moves as column vectors:

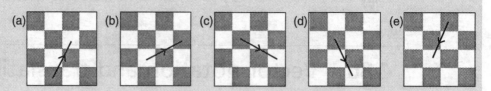

(a) (b) (c) (d) (e)

2 Draw the following vectors, remembering to mark the direction:

(a) $\begin{pmatrix} 2 \\ 3 \end{pmatrix}$ (b) $\begin{pmatrix} 5 \\ 2 \end{pmatrix}$ (c) $\begin{pmatrix} ^-2 \\ 4 \end{pmatrix}$ (d) $\begin{pmatrix} 6 \\ ^-1 \end{pmatrix}$ (e) $\begin{pmatrix} ^-3 \\ ^-4 \end{pmatrix}$

3 In each of the following, write the translation which takes A to A′ as a column vector.

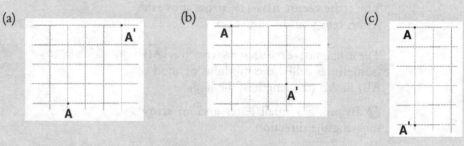

(a) (b) (c)

4 Translate the quadrilateral ABCD using the following vectors:

(a) $\begin{pmatrix} ^-1 \\ 4 \end{pmatrix}$ (b) $\begin{pmatrix} 2 \\ ^-3 \end{pmatrix}$ (c) $\begin{pmatrix} 0 \\ 2 \end{pmatrix}$

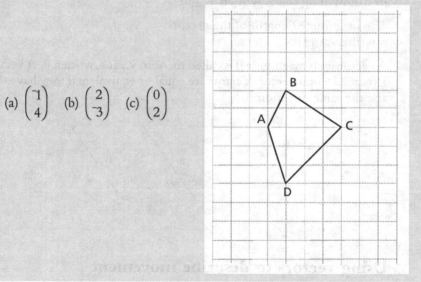

The **position vector** of a point A (x, y) represents the move from the origin O to A. It can be written like this:

$$\overrightarrow{OA} = \begin{pmatrix} x \\ y \end{pmatrix}$$

Using Pythagoras' theorem, the magnitude of OA is

$$|\overrightarrow{OA}| = \sqrt{x^2 + y^2}$$

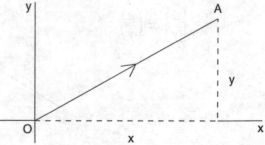

Inverse vectors

The **inverse** of a vector is a vector of equal magnitude (size) but in the opposite direction. The inverse of $\overrightarrow{AB}$ is $^-\overrightarrow{AB}$ or $\overrightarrow{BA}$.

The inverse of **a** is ⁻**a**.

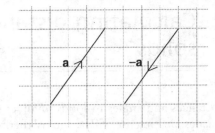

If $\mathbf{a} = \begin{pmatrix} x \\ y \end{pmatrix}$ then $^-\mathbf{a} = \begin{pmatrix} ^-x \\ ^-y \end{pmatrix}$.

5 Write down the inverse of each of the vectors in question 2.

6

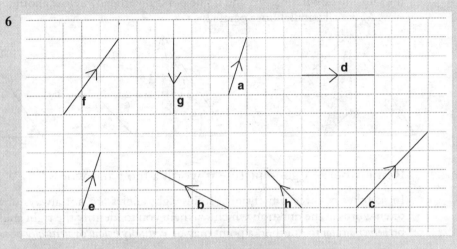

(a) Write down the column vector for each of the vectors **a** to **h**.
(b) Write down the inverse of each vector.
(c) Which pairs of vectors are equal?
(d) What is the magnitude of the vectors **d** and **g**?
(e) Using Pythagoras' theorem, calculate the magnitude of vectors **c** and **f**.

Scalars

A **scalar** is a quantity which has magnitude (size) but not direction. You can multiply a vector by a scalar to get another vector.

If a vector **a** is multiplied by a scalar k we get $k\mathbf{a}$.

$k\mathbf{a}$ is parallel to **a**, in the same direction if k is positive and in the opposite direction if k is negative. The length of $k\mathbf{a}$ is k times the length of **a**.

To multiply a column vector by a scalar you simply multiply each component by the scalar.

$$k\begin{pmatrix} x \\ y \end{pmatrix} = \begin{pmatrix} kx \\ ky \end{pmatrix}$$

7 Multiply $\begin{pmatrix} 2 \\ 4 \end{pmatrix}$ by each of the following scalars. Write your answers as column vectors.

(a) 3   (b) $\frac{1}{2}$ (c) ⁻2   (d) $^-\frac{1}{2}$

Remember: A vector has magnitude and direction. If you multiply a vector by a scalar the magnitude of the vector changes but the direction stays the same, unless the scalar is negative.

4.9a Calculating distances and angles in solids

Finding distances and angles in solids involves solving right-angled triangles viewed in different planes, making use of Pythagoras' theorem and the trigonometrical ratios sin, cos and tan.

It is very important to draw a simple diagram that helps you to see clearly the part of the solid that you are working on and the type of operation you need to perform. Your drawing should include all the information you need to answer the question and you should clearly label the things you need to find. Ignore what you don't need. Draw vertical lines up and down the page, and if one point is vertically below another then draw it that way. Make all parallel lines parallel.

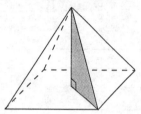 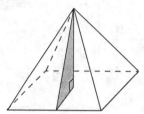 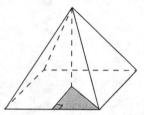

Remember: 'A good picture is worth a thousand words.'

In sketches of three-dimensional solids right angles are not always obvious. There are often words in the question which will help you to identify the right angles: one line may be *perpendicular* to another, a point may be *vertically below* or *vertically above* another point.

E.g. In a regular square based pyramid ABCDE the edge AB = 8 cm and the vertical height to the apex point E = 7 cm. Let X be the point on the base directly below E and let Y be the mid-point of AB.

(a) Calculate the angle EYX.
(b) Calculate the length of the slope EY.
(c) Calculate the area of the face ABE.

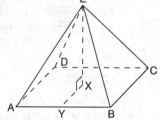

(a) To calculate $\angle$ EYX you need to draw the triangle EXY.

You know that EX = 7 cm. Because EX is vertical the angle EXY is a right angle. Because the pyramid is regular, X is in the middle of the base so XY is half the length of the base. Therefore XY = 4 cm.

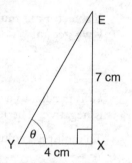

Looking at the diagram you can see that you know the opposite and adjacent sides to the angle you want to find. So use tan.

Let $\angle$ EYX = θ

$$\tan \theta = \frac{\text{opposite}}{\text{adjacent}} = \frac{7}{4}$$

$\boxed{7}$ $\boxed{\div}$ $\boxed{4}$ $\boxed{=}$ $\boxed{\text{INV}}$ $\boxed{\text{tan}}$ $\boxed{60.255119}$

$\angle$ EYX = 60·26° (to 2 d.p.)

(b) To calculate the length of the slope EY you can use Pythagoras' theorem in the triangle already drawn. (You could use the angle you have just found to calculate EY but if you got the angle wrong then you'd get the length of EY wrong too.)

Using Pythagoras, $\quad EY^2 = EX^2 + XY^2$
$$= 4^2 + 7^2$$
$$= 16 + 49$$
$$= 65$$
$$EY = \sqrt{65}$$
$$EY = 8.06 \text{ cm (to 2 d.p.)}$$

(c) To find the area of the triangle ABE you need a new diagram.

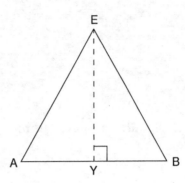

You know the length of EY from part (b).

Note: Do not use the rounded answer. It may create a rounding error. Use the **exact** value.

The exact value of EY is $\sqrt{65}$ cm. You know that AB = 8 cm.

Area of ABE $= \frac{1}{2}$ base × height
$$= \frac{1}{2} \times 8 \times \sqrt{65}$$
$$= 32.249031$$

The area of ABE = 32.25 cm² (to 2 d.p.)

Remember: If possible always use information that you have been given rather than your own answers.

1 ABCDEFGH is a regular cuboid with AB = 25 cm, BC = 10 cm and BF = 7 cm.

(a) Find the length EG.

Hint: Draw triangle EFG.

(b) Find the length AG.

Hint: Draw triangle AEG.

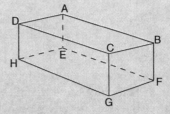

(c) Calculate the angle AGE.
(d) Find the length BG.
(e) Calculate the angle AGB.
(f) Calculate the area of the triangle ABG.

2 A snail is moving on a brick represented by the cuboid in question 1. The snail travels in a straight line from A to G along the shortest route.
(a) Calculate the length of the snail's trail.

Hint: Imagine the box opened out.

(b) Find the angle from AB that the snail will travel along.
(c) How far from the corner D will the snail cross the edge CD?

3 A flag pole stands exactly in the centre of a courtyard 3·6 m wide and 4·5 m long. The flag pole is supported by three cables attached to the pole at a point 7·6 m above the ground. The other ends of the cables are attached to points A, B and C on the ground. A and B are each half way along a side of the courtyard, and C is at one corner.

(a) Calculate the length of the cable attached to point A.
(b) Calculate the length of the cable attached to point B.
(c) Calculate the length of the cable attached to point C.

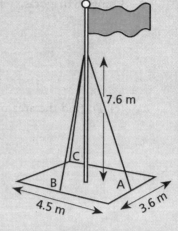

Remember: The most important thing to do in any 3D work is to draw a good diagram.

4.9b Congruent triangles

For any two shapes to be **congruent** to each other they must be *the same shape* and *the same size*. This means they fit onto each other exactly when rotated or reflected. For two polygons to be congruent all corresponding (matching) angles must be equal and all corresponding sides must be equal.

For two triangles to be congruent they must have:
      3 pairs of corresponding equal angles and
      3 pairs of corresponding equal sides

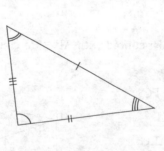
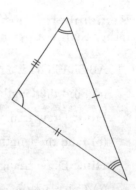

1 Which of these triangles are congruent? (They are not drawn accurately.) Explain in each case why you have or have not decided a pair are congruent.

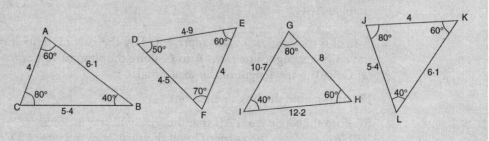

Congruent triangles are different to other shapes because you do not need to check all the sides and all the angles in a pair of triangles to be sure of congruence. If two triangles satisfy any *one* of the following conditions then they are congruent.

(i) Three sides of one triangle are equal to the three sides of the other.

An easy way to
remember this rule is:
SIDE, SIDE, SIDE or
SSS

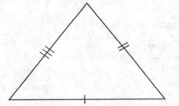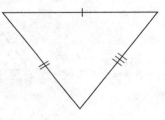

(ii) Two sides and the angle between them (the included angle) are the same in both triangles.

This is sometimes
referred to as the
included angle rule.
The pattern this time is
SIDE, ANGLE, SIDE
or **SAS**

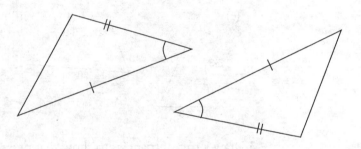

(iii) Two angles and a matching side are the same in both triangles.

The pattern this time
is ANGLE, ANGLE,
SIDE or **AAS**

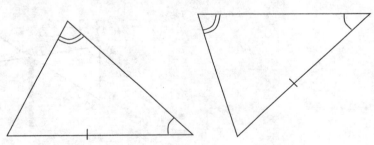

Hint: You can think of matching sides as being opposite the same sized angle.

(iv) The triangles are right-angled triangles with the same length hypotenuse and one other side the same length.

This pattern is
RIGHT ANGLE,
HYPOTENUSE,
SIDE or **RHS**

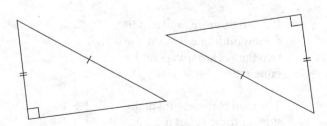

?

2 Which of the following pairs of triangles are congruent? (They are not drawn accurately.) Explain in each case why you have or have not decided a pair are congruent

(a)

(b)

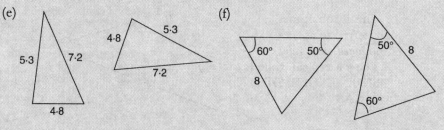

(c)

(d)

(e)

(f)

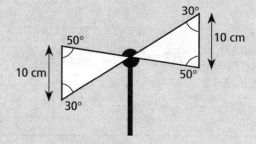

3 Draw a pair of triangles to show that two sides and an angle being equal does not prove congruence if the angle is not the included angle.

4 Jonathan has a windmill which he says is made of two congruent triangles.

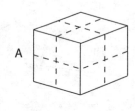

His brother says the triangles are not congruent. Who is correct and why?

4.9c   Areas and volumes of similar figures

If two figures are similar then corresponding edges on the two figures are always in the same ratio.

The ratio of the lengths of the sides of these cubes is 2 : 3.

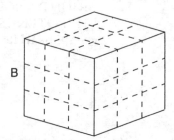

Ratio of areas

The area of a face on cube A is $2 \times 2 = 4$ square units.
The area of a face on cube B is $3 \times 3 = 9$ square units.
So the areas of the faces are in the ratio 4 : 9.
A cube has 6 faces so the surface area of A is $6 \times 4 = 24$ cm² and the surface area of B is $9 \times 4 = 54$ cm². The ratio of the surface areas is 24 : 54.
This can be simplified by dividing both numbers by 6 to give a ratio for the total surface areas of 4 : 9.

If you compare this result with the ratio of the lengths you should notice that the ratio of the **surface areas** of these two similar solids is the ratio of the **square** of the lengths of their sides.

If the ratio of the lengths is $A : B$
then the ratio of the areas is $A^2 : B^2$

Remember: Area is measured in **square** units. The ratio of the areas is the ratio of the **squares** of the lengths.

E.g. Triangles A and B are similar (they have the same angles). If the area of triangle A is 1·8 cm² what is the area of triangle B?

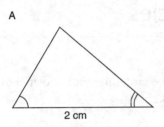
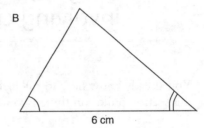

The ratio of the sides of the triangles is 2 : 6 which simplifies to 1 : 3.
The ratio of their areas will be $1^2 : 3^2 = 1 : 9$.
The area of A = 1·8 cm² therefore the area of B = $9 \times 1·8 = 16·2$ cm².

1 The surface area of cone C is 600 m². What is the surface area of cone D?

Ratio of volumes

Now consider the volume of the cubes A and B.
Volume of A = $2 \times 2 \times 2 = 2^3 = 8$ cubed units
Volume of B = $3 \times 3 \times 3 = 3^3 = 27$ cubed units
The ratio of the volumes is $2^3 : 3^3$ or 8 : 27.

If the ratio of the lengths is $A : B$
then the ratio of the volumes is $A^3 : B^3$

Remember: Volume is measured in **cubed** units. The ratio of the volumes is the ratio of the **cubes** of the lengths.

2 The radius of a small moon is 100 km. The moon orbits a planet with a radius of 5000 km.
(a) Calculate the ratio of the radius of the moon to the radius of the planet.
(b) Calculate the ratio of their surface areas.

Hint: You do not need to calculate the surface areas.

(c) Calculate the ratio of their volumes.

3 In a museum there is an exact replica of a steam locomotive. The model is 240 cm long and the real locomotive is 24 m long.
(a) Calculate the scale of the model in the form 1 : *k*.
(b) If it took 2 litres of paint to paint the model, how much paint would be needed to paint the real locomotive? (Ignore the thickness of the paint.)
(c) The real locomotive has a tank which holds 15 000 litres of water. How much water does the model tank hold?

4.9d Lengths, areas and volumes in shapes involving circles

You already know how to calculate the circumference and area of a circle. The work in this section builds on these two ideas.

Arcs

An **arc** is part of the circumference of a circle. If the circumference is cut in two then the arc which makes the larger angle at the centre is called the *major arc* and the arc which makes an angle of less than 180° at the centre is called the *minor arc*. If the circumference is cut exactly in half then two semicircular arcs are formed.

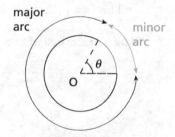

The length of the arc depends on the radius of the circle and the size of the angle turned through at the centre of the circle. If the angle turned through to produce the arc is θ and the diameter = *d*, radius = *r*, then

$$\text{Arc length} = \frac{\theta}{360} \times \pi d \qquad \text{or} \qquad \frac{\theta}{360} \times 2\pi r$$

E.g. Calculate the length of the minor arc AB given that $\angle$ AOB = 60° and *r* = 4 cm (π = 3·142).

$$\text{Length of arc AB} = \frac{\theta}{360} \times 2\pi r$$

$$= \frac{60}{360} \times 2 \times 3\cdot142 \times 4$$

$$= 4\cdot1893333$$

$$\text{AB} = 4\cdot19 \text{ cm (to 2 d.p.)}$$

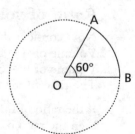

?

1 Work out the length of the minor arc in each of the following circles. (Answer to 2 d.p.)

(a)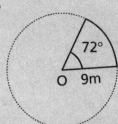

(b)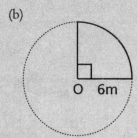

2 A groundsman has to set out a running track at a sports ground. The bends on the track are semicircles. The radius of the inner lane is 30 m.

Each lane is 1 m wide. If there are 8 lanes how long will the outside curve at one end of the track be?

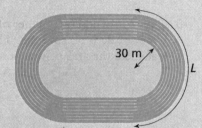

3 Hazel wants to make a witches hat for a fancy dress party using this pattern.

If Hazel's head measures 54 cm around and she has enough black card to draw a circle of radius 30 cm, calculate the angle θ of the piece of card she needs to cut out.

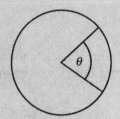

Hint: The arc length has to go round Hazel's head.

Sectors of circles

A **sector** of a circle is an area bounded (edged) by an arc and two radii. You can think of a sector as being the shape of a slice of pizza.

A *minor sector* is bounded by a minor arc and a *major sector* is bounded by a major arc.

In the same way that the length of an arc is a fraction of the circumference of the circle, the area of a sector is a fraction of the area of the circle.

Area of sector = $\dfrac{\theta}{360} \times \pi r^2$

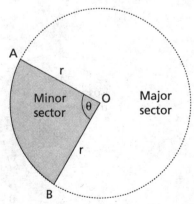

E.g. Calculate the area of the sector AOB where $\angle$ AOB = 90° and r = 10 m (π = 3·142).

Area of AOB = $\dfrac{\theta}{360} \times \pi r^2$

= $\dfrac{90}{360} \times 3\cdot142 \times 10^2$

Area of AOB = 78·55 m²

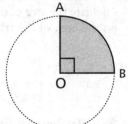

?

4 Calculate the area of the shaded sector AOB in each of the following circles. (Answer to 2 d.p.)

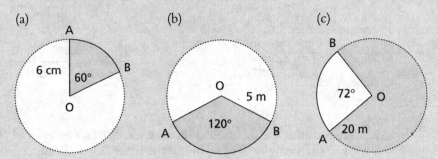

(a)   (b)   (c)

5 The rear windscreen wiper of a car rotates on an arm 45 cm long. The rubber wiper blade is 32 cm long. The wiper arm rotates through an angle of 110°. Calculate the area of windscreen cleared.

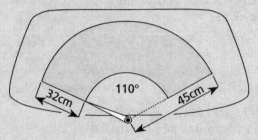

Hint: Calculate the area covered by the whole length of the arm then take away the area not cleared by the wiper blade.

Segments of a circle

A **segment** is an area of a circle bounded by a chord and an arc.

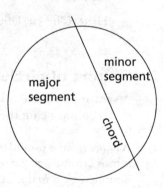

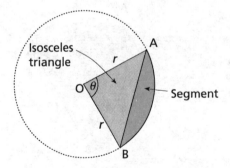

To calculate the area of a *minor segment* you first work out the area of the minor sector and then take away the area of the triangle formed by the chord and the two radii.

To calculate the area of a *major segment* you calculate the area of the major sector and then add on the area of the triangle.

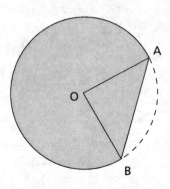

Area of segment = area of sector ± area of triangle

E.g. A gardener wishes to calculate the area of a flower bed which she knows forms a segment AB of a circle with radius 5 m. The angle subtended at the centre of the circle by AB is 130° (π = 3·142).

First find the area of the sector AOB.

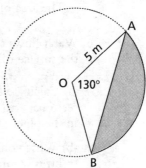

Area of sector $= \dfrac{\theta}{360} \times \pi r^2$

$\qquad\qquad = \dfrac{130}{360} \times 3\!\cdot\!142 \times 25$

$\qquad\qquad = 28\!\cdot\!365278$

Area of sector = 28·365 m² (to 3 d.p.)

Now find the area of the triangle. There are two ways to do this.

Method 1 Drop a perpendicular from O to the point X on AB. Since the triangle is isosceles, this line will cut AB in half at X.

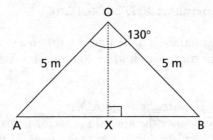

To calculate AX use sine in the triangle AOX with angle $\frac{1}{2}\theta$ and hypotenuse r.

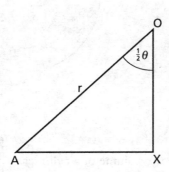

AX $= r \sin \frac{1}{2}\theta$
To calculate OX use cosine in the same triangle.
OX $= r \cos \frac{1}{2}\theta$
$\begin{aligned}
\text{Area of triangle} &= \tfrac{1}{2}\,\text{AB} \times \text{OX}\\
&= \text{AX} \times \text{OX}\\
&= r^2 \sin \tfrac{1}{2}\theta \cos \tfrac{1}{2}\theta\\
&= 5^2 \sin 65° \cos 65°\\
&= 9\!\cdot\!5755555
\end{aligned}$
Area of triangle $= 9\!\cdot\!576$ m² (to 3 d.p.)

Method 2 This method uses the formula $\quad$ Area $= \frac{1}{2}ab \sin C$
$\qquad\qquad\qquad\qquad\qquad\qquad\qquad$ (see unit **4.8b** question 7)

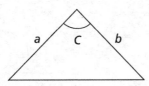

In this case the formula becomes
$\begin{aligned}
\text{Area} &= \tfrac{1}{2}r^2 \sin \theta\\
&= \tfrac{1}{2} \times 5^2 \sin 130°\\
&= 9\!\cdot\!5755555
\end{aligned}$

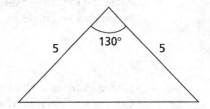

Area of triangle = 9·576 m² (to 3 d.p.)

Area of segment = area of sector − area of triangle
$$= 28{\cdot}365 \text{ m}^2 - 9{\cdot}576 \text{ m}^2$$
$$= 18{\cdot}789 \text{ m}^2$$
The area of the flower bed is 18·8 m² (to 1 d.p.).

?

6 Water flows through a circular pipe of radius 20 cm. A flow indicator floats on the surface of the water. The indicator shows a swing of 50° from the vertical.

(a) Calculate the cross-sectional area of the water in the pipe.

(b) What volume of water in litres would there be in a section of pipe 15 m long?

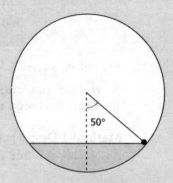

Remember: 1000 cm³ = 1 litre

7 A flat surface is to be milled (cut) on a steel bar with a radius of 25 mm. The width of the flat surface is to be 40 mm. This diagram shows a cross-section of the bar.

(a) Calculate the angle AOB.
(b) Calculate the area of the sector AOB.
(c) Calculate the area of the triangle AOB.
(d) Calculate the area of the segment to be removed from the bar.

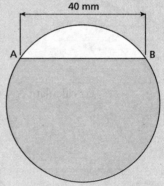

40 mm

A   B

Cylinders

You already know how to calculate the volume of a cylinder.
Volume of a cylinder = $\pi r^2 h$

Now we will look at the surface area of a cylinder. Imagine a hollow cylinder opened out. Each end of the cylinder becomes a circle and the curved surface of the cylinder becomes a rectangle.

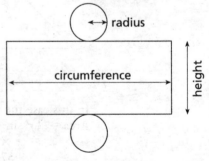

radius

circumference

height

Curved surface area of a cylinder = circumference × height
Curved surface area of a cylinder = $2\pi rh$
Adding on the area of the ends gives:
Total surface area of a cylinder = $2\pi r^2 + 2\pi rh$ or $2\pi r(r + h)$

E.g. Work out the total surface area of a cylinder with a radius of 20 cm and a height of 40 cm ($\pi = 3\cdot142$).

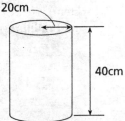

Surface area $= 2\pi r^2 + 2\pi rh = 2\pi r(r + h)$
$\qquad = 2 \times 3\cdot142 \times 20\ (20 + 40)$
$\qquad = 7540\cdot8$
Total surface area of cylinder $= 7540\cdot8$ cm²

8 A steel band uses oil drums with a diameter of 80 cm and a height of 100 cm. The drums are to be painted a new colour for a carnival.
(a) Calculate the curved surface area of each drum to be painted.
(b) If the band decides to paint the bottom ends of the drums as well what surface area of each drum will need to be painted?

Cones

A **cone** is a circular based pyramid.

A cone with its point (apex) above the centre of its base is a *right cone*.

A right cone is usually just called a cone.

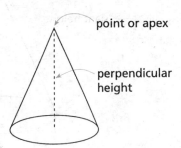

Cones can also be skewed (pushed over).

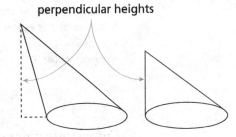

The volume of a cone (or any pyramid) is one third of the area of the base × the perpendicular height.
Volume of a cone $= \frac{1}{3}\pi r^2 h$

E.g. A pile of sand has been tipped in the shape of a cone. The diameter at the base of the pile is 1·8 m and the height is 0·6 m. Calculate the volume of sand to 1 decimal place ($\pi = 3\cdot14$).

Volume of a cone $= \frac{1}{3}\pi r^2 h$
$\qquad\qquad = \frac{1}{3} \times 3\cdot14 \times 0\cdot9^2 \times 0\cdot6$
$\qquad\qquad = 0\cdot50868$
Volume of sand $= 0\cdot5$ m³ (to 1 d.p.)

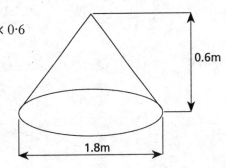

?

9 A drinking glass manufacturer wants to produce a conical wine glass. The height of the glass (excluding the stem) is to be 6 cm and the glass must have a capacity of 150 ml (millilitres). Calculate the radius at the top of the glass.

Note: 1 ml = 1 cm³

If you open out a hollow cone the base is a circle and the curved surface forms a sector of a larger circle.

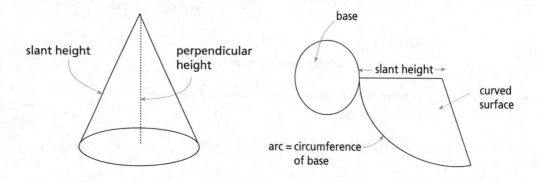

The arc length of this sector is equal to the circumference of the base and the radius of the sector is equal to the slant height l.

$$\text{Area of sector} = \frac{\text{arc length}}{\text{circumference}} \times \text{area of circle}$$

$$= \frac{2\pi r}{2\pi l} \times \pi l^2$$

Curved surface area of a cone = $\pi r l$

Adding on the area of the base gives:
Total surface area of a cone = $\pi r^2 + \pi r l$ or $\pi r(r + l)$

If you know the perpendicular height h then the slant height l is given by Pythagoras' theorem:

$$l = \sqrt{r^2 + h^2}$$

E.g.   Calculate the total surface area of a cone with a slant height of 13 cm and a base with a radius of 5 cm (π = 3·142).

$$\begin{aligned}
\text{Surface area} &= \pi r^2 + \pi r l = \pi\, r(r + l) \\
&= 3{\cdot}142 \times 5\, (5 + 13) \\
&= 282{\cdot}78 \text{ cm}^2
\end{aligned}$$

?

10 An ice cream cone has a radius at the open end of 3 cm and a perpendicular height of 12 cm. Calculate the surface area of the cone.

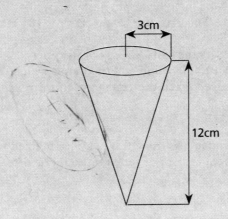

Spheres

Volume of a sphere = $\frac{4}{3}\pi r^3$

Surface area of a sphere = $4\pi r^2$

E.g. Find the volume and surface area of a football with a radius of 10 cm ($\pi = 3{\cdot}142$).

Volume = $\frac{4}{3}\pi r^3$
$= \frac{4}{3} \times 3{\cdot}142 \times 10^3$
$= 4189{\cdot}33$ cm³ (to 2 d.p.)

Surface area = $4\pi r^2$
$= 4 \times 3{\cdot}142 \times 10^2$
$= 1256{\cdot}8$ cm²

A **hemisphere** is half a sphere.

Volume of a hemisphere = $\frac{2}{3}\pi r^3$

Curved surface area of a hemisphere = $2\pi r^2$
Adding on the area of the flat circular face of a hemisphere gives:
Total surface area of a hemisphere = $3\pi r^2$

?

11 In the 1980s Saturn's most distant moon, Phoebe, was photographed by Voyager II. Phoebe has a diameter of 220 km.

(a) Calculate the volume of Phoebe.
(b) Calculate its surface area.

12 Tethys is another of Saturn's moons. It is notable for a huge hemispherical crater, Odysseus. The diameter of the crater is 100 km.

(a) Calculate the surface area of this crater.
(b) Calculate the volume of the moon which was removed when this crater was formed.

13 If the cone in question 10 is completely filled with ice cream and a hemispherical scoop is added on top, calculate the total volume of ice cream.

4.9e   Adding and subtracting vectors

Two vectors can be added or subtracted to produce a third vector, called the **resultant**. On a diagram the resultant vector is marked with a double arrow head.

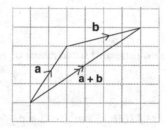

Addition

Adding two vectors means applying one vector and then applying the second. The second vector is drawn beginning at the end of the first. There are two laws governing the addition of vectors. One law says that going from A to B and then from B to C is the same as going directly from A to C. This is called the **triangle law**.

$$\overrightarrow{AB} + \overrightarrow{BC} = \overrightarrow{AC}$$

or

$$\mathbf{a} + \mathbf{b} = \mathbf{c}$$

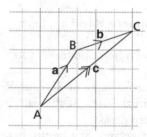

Remember: The second vector begins at the end of the first when you use the triangle law.

The second law says that going from A to C via D is the same as going from A to C via B. This is called the **parallelogram law**.

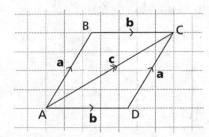

$$\vec{AB} + \vec{BC} = \vec{AC}$$

is the same as

$$\vec{AD} + \vec{DC} = \vec{AC}$$

The parallelogram law shows that the order in which you add vectors doesn't matter.

a + b = c = b + a

Subtraction

Subtracting a vector is the same as adding its inverse.

a – b is the same as **a + (–b)**

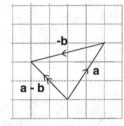

Remember: The inverse of a vector has the same magnitude (length) but goes in the opposite direction.

1 Given **a** and **b** as shown in the diagram, draw the following vectors:

(a) **a + b**
(b) **a – b**
(c) **a – 2b**
(d) **2a + 3b**

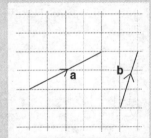

2 A quadrilateral ABCD has diagonals which intersect at E. Write each of the following as a single vector:

(a) $\vec{AB} + \vec{BC}$

(b) $\vec{AE} + \vec{ED}$

(c) $\vec{DC} + \vec{CA}$

(d) $\vec{EC} + \vec{AE}$

(e) $\vec{AE} - \vec{AD}$

(f) $\vec{BE} - \vec{BC}$

(g) $\vec{DA} + \vec{AB} + \vec{BC}$

(h) $\vec{CE} + \vec{BC} + \vec{EB}$

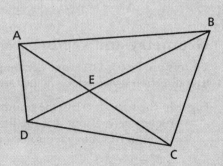

3 Find each of the following in terms of **a** and **b**. QX is $\frac{2}{3}$ QS.

(a) $\overrightarrow{QS}$

(b) $\overrightarrow{XS}$

(c) $\overrightarrow{RS}$

(d) $\overrightarrow{PX}$

(e) $\overrightarrow{XR}$

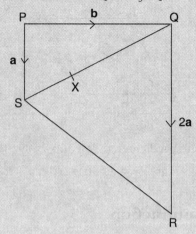

Column vectors

To add or subtract column vectors you simply add or subtract each component.

$$\begin{pmatrix} a \\ b \end{pmatrix} + \begin{pmatrix} c \\ d \end{pmatrix} = \begin{pmatrix} a+c \\ b+d \end{pmatrix}$$

4 Add the following vectors to find their resultants. (Draw the diagrams if it helps.)

(a) $\begin{pmatrix} 4 \\ 2 \end{pmatrix} + \begin{pmatrix} 1 \\ 3 \end{pmatrix}$

(b) $\begin{pmatrix} 3 \\ 1 \end{pmatrix} + \begin{pmatrix} 1 \\ 2 \end{pmatrix}$

(c) $\begin{pmatrix} 4 \\ 1 \end{pmatrix} + \begin{pmatrix} ^-1 \\ 6 \end{pmatrix}$

(d) $\begin{pmatrix} 3 \\ 4 \end{pmatrix} + \begin{pmatrix} 1 \\ ^-2 \end{pmatrix}$

(e) $\begin{pmatrix} 6 \\ 1 \end{pmatrix} + \begin{pmatrix} ^-2 \\ 2 \end{pmatrix}$

(f) $\begin{pmatrix} 3 \\ 2 \end{pmatrix} + \begin{pmatrix} 1 \\ 4 \end{pmatrix} + \begin{pmatrix} ^-2 \\ 2 \end{pmatrix}$

5 Find the resultants of the following. (Draw the diagrams if it helps.)

(a) $\begin{pmatrix} 2 \\ 3 \end{pmatrix} - \begin{pmatrix} 3 \\ 2 \end{pmatrix}$

(b) $\begin{pmatrix} 4 \\ 1 \end{pmatrix} - \begin{pmatrix} 3 \\ 2 \end{pmatrix}$

(c) $\begin{pmatrix} 3 \\ ^-4 \end{pmatrix} - \begin{pmatrix} 5 \\ 1 \end{pmatrix}$

(d) $\begin{pmatrix} 3 \\ 4 \end{pmatrix} - \begin{pmatrix} ^-2 \\ 1 \end{pmatrix}$

(e) $\begin{pmatrix} 2 \\ 2 \end{pmatrix} - \begin{pmatrix} 3 \\ ^-1 \end{pmatrix}$

(f) $\begin{pmatrix} 3 \\ 5 \end{pmatrix} - \begin{pmatrix} ^-2 \\ ^-3 \end{pmatrix}$

6 Given $\mathbf{r} = \begin{pmatrix} 4 \\ 1 \end{pmatrix}$ and $\mathbf{s} = \begin{pmatrix} ^-2 \\ 3 \end{pmatrix}$ write down the following vectors:

(a) $\mathbf{r} + \mathbf{s}$ (b) $\mathbf{r} - \mathbf{s}$ (c) $^-2\mathbf{s}$ (d) $2\mathbf{r} + 3\mathbf{s}$

Geometry and vectors

Vectors can be used to prove certain properties and results in geometry. Because vectors have direction as well as length, they are particularly useful for showing that lines are parallel.

E.g. In the triangle ABC the points X and Y are the mid-points of AB and AC respectively. Show that the line XY is parallel to BC and half its length.

In terms of vectors, you need to show that

$\overrightarrow{BC} = 2\,\overrightarrow{XY}$.

Then XY and BC must be parallel and

$|\overrightarrow{BC}| = |2\,\overrightarrow{XY}| = 2|\overrightarrow{XY}|$ so XY = $\frac{1}{2}$ BC.

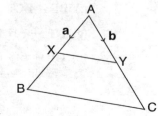

Let $\overrightarrow{AX} = \mathbf{a}$ and $\overrightarrow{AY} = \mathbf{b}$

$\overrightarrow{XY} = {}^-\mathbf{a} + \mathbf{b} = \mathbf{b} - \mathbf{a}$

$\overrightarrow{AX} = \frac{1}{2}\overrightarrow{AB}$ so $\overrightarrow{AB} = 2\mathbf{a}$

$\overrightarrow{AY} = \frac{1}{2}\overrightarrow{AC}$ so $\overrightarrow{AC} = 2\mathbf{b}$

$\overrightarrow{BC} = \overrightarrow{BA} + \overrightarrow{AC}$
$\qquad = {}^-2\mathbf{a} + 2\mathbf{b}$
$\qquad = 2\mathbf{b} - 2\mathbf{a}$
$\qquad = 2(\mathbf{b} - \mathbf{a})$

$\overrightarrow{BC} = 2\overrightarrow{XY}$

E.g. PQRS is a trapezium with $\overrightarrow{QP} = 2\mathbf{a}$, $\overrightarrow{RS} = \mathbf{a}$ and $\overrightarrow{QR} = \mathbf{b}$. If $\overrightarrow{XS} = \frac{1}{2}\mathbf{b}$ show that X is the mid-point of PR.

Express $\overrightarrow{PX}$ and $\overrightarrow{XR}$ in terms of $\mathbf{a}$ and $\mathbf{b}$.

By the triangle law,

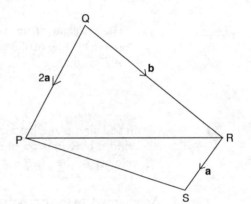

$\overrightarrow{PX} = \overrightarrow{PS} + \overrightarrow{SX}$

$\qquad = \overrightarrow{PQ} + \overrightarrow{QR} + \overrightarrow{RS} + \overrightarrow{SX}$
$\qquad = {}^-2\mathbf{a} + \mathbf{b} + \mathbf{a} - \frac{1}{2}\mathbf{b}$
$\qquad = \frac{1}{2}\mathbf{b} - \mathbf{a}$

$\overrightarrow{XR} = \overrightarrow{XS} + \overrightarrow{SR}$
$\qquad = \frac{1}{2}\mathbf{b} - \mathbf{a}$

Therefore $\overrightarrow{PX} = \overrightarrow{XR}$

$\overrightarrow{PR} = \overrightarrow{PX} + \overrightarrow{XR}$
$\qquad = 2\overrightarrow{PX}$

$\overrightarrow{PX}$ is in the same direction as $\overrightarrow{PR}$ so X must be on the line PR.

$|2\overrightarrow{PX}| = |\overrightarrow{PR}|$

$|\overrightarrow{PX}| = \frac{1}{2}|\overrightarrow{PR}|$

Therefore X is the mid-point of PR.

?

7 ABCD is a quadrilateral. The mid-points of AB, BC, CD and AD are W, X, Y and Z respectively. Show that the quadrilateral WXYZ is a parallelogram.

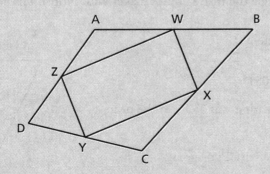

Hint: Show $\overrightarrow{WX} = \overrightarrow{ZY}$ and $\overrightarrow{XY} = \overrightarrow{WZ}$.

Solving problems with vectors

You can use vector addition and subtraction to solve problems involving vector quantities such as force and velocity. In doing this type of problem it is very important to draw a good diagram, taking special care over the direction of the vectors and labelling the resultant clearly.

One way to solve this type of problem is **by drawing** an accurate scale drawing and measuring the length and angle of the resultant.

E.g. The velocity of a plane in still air is 800 km/h (called the airspeed) on a bearing of 060°.

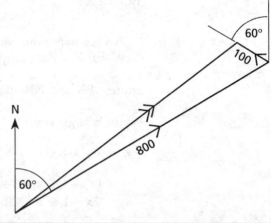

If the wind is blowing at 100 km/h from a bearing of 300° find the actual speed (called the ground-speed) and direction of the plane.

The actual velocity of the plane is the sum of its velocity in still air and the wind velocity.

The resultant of the two vectors gives a bearing of 053° and a speed of 750 km/h.

8 In still air a plane has air speed 300 km/h and flies on a bearing of 110°. If the wind is blowing at a speed of 100 km/h from a bearing of 060°, find the actual velocity of the plane.

Another way to solve problems involving vectors is **using trigonometry**, including the trigonometrical ratios and Pythagoras' theorem. This is easiest when the vectors are at right angles to each other.

E.g. A man rows from his house on the edge of a lake to an island 1 km due North in the middle of the lake. It takes him 30 minutes. When he reaches the island the man learns that the current is flowing due East with a speed of 1 km/h. What direction did the man have to row in to reach the island? How fast did he row?

To find the velocity of the man's course you have to subtract the velocity of the current from his actual velocity. The man took 30 minutes to travel 1 km so his actual speed was 2 km/h and his actual direction was North. The velocity of the current was 1 km/h East.

Let θ be the angle the man's course makes with North. His bearing will be $360° - \theta$.

$$\tan \theta = \frac{\text{opposite}}{\text{adjacent}} = \frac{1}{2}$$

$$\theta = 26 \cdot 565051°$$

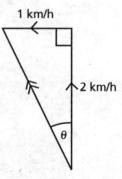

So the man's bearing was 333° (to the nearest degree).

To find his speed use Pythagoras:
$x^2 = 1^2 + 2^2 = 5$
$x = 2 \cdot 236068$

The man rowed at a speed of 2·24 km/h (to 2 d.p.).

9 A boat whose speed is 8 knots sets course on a bearing of 060°. If the tide is running at a speed of 3 knots from a bearing of 330°
(a) find the boat's actual speed to 1 d.p.
(b) find the direction of travel to the nearest degree.

Hint: The tide is perpendicular to the boat's direction.

If the two vectors and their resultant do not form a right-angled triangle you can use **components** to solve the problem. (At **level 10** you can use the sine and cosine rules.)

E.g. Paul and Susan are fighting over a ball. Paul is taller than Susan. He exerts a force of 70 N in a direction 30° above the horizontal. Susan exerts a force of 100 N in a direction 10° below the horizontal. Find the resultant force on the ball. Give your answer to the nearest whole units.

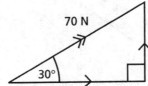

Let the force applied by Paul = **P** and the force applied by Susan = **S**.

Each force has a horizontal component and a vertical component. For example, for Paul :

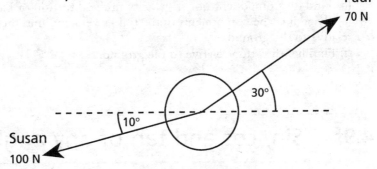

Imagine that 'up' is positive and 'towards Paul' is positive.

Horizontal component of **P** = 70 cos 30°
Vertical component of **P** = 70 sin 30°
Horizontal component of **S** = ⁻100 cos 10°
Vertical component of **S** = ⁻100 sin 10°

As you did with column vectors earlier in this unit, you can add the components of **P** and **S** to get the components of the resultant, **P** + **S**.

Horizontal component of **P** + **S** = 70 cos 30° + ⁻100 cos 10°
$\qquad\qquad$ = ⁻37·86 (to 2 d.p.)
Vertical component of **P** + **S** = 70 sin 30° + ⁻100 sin 10°
$\qquad\qquad$ = 17·64 (to 2 d.p.)

Use Pythagoras' theorem to find the magnitude of **P** + **S**:
$|P+S|^2 = (⁻37·86)^2 + (17·64)^2$
$|P+S| = 41·77$ (to 2 d.p.)

Use tan to find its direction:
$$\tan\theta = \frac{17\cdot64}{37\cdot86}$$
$\theta = 24·98°$ (to 2 d.p.)

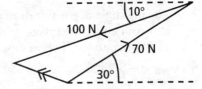

So the resultant is a force of 42 N in a direction 25° above the vertical towards Susan.

10 Jack and Jim are trying to move a piano. Jack can only push the piano forwards
and Jim can only push it sideways. Jack pushes three times as hard as Jim.
(a) Find the angle the direction of the piano makes with the forward direction.
(Give your answer to 2 d.p.)
(b) If Jim exerts a force of 40 N find the magnitude of the resultant force on the
piano. (Give your answer to 2 d.p.)

11 A train travels at 125 mph on a bearing of 030°. A child on the train runs across a
carriage at 5 mph. Her direction makes an angle of 45° clockwise with the
forward direction of the train.
(a) Find the component of the child's velocity in the direction of the train.
(b) What is her total speed in this direction relative to the ground?
(c) Find the component of the child's velocity in the direction of North.
(d) Find the component of her velocity in the direction of East.
(e) By adding the components of the train's velocity, find the child's speed
relative to the ground.
(f) Find her direction relative to the ground.

4.9f   Sin, cos and tan of any angle

You know that in a right-angled triangle sin, cos and tan are defined like this:

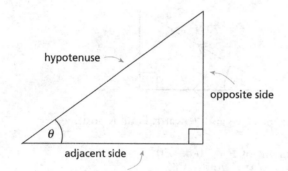

$$\sin \theta = \frac{\text{opposite}}{\text{hypotenuse}}$$

$$\cos \theta = \frac{\text{adjacent}}{\text{hypotenuse}}$$

$$\tan \theta = \frac{\text{opposite}}{\text{adjacent}}$$

But as you can see if you try to use your calculator, sin, cos and tan exist for all angles.

1 Write down the sin, cos and tan of the following angles to 3 d.p.
(a) 30°   (b) 144°   (c) 210°   (d) 300°
(e) ⁻40°   (f) 405°   (g) ⁻110°   (h) 520°

Note: Be careful not to omit negative signs.

To define sin, cos and tan for angles of any size you can use coordinates.

The point P with coordinates (x, y) moves on
a circle with centre O and radius 1 unit.

OP makes an angle θ with the positive x-axis.
The angle *increases* as P rotates *anticlockwise*.

For any angle θ, positive or negative, the sine
and cosine of θ are given by the coordinates
of P (because the 'hypotenuse' = 1).

$\sin \theta = y$

$\cos \theta = x$

$\tan \theta = \dfrac{\sin \theta}{\cos \theta} = \dfrac{y}{x}$

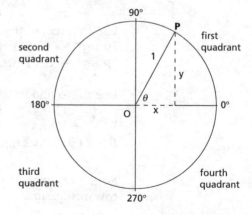

As OP rotates, the coordinates of P change sign.

In the first quadrant (from 0° to 90°) x and y are both positive.
In the second quadrant (90° to 180°) x becomes negative.
In the third quadrant (180° to 270°) y also becomes negative.
In the fourth quadrant (270° to 360°) x becomes positive again.

This means sin, cos and tan also change sign depending on which quadrant the angle is in. The following diagram shows which of the trig ratios are positive in each quadrant.

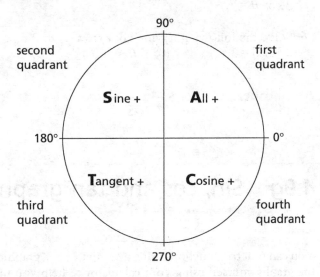

Remember: **C A S T**

After 360° angles continue to follow this same pattern with the point P continuing to rotate around the circle. Negative angles follow the same pattern with P rotating *clockwise* around the circle.

Repeating ratios

Look back at question 1. You may have noticed that apart from the + and − signs the answers to part (a) are the same as the answers to part (c). This is because as P rotates about O the coordinates keep on repeating the same values, with the sign being + or − depending on the quadrant. If you take an angle in the first quadrant you can find an angle in the second quadrant with the same sin, the same cos (but negative) and the same tan (but negative).

$\sin \theta = y$, $\cos \theta = x$, $\tan \theta = \dfrac{y}{x}$

$\sin (180° − \theta) = y$, $\cos (180° − \theta) = {}^-x$,

$\tan (180° − \theta) = \dfrac{{}^-y}{x}$

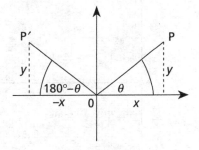

You can repeat this for any quadrant.

$\sin \theta = \sin (180° − \theta) = {}^-\sin (180° + \theta) = {}^-\sin (360° − \theta) = \sin (360° + \theta)$

$\cos \theta = {}^-\cos (180° − \theta) = {}^-\cos (180° + \theta) = \cos (360° − \theta) = \cos (360° + \theta)$

$\tan \theta = {}^-\tan (180° − \theta) = \tan (180° + \theta) = {}^-\tan (360° − \theta) = \tan (360° + \theta)$

2 (a) Write down an angle between 0° and 360° with the same sin as 52°.
   (b) Write down all the angles between 0° and 720° with the same cos as 75°.
   (c) Write down all the angles between ⁻360° and 360° with the same tan as 80°.

3 Write each of the following as the sin, cos or tan of an acute angle:
   (a) sin 528°   (b) cos 1079°   (c) tan ⁻413°

4 Find all the angles between 0° and 720° which satisfy the following equation:
   sin θ = 0·5

5 Find all the solutions between ⁻360° and 360° of the following equation:
   2 cos θ = √3

6 Solve the following, giving your answers to 2 d.p.
   8 tan θ − 3 = 0   (0° ≤ θ ≤ 360°)

Remember: Sin, cos and tan of θ repeat for 180° ± θ and 360° ± θ, with the + and − signs given by 'C A S T.

4.9g   Sin, cos and tan graphs

You can plot trig functions using a computer or a graphical calculator. You can also draw the graphs yourself using your calculator to help you make a table of values.

1 (a) Use your calculator to make a table of the values of sin x correct to 2 d.p. for values of x from 0° to 180° in steps of 10°.
   Use what you know from unit **4.9f** to extend your table for values of x from 180° to 360°.
   (b) Copy these axes and use the results in your table to plot the graph of y = sin x for 0° ≤ x ≤ 360°. (The first four points have been plotted for you.)

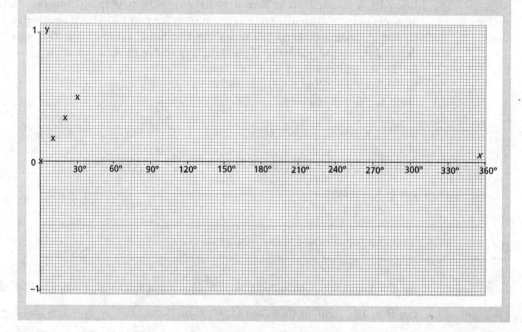

This very important graph is called a **sine curve** or sine wave. It is used to model many natural phenomena, including sound and light waves, heart beats and other types of regular motion. Because the sine function repeats every 360° the graph of y = sin x keeps on repeating the same pattern. The graph is described as **periodic** with period (wave length) 360°.

2 Repeat the method used in question 1 to draw the graph of $y = \cos x$ for $0° \leq x \leq 360°$. Use the same scale on the axes.

You should find that the graph of **cosine** is the same shape as the sine curve except that it has been translated (moved) 90° to the left. It is sometimes described as 90° *behind* the sine curve. The graph of cosine also repeats every 360°.

Note: Sine and cosine are always between 1 and ⁻1.

The graph of the **tangent** is a completely different shape to the graphs of the other two trig functions. The values of tan are not limited to lying between 1 and ⁻1.

3 Using your calculator and intervals of 10° try making a table of values of tan x for $0° \leq x \leq 180°$. Be careful not to omit the − signs.

Your calculator cannot give you a value for tan 90°. Explore what happens to tan x for values of x very close to 90°.

4 Using your table of values and the relationship $\tan \theta = \tan (180° + \theta)$ plot the graph of $y = \tan x$ for $0° \leq x \leq 360°$. Use the same horizontal axis as for the graphs of sine and cosine but you will need to alter the vertical axis.

You can see from the graph that although the curve of tan x gets very close to the lines $x = 90°$ and $x = 270°$ it never touches them. It gets very close from one side and then it jumps to negative values very close to the line but on the other side. These are described as *points of discontinuity*. The tangent of the angle cannot be calculated at these points. We say it tends to infinity.

Amplitude of sin and cos functions

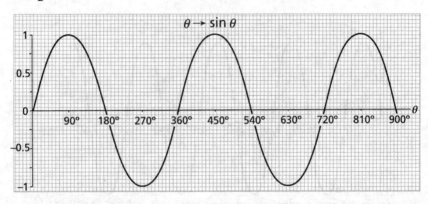

You have seen that the graph of sin θ oscillates between 1 and ⁻1. So the **amplitude** of the sine curve is 1.

The amplitude can be altered by multiplying sin θ by a number bigger than 1. This is the graph of 4 sin θ.

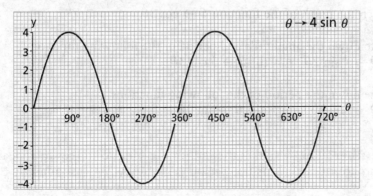

The amplitude of the wave has changed from 1 to 4 but the wave length is still 360°. It looks like the wave has been stretched vertically.

5 (a) What is the amplitude of this sine wave?
   (b) Write down the function in the form $\theta \rightarrow$

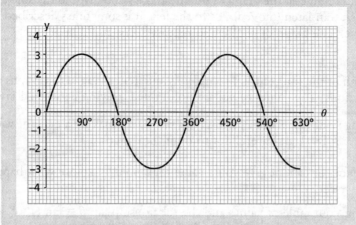

Remember: The amplitude tells you the maximum and minimum values. The amplitude is given by the multiplier of sin or cos.

Period of sin, cos and tan functions

The functions $\sin \theta$ and $\cos \theta$ have **period** (wave length) 360°. The period can be altered by replacing θ with a multiple of θ to give functions such as $\sin 2\theta$ or $\cos 7\theta$. This is the graph of $\sin 2\theta$.

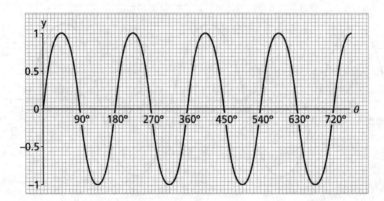

The period of the curve (the wave length) has changed from 360° to 180° because $\sin 2\theta$ repeats twice in 360°. It looks like the wave has been telescoped along the horizontal axis.

6 Sketch the graph of the function $\theta \rightarrow \cos 3\theta$.

7 Write down the amplitude and period of the following functions:
   (a) $\theta \rightarrow 4 \sin 2\theta$ (b) $\theta \rightarrow 5 \cos 3\theta$

8 Write down the period of the following functions:
   (a) $\theta \rightarrow \tan \theta$ (b) $\theta \rightarrow \tan 2\theta$

Remember: The period is the length the function takes to repeat itself. For sine and cosine functions the period is given by 360° divided by the multiplier of θ.

Solving equations

You can use graphs to solve equations involving trigonometrical functions.

E.g. Draw the graphs of $y = 6 \cos x$ and $y = 4$. Use these graphs to solve the equation $3 \cos x = 2$ for $0° \leq x \leq 360°$.

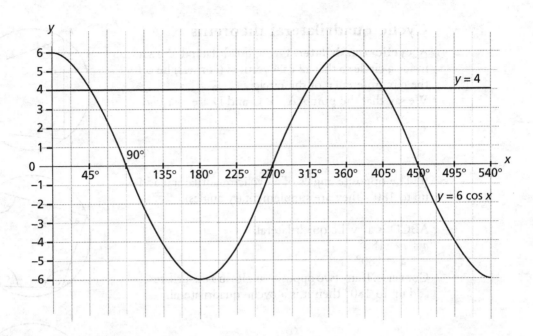

Where the graphs intersect, $6 \cos x = 4$. Dividing by 2 gives the equation you have been asked to solve. Therefore the points of intersection of the graphs will give you the solutions to the equation.
From the graph, the solutions are approximately 48° and 312°. (You can check these on your calculator.)

?

9 Draw the graphs of $y = 8 \sin x$ and $y = 2$. Use these graphs to solve the equation $\sin x = 0.25$ for $0° \leq x \leq 360°$.

4.9h Sin, cos and tan on a calculator or computer

To generate trigonometrical functions on a calculator it has to be able to plot graphs. There are various graphical calculators on the market which can do this but these calculators are usually programmable so they cannot be used in exams.

There are a number of software packages which can help you draw trigonometrical graphs on computer. Your school may have a copy of Omnigraph or a similar package. You can also write a simple programme in BASIC to draw trigonometrical curves.

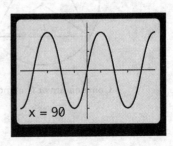

4.10a Circle theorems

Cyclic quadrilateral theorems

A **cyclic quadrilateral** is a quadrilateral drawn inside a circle so that all its 4 vertices (corners) lie on the circumference of the circle.
We say that the points A, B, C and D are *concyclic*.

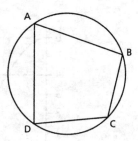

(i) The opposite angles of a cyclic quadrilateral add up to 180° (they are supplementary angles).

ABCD is a cyclic quadrilateral.
$a + c = 180°$
$b + d = 180°$
Converse: If any two opposite angles in a quadrilateral add up to 180° then it is a cyclic quadrilateral.

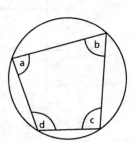

(ii) The exterior angle of a cyclic quadrilateral is equal to the interior angle opposite.

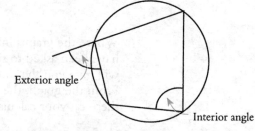

Exterior angle

Interior angle

Angle theorems

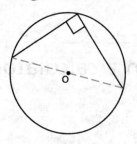

(i) The angle at the circumference subtended by (drawn from) a diameter is always a right angle.
Converse: When you draw a circle through the vertices of a right-angled triangle the hypotenuse forms a diameter of the circle.

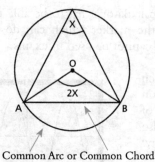

Common Arc or Common Chord

(ii) The angle subtended at the centre of a circle is twice the angle at the circumference subtended by the same chord or arc.

E.g.

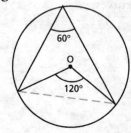
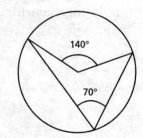

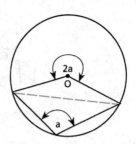

Note: When the angle at the circumference is drawn in the minor segment the angle at the centre becomes a reflex angle.

(iii) Angles at the circumference subtended by the same arc or chord are equal.

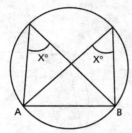

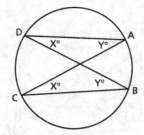

The angles marked *x* are subtended by the chord AB and the angles marked *y* are subtended by CD.

Converse: If two triangles are drawn with a common side and the same angle opposite this side then the vertices of the triangles are concyclic.

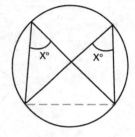

E.g. Find the missing angles in each of the following diagrams. Give reasons for each answer.

(a)

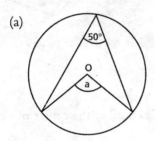

Angle at the centre = twice the angle at the circumference drawn from the same arc.
$a = 2 \times 50° = 100°$

(b)

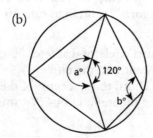

$a = 360° - 120° = 240°$
Angle at the centre = twice the angle at the circumference drawn from the same major arc.
$a = 2b$
$b = \frac{1}{2} \times 240° = 120°$

(c)

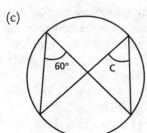

Angles drawn from the same arc are equal.
$c = 60°$

(d)

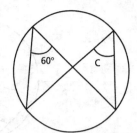

Angles drawn from the same arc are equal.
$d = 45°$
$e = 80°$

?

1 Find the missing angles marked in the following diagrams, giving reasons for your answers.

(a)

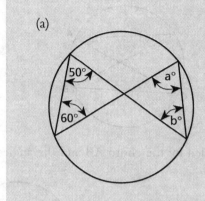

(b)

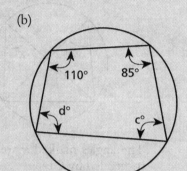

(c)

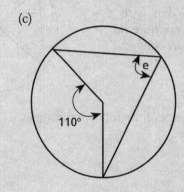

(d)

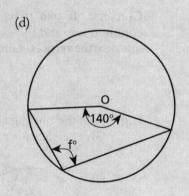

Chord theorems

(i) The line joining the mid-point of a chord to the centre of a circle is perpendicular to the chord.

Converse: A perpendicular line from the centre of a circle to a chord bisects the chord. This theorem is often used with Pythagoras' theorem to calculate the distance of a chord from the centre of the circle.

E.g. A chord 20 cm long is drawn in a circle of diameter 30 cm. Calculate the distance of the chord from the centre of the circle.

The shortest distance from the chord to the centre of the circle is along a line perpendicular to the chord. The theorem tells us that this perpendicular line bisects the chord.

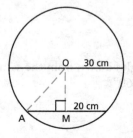

If A is an end-point and M is the mid-point of the chord and O is the centre of the circle then OA is equal to the radius = 15 cm and AM = $\frac{1}{2}$ × 20 cm = 10 cm.
Using Pythagoras, $OA^2 = AM^2 + OM^2$
$15^2 = 10^2 + OM^2$
$225 - 100 = OM^2$
$OM = \sqrt{125}$
$OM = 11·2$ cm (to 1 d.p.)

(ii) If two chords are the same length then they are the same distance from the centre of the circle.

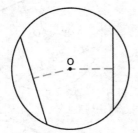

Converse: If two chords are the same distance from the centre of the circle then they are the same length.

Tangent theorems

A **tangent** to a circle is a line which touches the circle at only one point. A tangent is perpendicular to the radius at the point of contact.

(i) The two tangents to a circle from a given point are equal in length.

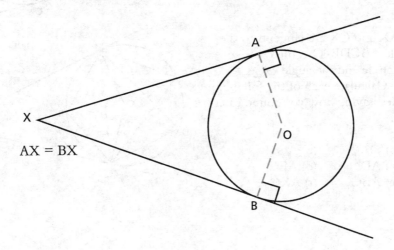

AX = BX

(ii) A line joining the centre of a circle to a point outside the circle:

(a) bisects the angle between the two tangents to the circle from that point.

(b) bisects the angle between the radii drawn perpendicular to the tangents.

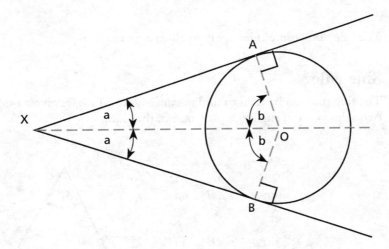

Problems on the circle often involve more than one of the theorems given in this section together with other simple angle theorems. Look for clues in the question to help you decide which theorems to use.

?

2 The radius of this circle is 5 cm. Chord AB is 8 cm long and chord CD is 3 cm from the centre of the circle. Show that the chords AB and CD are the same length.

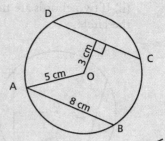

3 AB and BC are tangents to this circle. The angle between them is 50°. Calculate the size of angles x and y.

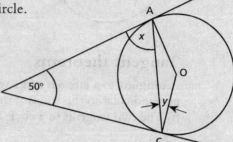

4 AX and CX are tangents to the circle ABCDE. O is the centre of the circle and the angle OCA = 30°. Calculate each of the following angles, saying how you found each one.

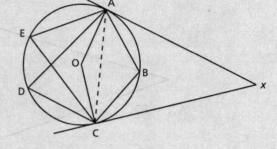

   (a) OAC   (b) AOC
   (c) ADC   (d) AEC
   (e) ABC   (f) AXC

4.10b Sine and cosine rules

The sine and cosine rules apply to all triangles.

Sine rule

The sine rule can be used to find missing sides and angles given a side and two angles or two sides and the angle opposite one of the sides.

$$\frac{a}{\sin A} = \frac{b}{\sin B} = \frac{c}{\sin C}$$

or

$$\frac{\sin A}{a} = \frac{\sin B}{b} = \frac{\sin C}{c}$$

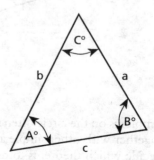

Finding missing sides

Given a side and two angles you can use the sine rule to find the other sides. You may first have to find the third angle using angle sum of a triangle = 180°.

E.g. During a survey of a triangular piece of land the following measurements were taken:

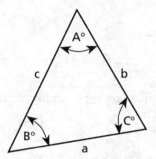

$a = 1000$ m
$B = 85°$
$C = 25°$

Calculate the length of side c.
First you need to find angle A.
$A + B + C = 180°$
therefore $A = 70°$

Using the sine rule, $\dfrac{\sin C}{c} = \dfrac{\sin A}{a}$

Rearranging, $c = \dfrac{a \times \sin C}{\sin A}$

Substituting in values, $c = \dfrac{1000 \sin 25°}{\sin 70°}$

`[1][0][0][0][×][2][5][sin][÷][7][0][sin][=]` `449.74096`

Side $c = 449.7$ m (to 1 d.p.)
(Remember to check: Does an answer of this size make sense?)

 1 Calculate the size of the missing side b.

Remember: Always use the given data rather than your calculated answers in case you have made a mistake!

Finding missing angles

Given two sides and the angle opposite one of these sides you can use the sine rule to find the angle opposite the second side. You can then find the third angle using angle sum of a triangle = 180°.

E.g. In this triangle, calculate the angle C given that $A = 72°$, $a = 6.3$ m and $c = 5.6$ m.

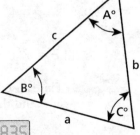

Using the sine rule, $\dfrac{\sin C}{c} = \dfrac{\sin A}{a}$

Rearranging, $\sin C = \dfrac{c \times \sin A}{a}$

Substituting in values, $\sin C = \dfrac{5.6 \sin 72°}{6.3}$

`[5][.][6][×][7][2][sin][÷][6][.][3][=]` `0.8453835`

Angle $C = 57.7°$ (to 1 d.p.)

 2 Find the third angle of this triangle.

3 Calculate the missing sides and angles in the following triangle.

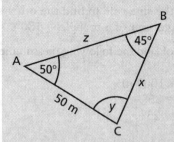

4 Two radar stations A and B pick up the same approaching aircraft at X. The distance between the stations is 143 km.
From A: The bearing of station B is 045°.
The bearing of the aircraft X is 322°.
From B: The bearing of the aircraft X is 312°.

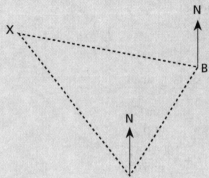

Calculate the distance of the aircraft from A.

Cosine rule

There are two ways to write the cosine rule, depending on whether you're finding a side or an angle.

(i) $\cos A = \dfrac{b^2 + c^2 - a^2}{2bc}$

This is used to find an angle when you know all the sides.

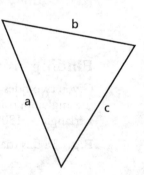

(ii) $a^2 = b^2 + c^2 - 2bc \cos A$

This is used to find a side when you have two sides and the angle between them.

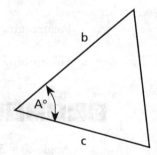

E.g. Find the missing angle A in this triangle.

$$\cos A = \frac{b^2 + c^2 - a^2}{2bc}$$

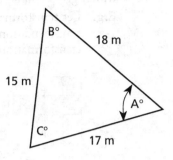

Substituting in values,

$$\cos A = \frac{17^2 + 18^2 - 15^2}{2 \times 18 \times 17}$$

$$= \frac{289 + 324 - 225}{612}$$

$$= \frac{388}{612}$$

$$\boxed{3}\,\boxed{8}\,\boxed{8}\,\boxed{\div}\,\boxed{6}\,\boxed{1}\,\boxed{2}\,\boxed{=}\quad \boxed{0.6339869}$$

$$\boxed{0.6339869}\,\boxed{INV}\,\boxed{cos}\quad \boxed{50.655113}$$

Angle $A = 50.7°$ (to 1 d.p.)

?

5 Calculate angle B and hence find angle C.

Remember: Once you know two angles you can find the third in the easiest way possible.

6 Ayemouth is due North of Beecastle and the bearing from Beecastle to Ceewick is 057°. If Beecastle is 9·7 km from Ayemouth and 11·4 km from Ceewick, how far is Ayemouth from Ceewick?

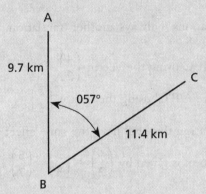

7 A pilot takes off from his home base at A and flies 56 miles south to town B. He flies home via town C, which is east of A and B. The distance from town B to town C is 70 miles and the distance from town C to home is 63 miles.
(a) Calculate his bearing on the flight from B to C.
(b) Calculate the angle of the turn to be made at C.

Remember: A good diagram helps.

The sine and cosine rules can also be used to solve problems in three dimensions by reducing the problem to a triangle in two dimensions.

4.10c Combinations and inverses of transformations

You have already carried out a variety of transformations on 2-dimensional shapes. This unit covers inverses of transformations and what happens when you combine two transformations.

To combine two transformations you perform the first transformation on an object, which gives you an image, and then apply the second transformation to the image.

E.g. Let transformation I be a rotation of 90° anticlockwise about the origin and let transformation II be a reflection in the y-axis. Carry out the combined transformation given by I followed by II on this flag.

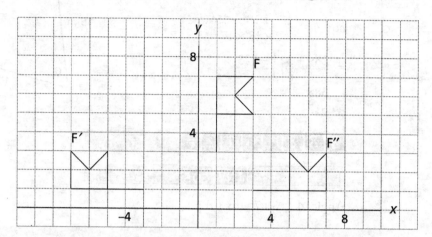

The *order* in which you combine two transformations is important. Sometimes combining two transformations in the opposite order would give the same result but often it gives a completely different result.

?

1 Carry out the transformations in the example above in the opposite order.

Translations

The **combination** of two translations is always another translation.

E.g.
(a) Translate the triangle ABC using the vector $\begin{pmatrix} 4 \\ 2 \end{pmatrix}$.
Label the result A'B'C'.
(b) Now translate the figure A'B'C' using the vector $\begin{pmatrix} 2 \\ 5 \end{pmatrix}$.
Label the result A"B"C".
(c) Give a single transformation that will have the same effect as the two carried out in (a) and (b).
The combined transformation is given by $\begin{pmatrix} 4 \\ 2 \end{pmatrix} + \begin{pmatrix} 2 \\ 5 \end{pmatrix} = \begin{pmatrix} 6 \\ 7 \end{pmatrix}$

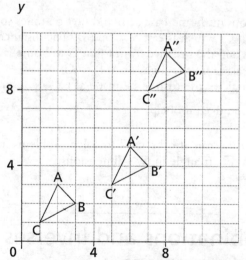

(d) Give a single transformation which will transform A"B"C" back onto ABC.
The work you have done on vectors should tell you that to return to the original position you need a vector of equal magnitude in the opposite direction.
The translation $\begin{pmatrix} -6 \\ -7 \end{pmatrix}$ is the **inverse** of the translation $\begin{pmatrix} 6 \\ 7 \end{pmatrix}$.

2

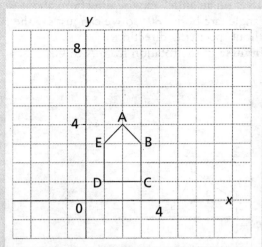

(a) Translate the figure ABCDE using the vector $\begin{pmatrix} ^-4 \\ 2 \end{pmatrix}$.
Label the image A'B'C'D'E'.
(b) Translate A'B'C'D'E' using the vector $\begin{pmatrix} 7 \\ 2 \end{pmatrix}$.
Label the image A"B"C"D"E".
(c) What single transformation has the same effect as the combination of these two transformations?
(d) Give the inverse of this combined transformation.

Rotations

If two rotations with the **same centre** are combined then the result is equivalent to a single rotation about the same centre.

E.g.

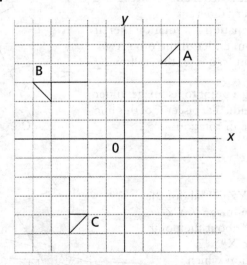

(a) Rotate the flag A $^+90°$ (anticlockwise) about the origin. Label the image B.
(b) Rotate B $^+90°$ about the origin. Label the image C.
(c) What single rotation will transform A onto C?
Since the two rotations performed were both about (0, 0) this will be the centre of rotation for the single equivalent rotation. The angle of rotation is the sum of the two angles turned through: $90° + 90° = 180°$.
(d) What rotation will transform C onto A?
There are two rotations which will take C back onto A.
(i) A rotation in the *opposite* direction to the rotation from A to C but of an equal magnitude about the same centre.
A rotation of $^-180°$ (clockwise) about (0, 0).

(ii) A rotation which *completes* a full circle about the same centre.
A rotation of ⁺180° (in an anticlockwise direction) about (0, 0).
In this case the angles are both 180° so we can just say the rotation is 180°
about (0, 0) without specifying direction.
This gives the **inverse** of the rotation from A to C.

3

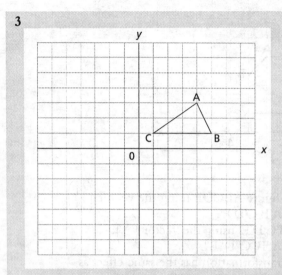

(a) Rotate the triangle ABC ⁻90° (clockwise) about (0, 0).
    Label the image of this rotation A'B'C'.
(b) Rotate A'B'C' 180° about (0, 0).
(c) What single transformation has the same effect as the combination of these
    two rotations?
(d) Give the two alternatives for the inverse of this combined transformation.

When two rotations with **different centres** are
combined the effect is very different.
If the equivalent transformation is a rotation then it
has a different centre from either of the other two.
To find this centre you can use the following
property of rotation:
If you draw a line joining a point to its image under
a rotation then the perpendicular bisector of this line
passes through the centre of rotation.

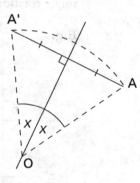

E.g. Rotate triangle XYZ 30° about the
point O. Label the image X'Y'Z'.
Rotate X'Y'Z' 50° about the point
P. Label the image X"Y"Z".
Find a single rotation which
takes XYZ to X"Y"Z".

Draw lines joining X to
X", Y to Y" and Z to Z".
Construct the perpendicular
bisectors of these lines. Where the
perpendicular bisectors meet will give
you the centre of the single equivalent
rotation, marked Q. To find the angle
of rotation measure the angle ZQZ".

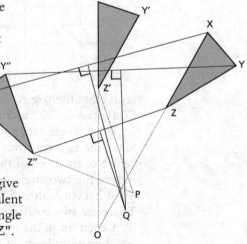

?

4

(a) Rotate the letter J 90° about (0, 0).
(b) Rotate the image of J 180° about the point (⁻3, ⁻2).
(c) Find a single transformation equivalent to the combination of these two rotations.
(d) Give the inverse of this transformation.

5 Draw a triangle with vertices D (5, 8), E (7, 5), F (5, 5). By rotating DEF 90° about (2, 2) and then rotating its image ⁻90° about (⁻1, ⁻3), find a single transformation equivalent to the combination of these two rotations.

Reflections

Reflecting a figure twice in the same line takes it back onto itself so a reflection is always its own **inverse**.
When you **combine** two reflections, the figure you are reflecting ends up back the right way up so the combination is equivalent to a single translation or a single rotation.
The effect of reflecting in two **parallel** lines is a translation.

E.g.

(a) Reflect the letter F in the line x = 3.
Call the image F'.
(b) Reflect F' in the line x = 0 (the y-axis).
Call this image F".
(c) What is the effect of combining these reflections?

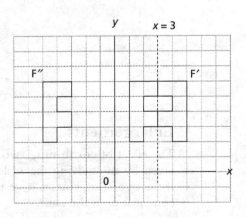

The figure has been translated 6 places to the left.

Describing this translation using a vector gives $\begin{pmatrix} ⁻6 \\ 0 \end{pmatrix}$.

?

6 (a) Reflect the letter N in the x-axis
($y = 0$) and label the image N'.

(b) Reflect N' in the line $y = 2$.
Label this image N".

(c) What single transformation has
the same effect as the combination of
these two parallel reflections?

(d) Give the inverse of this combined
transformation.

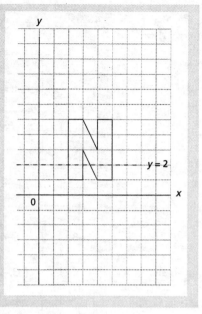

When a figure is reflected in lines which are **not
parallel** (skew) the combination of the reflections
will be equivalent to a single rotation.
The centre of the rotation is the point of
intersection of the two lines and the angle of
rotation is twice the angle between them.

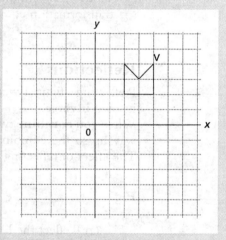

?

7 (a) Reflect the figure V in the line $x = 0$.
Label this reflection V'.

(b) Reflect V' in the line $y = x$.
Label this reflection V".

(c) Find a single rotation which
would take V to V".

(d) Give the inverse of this rotation.

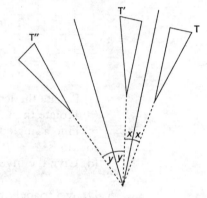

Enlargements

The effect of **combining** two enlargements is a single enlargement with a scale factor
given by multiplying the scale factors of the two individual enlargements together.
If the two enlargements have the **same centre** then the centre of enlargement of the
combination is the same.

E.g. (a) Enlarge the rectangle ABCD by a factor of $\frac{1}{3}$ using the centre of enlargement O.
Label the image of this enlargement A'B'C'D'.
(b) Enlarge A'B'C'D' by a factor of 2 using the same centre of enlargement.
Label the image of this enlargement A"B"C"D".

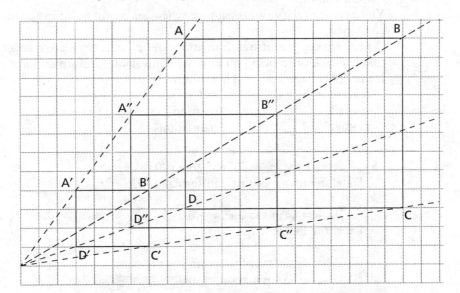

(c) What single transformation is equivalent to the combination of these two enlargements?
The single transformation which takes ABCD onto A"B"C"D" is clearly an enlargement with centre O. The scale factor is given by $\frac{1}{3} \times 2 = \frac{2}{3}$
(d) Give the inverse of the combined transformation.
The **inverse** of an enlargement is another enlargement with the same centre with the inverse (reciprocal) scale factor. In this case, the inverse transformation is an enlargement centre O with scale factor $\frac{3}{2}$.

If two enlargements with **different centres** are combined then you can use what you already know about finding a centre of enlargement to find the centre for the single equivalent enlargement.

?

8 (a) Enlarge the figure ABC by a factor of ¯2 using the origin as centre of enlargement.
Label the image A'B'C'.

Remember: A negative scale factor means the image will be on the other side of the origin.

(b) Enlarge the figure A'B'C' by a factor of ¯2 using (¯3, 0) as centre.

(c) Find a single transformation equivalent to the combination of these enlargements.

(d) Give the inverse of this transformation.

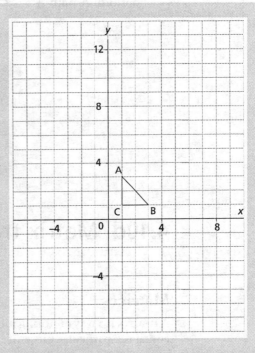

Combinations of congruent transformations

Translations, reflections and rotations are all called **congruent** transformations because the object and image are congruent (the same size and shape).

When you combine two congruent transformations the result must be a congruent transformation.

You have seen above what happens when congruent transformations of the same type are combined.

When two congruent transformations of different types are combined you can use this simple checklist to help you find the equivalent transformation:

Is the final image   Then it must be a

    reversed?   reflection

    rotated?   rotation

    neither?   translation

?

9 (a) Rotate the letter L 180° about (0, 0). Label the image of this transformation L'.

(b) Reflect L' in the line $x = 0$. Label the image L".

(c) What single transformation has the same effect as the combination of these transformations?

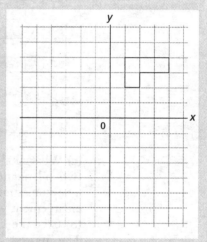

10 (a) Rotate flag A 180° about the origin. Label the image of this transformation A'.

b) Translate A' using the vector $\begin{pmatrix} ^-2 \\ ^-10 \end{pmatrix}$.

Label the image of this transformation A".

(c) Give a single transformation that will transform A onto A".

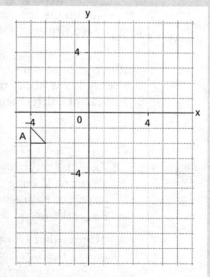

4.10d Matrix transformations

Matrices

A **matrix** is a way of storing information in columns and rows. Each position in the matrix contains a particular piece of information.

A position vector is an example of a matrix.

In the position vector $\overrightarrow{OP}$

$$\begin{pmatrix} x \\ y \end{pmatrix}$$

the number in the top row tells you the horizontal distance from O to P

the number in the bottom row tells you the vertical distance from O to P

A position vector is called a **2 x 1** matrix because it has **2** rows and **1** column. We say it has **order** (size) 2×1. A matrix with the same number of rows and columns is called a **square** matrix.

$$\begin{pmatrix} 1 \\ 2 \\ 3 \\ 4 \end{pmatrix} \quad \begin{pmatrix} 1 & 2 & 7 & 4 \\ 3 & 0 & 1 & 4 \end{pmatrix} \quad \begin{pmatrix} 7 & 1 & 2 \\ 3 & 0 & 1 \\ ^-2 & 4 & ^-5 \end{pmatrix}$$

4×1 2×4 3×3

Matrices are labelled with capital letters and, like vectors, they are printed in bold type but in handwriting they are underlined with a straight or wavy line.

$$\mathbf{M} = \begin{pmatrix} a & b \\ c & d \end{pmatrix} \text{ or } \underline{M} = \begin{pmatrix} a & b \\ c & d \end{pmatrix} \text{ or } \underset{\sim}{M} = \begin{pmatrix} a & b \\ c & d \end{pmatrix}$$

Multiplication

Matrices can be multiplied together provided they have the right number of rows and columns. You can **pre-multiply** a 2×1 matrix (vector) by a 2×2 matrix and the result is another vector. This is written like this:

$$\mathbf{M} \begin{pmatrix} x \\ y \end{pmatrix} = \begin{pmatrix} x' \\ y' \end{pmatrix}$$

First you multiply *along* the **top** row of the matrix and *down* the vector, multiplying the first number in the row by the first number in the column and the second number in the row by the second number in the column and adding the results. The answer goes in the **top** row of the resulting vector.

$$\rightarrow \begin{pmatrix} a & b \\ c & d \end{pmatrix} \begin{pmatrix} x \\ y \end{pmatrix} = \begin{pmatrix} ax + by \\ \end{pmatrix}$$

You then repeat this process for the bottom row.

$$\begin{pmatrix} a & b \\ c & d \end{pmatrix} \begin{pmatrix} x \\ y \end{pmatrix} = \begin{pmatrix} ax + by \\ cx + dy \end{pmatrix}$$

When the second matrix has more than one column you treat each column in turn. Multiply along the nth row and down the mth column to get the answer in the nth row of the mth column

Hint: Imagine the two matrices superimposed. Where the row and column overlap tells you where to put the answer.

You should notice that you can only multiply two matrices if the number of columns in the matrix on the left is the same as the number of rows in the matrix on the right. Matrices can also be multiplied by scalars. Like with vectors, every element of the matrix is multiplied by the scalar.

$$k\mathbf{M} = k \begin{pmatrix} a & b \\ c & d \end{pmatrix} = \begin{pmatrix} ka & kb \\ kc & kd \end{pmatrix}$$

?

1 Multiply the following matrices:

(a) $\begin{pmatrix} 1 & 2 \\ 0 & 1 \end{pmatrix}\begin{pmatrix} 3 & 1 \\ 2 & 0 \end{pmatrix}$　　(b) $\begin{pmatrix} 1 & 0 & 3 \\ 2 & 1 & 5 \end{pmatrix}\begin{pmatrix} 1 & 0 \\ 2 & ^-1 \\ 4 & 1 \end{pmatrix}$　　(c) $7\begin{pmatrix} 1 & 0 \\ 2 & ^-1 \end{pmatrix}$

If you multiply by the matrix $\begin{pmatrix} 1 & 0 \\ 0 & 1 \end{pmatrix}$ you will find that it has no effect.

$\begin{pmatrix} 1 & 0 \\ 0 & 1 \end{pmatrix}\begin{pmatrix} x \\ y \end{pmatrix} = \begin{pmatrix} x \\ y \end{pmatrix}$ for all x and y

The matrix $\begin{pmatrix} 1 & 0 \\ 0 & 1 \end{pmatrix}$ is called the **identity matrix**. It is often written **I**.

(This is true for all matrices with 1's on the leading diagonal and zeros everywhere else.)

Transformations

2×2 matrices can be used to represent 2-dimensional transformations. To apply the transformation represented by **M** to a point P you pre-multiply the position vector $\overrightarrow{OP}$ by **M**.

The point (0, 0) will always remain fixed because

$\begin{pmatrix} a & b \\ c & d \end{pmatrix}\begin{pmatrix} 0 \\ 0 \end{pmatrix} = \begin{pmatrix} 0 \\ 0 \end{pmatrix}$ for all a, b, c and d

This means that if a matrix represents an enlargement or a rotation then (0, 0) must be the centre. And if a matrix represents a transformation with a fixed line (such as a reflection or a stretch) the line must pass through the point (0, 0).

E.g. Transform the rectangle OABC using the matrix $\begin{pmatrix} 1 & 0 \\ 0 & 2 \end{pmatrix}$.

First write down the position vectors of A, B and C.
(The point O will remain fixed.)

$\overrightarrow{OA} = \begin{pmatrix} 0 \\ 2 \end{pmatrix}$　$\overrightarrow{OB} = \begin{pmatrix} 3 \\ 2 \end{pmatrix}$　$\overrightarrow{OC} = \begin{pmatrix} 3 \\ 0 \end{pmatrix}$

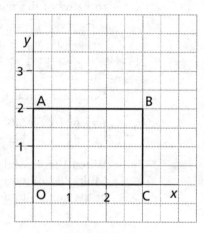

Method 1 Multiply each position vector separately.

To find the position of A':

$\begin{pmatrix} 1 & 0 \\ 0 & 1 \end{pmatrix}\begin{pmatrix} 0 \\ 2 \end{pmatrix} = \begin{pmatrix} 1\times0+0\times2 \\ 0\times0+2\times2 \end{pmatrix} = \begin{pmatrix} 0 \\ 4 \end{pmatrix}$ therefore $\overrightarrow{OA'} = \begin{pmatrix} 0 \\ 4 \end{pmatrix}$

To find the position of B':

$\begin{pmatrix} 1 & 0 \\ 0 & 2 \end{pmatrix}\begin{pmatrix} 3 \\ 2 \end{pmatrix} = \begin{pmatrix} 1\times3+0\times2 \\ 0\times3+2\times2 \end{pmatrix} = \begin{pmatrix} 3 \\ 4 \end{pmatrix}$ so $\overrightarrow{OB'} = \begin{pmatrix} 3 \\ 4 \end{pmatrix}$

To find the position of C':

$\begin{pmatrix} 1 & 0 \\ 0 & 2 \end{pmatrix}\begin{pmatrix} 3 \\ 0 \end{pmatrix} = \begin{pmatrix} 1\times3+0\times0 \\ 0\times3+0\times2 \end{pmatrix} = \begin{pmatrix} 3 \\ 0 \end{pmatrix}$ so $\overrightarrow{OC'} = \begin{pmatrix} 3 \\ 0 \end{pmatrix}$

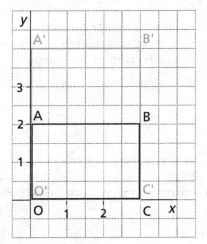

Method 2 Put the position vectors together to form a single matrix with 3 columns.

$$\begin{matrix} A & B & C \end{matrix}$$
$$\begin{pmatrix} 0 & 3 & 3 \\ 2 & 2 & 0 \end{pmatrix}$$

$$\begin{pmatrix} 1 & 0 \\ 0 & 2 \end{pmatrix}\begin{pmatrix} 0 & 3 & 3 \\ 2 & 2 & 0 \end{pmatrix} = \begin{matrix} A' & B' & C' \end{matrix} \\ \begin{pmatrix} 0 & 3 & 3 \\ 4 & 4 & 0 \end{pmatrix}$$ which gives the same results.

This matrix represents a stretch factor 2 parallel to the y-axis.

Note: Use the method you find easier.

Recognising transformations

You need to be able to work out from a matrix what transformation it represents. You can always do this by drawing an object and its image (as in the example above) and looking at the effect. If you are not given an object to transform then use the square with vertices (0, 0), (1, 0), (1, 1) and (0, 1), called the **unit square**.

Given any matrix you already know that (0, 0) is fixed. The matrix also tells you immediately what happens to the points (1, 0) and (0, 1).

$$\begin{pmatrix} a & b \\ c & d \end{pmatrix}\begin{pmatrix} 1 \\ 0 \end{pmatrix} = \begin{pmatrix} a \\ c \end{pmatrix} \text{ and } \begin{pmatrix} a & b \\ c & d \end{pmatrix}\begin{pmatrix} 0 \\ 1 \end{pmatrix} = \begin{pmatrix} b \\ d \end{pmatrix}$$

So the first column of the matrix tells you the image of (1, 0) and the second column tells you the image of (0, 1).

Knowing what happens to these three points may be enough to describe the transformation. To be sure you can also find the image of (1, 1) and then you know how the matrix transforms the unit square.

The simplest transformations are given by matrices with $b = c = 0$ or $a = d = 0$.
If $b = c = 0$ then

$$\begin{pmatrix} a & 0 \\ 0 & d \end{pmatrix}\begin{pmatrix} x \\ y \end{pmatrix} = \begin{pmatrix} ax \\ dy \end{pmatrix}$$

so the effect of the matrix may be to multiply the x and y coordinates by a factor or to change their signs.

Here are the matrices of some common transformations with $b = c = 0$.

(i) You have already seen above what happens when $b = c = 0$ and $a = d = 1$.

$$\begin{pmatrix} 1 & 0 \\ 0 & 1 \end{pmatrix}$$ is the identity matrix.

(ii) $\begin{pmatrix} ^-1 & 0 \\ 0 & 1 \end{pmatrix}$ Here the *a* value has become negative.

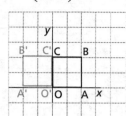

The effect is to change the sign of the *x* coordinates in the position vectors and leave the *y* coordinates unchanged. This is a **reflection** in the *y*-axis.

(iii) $\begin{pmatrix} ^-1 & 0 \\ 0 & ^-1 \end{pmatrix}$ Here both the *a* and *d* values are negative.

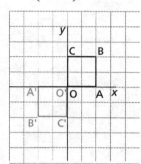

This matrix represents a **rotation** of 180° about (0, 0).

(iv) $\begin{pmatrix} 2 & 0 \\ 0 & 1 \end{pmatrix}$ Here the *a* value has been multiplied by 2.

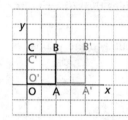

This has the effect of doubling *x* coordinates and leaving *y* coordinates unchanged.
So this matrix represents a **stretch** factor 2 parallel to the *x*-axis.

(v) $\begin{pmatrix} 2 & 0 \\ 0 & 2 \end{pmatrix}$ Here *a* and *d* have been multiplied by the same amount.

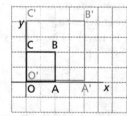

This matrix represents an **enlargement** centre (0, 0) with scale factor 2.

2 Describe the transformation produced by each of the following matrices:

(a) $\begin{pmatrix} 1 & 0 \\ 0 & 3 \end{pmatrix}$ (b) $\begin{pmatrix} 1 & 0 \\ 0 & ^-1 \end{pmatrix}$

If $a = d = 0$ then

$$\begin{pmatrix} 0 & b \\ c & 0 \end{pmatrix}\begin{pmatrix} x \\ y \end{pmatrix} = \begin{pmatrix} by \\ cx \end{pmatrix}$$

so the *x* and *y* coordinates are exchanged. They may also be multiplied by a factor and have their signs changed.

Here are the matrices of some common transformations with $a = d = 0$.

(vi) $\begin{pmatrix} 0 & 1 \\ 1 & 0 \end{pmatrix}$ This matrix exchanges the x and y coordinates.

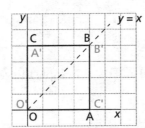

The effect of this is a **reflection** in the line $y = x$.

(vii) $\begin{pmatrix} 0 & ^-1 \\ 1 & 0 \end{pmatrix}$ Here the b value is negative.

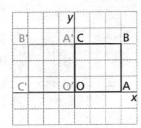

This matrix represents a **rotation** of 90° (anticlockwise) about the origin.

(viii) $\begin{pmatrix} 0 & ^-1 \\ ^-1 & 0 \end{pmatrix}$ Here the b and c values are both negative.

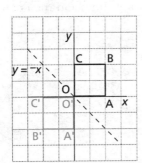

This matrix not only exchanges x and y coordinates but also makes all the resulting values negative. The effect is a **reflection** in the line $y = ^-x$.

3 Describe the transformation produced by each of the following matrices:

(a) $\begin{pmatrix} 0 & 1 \\ ^-1 & 0 \end{pmatrix}$ (b) $\begin{pmatrix} 0 & 3 \\ 1 & 0 \end{pmatrix}$

Combining matrices

You have seen what happens when transformations are combined. To combine matrix transformations you multiply the matrices.

Remember: The order matters.

You always **pre-multiply** so to transform a point (x, y) by the matrix **A** and then by the matrix **B** you would multiply the position vector by **A** and then by **B**.

If $\mathbf{A} = \begin{pmatrix} a & b \\ c & d \end{pmatrix}$ and $\mathbf{B} = \begin{pmatrix} e & f \\ g & h \end{pmatrix}$

$\mathbf{A} \begin{pmatrix} x \\ y \end{pmatrix} = \begin{pmatrix} ax + by \\ cx + dy \end{pmatrix}$

$$\mathbf{BA}\begin{pmatrix} x \\ y \end{pmatrix} = \begin{pmatrix} e & f \\ g & h \end{pmatrix}\begin{pmatrix} ax+by \\ cx+dy \end{pmatrix}$$

$$= \begin{pmatrix} aex+bey+cfx+dfy \\ agx+bgy+chx+dhy \end{pmatrix}$$

$$= \begin{pmatrix} aex+cfx+bey+dfy \\ agx+chx+bgy+dhy \end{pmatrix}$$

Another way to do this is to multiply **A** and **B** and then multiply the vector by the result:

$$\mathbf{BA} = \begin{pmatrix} e & f \\ g & h \end{pmatrix}\begin{pmatrix} a & b \\ c & d \end{pmatrix} = \begin{pmatrix} ae+cf & be+df \\ ag+ch & bg+dh \end{pmatrix}$$

$$\mathbf{BA}\begin{pmatrix} x \\ y \end{pmatrix} = \begin{pmatrix} ae+cf & be+df \\ ag+ch & bg+dh \end{pmatrix}\begin{pmatrix} x \\ y \end{pmatrix}$$

$$= \begin{pmatrix} aex+cfx+bey+dfy \\ agx+chx+bgy+dhy \end{pmatrix} \text{ which gives the same results.}$$

?

4 (a) Illustrate the effect of applying $\begin{pmatrix} 1 & ^-1 \\ 1 & 1 \end{pmatrix}$ followed by $\begin{pmatrix} ^-1 & 0 \\ 0 & 1 \end{pmatrix}$ to the unit square.

(b) Write down the matrix of this combined transformation.

(c) Describe the effect of this matrix.

You may be given a question involving the repeated application of the same matrix.

E.g. What is the effect of applying the matrix transformation $\begin{pmatrix} 0 & ^-2 \\ 1 & 0 \end{pmatrix}$ 4 times?

Method 1 Multiply the matrix by itself 4 times and then consider the transformation given.

Let $\mathbf{M} = \begin{pmatrix} 0 & ^-2 \\ 1 & 0 \end{pmatrix}$

M multiplied by itself n times is written $\mathbf{M}^n$.

$$\mathbf{M}^2 = \begin{pmatrix} 0 & ^-2 \\ 1 & 0 \end{pmatrix}\begin{pmatrix} 0 & ^-2 \\ 1 & 0 \end{pmatrix} = \begin{pmatrix} ^-2 & 0 \\ 0 & ^-2 \end{pmatrix}$$

$$\mathbf{M}^3 = \begin{pmatrix} 0 & ^-2 \\ 1 & 0 \end{pmatrix}\begin{pmatrix} ^-2 & 0 \\ 0 & ^-2 \end{pmatrix} = \begin{pmatrix} 0 & 4 \\ ^-2 & 0 \end{pmatrix}$$

$$\mathbf{M}^4 = \begin{pmatrix} 0 & ^-2 \\ 1 & 0 \end{pmatrix}\begin{pmatrix} 0 & 4 \\ ^-2 & 0 \end{pmatrix} = \begin{pmatrix} 4 & 0 \\ 0 & 4 \end{pmatrix}$$

This is the identity matrix multiplied by 4.

So applying **M** 4 times has the effect of multiplying the x and y coordinates by 4. This gives an enlargement factor 4 centre (0, 0).

Method 2 Apply the matrix four times to the unit square.

(Sometimes it can be clear from applying it once what would be the effect of four successive applications.)

Step 1 $\begin{pmatrix} 0 & ^-2 \\ 1 & 0 \end{pmatrix}\begin{pmatrix} 1 & 0 & 1 \\ 0 & 1 & 1 \end{pmatrix} = \begin{pmatrix} 0 & ^-2 & ^-2 \\ 1 & 0 & 1 \end{pmatrix}$

Step 2 $\begin{pmatrix} 0 & ^-2 \\ 1 & 0 \end{pmatrix}\begin{pmatrix} 0 & ^-2 & ^-2 \\ 1 & 0 & 1 \end{pmatrix} = \begin{pmatrix} ^-2 & 0 & ^-2 \\ 0 & ^-2 & ^-2 \end{pmatrix}$

Step 3 $\begin{pmatrix} 0 & ^-2 \\ 1 & 0 \end{pmatrix} \begin{pmatrix} ^-2 & 0 & ^-2 \\ 0 & ^-2 & ^-2 \end{pmatrix} = \begin{pmatrix} 0 & 4 & 4 \\ ^-2 & 0 & ^-2 \end{pmatrix}$

Step 4 $\begin{pmatrix} 0 & ^-2 \\ 1 & 0 \end{pmatrix} \begin{pmatrix} 0 & 4 & 4 \\ ^-2 & 0 & ^-2 \end{pmatrix} = \begin{pmatrix} 4 & 0 & 4 \\ 0 & 4 & 4 \end{pmatrix}$

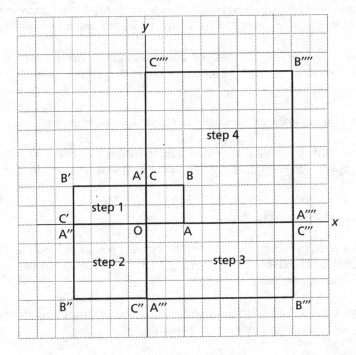

The matrix has the effect of a stretch factor 2 parallel to the y-axis followed by a rotation of 90°.

Applying it four times will rotate the square through a full circle and stretch it by a factor of 2 twice in each direction. So the net effect of four applications is an enlargement scale factor 4 centre (0, 0).

5 Describe and illustrate the effect of applying the matrix transformation $\begin{pmatrix} ^-2 & 0 \\ 0 & 1 \end{pmatrix}$ 4 times to the unit square.

Remember: You can always work out the effect of a matrix by seeing what happens to the unit square.

5.6a   Designing a questionnaire

Before you begin to collect data it is important that you have a clear idea of what data you need and how you intend to use it. Always write this down clearly so that anyone looking at your work can see why you are doing the survey and how it will produce the data you need.

There are many things that you could investigate using a survey: family size, pocket money, school meals, how people get to school, favourite subjects, etc. The list is as long as your imagination.

When you design a questionnaire keep the following points in mind:

1 Your survey should gather all the information you need. Too much will be difficult to interpret, not enough and you may be unable to answer the question.

2 Your questionnaire should not be too long. How long it can be depends on the time and resources available.

3 You need to survey enough people for your results to have any meaning. If you give four choices of answer then you need 20 to 50 responses. Collecting more would help make your figures more accurate.

4 Questions should only have one meaning. People must be clear what a question means and which category their answer goes in.

5 How to answer the question should be clear. Always state whether the question requires a yes/no answer, a tick in a box, ringing with a circle or some other form of response.

6 Always provide answers to choose from. Otherwise every person who answers the questionnaire will say something different and there's no way to collate the results.

7 Offer a reasonable number of choices. Too little choice and the results won't tell you anything new, too much choice and you won't be able to draw any conclusions. Offer at least three alternatives.

E.g.   Here are three suggested questions for a holiday survey. Which is the best question?
1 Where would you like to go on holiday? – Too much choice.
2 Would you prefer to go on holiday or to school? – Too little choice or even no choice at all!
3 Where would you prefer to go on holiday?
(a) Spain   (b) Greece   (c) the USA   (d) in this country
– This question gives 4 choices so it is the most likely to give you useful results.

8 You must cover all possible answers to a question. If you give people boxes to tick then there must always be a box which applies to them.

9 Don't ask people to make a value judgement. Don't ask them if they do something 'rarely' or 'often', or if they are 'small' or 'young'. Always give specific measurements of time, height, age etc.

?

> **1** Using the points listed above, suggest improvements to the following questionnaire for cinema customers.

Name ....

1 How old are you?   Under 11   11–17   18–25   26–35   36–45
2 Are you   Male   Female
3 Are you   Single   Married
4 How many times have you been to the cinema in the last 12 months?
    1–5   6–10   11–20   20 or more
5 What type of films do you prefer?

    Adventure   Comedy   Romance   Horror   Musical   Other

6 Which one of the following would you like to see at the cinema you use most often?
    Cheaper seats   More choice   Better refreshments   No smoking

Before you continue, check the answers to see what is wrong with the questionnaire.

Taking account of bias

The results of a survey can be affected by the **bias** of people responding to the survey. For example, if the questionnaire above were only given to smokers then the answers to question 6 might give a false impression.

You should try to take account of bias when you design your survey. To take account of smokers being biased you could add a question asking people whether they smoke.

E.g.   120 people were surveyed and asked which in their opinion was the best football team in the British Isles. The results are given below.

Liverpool	57
Everton	56
Tranmere	5
Arsenal	1
Manchester Utd.	1

You can easily guess this survey was carried out in Liverpool.
    To take into account the bias of the people replying you could add a question asking people which is their favourite team. (You could help avoid bias by doing the survey in different areas.)

Your conclusions should also take account of bias. For example, the survey above tells you that nearly half the people in Liverpool think that Everton is the best football team in the British Isles. From this survey you cannot conclude that half the people in Britain think Everton is the best team.

?

2 You are doing a survey to find out whether people would prefer the local community centre to be used as a youth club on Friday nights or for an over 60's evening.
    (a) What is the major factor which will affect people's responses?
    (b) How could you take this bias into account?
    (c) Can you think of any other factors which may cause bias?

Using your results

Once you have collected your data it has to be **collated** (put together) so that it can be read more easily. To collate the responses to a particular question you would usually start with a tally chart. Then you could present the results in a frequency table, a bar chart or a pie chart.
    This could help you to draw conclusions like the following:
40% of customers prefer adventure films.
The least important improvement to make is better refreshments.
    If you want to combine the answers to more than one question then you could use a computer database to help you with this work. There are a number of database programmes available.

This could help you to draw conclusions like the following:
Single people go to the cinema more often than married people.
Children under 11 prefer comedy films to romances.

You should display your results clearly in an ordered way to allow you and anyone looking at your results to see immediately what information you've found.

Analysing your work will involve examining your results and stating what conclusions you can make. Be careful not to assume too much. Take into account any factors you can think of which might affect your results.

For example, a survey conducted at 11 o'clock on a Monday morning asking people why they use a local shopping centre wouldn't tell you very much about why people use the centre on a Saturday.

?

> **3** Fifty people were asked the following question:
> Where would you prefer to go on holiday?
> (A) Spain   (B) Greece   (C) the USA   (D) in this country
>
> The responses were: A, B, A, C, C, D, A, C, B, A, C, C, B, A, D, C, B, C, B, A, A, D, C, C, D, C, A, B, A, B, A, D, C, D, A, C, B, A, C, D, B, A, D, C, B, C, B, C, C, D
> (a) Collate this data.
> (b) Write a brief analysis of the results.

5.6b   Scatter graphs and correlation

Analysing data often involves investigating the relationship between two variables.

You might want to answer questions like "If you're good at Maths are you likely to be good at Science too?" or "Are people with longer names generally taller than people with shorter names?"

One method of finding out if there is a relationship between two groups of data is to draw a **scatter graph**.

E.g.   The height and assessment test results in Maths and Science of a class of 25 pupils are given below. Draw a scatter graph of their Maths and Science results.

Name	Scott	Tim	Keith	Ian	Tony	Carl	Paul	Melvin	Kieran	Mark
Height (cm)	143	172	162	135	156	127	173	155	147	163
Maths	60	27	42	56	26	36	20	52	22	43
Science	48	30	45	52	22	40	25	58	26	48

Name	Lynne	Rosie	Jo	Vicky	Sarah	Tanya	Dawn	Jean	Omar	Sally
Height (cm)	153	165	170	139	167	157	149	152	161	163
Maths	32	54	17	57	47	45	38	28	40	30
Science	38	46	24	63	39	45	35	26	42	36

Name	Lisa	Peter	Robert	Abigail	Keely
Height (cm)	153	147	139	145	142
Maths	48	40	17	42	53
Science	23	46	30	43	47

Draw a pair of axes with Maths results on one axis and Science results on the other. Plot the scores of each pupil like a pair of coordinates. For example, Scott's results go on the graph at (60, 48).

The results of the first ten pupils on the list have been marked on this scatter graph.

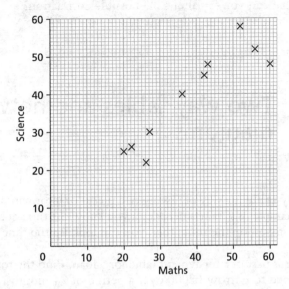

1 Complete the scatter graph by marking on the results of the remaining 15 pupils (from Lynne to Keely).

Correlation

There is a **correlation** between two variables when changes in one variable are linked to changes in the other.

Look at your scatter graph. Although the points are scattered they are mainly in a band going from the origin (0, 0) diagonally across the graph. This indicates that the better a pupil is at Maths the better they are likely to be at Science. So there is a **positive correlation** between Maths results and Science results.

If one variable increases as the other increases then their correlation is described as **positive**.

The graph will look something like this.

An example of this might be the amount of pocket money you receive and the amount you spend.

If one variable increases as the second decreases the correlation is described as **negative**.

The graph will look something like this.

An example of this might be the more study you do now the less you will have to do in the future.

There is not necessarily any relationship between two quantities.

If the points are spread all over the graph so that there appears to be no pattern then we say that there is **no correlation**.

?

2 (a) Draw a scatter graph of the heights of the pupils and their Maths results.
(b) What can you say about the possible correlation?

5.6c Two way tables and network diagrams

A **two way table** is a way of linking two pieces of information to get a result. One of the simplest examples is a train timetable. If you know the time of the train's departure and the name of a station on the route then you can look up the time of arrival at that station.

E.g. This is part of a repayment table for a loan. Find the total you would repay if you needed to borrow £2000 over a period of 24 months.

Amount of loan	LOANS UNDER £2,000 APR 25.9%				LOANS OF £2,000 AND OVER APR 23.4%				
	£100	£500	£900	£1,000	£2,000	£5,000	£10,000	£100★	£500★
12 MONTHS Total to repay £	121.44	607.44	1093.44	1214.88	2403.00	6007.68	12015.60	120.00	600.60
Monthly repayments £	10.12	50.62	91.12	101.24	200.25	500.64	1001.30	10.00	50.05
24 MONTHS Total to repay £	139.68	699.12	1258.56	1398.48	2738.16	6846.00	13692.00	136.80	684.48
Monthly repayments £	5.82	29.13	52.44	58.27	114.09	285.25	570.50	5.70	28.52
36 MONTHS Total to repay £	159.48	799.92	1440.36	1600.20	3103.20	7758.72	15517.44	154.80	775.80
Monthly repayments £	4.43	22.22	40.01	44.45	86.20	215.52	431.04	4.30	21.55
48 MONTHS Total to repay £	181.92	910.56	1638.72	1820.64	3497.28	8743.20	17486.88	174.72	874.08
Monthly repayments £	3.79	18.97	34.14	37.93	72.86	182.15	364.31	3.64	18.21

To do this you find the **column** which represents £2000 and the **row** which shows 24 months. You go down the column and along the row. Your answer is at the point where they meet.

You would have to repay £2738·16.

1 (a) What is the monthly repayment on a loan of £1000 over 12 months?
(b) What is the total amount you would have to repay if you borrowed £10 000 over a period of 3 years?

By putting results from the table together you can work out values of odd amounts. You can also use the table in the reverse way: if you know a result then you can find the information which produced that result.

2 (a) Work out the repayments on a loan of £1500 over 48 months.
(b) If someone is repaying £10·12 per month how much did they borrow?

Networks

This is part of a map of the London Underground.

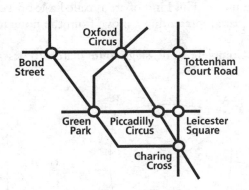

From the diagram you can see that it is possible to travel from Green Park to Charing Cross without passing through another station. You could describe this as a single move. To travel from Charing Cross to Oxford Circus you would have to go through at least one other station so between these two stations there is no possible single move.

The Underground map is not like an ordinary map because it doesn't show the correct positions of the stations and the distances between them are not drawn to scale. It only shows the connections between stations. This 'map' of the Underground is really a **network diagram**.

In a network diagram the term used to describe the points where the lines meet is NODES.

The lines joining the nodes are called ARCS.

The areas inside and outside the lines are called REGIONS

The information given in a network diagram can also be displayed in the form of a table like this.

In this diagram a 1 indicates a single move and a 0 indicates that a single move is not possible.

The squares representing moves from the station to itself have been blanked out because it is impossible to get from any of these stations back to itself without going through another.

	Bs	Oc	Tcr	Gp	Pc	Ls	Cc
Bs		1					
Oc							
Tcr						1	
Gp		0					
Pc							
Ls							
Cc	0			1	1	1	

 3 Complete the table to show the possible moves between stations.

A table of information displayed like this is called a **route matrix**. (If you have more than one matrix they are called matrices.) The matrix above is a **one-stage** route matrix because it deals with single (one-stage) moves.

In each square of the matrix you put the number of ways of getting between the nodes in a single move. When there is no possible single move from one node to another you put a 0 in the square.

Sometimes on a network you can go from a node back to the same node in a single move. This kind of arc is called a **loop route**. For a loop route you put a 1 in the square representing a move from the node to itself.

E.g. Complete a one-stage route matrix to describe this network.

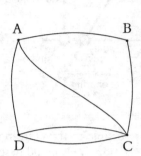

		To			
		A	B	C	D
	A	0	1	1	1
From	B	1	0	1	0
	C	1	1	0	2
	D	1	0	2	0

Note: This means that there are two different ways to get between C and D in a single move.

4 Complete a one-stage route matrix for each of the following networks:

(a)   (b)

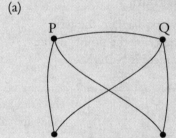

5 Draw the networks described by the following one-stage matrices:

(a)

	A	B	C	D
A	0	1	0	0
B	1	0	1	1
C	0	1	0	1
D	0	1	1	0

(b)

	M	N	O	P
M	1	2	1	0
N	2	0	1	1
O	1	1	0	1
P	0	1	1	0

You can also look at the ways of going from one node to another in two moves. This means passing through one other node on the way. A matrix which shows the possible two-stage routes between nodes is called a **two-stage** route matrix.

E.g. Complete a two-stage route matrix for the network in question 4(a).
You can go from P to Q via R or via S so there are 2 two-stage routes from P to Q.
You can go from P to itself via R or S or Q so there are 3 two-stage routes from P to P.

	P	Q	R	S
P	3	2	1	1
Q	2	3	1	1
R	1	1	2	2
S	1	1	2	2

?

6 Complete a two-stage route matrix for this network.

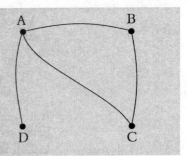

The networks you have looked at so far have all had arcs which can be travelled in both directions (two-way arcs). Just like streets, arcs can sometimes be one-way.

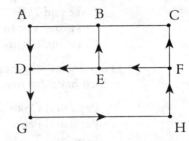

?

7 Complete a one-stage route matrix for this network.

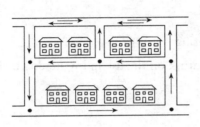

8 This a one-stage route matrix.

(a) Draw the network it represents.
(b) Complete a two-stage matrix for the network.

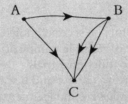

		To	
	A	B	C
From A	1	1	2
B	0	0	1
C	0	0	0

5.6d Combining independent events

Two events are described as **independent** if they have no effect on each other. Rolling dice, tossing coins and any other actions you can repeat in exactly the same way over and over again will give independent events.

If you choose two items **with replacement** then events will be independent because the second choice will not be affected by the first choice.

When you combine two trials and events are independent then all the different combinations of outcomes of the two events are possible. (This is not true when events are not independent. Think of being dealt two cards: they can't both be the Ace of Hearts.)

E.g. A drinks machine contains Coke, Pepsi, Tango, 7UP, Vimto and Citrus Spring. List all the possible combinations of drinks that Amit and Tim might choose, assuming that they choose independently of each other. (This is like choosing with replacement.)

You could list all the possible combinations in any order as you thought of them.

Coke and Coke
7UP and Vimto
Pepsi and Tango …

But then it's very hard to see if you've missed a possible combination. It is better to list the combinations in a systematic way, following a pattern.
List all the combinations which have Coke first:

Coke and Coke
Coke and Pepsi
Coke and Tango
Coke and 7UP
Coke and Vimto
Coke and Citrus Spring

Then look at the next drink on the list and write down all the combinations which have this first.

Pepsi and Coke
Pepsi and Pepsi
Pepsi and Tango
Pepsi and 7UP
Pepsi and Vimto
Pepsi and Citrus Spring

Always use the same order for the second choice.
To calculate the number of possible combinations, you multiply the number of possible outcomes for the individual trials.
There are 6 ways for Amit to choose and 6 ways that Tim could choose. Tim's choice and Amit's choice are independent so whatever Amit chooses there are still 6 possible choices for Tim. The total number of ways Amit and Tim can choose their drinks is $6 \times 6 = 36$.
It is useful to work this out to check that you have found all the possible combinations. Another way to display all the possible outcomes is to use a table called a **sample space**.

Amit

		C	P	T	7	V	S
	C	CC	CP	CT	C7	CV	CS
	P	PC	PP	PT	P7	PV	PS
Tim	T	TC	TP	TT	T7	TV	TS
	7	7C	7P	7T	77	7V	7S
	V	VC	VP	VT	V7	VV	VS
	S	SC	SP	ST	S7	SV	SS

The more possible outcomes each trial has the easier it is to find all the combinations using a sample space. You can clearly see all 36 combinations.

?

1 (a) How many different possible outcomes are there when you roll two dice?

(b) Draw a sample space to show all the possible outcomes.

You can also display the possible outcomes of two events using a **tree diagram**.

E.g. This is a tree diagram showing the results of tossing a coin twice.

Remember: Put the outcomes of the second trial in the same order as the first.

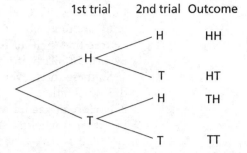

2 (a) There are three cards A, B and C face down on a table. One card is picked up and then replaced and then a second card is picked up. List the possible ways in which they could be chosen.
(b) Complete this sample space to show the possible ways of picking up the cards.
(c) Draw a tree diagram to show the possible ways of picking up the cards.

1st	2nd		
	A	B	C
A			
B			
C			

3 There are 3 children in the Webb family. Assuming there is an even chance of having boys and girls, complete a tree diagram to show the possible combinations of sexes for the children.

5.6e Mutually exclusive and complementary events

Two events are **mutually exclusive** if when one of them happens it stops the other happening. For example, we cannot both eat the last piece of cheesecake in the fridge. Either I eat it or you eat it (unless we are prepared to share). The events 'I eat it' and 'you eat it' are mutually exclusive.

Note: The words 'either... or...' often give a clue to events being mutually exclusive.

When events are mutually exclusive then there is no overlap.

'Choosing a Heart' and 'choosing a Spade' are mutually exclusive events because no card can be a Heart and also a Spade. 'Choosing a Heart' and 'choosing a King' are **not** mutually exclusive events because you could choose the King of Hearts.

The total sum of the probabilities of mutually exclusive events in any trial is always 1. This is because the mutually exclusive events together cover all the possible outcomes and there is no overlap.

E.g. (a) When you toss a coin it can't come down on both sides at once so 'getting a Tail' and 'getting a Head' are mutually exclusive events.
p(getting a Tail) = $\frac{1}{2}$
p(getting a Head) = $\frac{1}{2}$
So p(getting a Tail) + p(getting a Head) = $\frac{1}{2}$ + $\frac{1}{2}$ = 1

(b) In a game it is known that the probability of Rachel winning is 0·3 and the probability of Lubna winning is 0·4. What is the probability that neither Rachel nor Lubna will win?

We have three events: 'Rachel wins', 'Lubna wins' and 'neither Rachel nor Lubna wins'. Rachel and Lubna cannot both win so 'Rachel wins' and 'Lubna wins' are mutually exclusive events. Clearly if Rachel wins then it cannot also be true that 'neither Rachel nor Lubna wins' so these are mutually exclusive events. (Similarly if Lubna wins.)

So these three events are mutually exclusive and between them they cover all the possibilities.

Therefore p(Rachel wins or Lubna wins or neither) = 1

p(neither Rachel nor Lubna wins) = 1 − (0·3 + 0·4)

= 0·3

If mutually exclusive events are equally likely then the probability of each event is 1 divided by the number of events.

E.g. A bag contains five different coloured balls: a green one, a red one, a blue one, an orange one and a white one. What is the probability of choosing a ball of a particular colour?

A ball cannot be two colours at once so the events are mutually exclusive. The sum of all the probabilities must be 1.

p(green) + p(red) + p(blue) + p(orange) + p(white) = 1

But you are just as likely to choose a ball of one colour as a ball of another colour so all these probabilities are equal.

Therefore 5 × p(green) = 1

p(green) = $\frac{1}{5}$

This is the same for any colour.

Complementary events

The two events given by something 'happening' and 'not happening' are called **complementary** events. For example, the event 'throwing a 6' has the complementary event 'not throwing a 6' and 'getting a Tail' has the complementary event 'getting a Head'. If something is happening then it can't also not happen so complementary events are clearly mutually exclusive. Any two complementary events cover the whole range of possibilities because something must either happen or not happen. Using the fact that the total sum of mutually exclusive events is always 1,

p(event) + p(not event) = 1

This is very useful because it means that if you know the probability of something happening you can work out the probability of it not happening. Sometimes when you want to find the probability of an event it's far easier to calculate the probability of it not happening then take that away from 1.

E.g. If a fair die is rolled what is the probability of getting 1, 2, 3, 4 or 5?
This is the same as not getting a 6.
The probability of getting a 6 is $\frac{1}{6}$ so
p(not getting a 6) = 1 − p(getting a 6) = 1 − $\frac{1}{6}$ = $\frac{5}{6}$
Hence p(getting 1, 2, 3, 4 or 5) = $\frac{5}{6}$

1 (a) What is the probability of getting a 1 on a fair icosahedral die with 20 faces?
(b) Use this to calculate the probability of not getting a 1.

2 The probability of drawing a picture card (K, Q, J, A) from a pack is $\frac{4}{13}$. What is the probability of not choosing a picture card?

3 In a game of chance the probability of winning is $\frac{1}{5}$. What is the probability of losing?

4 There are red and blue counters in a bag. If the probability of choosing a red counter is $\frac{5}{8}$ what is the probability of choosing a blue counter?

5.7a   Specifying and testing a hypothesis

Believing that something is true is not a good enough basis for making what could be major decisions. You need to check whether or not it really is true.

First you need to state exactly what it is you believe to be true. This is called making a **hypothesis**. Then you need to decide what evidence you need to test your hypothesis.

Depending on what your hypothesis is, you may need to use an observation sheet or a survey to test it, or you may need to do an experiment. Before you start collecting data you need to work out exactly how you are going to use the results to prove or disprove the hypothesis. Write down in advance what results you expect to see if the hypothesis is true. Always state your hypothesis as clearly as you can so that anyone reading it will know what you mean. Don't make it too vague (e.g. "Girls are better than boys") or it may be impossible to test.

E.g.   (a) "All children would like to go to Disneyland."
This is a hypothesis. To check this hypothesis you would need to ask a sample of children the question 'Would you like to go to Disneyland?'
If the hypothesis is true then you would expect 100% of the answers to be 'Yes'. You might say the hypothesis is true if you get 97% or more 'Yes' answers.

(b) "Football teams that play in red strips are more successful than teams that play in blue strips."
(i)   What information do you need to collect to test this hypothesis?
You need to record the results of a sample of matches. This sample must be large enough for you to be able to draw conclusions from the results. By recording games won, lost and drawn by teams wearing red and teams wearing blue for all the clubs in the football league on a number of Saturdays you should have sufficient data.
(ii)   How can you use this data to test the hypothesis?
Tally the number of games won, lost and drawn for blue teams and for red teams. Giving 0 points for a game lost, 1 point for a draw and 2 points for a win, calculate a total score for blue teams and a total score for red teams.
Score = 2 × number of games won + number of games drawn
Calculate the mean score per game in each case. (If you have observed the same number of games for blue teams and for red teams then you can compare the scores directly.) If the hypothesis is true then the mean score will be higher for teams which play in red.

If your results support your hypothesis you need to obtain more results to check your first set. For the hypothesis to be generally true it must work every time you test it. Otherwise it may just have been true in one particular week or in one particular town or among one particular class of pupils. If your results don't support your original hypothesis you may wish to change it and try again.

You need to be clear about what conclusions you can draw from a particular test. Be careful not to assume too much.

?

1   Ian believes that boys are better at Maths than girls.
(a) Who does Ian need to survey to test his hypothesis?
(b) What two pieces of information does he need to collect?
(c) Use the Maths scores in **unit 5.6b** to test Ian's hypothesis.
(d) What are the limitations of the test you have done?

2   Below are two hypotheses. In each case, write down who you would survey and what information you would need to collect to test the hypothesis.
(a) Motorists would be happy to pay more for unleaded petrol.
(b) Your school day should start at 8 am and finish at 2 pm with no lunch break.

5.7b Calculating the mean from a grouped frequency table

You already know how to create a grouped frequency table from a set of data. It is very important when grouping data that you choose suitable class intervals.

If you have to choose your own class intervals first find the range of the data and decide how many intervals you want.

E.g. These are the weights in kilograms of 24 pupils in class 8M.

32	43	37	53	41	29	45	35	36	42	46	33
32	45	55	35	39	46	47	52	49	47	46	43

Make a grouped frequency table of these results.
The weights go from 29 to 55, giving a range of 26. Using a class interval of 5 kg will give you 6 intervals starting at 26 and ending at 55.

Class interval	Tally	Frequency
26 – 30	I	1
31 – 35	IIIII	5
36 – 40	III	3
41 – 45	IIIII I	6
46 – 50	IIIII I	6
51 – 55	III	3

Grouping this data in classes of 5 kg gives 6 class intervals which shows how the weights are distributed.

If the same information were grouped using class intervals of 10 kg this would not show how the weights are spread. Using class intervals of 2 kg would do little to simplify the original data.

1 David records the number of cars which pass his house between 6:00 and 6:15 each evening for 30 days.

24	35	47	53	42	34	45	35	42	36
28	19	16	32	24	26	29	21	36	30
20	26	42	27	28	31	39	16	27	23

(a) Using suitable class intervals tally the number of cars seen each day.
(b) Create a grouped frequency table from this information.

Calculating the mean

E.g. The examination marks of 250 pupils are recorded below. What was the mean mark?

Class interval	0 – 9	10 – 19	20 – 29	30 – 39	40 – 49	50 – 59	60 – 69	70 – 79	80 – 89	90 – 99
Frequency	0	2	6	24	36	47	55	40	27	13

To calculate the mean you would normally add up all the values and then divide by the total number of values (in this case 250). You cannot do that with this information because you only know that a value is between say 20 and 29 and not exactly what the value is. With grouped data you use the middle value of each class interval and multiply by the frequency for the class.

Then divide by the total frequency.

$$\text{Mean} = \frac{\text{Total (mid-value} \times \text{frequency)}}{\text{Total frequency}}$$

Class interval	Mid-value	Frequency	Mid-value × frequency
0 – 9	4·5	0	0
10 – 19	14·5	2	29
20 – 29	24·5	6	147
30 – 39	34·5	24	828
40 – 49	44·5	36	1602
50 – 59	54·5	47	2561·5
60 – 69	64·5	55	3547·5
70 – 79	74·5	40	2980
80 – 89	84·5	27	2281·5
90 – 99	94·5	13	1228·5
		Total 250	Total 15 205

$$\text{Mean} = \frac{\text{Total (mid-value} \times \text{frequency)}}{\text{Total frequency}} = \frac{15\ 205}{250} = 60·82$$

?

2 The weights of 24 pupils in 8M are given in the example at the start of this unit.
(a) Using the class intervals given in the example, write down the mid-class values.
(b) Calculate the mean weight of the pupils.

3 Using your answers to question 1, calculate the mean number of cars passing David's house between 6:00 and 6:15 each day.

5.7c Comparing data using the mean, mode, median and range

You already know how to find the mean, mode, median and range of a set of data which is not grouped. With grouped data you cannot find the exact mean, mode, median and range because you do not know the exact values of the data, but only which class a value is in. To overcome this you use the class mid-value to represent the class.

You have seen in **unit 5.7b** how to calculate the mean of a set of grouped data.

$$\text{Mean} = \frac{\text{Total (mid-value} \times \text{frequency)}}{\text{Total frequency}}$$

Modal group or class = class with the highest frequency
The mid-point of the modal class gives an approximate value for the mode.

Median class = class which contains the middle value
The mid-point of the median class gives an approximate value for the median.

Range = maximum value (upper boundary of highest class) − minimum value (lower boundary of lowest class)

E.g. On the next page are two sets of grouped data. Calculate the mean, mode, median and range of each set of data.

Height (in cm) of 80 girls in Year 8

Height (h)	Girls
$120 \leq h < 125$	1
$125 \leq h < 130$	3
$130 \leq h < 135$	6
$135 \leq h < 140$	12
$140 \leq h < 145$	17
$145 \leq h < 150$	18
$150 \leq h < 155$	15
$155 \leq h < 160$	5
$160 \leq h < 165$	2
$165 \leq h < 170$	1

To calculate the mean you first multiply the class mid-values by the frequencies.

$122 \cdot 5 \times 1 + 127 \cdot 5 \times 3 + 132 \cdot 5 \times 6 + 137 \cdot 5 \times 12 + 142 \cdot 5 \times 17 + 147 \cdot 5 \times 18 + 152 \cdot 5 \times 15 + 157 \cdot 5 \times 5 + 162 \cdot 5 \times 2 + 167 \cdot 5 \times 1 = 11\ 595$

Then divide by the total frequency.

$$\text{Mean} = \frac{11\ 595}{80} = 144 \cdot 9 \text{ (to 1 d.p.)}$$

The 40th and 41st girls are both in the class $145 \leq h < 150$ so this is the median class.

$145 \leq h < 150$ is also the modal class because it has the highest frequency (18).

The range is $170 - 120 = 50$

Height (in cm) of 80 boys in Year 8

Height (h)	Boys
$120 \leq h < 125$	1
$125 \leq h < 130$	4
$130 \leq h < 135$	8
$135 \leq h < 140$	16
$140 \leq h < 145$	20
$145 \leq h < 150$	14
$150 \leq h < 155$	10
$155 \leq h < 160$	4
$160 \leq h < 165$	2
$165 \leq h < 170$	1

Multiplying the class mid-value by the frequency gives

$122 \cdot 5 \times 1 + 127 \cdot 5 \times 4 + 132 \cdot 5 \times 8 + 137 \cdot 5 \times 16 + 142 \cdot 5 \times 20 + 147 \cdot 5 \times 14 + 152 \cdot 5 \times 10 + 157 \cdot 5 \times 4 + 162 \cdot 5 \times 2 + 167 \cdot 5 \times 1 = 11\ 455$

Dividing by the total frequency

$$\text{Mean} = \frac{11\ 455}{80} = 143 \cdot 2 \text{ (to 1 d.p.)}$$

Median class is $140 \leq h < 145$

Modal class is $140 \leq h < 145$

Range is again $170 - 120 = 50$

Although the range of both sets of data is the same, the mean, median and modal scores are greater for the girls in Year 8 than for the boys. This shows that the girls are generally taller than the boys.

1 Kevin and Scott carried out a survey to find out whether buses were later on a Monday than a Saturday. They observed 19 buses each day and recorded how many minutes late each bus was. They included buses that were on time but ignored buses that were early.

Monday						
Minutes late	0–2	3–5	6–8	9–11	12–14	15–17
No. of buses	2	5	7	4	1	0
Saturday						
Minutes late	0–2	3–5	6–8	9–11	12–14	15–17
No. of buses	1	9	4	2	1	2

(a) Calculate the mean, median, mode and range of the data collected on Monday.
(b) Calculate the mean, median, mode and range of the data collected on Saturday.
(c) Use your answers to (a) and (b) to compare the two sets of data.

5.7d   Frequency polygons

A **frequency polygon** is a line graph which shows the shape of a grouped frequency distribution.

If you already have a bar chart you can draw a frequency polygon from it by joining the mid-points of the top of each bar. To draw a frequency polygon without first drawing the bar chart you plot the class mid-values against frequency.

E.g.   This is a grouped frequency table of standard assessment test results achieved by 120 pupils in Year 9 in 1992.

Score	0–9	10–19	20–29	30–39	40–49	50–59	60–69	70–79	80–89	90–99
Frequency	2	4	10	16	24	26	18	12	5	3

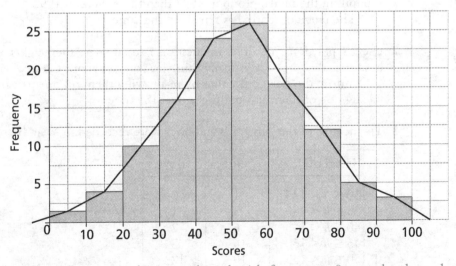

Note: Add an extra class at each end with frequency 0 to make the polygon touch the horizontal axis.

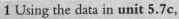

1 Using the data in **unit 5.7c,**
(a) draw a frequency polygon for the heights of the girls in Year 8.
(b) draw a frequency polygon for the heights of the boys in Year 8.

Comparing frequency polygons

To compare two sets of data it is very useful to draw the two frequency polygons on the same pair of axes. Then you can easily compare their shapes.

E.g. You have already seen the SAT results for 1992. Below are the results for the 120 pupils sitting the same tests in 1993.

1993 SAT scores

Score	0-9	10-19	20-29	30-39	40-49	50-59	60-69	70-79	80-89	90-99
Frequency	1	3	6	13	18	28	25	15	7	4

Use frequency polygons drawn on the same axes to compare the results of the two year groups.

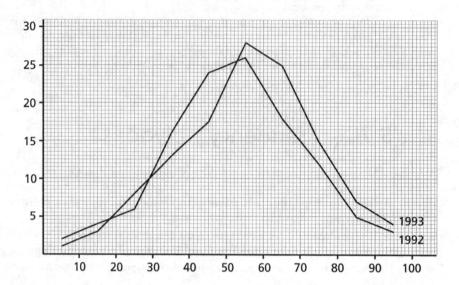

The shapes of the polygons are similar but the line of the 1993 polygon has moved to the right. Scores are generally better in 1993. There are fewer low scoring pupils and more high scoring pupils.

The 1993 polygon has a higher peak. This means that there were more pupils in the modal group in 1993 than there were in 1992.

The range of scores has remained the same.

?

2 Use the polygons you drew in question 1 to compare the heights of the boys and the girls. Say as many things as you can about the frequency polygons.
   Compare the polygons either by re-drawing them on one pair of axes or by tracing one of them and putting it over the other.

3 The heights of the same girls and boys were recorded in Year 10.

Height (h)	Girls	Boys
$130 \leq h < 135$	1	0
$135 \leq h < 140$	3	1
$140 \leq h < 145$	6	2
$145 \leq h < 150$	10	8
$150 \leq h < 155$	19	12
$155 \leq h < 160$	17	15
$160 \leq h < 165$	15	17
$165 \leq h < 170$	5	16
$170 \leq h < 175$	3	5
$175 \leq h < 180$	1	3

(a) Draw a frequency polygon for each set of data on the same pair of axes.
(b) Use the polygons to compare the two frequency distributions.

5.7e   Drawing a line of best fit

The points that are plotted on a scatter graph do not usually lie in a straight line but you have seen that when there is a positive or negative correlation the points tend to lie within a band across the graph.

The points look as though they are clustered around a single line. This line is called the **line of best fit**. This line is extremely useful because you can find the equation of the line and then use it to generate a formula linking the two variables. This allows you to predict the approximate value of one variable given the value of the other.

You can draw in the line of best fit 'by inspection' ('by eye') if you can see the line suggested by the points. You should try to get as many points on the line as possible and an equal number of points on either side. (You can ignore very way out points.)

If there are only a small number of points, you can calculate the mean point and then position the line so that it goes through the mean point with an equal number of the other points on each side of the line.

E.g.   This is the scatter graph from **unit 5.6b** of the Maths and Science marks for the first 10 pupils. Draw a line of best fit on this graph.

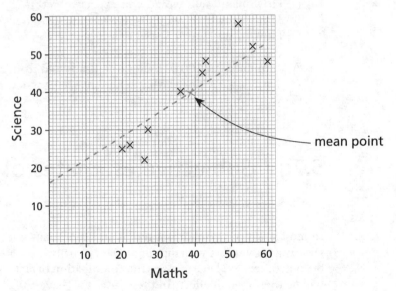

First find the mean Maths score and the mean Science score.

$$\text{Mean Maths score} = \frac{384}{10} = 38{\cdot}4 \qquad \text{Mean Science score} = \frac{394}{10} = 39{\cdot}4$$

Plot the mean point (38·4, 39·4) on the graph. Then draw in the line of best fit.

?

1 Using the remaining values from **unit 5.6b**, draw a new scatter graph and find its line of best fit.

2 Use your graph to predict what you might expect to get in Science if you got the following Maths results:
(a) Maths 10   (b) Maths 30   (c) Maths 50

5.7f   Relative frequency

In some situations you can use symmetry to work out the probability of an event happening. For example, on a fair die the chance of getting any given number is 1 in 6 because there are six possible equally likely outcomes.

You can also estimate probability by repeating an experiment a large number of times and finding what proportion of the time you get the result you want. This is called **relative frequency**.

It is given by:
$$\frac{\text{number of results which give the event you want}}{\text{number of trials}}$$

Using symmetry is more accurate because in reality you have to do a very large number of trials before the relative frequency of the event gets close to the true probability.

> **?**
>
> 1 Toss a coin ten times and record the number of Heads you get. Use your result to estimate the probability of getting Heads.
>
>   Repeat this experiment several times.

You may have got 5 Heads, you may not. You can see that you don't always get 5 Heads. The more times you toss the coin the closer the experimental results will come to the number you would expect.

If you only tossed the coin once and it came up Heads then after the first trial you would estimate p(Heads) = 1 and p(Tails) = 0!

> **?**
>
> 2 Use relative frequency to estimate the following:
>   (a) How many Tails would you expect to get in 20 tosses of a coin?
>   (b) How many times would you expect to get a 6 if you rolled a fair die 18 times?
>   (c) How many Hearts would you expect if you were dealt 12 cards at random?
>
> 3 At a summer fair 100 winning tickets are sold from a total of 800 tickets. If Gillian bought 1 ticket what is her chance of winning a prize?

5.7g   Subjective estimates of probability

In most situations you cannot repeat an experiment over and over again in exactly the same way, as you can with flipping a coin. Usually there are too many factors which affect the outcome. You have to assess the combination of factors and work out what you think will be their overall effect. In these cases you have to fall back on a subjective estimate of the probability. In other words, given the information you have to make your best guess!

E.g.   What is the probability that it will rain tomorrow?
     This could depend on today's weather, the time of year, where you are, etc. Your estimate of the likelihood of rain is therefore subject to information which only you can assess at the time.

> **?**
>
> 1 Make what you consider to be a reasonable estimate of the probabilities of the following events.
>
>   (a) The next train you catch will be on time.
>   (b) The next car you see will be a Ford.
>   (c) There will be a frost next week.

5.7h   Adding probabilities of mutually exclusive events

You already know that events are mutually exclusive if they can't both happen at the same time.

E.g.   If Andy, Bev, Carl and Diane have a race and Bev wins, then Andy, Carl and Diane must lose. The events 'Andy wins', 'Bev wins', 'Carl wins' and 'Diane wins' are mutually exclusive.

Combining events

There are two ways to combine events.

❶ Using AND. This gives events of the form 'Andy wins **and** Bev comes second'. You are interested in events both happening.

With mutually exclusive events you know that the probability of two events both happening is always zero.

❷ Using OR. This gives events of the form 'Andy **or** Bev wins'. You are interested in at least one event happening.

With mutually exclusive events there is no overlap so **either** Andy wins **or** Bev wins **but not both**.

If you wish to work out the probability of **either** A **or** B you simply add the probabilities.

p(either A or B) = p(A) + p(B)

So p(Andy or Bev wins) = p(Andy wins) + p(Bev wins)

E.g.   A family bag of crisps contains 6 packets of crisps: 3 plain, 2 cheese and onion and 1 smoky bacon. What is the probability of picking plain or smoky bacon if you choose a packet without looking?
The events are mutually exclusive because a packet of crisps cannot be plain and smoky bacon flavour at the same time.
p(choosing plain) = $\frac{3}{6}$
p(choosing smoky bacon) = $\frac{1}{6}$
p(choosing plain or smoky bacon) = $\frac{3}{6} + \frac{1}{6} = \frac{4}{6} = \frac{2}{3}$

Note: Do not cancel any fractions until the final stage.

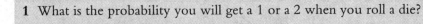

1   What is the probability you will get a 1 or a 2 when you roll a die?

2   A biscuit jar contains 3 chocolate, 4 cream, 2 wafer and 1 plain biscuits.
   (a) Why are choosing a cream biscuit and choosing a wafer biscuit mutually exclusive?
   (b) What is the probability of choosing a cream or a wafer biscuit if you choose without looking?
   (c) What is the probability of choosing a chocolate or a cream biscuit if you choose without looking?

3 Jess always goes to school in one of the following ways:

	probability
by bicycle	0·4
by car	0·1
by bus	0·3
on foot	0·2

   (a) Calculate the probability that she will either walk or go by bus.
   (b) Calculate the probability that she will go to school in a vehicle.

Remember: When events are mutually exclusive then you add probabilities.

5.8a   Cumulative frequency tables

In data handling the frequency tells you how often a particular result was obtained. **Cumulative frequency** indicates how often a result was obtained which was less than (<) or less than or equal to (≤) a stated value in a collection of data.

Cumulative frequency can only be used when information has a clear order, such as measurements of height, age, weight, or quantities such as numbers of goals scored etc.

E.g.   This table of results shows the frequency distribution of a set of test marks for 120 children.
   The cumulative frequency is found by adding together the frequencies to give a running total.

Marks	Number of candidates (Frequency)	Candidates up to this point (Cumulative frequency)
1 – 10	1	1
11 – 20	3	4
21 – 30	7	11
31 – 40	11	22
41 – 50	21	43
51 – 60	34	77
61 – 70	25	...
71 – 80	13	...
81 – 90	4	...
91 – 100	1	...

Note: The numbers in this column are obtained by adding those in the frequency column together.

The cumulative frequency of a class of marks tells you how many candidates obtained marks in that class or lower.

1 (a) Complete the table.
   (b) Use the table to find the number of pupils who scored 30 marks or less.
   (c) Use the table to find the number of pupils who scored more than 70 marks.

Note: The last entry in the cumulative frequency column = total frequency.

2 These are the heights of a class of 32 pupils measured to the nearest cm.

155	134	162	174	126
158	148	163	142	154
159	176	145	136	184
166	151	131	173	168
157	143	165	152	140
149	154	167	172	157
160	158			

(a) Construct a cumulative frequency table for this data, grouping the heights in intervals of 10 cm starting at 120 cm.
(b) To get into a theme park half price children have to be under 150 cm tall. How many of these pupils can get in for half price?
(c) To ride the 'Looper' at the same park people have to be a minimum height of 160 cm. How many of this group can ride the 'Looper'?

?

3 Below are the approximate birth weights of 20 babies.

Birth weights (g)				
3270	3550	4225	2680	3140
3380	2150	3750	3227	4050
3760	4210	3900	3670	3420
2850	3270	3600	4515	3880

(a) Choosing suitable intervals construct a cumulative frequency table of this information.
(b) Use your table to find out how many of these babies weighed between 2·5 kg and 3·5 kg at birth.

5.8b Cumulative frequency curves

To draw a **cumulative frequency curve** for a set of grouped data you plot the upper boundary of each class of data against the cumulative frequency for that class. The cumulative frequency always goes on the vertical axis.

E.g. Draw a cumulative frequency curve for the test marks given in **unit 5.8a**.
Plot the upper boundary of each class against the cumulative frequency.

You get a curve which has a very distinctive S shape.

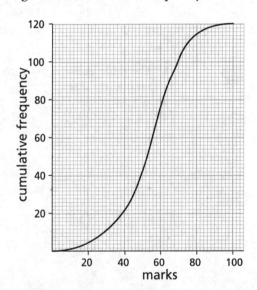

You have already seen how you can use a cumulative frequency table to find the number of results which are above or below a particular class boundary.

A cumulative frequency curve gives a continuous line so you can use it to estimate the number of results above or below any given value.

E.g. A group of children were asked how may pieces of fruit they eat each week. The results are shown on this cumulative frequency graph.

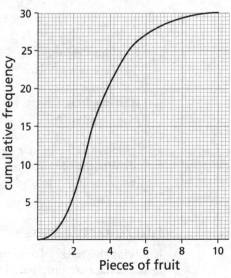

Calculate the number of children who eat up to 5 pieces of fruit.
Find 5 on the horizontal axis. Draw a line vertically from there to the curve and then horizontally to the cumulative frequency axis. Read off the answer:

25 children eat up to 5 pieces of fruit per week.

You can also use a cumulative frequency curve in the reverse way to find the value in a given position, e.g. the tenth highest value or the middle value (median).

Median

To find the median of a set of data you usually arrange the values in order and find the middle value. If n is the total number of values then the median is the $\frac{1}{2}(n + 1)$th value.

This suggests that to find the median from a cumulative frequency curve you find $\frac{1}{2}(n + 1)$ on the vertical axis (where n is the total frequency), draw a horizontal line to the curve and read off the corresponding value from the horizontal axis.

But if the total frequency is large then there is very little difference between the $\frac{1}{2}n$th value and the $\frac{1}{2}(n + 1)$th value. Also it is not very practical to find $\frac{1}{2}(n + 1)$ on the cumulative frequency axis.

So when the total frequency is large you draw a line from the half way mark on the vertical axis to the curve and then down to the horizontal axis, and read off the value.

E.g. From the cumulative frequency curve in the example above find out how many pieces of fruit the average (median) child eats per week.
Draw a line horizontally from the middle child on the cumulative frequency axis to the curve and then vertically down to the horizontal axis.
The average child eats 3 pieces of fruit per week.

Note: Even if your graph is incorrect you will get marks for drawing in the lines to show you used the right method.

1 The table below shows the number of hours of television watched by a group of people per week.

Hours watched	Number of people	Cumulative frequency
< 15	1	1
< 20	2	3
< 25	7	10
< 30	11	21
< 35	25	46
< 40	23	...
< 45	17	...
< 50	10	...
< 55	3	...
< 60	1	...

(a) Complete the table.
(b) Draw a cumulative frequency graph using the information from the table.

Remember: Check your final cumulative frequency equals the total number of people surveyed.

(c) How many people watch under 30 hours of television?
(d) What is the median amount of time spent watching television?
(e) What is the tenth highest amount of television watched?

Interquartile range

Knowing the range of a frequency distribution only tells you the extreme values. To see how the data are distributed around the median the range is divided into four quarters.
The value one quarter of the way from the lower end of the range is called the **lower**

quartile (or first quartile). The middle value or **second quartile** is the median itself. The value three quarters of the way from the lower end of the range is called the **upper quartile** (or third quartile).

If the total frequency, n, is large then the 1st quartile has cumulative frequency $\frac{1}{4}n$ and the 3rd quartile is at $\frac{3}{4}n$. If n is small then the 1st quartile is at $\frac{1}{4}(n+1)$ and the 3rd quartile is at $\frac{3}{4}(n+1)$.

The difference between the lower and upper quartiles is called the **interquartile range**. In any frequency distribution half of the data lies in the interquartile range. This is a very useful way to measure the spread of a set of data, since it only includes the half of the data which is closest to the median, and avoids distortions caused by unusually large or small values.

E.g. Describe the distribution of the time spent by people watching television in question 1.

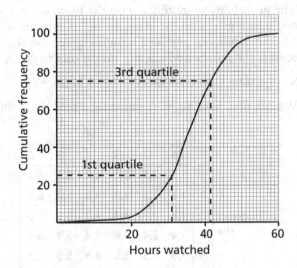

From the curve, 1st (lower) quartile = 31 hours
3rd (upper) quartile = 41 hours
The interquartile range is 31–41 = 10 hours.
From this you can say that half the people surveyed watch between 31 and 41 hours of television a week.

?

2   The table below gives the mass to the nearest kg of 180 pupils.

(a) Draw a cumulative frequency curve for this information. Use a scale of 1 cm = 20 pupils on the vertical axis and 1 cm = 5 kg on the horizontal axis.
(b) Use your curve to work out the following:
   (i) the number of pupils under 40 kg
   (ii) the number of pupils over 59 kg
   (iii) the median mass of the pupils
   (iv) the lower quartile
   (v) the upper quartile
   (vi) the interquartile range
(c) What does the interquartile range tell you in this case?

Mass (kg)	Frequency
< 30	0
< 35	1
< 40	6
< 45	11
< 50	25
< 55	43
< 60	42
< 65	26
< 70	16
< 75	8
< 80	2

5.8c Calculating probabilities when independent events are combined

The probability of two independent events both happening is less than the probability for each of the individual events (unless one of the probabilities is 0 or 1).

E.g. You roll two fair dice, one green and one black. How does the probability of getting a 6 on both dice compare with the individual probabilities of getting a 6? You have already seen that when you combine two trials which involve independent events all the combinations of outcomes are possible. So there are $6 \times 6 = 36$ possible combinations for the scores on the dice.

The probability of getting a 6 on the black die is $\frac{1}{6}$ so the number of outcomes which give 6 on the black die is $\frac{1}{6} \times$ number of outcomes $= \frac{1}{6} \times 36 = 6$.

The probability of getting a 6 on the green die is also $\frac{1}{6}$ so of these 6 outcomes the number which also give 6 on the green die is $\frac{1}{6} \times 6 = 1$.

So p(getting 6 on both dice) = 1 out of 36 $= \frac{1}{36}$

We can illustrate this by completing a probability space.

		black die				
	1	**2**	**3**	**4**	**5**	**6**
1	1,1	2,1	3,1	4,1	5,1	6,1
2	1,2	2,2	3,2	4,2	5,2	6,2
3	1,3	2,3	3,3	4,3	5,3	6,3
4	1,4	2,4	3,4	4,4	5,4	6,4
5	1,5	2,5	3,5	4,5	5,5	6,5
6	1,6	2,6	3,6	4,6	5,6	6,6

green die (rows 3 and 4 labelled)

You can see that there are 36 different possible results and that only one of these gives you two 6's.

If the probability of one event is 0 that means it can't happen so the probability of it and another event both happening must also be 0.

If the probability of one event is 1 that means it must happen so the probability of both events happening will be the same as the probability for the other event.

?

1 If you have a 50p coin, a 10p coin, a 5p and a 2p in your purse what is the probability that if you take out two coins they will be a 50p coin and a 1p coin?

2 (a) Each day 1 pupil from a mixed class is chosen at random to take the register to the school office. The probability that a girl will be chosen to take the register is p. Is the probability that a girl will be chosen 2 days running
   (i) the same as p?   (ii) less than p?   (iii) greater than p?
   (b) Which of the following is the lowest?
   (i)   the probability that a boy will be chosen on the first day of term
   (ii) the probability that a girl will be chosen on the second day of term
   (iii) the probability that a boy will be chosen on the first day and a girl will be chosen on the second day

You saw above that the probability of getting a 6 on two dice at the same time is $\frac{1}{36}$. This is the same as what you get if you multiply the individual probabilities together.

p(6 on both dice) $= \frac{1}{6} \times \frac{1}{6} = \frac{1}{36}$

When two events are independent then

p(event 1 **and** event 2) = p(event 1) $\times$ p(event 2)

E.g. A bag contains 3 red counters, 4 blue counters and 5 white counters. A counter is chosen at random from the bag and then replaced and a second counter is chosen. What is the probability of choosing two red counters?

You know that when items are chosen **with replacement** then events are independent.

The first counter has been replaced so the probabilities in the second trial are the same as those in the first trial.

The probability of choosing a red counter,

$$p(\text{red}) = \frac{3}{(3+4+5)} = \frac{3}{12} = \frac{1}{4}$$

$$p(\text{red then red}) = p(\text{red}) \times p(\text{red}) = \frac{1}{4} \times \frac{1}{4}$$
$$= \frac{1}{16}$$

So the probability of choosing two red counters is $\frac{1}{16}$.

?

3 If you roll a die and toss a coin what is the probability of getting a 5 and Heads?

Diagrams

One way to illustrate the probabilities for combined events is using a **probability space**.

E.g. What is the probability of taking a picture card from a pack, returning it and then taking a second picture card? Illustrate this using a probability space.

The probability of taking a picture card (A, K, Q, J) is $\frac{16}{52}$ which simplifies to $\frac{4}{13}$.

$$p(\text{picture}) = \frac{4}{13} \qquad p(\text{not picture}) = 1 - \frac{4}{13} = \frac{9}{13}$$

There are 13 different types of card, of which 4 are picture cards.

Choosing with replacement gives independent events so all combinations of outcomes are possible. Therefore choosing 2 cards gives $13 \times 13 = 169$ possibilities.

Of these, $4 \times 4 = 16$ give 2 picture cards.

So the probability of choosing 2 picture cards is $\frac{16}{169}$.

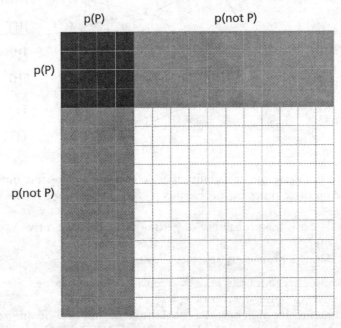

The probability space shows that out of 169 possibilities there are 16 outcomes which give 2 picture cards.

Another way to illustrate the probabilities for combined events is using a **tree diagram**.

Note: The greatest problem most people find in drawing this type of diagram is in the layout. Before you start drawing work out how many branches there are going to be!

Keep the outcomes in the same order for each trial. Remember the probabilities should add up to 1 for each group of branches.

Leave any simplification of fractions to the final calculation rather than simplifying fractions on the diagram.

E.g. Draw a tree diagram to illustrate the probability of taking a picture card from a pack, returning it and then taking a second picture card.

Let P be the event 'taking a picture card' and N be the complementary event 'not taking a picture card'.

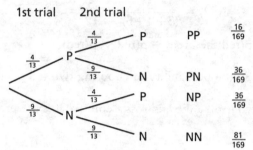

To calculate probabilities from a tree diagram you multiply along the branches.
p(2 picture cards) = p(P) × p(P)

$$= \frac{4}{13} \times \frac{4}{13}$$

$$= \frac{16}{169}$$

If you go on to three trials the probability space diagram becomes impractical. But you can draw a tree diagram for any number of trials.

E.g. Draw a tree diagram to illustrate the probabilities when tossing a coin three times.

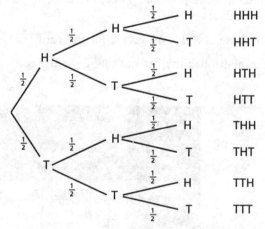

In each case the probability is $\frac{1}{2}$ so each of the possible outcomes of tossing the coin three times has probability $\frac{1}{2} \times \frac{1}{2} \times \frac{1}{2} = \frac{1}{8}$ or 0·125.

?

4 (a) What is the probability of getting more than 4 on two successive rolls of a fair die?

(b) Draw a probability space to illustrate your answer.

5 Lisa uses her mountain bike to ride to her friend's house. She has to go through two sets of traffic lights on the way.
At the first set of lights the probability that they will be on green is 0·6.
At the second set of traffic lights the probability that they will be on green is 0·5.
(a) Calculate the probability that the first set of traffic lights will not be green.
(b) Calculate the probability that the second set of traffic lights will not be green.
(c) Draw a tree diagram to illustrate the probabilities of the two sets of lights being green or not green.
(d) Calculate the probability that Lisa will be able to ride to her friend's house without having to stop at any traffic lights.

5.9a Histograms

You have already drawn many bar charts. A histogram looks very like a bar chart but there are important differences.

Bar charts

❶ All the bars are the same width.
❷ The height or length of the bar indicates the frequency.
❸ Only one axis has a scale. The other may be colours, types of car, numbers of children in a family etc.

Histograms

❶ The width of each column is in proportion to the size of the class or group of data it represents (with no spaces between the columns). The columns may have different widths.
❷ The quantity on the vertical axis is **frequency density** (or frequency per class of a given size).
❸ The frequency for a particular class of data is given by the **area** of the column representing that class.
❹ The horizontal axis must have a scale. This acts like a normal scale on a graph, with the same distance always representing the same number of units.

Note: Histograms are usually used with grouped data.

E.g. A school runs a cafeteria system at lunch times. The table below shows how much 600 pupils spent on lunch in a particular week. Draw a histogram of this information.

Amount spent (£)	Frequency
0 – 0·99	4
1·00 – 1·99	7
2·00 – 2·99	14
3·00 – 3·99	35
4·00 – 4·99	98
5·00 – 5·99	125
6·00 – 6·99	194
7·00 – 7·99	107
8·00 – 8·99	13
9·00 – 9·99	3

The classes given in this table are all the same size so if you drew a histogram using these class intervals then the columns would all have the same width. Therefore the areas of the columns would only depend on their heights.

The frequencies here range from 3 to 194 and on a histogram the frequency is equal to the area of the column so the tallest column would be about 65 times as tall as the shortest column. You can regroup the data using different class intervals to produce a more balanced histogram.

The range of frequencies is now 60 to 194. Now you need to work out the height and width of each column. The width is given by the class interval. To calculate the height (or frequency density) of a column you divide the frequency by the width.

Amount spent (£)	Frequency
0 – 3·99	60
4·00 – 4·99	98
5·00 – 5·99	125
6·00 – 6·99	194
7·00 – 9·99	123

frequency (area) = height × width

$$\text{height (frequency density)} = \frac{\text{frequency}}{\text{class interval}}$$

Frequency	Amount spent (£)	Frequency density
60	0 – 3·99	0·15
98	4·00 – 4·99	0·98
125	5·00 – 5·99	1·25
194	6·00 – 6·99	1·94
121	7·00 – 9·99	0·40

You can now draw a histogram of this data.

Amount spent in the school cafeteria in a week (pence)

Interpreting histograms

If the columns in a histogram are all the same width then you can compare the frequencies of the classes by comparing the heights of the columns. The tallest column indicates the modal class.

If the columns are of different widths then you must compare the **areas** of the columns to compare frequencies. You don't always need to work out the actual areas. For example, if two columns are about the same height and one is twice the width then you can see that the wider column has about twice the area. In other words, if the columns are about the same height and the class interval is doubled then the frequency will be about doubled. The column with the largest area indicates the **modal class**.

The **height** of a column is like averaging out the frequency over all the values in the class.

$$\text{height} = \frac{\text{frequency}}{\text{class interval}}$$

So the taller the column the greater the average frequency for the values in that class. This means that the **mode** is probably in the class with the tallest column, even if this is not the modal class. You can find the total frequency by adding together the areas of all the columns.

E.g. What can you say about the distribution of spending in the school cafeteria by looking at the shape of the histogram in the example above?

First consider the areas of the columns. The tallest column must have a greater area than the other 2 columns with the same width. It also clearly has a greater area than the column on the far left, which is thinner and shorter.

The column on the far right is 3 times the width of the tallest column but less than $\frac{1}{4}$ of the height so its area must be less than $\frac{3}{4}$ of the area of the tallest column.

Therefore in this histogram the tallest column also has the greatest area. Therefore the class £6·00–6·99 is the modal class and also contains the mode.

This means there are more pupils spending £6·00–6·99 than the amount in any of the other classes. And the most frequently spent amount is somewhere between £6 and £6·99.

You could also say that the majority of children spend between £4 and £7 a week in the cafeteria because this range contains most of the area of the histogram.

?

1 The distances travelled to school by 330 pupils are shown in the grouped frequency table below.

Distance (km)	Frequency
$0 \leq d < 0{\cdot}5$	4
$0{\cdot}5 \leq d < 1{\cdot}0$	17
$1{\cdot}0 \leq d < 1{\cdot}5$	30
$1{\cdot}5 \leq d < 2{\cdot}0$	54
$2{\cdot}0 \leq d < 2{\cdot}5$	62
$2{\cdot}5 \leq d < 3{\cdot}0$	79
$3{\cdot}0 \leq d < 3{\cdot}5$	52
$3{\cdot}5 \leq d < 4{\cdot}0$	27
$4{\cdot}0 \leq d < 4{\cdot}5$	11
$4{\cdot}5 \leq d < 5{\cdot}0$	2
$5{\cdot}0 \leq d < 5{\cdot}5$	1
$5{\cdot}5 \leq d < 6{\cdot}0$	1

(a) Regroup this data so that each new class interval has at least 40 pupils in it.

(b) Calculate the frequency density for each of these classes.

(c) Use your new classes to draw a histogram of distances travelled to school.

(d) Say as much as you can about the distribution of distances travelled by looking at the shape of the histogram.

Remember: In a histogram the frequency is given by the area of the column.

5.9b Presenting complex data in a simplified form

You have already seen many different ways to display statistical data. These include bar charts, pictograms, pie charts, histograms, scatter graphs, frequency polygons, cumulative frequency curves, etc.

The most appropriate way to display data depends on the type of data collected and what you want to use it for.

❶ Data collected from an opinion poll or observation sheet can be tallied and then displayed in a table or as a bar chart or pie chart. A bar chart shows the frequencies as numbers and a pie chart shows the frequencies as percentages or fractions of the total frequency.

❷ Data involving measurement can be displayed on a cumulative frequency curve, as a frequency polygon or in a histogram.

❸ To compare the relationship between two variables use a scatter diagram.

E.g. Sean wants to know whether people get better at crosswords with practice so he does an experiment. He does a large number of crosswords and for each one he records the percentage of correct answers he gets and the number of crosswords he has already done.

There are two variables in Sean's experiment and he wants to know whether there is any correlation (relationship) between them. This suggests that a scatter graph is the best way to display this data. By plotting the number of crosswords already done on one axis and the percentage of correct answers on the other axis and looking at the distribution of the points he can find out if any correlation exists.

Using a database

If you have more complex data, such as the results of a survey with several questions or an experiment involving several variables, you will need to use a database (usually a computer database) to store the information.

Using the correct software on a computer you can select a particular variable or combination of variables which you wish to examine. The computer will also be able to present the data in a variety of different forms.

If you do not have a computer and the appropriate software of your own you should be able to practise these skills at school. Using this approach can improve the presentation of any topic work which you may have to do in a wide variety of subjects.

1 Use the data in the table to complete tasks (a) to (c) below.

	1969	1979	1988	1989
United Kingdom population (*millions*)	55.5	56.2	57.1	57.2
England (130,439 sq km)	na	46.7	47.5	47.7
Scotland (78,772 sq km)	5.2	5.2	5.1	5.1
Wales (20,768 sq km)	na	2.8	2.9	2.9
Northen Ireland (14,121 sq km)	1.5	1.5	1.6	1.6
England and Wales (151,207 sq km)	48.7	49.5	50.4	50.6
Males	26.9	27.4	27.8	27.9
Females	28.6	28.9	29.3	29.3
% of the population between 16 and retirement age	60.1[1]	59.0	61.3	61.4
% of the population over retirement age	15.9	17.3	18.2	18.2
% of the population aged 75+	4.6	5.4	6.6	6.7
(*thousands*)				
Live births	920.3	734.6	787.6	777.3
Deaths	659.5	675.5	649.2	657.7
Migrant inflow[2]	206	195	216	250
Migrant outflow[2]	293	189	237	205
Net migration	−87	+6	−21	+44
(*thousands*)				
Marriages	452	417	394	392
of which:				
Remarriages (one or both parties)	71	130	141	139
Divorces	55	148	166	na
Households (*millions*)	na	na	22.0	na
Average household size (GB)	na	2.67	2.48	2.51
Life expectation at birth (*years*)				
Males	68.5	70.0	72.2	72.4
Females	74.7	76.1	77.9	78.0
Infant mortality (*deaths per thousand live births*)	17.1	9.5	9.0	8.4
Legal abortions in Great Britain (UK residents)(*thousands*)	na	130.8	181.0	183.2
Deaths (*thousands*) due to:				
Cancer (malignant)	130.1	145.1	160.6	161.9
Heart disease	216.5	231.3	206.8	204.3
Respiratory diseases	94.6	94.8	69.8	78.3
Road accidents	7.7	7.0	5.3	5.6
All other accidents	12.3	11.2	8.4	8.5

[1] Percentage of population between 15 and retirement age.
[2] Excludes movement to and from the Irish Republic.

(a) Choose an appropriate way to illustrate the population growth in the United Kingdom from 1969 to 1989.

(b) Choose an appropriate way to illustrate the main causes of death in the United Kingdom in 1969.

(c) Draw a line graph to show the increase in the life expectancy of males and females since 1969.

5.9c   Sampling

In data handling the word **population** is used for a collection or group of objects which are being studied. A **sample** is a smaller group selected from a population.

When a large population is being studied it is not usually possible to collect data on every member of the population so a sample (or several samples) of the population is studied and conclusions are drawn about the population as a whole. This means that it is very important to choose a sample which is representative of the whole population. Otherwise the conclusions drawn may be very inaccurate.

Sampling is widely used in market research and polling where it is not possible to survey the entire population of a country every time you want to find out about product preference or voting habits.

Sampling is also very important in quality control in industry where it is used not only to check the quality of manufactured products but also to monitor efficiency and standards. Sampling is particularly important for things which can only be tested by wearing them out, such as the length of time a light bulb will last. With most products it would be too expensive to test every single item produced and it is not necessary to do so. No-one would be prepared to pay the extra cost involved in making sure that every single box of their favourite cereal contained exactly the stated weight: it's not that important.

However, there are some things which must work every time so every single item must be tested. A good example of this is the brakes on a car.

Choosing a sample

There are two factors that you need to consider when choosing a sample.
❶ The size of the sample. The sample must be a large enough proportion of the population for the results to be significant. The larger your sample the more accurate your results.

However, there is usually a limit to the size of sample you can have because a larger sample requires more resources to test it. In cases where a product is tested to destruction, such as the life of a light bulb, choosing a very large sample would mean destroying most of your output!
❷ The way the sample is chosen. The sample should be representative of the population. This means it should take account of variations in the characteristics of the population. These variations should be represented in the sample in the same ratios as in the total population.

For example, if the population to be surveyed contains twice as many women as men then the sample should also contain twice as many women as men.

This type of sampling is called **quota sampling** or **stratified sampling**.

E.g.   (a) A researcher may be given a quota of people to interview:
  10 housewives with children
  2 housewives without children
  6 women who work full-time and have children
  12 women who work full-time and don't have children
(b) A sample may be stratified by age, so that the percentage of the sample in a particular age group is the same as the percentage of the total population in that age group. Then the results can be analysed by age.
(c) A sample of manufactured products from a factory must include the correct proportion of products from each shift and from each machine in order to be representative of the total output.

1 Say which of the following you would study by sampling. Give reasons for your answers. What are the factors you would take into account in the cases you would test by sampling?

(a) The average life of a battery.
(b) The type of cat food most cats prefer.
(c) The top ten singles sold last week.
(d) The cables on a lift.

Sometimes you have no information about the characteristics of a population. Then you should choose a sample in which all items are equally likely to be chosen. This is called a **random sample**.

To ensure the sample is random and as accurate as possible it should be repeated a number of times. The random samples can then be averaged.

2 To carry out the following experiment you will need 100 counters or other objects which are the same except for their colour. Put the counters in a bag. Choose a colour.

Experiment: Take 10 counters without looking and record the number of your chosen colour. Multiply the result by 10 to predict how many of your chosen colour are in the bag. Replace the counters.
Repeat the experiment 10 times, recording your results in a table.
Average out the results of the 10 experiments to find the mean number of counters you picked of your chosen colour.
Multiply the mean by 10 to get an estimate for the total number of counters of that colour.
Empty the bag and count how many counters of your chosen colour there are. Compare this with your first prediction and the final mean estimate.

You should have found that the results obtained by repeating the trial were more accurate because they were based on more information.

The technique of random sampling can be used to estimate the size of a population.

E.g. The crested newt is an endangered species. Conservationists want to find out the number of crested newts in a pond. To do this they catch 10 newts and mark them in a harmless way.

The newts are released back into the pond and the next day 10 more newts are caught. Of the 10 newts 2 are found to have been marked the previous day. The result on the 2nd day is that 2 out of a sample of 10 newts are marked.

Applying the results of this sample to the whole population means that 20% of the population should be marked. But the conservationists know that 10 newts are marked. So 20% of the population is about 10 newts.

Let the size of the total population be P.

$$\frac{20}{100} \times P \approx 10$$

$$\frac{1}{5} \times P \approx 10$$

$$P \approx 50$$

So there are about 50 newts in the pond.

5.9d   Conditional probabilities

If the probability of an event happening depends on whether another event took place or not, then we say the events are **dependent**. The probability is said to be **conditional**.
Whenever the outcome of one trial affects the possible outcomes of a second trial then

events are dependent. If two items are chosen **without replacement** then the item chosen first cannot be chosen again so the probabilities for the second choice are conditional on what was chosen first.

E.g. In a biscuit barrel there are 5 chocolate biscuits, 4 plain and 6 wafers.
(a) A biscuit is taken at random and eaten. Write down the probability of choosing each type of biscuit.
(b) A second biscuit is taken. What is the probability that both biscuits were chocolate?
(a) The total number of biscuits is $5 + 4 + 6 = 15$. The words 'at random' tell you that each biscuit is equally likely to be chosen so

p(choosing chocolate) $= \frac{5}{15}$
p(choosing plain) $= \frac{4}{15}$
p(choosing wafer) $= \frac{6}{15}$

(b) If the first biscuit is eaten then it cannot be replaced! So the probabilities for the second choice are conditional on which biscuit was chosen first.

The probability of choosing a chocolate biscuit in the first trial was $\frac{5}{15}$.

If that biscuit is eaten then there will only be 4 chocolate biscuits left and only 14 left in the barrel. This means that on the second occasion the probability of choosing a chocolate biscuit is $\frac{4}{14}$. This is conditional on having chosen chocolate in the first trial.

We write this as p(chocolate 2nd choice given chocolate 1st choice) or p(chocolate/chocolate).

The probability of choosing 2 chocolate biscuits is

p(chocolate 1st choice) × p(chocolate 2nd choice given chocolate 1st choice)

$p(C) \times p(C/C) = \frac{5}{15} \times \frac{4}{14}$

$= \frac{2}{21}$

The tree diagram looks like this. To get the combined probabilities you multiply along the branches. Do your simplifying in the calculation and not on the diagram.

Remember: In the 2nd trial the number you are choosing from is 1 less.

1st trial	2nd trial	Outcome	Combined Probability
C ($\frac{5}{15}$)	C ($\frac{4}{14}$)	CC	$\frac{5}{15} \times \frac{4}{14} = \frac{2}{21}$
	P ($\frac{4}{14}$)	CP	$\frac{5}{15} \times \frac{4}{14} = \frac{2}{21}$
	W ($\frac{6}{14}$)	CW	$\frac{5}{15} \times \frac{6}{14} = \frac{1}{7}$
P ($\frac{4}{15}$)	C ($\frac{5}{14}$)	PC	$\frac{4}{15} \times \frac{5}{14} = \frac{2}{21}$
	P ($\frac{3}{14}$)	PP	$\frac{4}{15} \times \frac{3}{14} = \frac{2}{35}$
	W ($\frac{6}{14}$)	PW	$\frac{4}{15} \times \frac{6}{14} = \frac{4}{35}$
W ($\frac{6}{15}$)	C ($\frac{5}{14}$)	WC	$\frac{6}{15} \times \frac{5}{14} = \frac{1}{7}$
	P ($\frac{4}{14}$)	WP	$\frac{6}{15} \times \frac{4}{14} = \frac{4}{35}$
	W ($\frac{5}{14}$)	WW	$\frac{6}{15} \times \frac{5}{14} = \frac{1}{7}$

With conditional probability the probability of A followed by B is written

$p(A \text{ and } B) = p(A) \times p(B \text{ given } A)$ or $p(A \text{ and } B) = p(A) \times p(B/A)$

1 In a class there are 14 girls and 13 boys. Two pupils are to be chosen at random to give books out. Draw a tree diagram to illustrate the probabilities.

2 Mark has bought a packet of 9 hyacinth bulbs which all look the same. 4 of the bulbs will have red flowers, 3 blue and 2 white.
(a) If Mark chooses 2 bulbs from the packet calculate the probability that they will both have blue flowers.
(b) Calculate the probability that the first bulb chosen will have white flowers and the second will have red flowers.

An alternative to drawing a tree diagram to represent dependent probabilities is to use a sample space. This shows all the possible outcomes. If a combination is not possible then you blank out that square.

E.g. A teacher needs two pupils to help on parents' evening. Two pupils are to be chosen at random from Alice, Brian, Claire, Derek and Elaine.
Illustrate the possible combinations for choosing two pupils from these five.

Followed by

		A	B	C	D	E
	A		AB	AC	AD	AE
First	B	BA		BC	BD	BE
choice	C	CA	CB		CD	CE
	D	DA	DB	DC		DE
	E	EA	EB	EC	ED	

Note: Since you need two pupils this is without replacement.

You cannot choose Alice and then Alice again so that choice can be blanked out.
The number of possibilities for the first choice is 5 but the number of possibilities for the second choice is 1 less. So the total number of possible combinations is $5 \times 4 = 20$.

3 In a packet of yoghurts there are 4 different varieties: strawberry, raspberry, lemon and blackcurrant. Mr Smith has one today and one tomorrow.
Illustrate Mr Smith's choices using a sample space.

5.10a Dispersion and standard deviation

Dispersion is the name given to the way data are distributed. You are already familiar with two ways to describe dispersion.

❶ Range. This tells you the difference between the largest and smallest values.

❷ Interquartile range. The difference between the first and third quartiles. This removes values from the range which are unusually large or small.

There are a number of more accurate ways in which you can measure the spread of a set of data.

Deviation from the mean

The distance of a value from the mean is called its **deviation** from the mean.

E.g. The ages of the five members of the Smith family are 8, 10, 12, 32, 38.
Their mean age is 20.

   The deviation from the mean is found by subtracting the mean from each of the values in the original list.

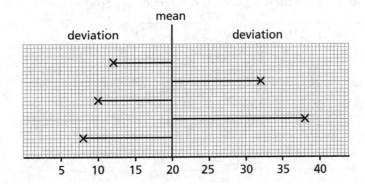

Age (x)	Mean ($\bar{x}$)	Deviation ($x - \bar{x}$)
8	20	⁻12
10	20	⁻10
12	20	⁻8
32	20	12
38	20	18

Mean deviation

If you try to find the mean of the deviations in the usual way you will find that the value is 0.

$$\frac{^-12 + {}^-10 + {}^-8 + 12 + 18}{5} = 0$$

Finding the mean of the deviations in this way takes into account which side of the mean the values are (i.e. whether the deviation is positive or negative). But this is not necessary.

   To make the values more useful just consider the **size** of each deviation and ignore the direction. This positive value is called the **modulus** (sometimes shortened to **mod**) and is written like this:

$$\left| x - \bar{x} \right|$$

The mean size of the deviations can now be calculated.

Mean deviation = $\dfrac{\sum \left| x - \bar{x} \right|}{n}$

$\sum$ is the Greek letter, sigma. It means sum (add up) all the values. n is the number of values which have been added.

E.g. Calculate the mean deviation of the ages of the Smiths.

Age (x)	Modulus of the deviation $\lvert x - \bar{x} \rvert$
8	12
10	10
12	8
32	12
38	18

Mean deviation $= \dfrac{12 + 10 + 8 + 12 + 18}{5} = 12$

So the average distance of the values from the mean is 12 years.

Variance

An alternative way to get positive values for the deviation from the mean is to square the deviation. The squares of the deviations can then be added and their mean value calculated. This mean of the squares of the deviations is called the **variance**.

Variance $= \dfrac{\sum \left(x - \bar{x}\right)^2}{n}$ where n is the total number of values

E.g. Find the variance for the ages of the Smiths.

Age (x)	$\bar{x}$	$(x - \bar{x})$	$(x - \bar{x})^2$
8	20	⁻12	144
10	20	⁻10	100
12	20	⁻8	64
32	20	12	144
38	20	18	324

Variance $= \dfrac{\sum \left(x - \bar{x}\right)^2}{n} = \dfrac{144 + 100 + 64 + 144 + 324}{5} = 155 \cdot 2$

Since the original problem was to measure the spread of ages in the Smith family an answer of 155·2 does not seem to make much sense. This is because the deviations were squared. This can be corrected by taking the square root of the variance.

Standard deviation

The square root of the variance is called the **standard deviation**. The standard deviation is given by

$$\sigma = \sqrt{\dfrac{\sum \left(x - \bar{x}\right)^2}{n}}$$

For the ages of the Smith family the standard deviation $= \sqrt{155 \cdot 2} = 12 \cdot 46$ (to 2 d.p.)
For a general frequency distribution

Variance $= \dfrac{\sum \left(x - \bar{x}\right)^2 f}{\sum f}$ where f is the frequency of the value x.

Standard deviation $= \sqrt{\dfrac{\sum \left(x - \bar{x}\right)^2 f}{\sum f}}$

Note: If you are using grouped data the class mid-value is used for x.

E.g. Sam records the number of birds visiting a bird table between 12 noon and 12:15 each day for 20 days. Her results are given below.
Calculate the mean and standard deviation of the number of visiting birds.

3	8	9	2	5	6	4	8	6	3
2	6	8	4	5	3	5	2	7	4

Birds (x)	Frequency(f)	xf
2	3	6
3	3	9
4	3	12
5	3	15
6	3	18
7	1	7
8	3	24
9	1	9
	Total = 100	

Mean = $\dfrac{\sum x}{n}$ or $\dfrac{\sum xf}{\sum f}$

Mean = $\dfrac{100}{20} = 5$

There are on average 5 birds visiting the table each day between 12 and 12:15.

Birds (x)	Deviation($x - \bar{x}$)	$(x - \bar{x})^2$	Frequency(f)	$(x - \bar{x})^2 f$
2	⁻3	9	3	27
3	⁻2	4	3	12
4	⁻1	1	3	3
5	0	0	3	0
6	1	1	3	3
7	2	4	1	4
8	3	9	3	27
9	4	16	1	16
				Total = 92

Standard deviation = $\sqrt{\dfrac{\sum (x - \bar{x})^2 f}{\sum f}}$

$= \sqrt{\dfrac{92}{20}}$

$= \sqrt{4 \cdot 6}$

$= 2 \cdot 14$ (to 2 d.p.)

This tells us that the number of birds visiting the table will normally be within about 2 of the mean. In other words the number of visiting birds will usually be between 3 and 7.

?

1 The efficiency of an office junior is being checked. He completes the following number of pieces of work per hour over 20 hours.

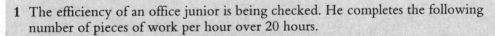

5	2	6	4	4	5	4	3	4	5
5	6	8	8	7	4	2	9	1	8

Calculate the mean and standard deviation of the number of pieces of work completed.

2 Use the data given in **unit 5.7c** to answer the following:
   (a) Calculate the standard deviation for the heights of the girls in Year 8.
   (b) Calculate the standard deviation for the heights of the boys in Year 8.
   (c) Compare the mean and standard deviations for the two sets of data.

Using the standard deviation

Approximately 68% of any population is within one standard deviation of the mean: 34% on either side. Within two standard deviations you would expect approximately 96% of any population.

34% | 34%

14% | 14%

E.g. A drinks machine contains a selection of milk shakes which it dispenses in 500 ml cups. The mean quantity of milk shake dispensed is 500 ml, with a standard deviation of 7·5 ml. Estimate the probability that a drink from the machine will contain less than 480 ml.

480 ml is 20 ml below the mean. The standard deviation is 7·5 ml so two standard deviations would be 15 ml. 480 ml is therefore more than two standard deviations below the mean.

Only 4% of the population is more than two standard deviations from the mean. Therefore 2% of the population is more than two standard deviations **below** the mean (and 2% is more than two standard deviations above). This means that under 2% of drinks dispensed will contain less than 480 ml so the probability of a drink containing less than 480 ml is under 0·02.

?

3 What is the maximum amount of drink that could be dispensed by the machine in the example above if the drink was within one standard deviation of the mean?

4 What percentage of drinks dispensed are between one and two standard deviations above the mean?

5.10b Comparing histograms

One way to compare two frequency distributions is to compare the shapes of their histograms.

E.g. Two samples of 50 people were asked a question with responses ranging from strongly agree (1) to strongly disagree (5). Below are the results.

(a) 1 1 1 1 1 1 1 1 1 1
    1 1 1 1 1 1 1 1 1 1
    1 1 1 1 1 1 1 1 1 1
    1 1 1 1 1 2 2 4 4 4
    4 5 5 5 5 5 5 5 5 5

(b) 1 1 1 1 1 1 1 1 1 1
    1 1 1 1 1 2 2 2 2
    2 2 2 2 2 2 2 2 2 2
    2 2 2 2 2 2 2 2 2 2
    3 3 3 3 3 4 4 4 4 5

Both sets of data have the same mean (2) and the same range but their histograms show that the responses are distributed very differently.

(a)

(b)

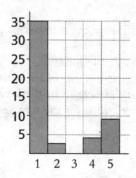

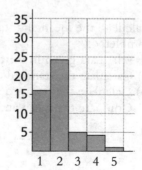

In histogram (a) there is no regularity. The values are concentrated at the extremes with 1 being exceptionally large in comparison with the other responses. 13 people were more than 1 place away from the mean and 9 were more than 2 places away.

In (b) the responses are grouped near the mean. The frequencies are higher the nearer the mean you get, but with more people answering 1 than any single response above the mean. 2 is the modal response as well as the mean. Only 5 people were more than 1 place away from the mean, and only 1 person was more than 2 away from the mean.

In sample (a) there was a much wider spread of opinion than in sample (b). In (a) more people felt strongly one way or the other and this averaged out. In (b) more people answered 2 or near 2.

In both cases the mean response is 2. In (a) this represents the average of people's views but it is not the view of many people. In sample (b) the mean response is much more representative of people's views.

?

1 Compare the frequency distributions represented by the following histograms. Say as much as you can about the position of the mean and the spread of the data.

(a)　　　　　　　(b)　　　　　　　(c)

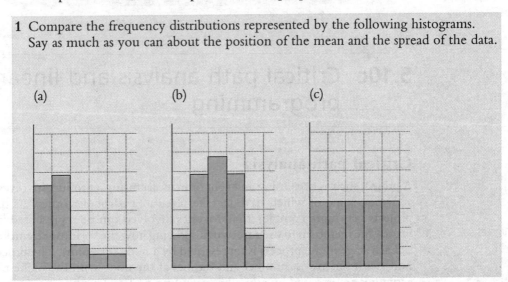

Normal distribution

In a set of unbiased continuous data, such as measurements of height or weight, you would expect values to be concentrated around the mean, with the mean having the highest frequency and the frequency decreasing the further away from the mean you get.

You would also expect the distribution to be symmetrical about the mean. This gives mean = mode = median.

A distribution which has these characteristics and which is often used to provide a comparison with other distributions is the **normal distribution**. This type of distribution occurs in many natural phenomena.

A graph of values against frequency for the normal distribution gives a very distinctive symmetrical bell-shaped curve with the highest point at the mean.

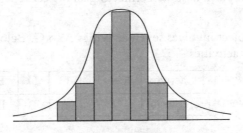

A histogram representing a normal distribution has a similar bell-like shape.

In this type of histogram the mean, median and mode are all equal and the histogram is symmetrical about the mean. In the example above, the responses in sample (b) are distributed more 'normally' than those in sample (a). Histograms which are not 'normally' distributed can be compared with the normal distribution.

2 (a) Which of the following frequency distribution graphs do you think best represents the amount of long French words spoken by the average pupil in Year 7?

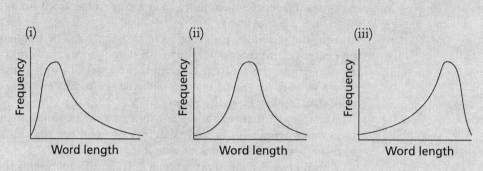

(i)   (ii)   (iii)

(b) Which of the graphs do you think best represents the amount of long French words a French person would use in everyday conversation?

5.10c Critical path analysis and linear programming

Critical path analysis

A project such as organising an event or manufacturing a product involves a sequence of activities, some of which have to take place in a particular order. As the planning of projects gets more complex the processes involved can be represented in a number of ways. One method is to use a **network** showing how the various activities are connected.

Each stage in the process is represented by a node (or point). The process starts at the node with the lowest number and finishes at the node with the highest number. Each activity is represented by a line between two nodes. This line represents an activity B which starts at point 2 and continues to point 3.

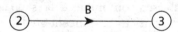

If an activity B cannot take place until another activity A is completed then A is called a **prerequisite** of B. A must appear at an earlier stage than B in the network.

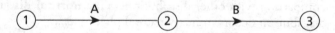

The shortest possible route connecting all the activities in a process is called the **critical path**.

E.g. A project involves seven activities A to G. Below is a table of prerequisites for these activities:

activity	A	B	C	D	E	F	G
prerequisite	–	A	A	B	B	C,D	E,F

Draw a critical path network to represent this project.

Look at the table. A has no prerequisite so it can happen before any other activity has taken place. So start with A going from node 1 to node 2.

Now A is a prerequisite of B and C, which do not depend on each other, so the network can have two branches leading from node 2, one representing B and one representing C.

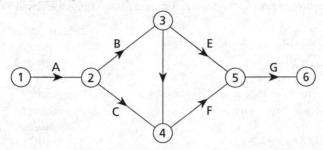

1 A firm wants to start manufacturing televisions. This involves the following activities. Complete a table of prerequisites and hence draw a critical path network for this process.

(A) Order components   (B) Order packing

(C) Manufacture parts   (D) Set up testing procedures

(E) Assemble sets   (F) Test sets

(G) Pack sets   (H) Dispatch sets to wholesalers

Critical path analysis can be used to work out the timing for an entire process and also for various stages of the process.

Given a starting time of 0 for the whole path you can work out the earliest starting time (ES) for each activity. The earliest starting time for the final stage tells you how long the entire process will take.

E.g. The following table shows the time needed for each of the activities listed in question 1 involved in the manufacture of television sets. Work out the minimum time the manufacturers need to allow to produce the televisions.

activity	A	B	C	D	E	F	G	H
time needed (days)	5	4	6	3	1	1	1	1

This involves looking at the critical path network. Check your answer to question 1 if you haven't already done so.

Earliest starting time

at node 1 = 0

at node 2 = 0 + 5 = 5 days   This represents the time needed to complete A.

at node 3 = 5 + 6 = 11

at node 5 = 11 + 1 = 12   Note: You are only recording the longest route here.

at node 7 = 12 + 1 = 13

at node 8 = 13 + 1 = 14

at node 9 = 14 + 1 = 15 days

So the manufacturing process must be started at least 15 days before the expected completion of the work.

If you know the minimum time the process will take and the time or date when the process must be finished then you can work out the latest possible starting time for the project.

?

2 Claire is having a party. She has made a list of all the things which need to be done in preparation and an estimate of how long they will take.

A	Buy food	2 hours
B	Get the house ready	40 minutes
C	Have a bath	15 minutes
D	Make food	2 hours
E	Collect records from friend's house	5 minutes
F	Decide on menu	20 minutes
G	Put out the food	10 minutes
H	Get dressed	25 minutes
I	Start the party	

Two of Claire's friends have offered to help so up to three activities can take place at the same time.

(a) Draw a critical path network to show how Claire and her friends need to organise their tasks.

(b) Calculate the minimum time needed to prepare for the party if each task is done by one person.

(c) If the party is to start at 7:30 what is the latest time they can start the preparations?

Linear programming

You have already seen how you can find a set of solutions which satisfy several inequalities at the same time by drawing a graph of the inequalities.

Linear programming uses the method of graphing inequalities to find solutions in situations where there are several limits or conditions. The best (or optimum) solution is then chosen from the set of possible solutions. Linear programming is used in business management to determine **maximum** profits, **minimum** cost or overheads etc. When several inequalities are graphed a triangle or polygon is produced. The points within this shape give all the possible solutions. The maximum or minimum values occur at the vertices (corners).

E.g. A greengrocer makes a special offer to customers who buy at least 1 lb of apples and 1 lb of pears. The offer is limited to a total of 5 lb of fruit.

(a) Write down the three inequalities that represent these conditions.

(b) Draw graphs on the same axes to represent these conditions.

(c) If the profit on apples is 40p per lb and the profit on pears is 55p per lb, what combination of fruit will give the shop its greatest profit?

(d) What will the maximum profit be?

(a) Let x lb be the quantity of apples bought. Let y lb be the quantity of pears bought. Hence $x \geq 1$, $y \geq 1$ and $x + y \leq 5$

(b)

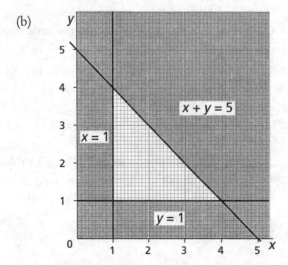

(c) The maximum profit must occur when the most possible fruit is sold so it will be on the line $x + y = 5$.

The profit on pears is greater than on apples so look for the point on this line which gives the greatest quantity of pears. This will be at one of the vertices of the triangular region bounded by the inequalities. The two vertices which touch the line $x + y = 5$ have coordinates (1, 4) and (4, 1). (1, 4) gives more pears.

Hence the maximum profit the shop will make is when the customer buys 1 lb of apples and 4 lb of pears.

(d) The profit is given by the equation $40x + 55y$.

Substituting the values $x = 1$ and $y = 4$ into the equation gives

$$40 \times 1 + 55 \times 4 = 260$$

So the maximum profit is £2·60.

?

3 The post office is planning a new book of stamps for business users containing 24 pence and 32 pence stamps. Market research has come up with the following requirements:
(i) There should be more 24 pence stamps than 32 pence stamps.
(ii) There should be at least 20 stamps in total.
(iii) The cost should not be more than £9·60.
(a) Write down the inequalities representing these requirements.
(b) By drawing a graph find the largest number of 32 pence stamps that can be included in the book.

4 A builder plans to build houses and bungalows on a 6000 m² plot of land. He allows 300 m² for each bungalow and 400 m² for each house.
The local council insists on the following restrictions:
There must be more than 6 houses.
There must be more bungalows than houses.
Draw the regions which represent these conditions on one pair of axes. Use your graph to calculate the following:
(a) the maximum number of bungalows that he can build.
(b) the maximum number of houses that he can build.

Remember: The maximum or minimum values in linear programming are calculated at the vertices of the solution region.

5.10d Calculating the probability for any two events

You know how to calculate probabilities when events are independent or dependent or mutually exclusive. You now need to be able to apply what you know about probability to be able to calculate the probability for any two events.

There are a number of questions you should ask yourself before you start calculating the probabilities.

Step 1 What event are you looking for the probability of?

Step 2 Can you use the fact that p(event) = 1 – p(not event) to save you work? (You may already have calculated p(not event).)

Step 3 Is the event a combination of two or more mutually exclusive events whose probabilities you can add?

Step 4 Are these events themselves combinations of two other events, either dependent or independent?

Here is an example to show how useful these steps can be.

E.g. Find the probability of getting a 5 or Heads (or both) if you toss a coin and roll a fair die.

Without using the steps above:

It is possible to get a 5 and Heads at the same time so the events 'getting a 5' and 'getting Heads' are not mutually exclusive. In fact the event 'getting a 5 or Heads or both' is a combination of **three** mutually exclusive events:

'5 and not Heads', 'Heads and not 5' and '5 and Heads'

p(5 or H or both) = p(5 and not H) + p(H and not 5) + p(5 and H)

The result you get on the coin will have no effect on the result on the die (and vice versa) so the individual events involved are independent and you can multiply the probabilities.

Hence p(5 and not H) = p(5) × p(not H)

$= \frac{1}{6} \times \frac{1}{2}$

$= \frac{1}{12}$

p(H and not 5) = p(H) × p(not 5)

$= p(H) \times [1 - p(5)]$

$= \frac{1}{2} \times \frac{5}{6}$

$= \frac{5}{12}$

p(5 and H) = p(5) × p(H)

$= \frac{1}{6} \times \frac{1}{2}$

$= \frac{1}{12}$

Adding the probabilities of these mutually exclusive events gives
p(5 or H or both) $= \frac{1}{12} + \frac{5}{12} + \frac{1}{12}$

$= \frac{7}{12}$

This is easier to see if you draw a tree diagram.

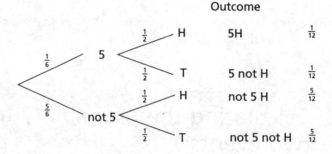

It is easier still if you use the steps given on the previous page.

Step 1   event = 5 or Heads or both

Step 2   p(5 or Heads or both) = 1 − p(neither 5 nor Heads)

Step 4   neither 5 nor Heads = not 5 **and** not Heads

'not 5' and 'not Heads' are two independent events so multiply the probabilities:

p(not 5 and not Heads) = p(not 5) × p(not Heads)

$= \frac{5}{6} \times \frac{1}{2}$

$= \frac{5}{12}$

So p(5 or Heads or both) $= 1 - \frac{5}{12}$

$= \frac{7}{12}$

Remember: Whenever you can, use the fact that p(event) = 1 − p(not event) to make things easier.

You can see from this example that sometimes it's much quicker not to draw a diagram.

E.g. A bag contains 2 red counters, 7 orange counters and 3 yellow counters. A counter is chosen without looking and then replaced. A second counter is then chosen. Calculate the probability that the two counters will be the same colour.

Step 3   p(2 same colour) = p(2 red) + p(2 orange) + p(2 yellow)

Events are independent because the counters are replaced. The probabilities are the same each time a choice is made.

Step 4   p(2 same colour) = p(red) × p(red) + p(orange) × p(orange)

$$+ \; p(yellow) \times p(yellow)$$

$$= \tfrac{2}{12} \times \tfrac{2}{12} + \tfrac{7}{12} \times \tfrac{7}{12} + \tfrac{3}{12} \times \tfrac{3}{12}$$

$$= \tfrac{4}{144} + \tfrac{49}{144} + \tfrac{9}{144}$$

$$= \tfrac{31}{72}$$

1 A card is drawn at random from a pack of 52 and then replaced. A second card is then chosen. Calculate the probability that:
(a) both cards will be picture cards. (These include Aces.)
(b) neither card will be a picture card.
(c) at least one card will be a picture card.

When items are chosen without replacement then the probabilities are different for the second trial (conditional probability). In this case it may well be easier if you draw a diagram, especially if there are several parts to the question. Once you've drawn the diagram you can read off the probabilities required to answer the various parts of the question.

E.g. Simon's drawer contains 3 black socks, 4 grey socks and 5 white socks. Simon pulls two socks from the drawer without looking.
(a) What is the probability he chooses 2 socks of the same colour?
(b) What is the probability he chooses first a grey and then a black sock?
(c) What is the probability that one sock will be grey and the other black?
Simon is choosing without replacement so the events are dependent.

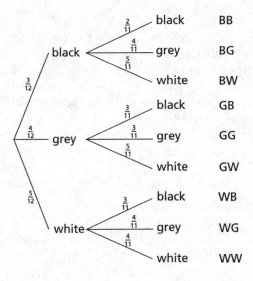

(a) p(2 same colour) = p(2 black) + p(2 grey) + p(2 white)

$$= \tfrac{3}{12} \times \tfrac{2}{11} + \tfrac{4}{12} \times \tfrac{3}{11} + \tfrac{5}{12} \times \tfrac{4}{11}$$

$$= \tfrac{19}{66}$$

(b) p(grey then black) = p(grey) × p(black/grey)

$$= \frac{4}{12} \times \frac{3}{11}$$

$$= \frac{1}{11}$$

(c) There are two ways to get a grey sock and a black sock: first grey then black or first black then grey.

p(grey and black) = p(grey then black) + p(black then grey)

From (b), p(grey then black) = $\frac{1}{11}$

$$= \frac{1}{11} + p(black) \times p(grey/black)$$

$$= \frac{1}{11} + \frac{3}{12} \times \frac{4}{11}$$

$$= \frac{2}{11}$$

2 A car dealer has 6 red cars, 5 blue cars and 2 white cars. He sells one car in the morning and a second in the afternoon.

(a) Draw a tree diagram to illustrate the probabilities.

(b) What is the probability that
   (i) the cars are both blue?
   (ii) the cars are both the same colour?
   (iii) at least one car is blue?

3 Sajpal and Michael carry out a survey of 120 Year 7 pupils to find out whether they watch BBC or ITV television, both or neither.
The results are as follows:

BBC	22
ITV	29
neither	6
both	63

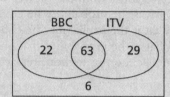

(a) If a child is chosen at random, what is the probability that he or she watches at least some BBC programmes?

(b) Given that Sarah watches ITV, what is the probability that she also watches BBC?

(c) If two children are chosen at random, what is the probability that they both watch television but not the same channel?

Exam questions

1 The diagram below shows how the 55p cost of a bottle of mineral water is made up.

(a) Express the cost of water as a percentage of the total cost of a bottle of mineral water. Give your answer correct to one decimal place. (4 marks)
The cost of the glass for the bottle increases by 25%.
The cost of all other items is unchanged.
(b) Calculate the new cost of a bottle of mineral water. (2 marks)
(ULEAC)

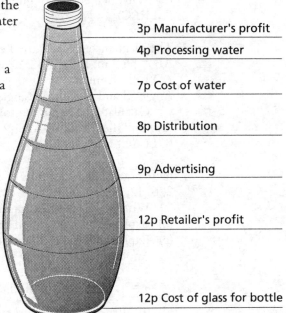

3p Manufacturer's profit
4p Processing water
7p Cost of water
8p Distribution
9p Advertising
12p Retailer's profit
12p Cost of glass for bottle

2 Factorise completely
(a) $x^2 - 3x$ (2 marks)   (b) $2p^2q + pq^2$ (2 marks)   (ULEAC)

3 A fire escape ladder AB is mounted on the back of a fire engine at a height of 2·3 m above the ground. The ladder is extended to a length of 27 m and makes an angle of 14° with the vertical. The fire engine is parked so that the top of the ladder touches a building at B as shown in the diagram. Calculate
(i) the horizontal distance, AC, from the foot of the ladder to the building,
(ii) the height of the top of the ladder above the ground.
(WJEC)

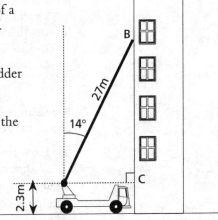

4 A plastic marker buoy floating in the sea consists of a cone attached to a hemispherical base, as shown in the diagram below. The radius of the hemispherical base is 0·95 metres, and the height of the cone is 1·2 metres.
Calculate the volume of the buoy. (4 marks)
(WJEC)

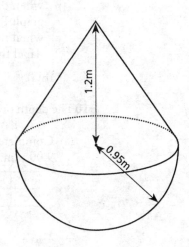

5 Gunpowder is made up of potassium nitrate, sulphur and charcoal mixed in the ratio 33 : 5 : 7.
   (a) 10 kg of sulphur and 14 kg of charcoal are mixed. How much potassium nitrate must be added to make gunpowder? (2 marks)
   (b) How much charcoal is needed to make 900 kg of gunpowder? (3 marks)
   (c) What percentage of gunpowder is made up of sulphur? (3 marks)
   (ULEAC)

6 The diagram represents the Leaning Tower of Pisa.
   AB = 55·9 m, BC = 13·2 m and CD = 54·8 m.
   AD is horizontal.
   Angles B and C are right angles.
   (a) Calculate the angle the tower makes with AD. (5 marks)
   (b) Find the length of AD. (2 marks)
   (ULEAC)

7 Here are the first six terms of a sequence of numbers.
   2, 6, 12, 20, 30, 42
   (a) Write down the next number in the sequence. (1 mark)
   (b) Explain how you found this number. (2 marks)
   (c) Explain why all the numbers in the sequence will be even. (1 mark)
       Another sequence may be obtained by substituting, in order,

   $$n = 1, n = 2, n = 3, \text{ in the formula } s = \frac{n(n+1)}{2}$$

   (d) (i) Write down the first six terms of this sequence. (2 marks)
       (ii) Use this answer to help you find a formula for working out the first sequence. (2 marks)
   (ULEAC)

8 A large locust swarm contains 40 000 000 000 locusts.
   (a) Each locust needs to eat about 2 g of food a day. How much will the whole swarm eat in a day, in kg?
   (b) In Africa farmers grow about 1000 kg of maize to the acre. If a swarm of locusts invades an area growing maize, how many acres of this crop would be destroyed in a day?
   (MEG SMP 11–16)

9 A container has a capacity of 2 litres. Water is poured into the container at a rate of 125 ml per second.

   (a) How many seconds will it take to fill the container?
       (2 marks)
   (b) The container has a height of 18 cm.

   Sketch graphs to show how the depth of water increases with time:

   (i) when the container is cylindrical (label the graph I),
   (ii) when the container is an inverted cone (label the graph II). (4 marks)

   (MEG)

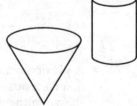

10 The depth of water, d metres, in a harbour at t hours after noon is given by the formula
   $$d = 6 + 4 \cos(30t)°$$
   (a) Complete the following table for values of d at hourly intervals from noon until 9.00 p.m. (2 marks)

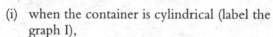

t	0	1	2	3	4	5	6	7	8	9
d	10	9.46	8	6			2			

(b) On the grid below, draw a graph of d against t. (3 marks)

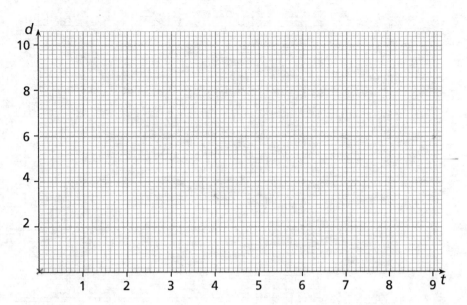

(c) From the graph, obtain the times between which a fully laden boat, requiring a depth of at least 5 metres of water, would be unable to enter harbour. (2 marks)
(MEG)

11 The equation
$$x(x + 1) = 10$$
has a solution between 2 and 3. Using decimal search or otherwise, find this value of x, giving your final answer correct to 2 decimal places. Show your working clearly. (MEG SMP 11-16)

12 The diagram shows a circle, centre O. AT and BT are tangents to the circle and P and Q are points on its circumference.

Angle AOB = 100° and angle QAT = 30°

Stating your reasons and showing your working, calculate the size of
(i) angle ATB,
(ii) angle BPQ.
(NEAB)

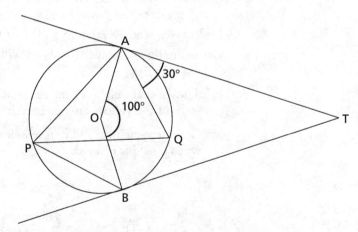

13 A surveyor measures a field and makes a rough sketch of it, shown below. Calculate the distance AC. (4 marks)
(WJEC)

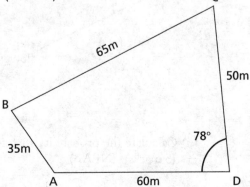

14 (a) Find the gradient of the line $2y = x + 4$. (1 mark) $y = \frac{x + 4}{2}$ g is $\frac{1}{2}$

(b) On the grid below, draw and label the lines $2y = x + 4$ and $y = 4 - x$. (4 marks)

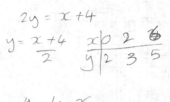

$2y = x + 4$

$y = \frac{x+4}{2}$

x	0	2	6
y	2	3	5

$y = 4 - x$

x	1	2	4	-1
y	3	2	0	5

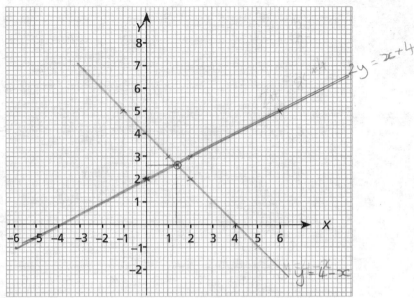

(c) Obtain the solution of the simultaneous equations

$2y = x + 4$ $x = 1.4$
$y = 4 - x$ $y = 2.6$

giving the value of x and the value of y correct to one decimal place. (2 marks)
(MEG)

15 Solve the equation

$7 \tan x° - 4 = 0$, for $0 \le x \le 360$. (3 marks)

(SEB)

16 A packet contains the seeds of flowers which will be either red or yellow. $\frac{2}{3}$ of the seeds will produce red flowers and $\frac{1}{3}$ will produce yellow flowers.

(a) I select two seeds at random and plant them.

Calculate the probability that both will be the seeds of a yellow flower.

(1 mark)

(b) It is known that only $\frac{4}{5}$ of the seeds of the red flowers germinate, while $\frac{9}{10}$ of the seeds of the yellow flowers germinate.

(i) Complete the probability tree below, which shows the possible outcomes when a seed is planted.

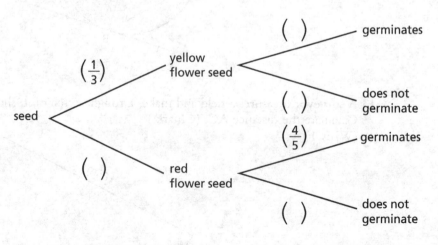

(ii) Calculate the probability that a seed chosen at random will germinate.
(5 marks) (NEAB)

17 This table gives the first four terms of a sequence *u*.

u_1	u_2	u_3	u_4
3	6	12	24

(a) There is a simple relationship connecting each term with the next one. What is the relationship? Write it in words or in symbols.

(b) Write down a formula for the *n*th term u_n in term of *n*.
(MEG)

18 A cylindrical tank, 5 metres long, is used to store a hazardous liquid as shown in Figure 1.

A dipstick is used to measure the depth of the liquid.

The dipstick passes through the centre, O, of a cross-section of the tank as shown in Figure 2.
The diameter of the cross-section of the tank is 2 metres.

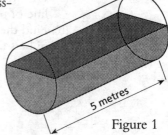

Figure 1

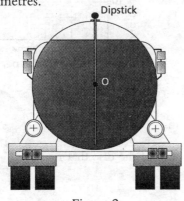

Figure 2

To satisfy safe storage conditions, the horizontal surface area of the liquid in the tank must not be less than 2 square metres.

(a) Explain why the width of the horizontal surface of the liquid must not be less than 0·4 metres. (2 marks)

(b) The depth of the liquid in the tank is found to be 1·8 metres.

Can this volume of liquid be stored safely in the tank?

Justify your answer. (5 marks) (SEB)

19 An expression for the volume and an expression for the surface area of the capsule shown in the diagram are contained in the following list.

$\pi d + 2h$
$\pi d^2 + \frac{1}{4}\pi d^2 h$
$\pi d^2 + \pi dh$
$\frac{1}{6}\pi d^3 + \frac{1}{4}\pi d^2 h$
$\frac{1}{6}\pi d^3 + \pi dh$

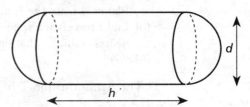

(a) (i) Write down the expression for the volume. (2 marks)

   (ii) Give a reason for your choice. (2 marks)

(b) Write down the expression for the surface area. (2 marks)
(MEG)

20 Mrs. McDonald lives 8 miles from the nearest railway station, and it takes her 20 minutes, travelling at constant speed, to drive there in her car

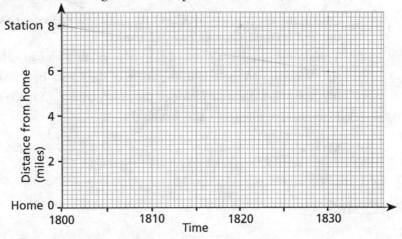

(a) She sets off from home at 1810 to meet her son at the station. On the grid above, draw a travel graph for her journey. (3 marks)

(b) Mrs. McDonald's son arrived at the station at 1800 and started to walk along the road towards home. He walked at 4 miles an hour.
On the grid above, draw a travel graph for his walk. (3 marks)
(MEG)

21 This scatter diagram represents the number of road deaths per 100 000 population (y) and the number of vehicles per 100 population (x) in ten countries.

(a) On the diagram, draw the line of best fit. (2 marks)

(b) Find the equation of the line of best fit. (3 marks)
(MEG)

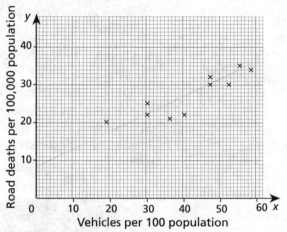

22 This is a floppy disc for a micro-computer.
The useful area is shaded.
(a) Find the area of the whole disc.
(b) Find the shaded area.
(c) Find the percentage of the area of the disc that is useful.
(MEG SMP 11-16)

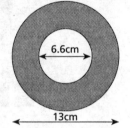

23 The distances, in kilometres, of five planets from the sun are as follows:

Planet A	$1 \cdot 43 \times 10^9$	Planet D	$2 \cdot 87 \times 10^9$
Planet B	$5 \cdot 97 \times 10^7$	Planet E	$1 \cdot 50 \times 10^8$
Planet C	$7 \cdot 78 \times 10^8$		

(a) Find the ratio of the distance of Planet D from the sun to the distance of Planet B from the sun. Give your answer in the form $k : 1$. (3 marks)

(b) Light travels at a speed of $3 \cdot 00 \times 10^5$ km/s. Calculate the time, correct to the nearest minute, that light takes to travel from the sun to Planet C. (3 marks)
(MEG)

24 The transformation T of the plane is represented by the matrix **M**

where $\mathbf{M} = \begin{pmatrix} 1 & 1 \\ -1 & 1 \end{pmatrix}$

The images of the points O(0, 0), A(5, 0) and B(0, 3) under this transformation are O, A' and B' respectively.

(a) Obtain the coordinates of A' and B', and show triangles OAB and OA'B' on the grid on the following page. (3 marks)

(b) Transformation T is a combination of a rotation and an enlargement.
(i) Write down the size of the angle of the rotation. (1 mark)
(ii) Calculate the scale factor of the enlargement. (2 marks)

(c) Find positive integers n and k such that

$$\mathbf{M}^n = k \begin{pmatrix} 1 & 0 \\ 0 & 1 \end{pmatrix}.$$

(3 marks)

(MEG)

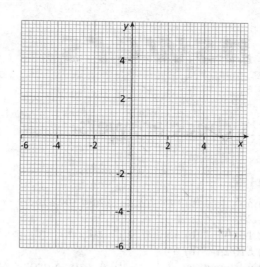

25 When a ball is dropped from a height, it bounces to 70% of its starting height.
A ball is dropped from a height of 2 metres and bounces three times.
How high does it reach on its third bounce?
Give your answer in centimetres and express it correct to 2 significant figures.
(SEB)

26 (a) Express $x^2 + 5x - 7$ in the form $(x + a)^2 + b$.
(b) Hence, solve $x^2 + 5x - 7 = 0$. (4 marks)
(NEAB)

27 The diagram below shows the graph of $y = x^2 - \dfrac{1}{x}$

(a) From this graph write down
(correct to the nearest integer)
the solutions of the equation
$$x^2 - \frac{1}{x} = 10$$
The solutions of $x^2 - \dfrac{1}{x} = 10$ may

also be found by iteration.

(b) One method is to re-write the

equation as $x = \sqrt{10 + \dfrac{1}{x}}$ and use

the iteration $u_{n+1} = \sqrt{10 + \dfrac{1}{u_n}}$

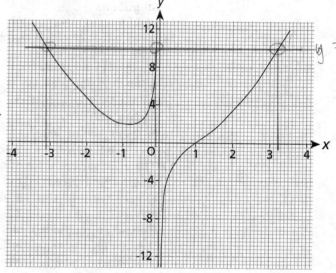

(i) Using this iteration with $u_1 = 3$ find u_2 and u_3, writing down all the figures
shown on your calculator.
(ii) Hence write down, correct to 2 decimal places, one solution of the
equation.

(c) (i) Show that the equation may also be re-written as
$$x = \frac{1}{x^2 - 10}.$$
(ii) Use the iteration $u_{n+1} = \dfrac{1}{u_n^2 - 10}$ to find a second solution, correct to 2
decimal places, of the equation.

(d) Use a modification of the iteration in (b) to find the third solution, correct to 2
decimal places, of the equation.

(10 marks)

(MEG SMP 11-16)

Answers

Letts check answers

Level 3

1 (a) 365   (b) two hundred and sixty four   (c) 675, 360, 125, 5

2 (a) 20   (b) 8   (c) 15   (d) 5   (e) 17

3 (a) 14   (b) 45   (c) 80   (d) 16

4 (a) £10·24   (b) 6

5 (a) 6 remainder 2   (b) 4 cars, 3 people in the car which is not full

6 (a) about 2 metres   (b) about 70 cm

7 (a) £20   (b) £500

8
$$\begin{array}{r} £1·36 \\ +£3·24 \\ \hline £4·60 \end{array}$$

9 -3°C

10 29·7 cm

11 (a) 1000   (b) 60   (c) 1000   (d) 7   (e) 100 000

12 (a) feet and inches or metres or centimetres

    (b) milk, orange juice, water ...

    (c) stopwatch

    (d) minutes

13 (a) 113   (b) 42

14 (a) 15, 18, 21 Each number is 3 more than the last number. They are multiples of 3 (3 times table).

    (b) 39 + 11 = 50, 49 + 11 = 60, 59 + 11 = 70

15 (a) 32, 302, 56, 200, 18, 160, 470

    (b) 65, 35, 200, 160, 470

    (c) 200, 160, 470

16 (a) 2500 (half of 5000)

    (b) 1 step forward, 6 steps to the left, 4 steps back, 2 steps right, 3 steps back

17 There are various ways of doing this. Here are some examples:

Objects with curved edges: tennis ball, round cushions, Frisbee, oval mirror

Objects with right angles: work-out video, building blocks, poster, shoe box, CD player

Cuboid objects: video, blocks, shoe box, CD player

Regular objects: tennis ball, blocks

'Flat' objects: poster, Frisbee, mirror

18 (a) 2   (b) 1   (c) 6

19 (a) NE   (b) SE

20 £4·29

21

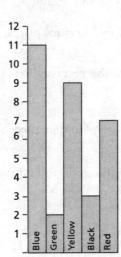

22 Event (b) is most likely. Only you can place the other events.
23 (c) and perhaps (b) but probably not (a)
24 (a) not fair   (b) not fair   (c) fair

Level 4

1 (a) sixty thousand, two hundred and fifty four
(b) 3 701 875
(c) 43 692, 42 732, 10 515, 8260, 4037, 3175, 2065, 318
2 (a) 48   (b) 63   (c) 3   (d) 8
3 (a) 111 kg   (b) 31 g
4 (a) 721   (b) 833   (c) 657   (d) 408
5 (a) 576   (b) £4·41   (c) 25   (d) 12
6 (a) 6·92 m   (b) 1·22 kg   (c) 3·6
7 (a) 50   (b) 90   (c) 50   (d) 60
8 (a) 360   (b) 840   (c) 2300   (d) 4800

9 (a)   (b)

(c) 60   (d) 9
10 (a) 45 mm   (b) 2·7 cm
11 (a) 50%   (b) 9
12 (a) 2048 mm (b) 8
13 (a) 1·06 m   (b) $(2 \times 2\cdot56) + 3\cdot18 + 1\cdot06 = 9\cdot36$ m   (c) $25 - (2 \times 9\cdot36) = 6\cdot28$ m
14 (a) 1, 2, 4, 5, 10, 20   (b) 1, 2, 3, 4, 6, 12
15 7, 14, 21, 28, 35
16 (a) 4   (b) 25   (c) 100
17 (a) 5   (b) 9   (c) 7
18 (a) 128   (b) 128
19 (a) 36   (b) 2352
20 (a) 10   (b) 16   (c) 7 (d) 5
21 12
22 A (1, 2)   B (3, 4)   C (4, 2)   D (5, 0)
23

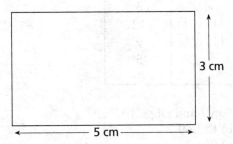

24

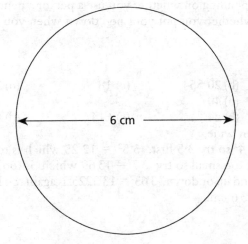

25

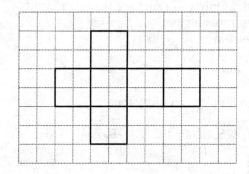

26 (a) parallel   (b) obtuse   (c) vertical
    (d) horizontal   (e) reflex   (f) acute

27

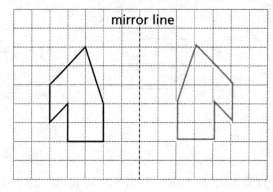

28 C and E are congruent
29 A is at a distance of 2·2 units at an angle of 63°, B (5, 53°), C (4·5, 27°), D (5, 0°)
30 (a) 5   (b) 4   (c) 3
31 (a) 20 cm   (b) 24 cm²
32 140

33

No. of birds	Tally	Frequency
0 – 9		0
10 – 19	|||	3
20 – 29	⊬⊬⊤ ⊬⊬⊤ ||	12
30 – 39	⊬⊬⊤ ||||	9
40 – 49	⊬⊬⊤	5
50 – 59	|	1

34 mean 6·6, mode 7, median 7 and range 10
35 (a) $16.80   (b) £13.40
36 (a) 1   (b) 0
    (c) Your estimate, depending on whether you use a pen or a pencil, what colour pen
    you usually use, whether you put your pen down when you read questions.

Level 5

1 (a) 9315   (b) 20 554   (c) 18   (d) 35
2 (a) 35 000   (b) 40
3 (a) 12   (b) 24   (c) £14   (d) £48
4 4·8 m long and 3·6 m wide
5 13 is between 3^2 and 4^2 so try 3·5 first. $3·5^2 = 12·25$ which is too small so try $3·6^2$ $= 12·96$ which is still too small so try $3·7^2 = 13·69$ which is too large. Try $3·65^2$ to check whether to round up or down. $3·65^2 = 13·3225$ is again too large so the solution to 1 decimal place is 3·6 cm.

6 (a) 2·54   (b) 15·7   (c) 3·142
7 (a) 2300   (b) 5000   (c) 36 000
8 (a) 250 g   (b) 1 kg   (c) 5 litres   (d) 24 km
9 (a) 1·1 m   (b) 2500 g   (c) 3·7 m
10 -5, -2, 0, 3, 4
11 (a) -5 °C   (b) -4°C
12 (a) 2^6 (b) 3^4 (c) 4^5
13 (a) 1, 1, 2, 3, 5, 8, 13, 21
     (b) 1, 2, 4, 8, 16, 32, 64, 128
     (c) 1, 3, 6, 10, 15, 21, 28, 36
14 (a) square   (b) cube   (c) prime   (d) prime   (e) square and cube

15 (a) $117n$ seconds   (b) $\dfrac{m}{117}$

16 10 cm²
17

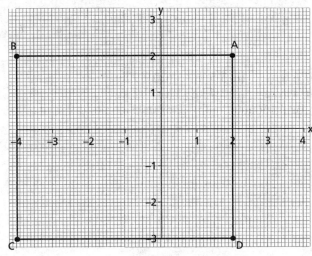

18 (a) 60°   (b)   140°   (c)   290°
19 (a) $a = c = e = g$ because c is opposite a, e is alternate to c and corresponding to a, and g is opposite e and corresponding to c.
     (b) 180°
20 (a) 4   (b) infinity
21 London, Bristol, Birmingham, Manchester, Leeds and back to London (or the reverse of this route): 520 miles total.
22 1800 cm³
23

Height	Tally	Frequency
$130 \leqslant h < 135$	I I	2
$135 \leqslant h < 140$	I I I	3
$140 \leqslant h < 145$	I I I	3
$145 \leqslant h < 150$	⤗I	5
$150 \leqslant h < 155$	I I I I	4
$155 \leqslant h < 160$	I I I	3

24 15%
25

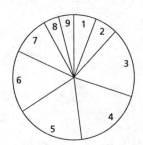

26 (a)

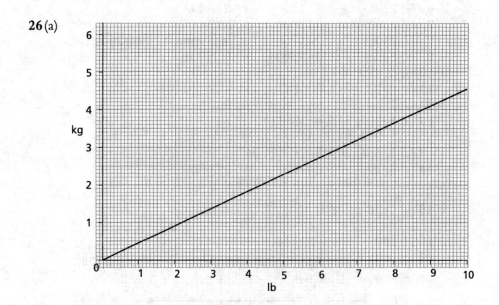

(b) (i) 6·6 lb   (ii) 5·5 lb   (iii) 9.9 lb

(c) (i) 4·1 kg   (ii) 2·7 kg   (iii) 0·2 kg

27 (a) $\frac{1}{6}$ or 0·1666666   (b) $\frac{1}{20}$ or 0·05

Section 2 answers

2.6a

1 $0·016$, $0·1$, $0·1006$, $0·106$, $0·16$

2 (a) $\frac{4}{10}$ (4 tenths)   (b) $\frac{2}{100}$ (2 hundredths)   (c) $\frac{7}{1000}$ (7 thousandths)

  (d) $\frac{8}{100}$ (8 hundredths) (e) 7 units

2.6b

1 (a) equivalent   (b) equivalent   (c) not equivalent (d) equivalent

2 (a) $\frac{14}{3}$ (b) $4\frac{1}{2}$

3 (a) $\frac{3}{4} + \frac{1}{3} = \frac{9}{12} + \frac{4}{12} = \frac{13}{12} = 1\frac{1}{12}$ (b) $\frac{2}{5} - \frac{1}{4} = \frac{8}{20} - \frac{5}{20} = \frac{3}{20}$ (c) $\frac{7}{8}$ (d) $\frac{1}{4}$

4 (a) $3 : 2$ (b) $3 : 4$ (c) $3 : 2$ (d) $3 : 2$

5 (a) $2·4$ m   (b) $4·8$ m

6 (a) $0·25$ or 25% (b) $0·2$ or 20%   (c) $0·4$ or 40%   (d) $0·1$ or 10%

2.6c

1 (a) $0·35$ (b) $0·625$ (c) $0·8125$ (d) $0·\dot{5}\dot{7}$ (= $0·575757...$)   (e) $0·1\dot{4}285\dot{7}$

2 (a) 50%   (b) 75%   (c) 37·5%   (d) 6%   (e) 60%   (f) 17·5%

3 (a) $\frac{9}{50} = 0·18 = 18\%$ (b) $\frac{1}{5} = 0·2 = 20\%$ (c) $\frac{5}{6} = 0·8\dot{3} = 83·\dot{3}\%$

2.6d

1 (a) £70   (b) £100   (c) £48   (d) £18

2 (a) £280   (b) 92·8 m   (c) 8125   (d) £2616   (e) £1762·50

3 (a) £138   (b) £220   (c) £9775   (d) 799

4 (a) 8%   (b) 4%   (c) 7%

2.6e

1 (a) $1 : 3$ (b) $9 : 1$

2 (a) 6 cubic metres   (b) 5 cubic metres   (c) 6 cubic metres

3 2000 g stewing steak, 75 g plain flour, about $2\frac{1}{2}$ medium onions, about $7\frac{1}{2}$ medium leeks, 250 g button mushrooms, 125 g lard, 1000 g tinned tomatoes. (You can divide by 2 and multiply by 5 or use the multiplier 2·5.)

4 375 g apples, 150 g flour (You can divide by 4 and multiply by 3 or use the multiplier 0·75.)

2.6f

1 (a) $10 \times £10 = £100$ (b) $20 \times £5 = £100$ (c) 300×30 mm $= 9$ m

  (d) $20 \times £10 = £200$

2 (a) £115·74   (b) £81·60   (c) 8·216 m   (d) £189·81

3 (a) $\dfrac{15 \times 90}{5} = 3 \times 90 = 270$ (b) $\dfrac{40 \times 70}{40} = 70$ (c) $\dfrac{900}{30 \times 10} = 3$

(d) $\dfrac{30 \times 60}{10 \times 20} = 9$ or $\dfrac{24 \times 60}{12 \times 20} = 6$

4 (a) 267   (b) 76·46 (to 2 d.p.)   (c) 2·64 (to 2 d.p.)   (d) 6·60 (to 2 d.p.)

2.7a

1 (a) 600   (b) 3200   (c) 5400   (d) 2000
  (e) 8000   (f) 18 000   (g) 210 000   (h) 240 000

2 (a) 30   (b) 50   (c) 50   (d) 20   (e) 25

3 (a) 1·2   (b) 150   (c) 24
  (d) 10   (e) 400   (f) 200
  (g) 10 000   (h) 400   (i) 500

2.7b

1 (a) $(2·538)^2 \times 12^2 = 927·568$ cm² (to 3 d.p.)
  (b) $187·8 \div 2·538 = 74$ inches (to nearest inch)

2 (a) 48 mph   (b) 1 hour 5 minutes

3 549 miles (to the nearest mile)

4 71·76 square yards (to 2 d.p.)

2.7c

1 (a) £29·38   (b) £42·30   (c) £293·75   (d) £209·81

2 100, 50, 25, 12·5, 6·25, 3·125, 1·5625, 0·78125

3 (a) 14   (b) 18   (c) 10   (d) 6

4 (a) 9·2   (b) 7·2   (c) 8·0   (d) 9·2
  (e) 33 929·2 mm³

5

x	-2	-1	0	1	2
y	24	5	0	3	8

2.7d

1 (a) A protractor or angle measurer (to the nearest degree)
  (b) A stop watch (to the nearest 0·01 seconds or $\frac{1}{100}$ of a second)
  (c) A scale ruler (to the nearest mile)
  (d) A mileometer (to the nearest $\frac{1}{10}$ of a mile)
  (e) A speedometer (to the nearest mile per hour or kilometre per hour)
  (f) A thermometer (to the nearest degree)
  (g) Bathroom scales (to the nearest kg or pound)
  (h) Kitchen scales (to the nearest oz or 25 g)

2 (a) 2 mm   (b) 72·9 kg or 73 kg

2.7e

1

	Measurement	Minimum	Maximum	Range
Height	158 cm	157·5 cm	158·5 cm	157·5 cm ≤ x < 158·5 cm
Weight	48 kg	47·5 kg	48·5 kg	47·5 kg ≤ x < 48·5 kg
Waist	67 cm	66·5 cm	67·5 cm	66·5 cm ≤ x < 67·5 cm
Neck	32 cm	31·5 cm	32·5 cm	31·5 cm ≤ x < 32·5 cm
Leg	70 cm	69·5 cm	70·5 cm	69·5 cm ≤ x < 70·5 cm

2.7f

1 (a) $\dfrac{120 \text{ miles}}{3 \text{ hours}} = 40$ mph   (b) 6 mph × 0·5 hours= 3 miles   (c) $\dfrac{40 \text{ km}}{8 \text{ km}/\text{h}} = 5$ hours

2 (a) 19·3 × 20 = 386 g   (b) $\dfrac{810}{2\cdot7} = 300$ cm³   (c) $\dfrac{26\cdot7}{3} = 8\cdot9$ g/cm³

3 (a) To 2 decimal places, $\dfrac{500}{99} = 5\cdot05$ g/p and $\dfrac{200}{63} = 3\cdot17$ g/p so the 500 g bag is better value.

   (b) To 2 decimal places, $\dfrac{2000}{875} = 2\cdot29$ g/p and $\dfrac{454}{175} = 2\cdot59$ g/p so the 454 g box of chocolates is better value.

2.7g

1 2, 3, 5, 7, 11, 13, 17, 19, 23, 29

2 There are a variety of ways in which each of these diagrams can be produced. However, they all give the same answers.

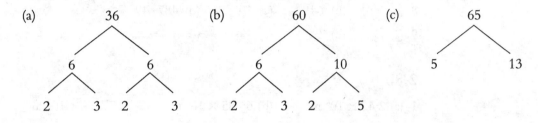

3

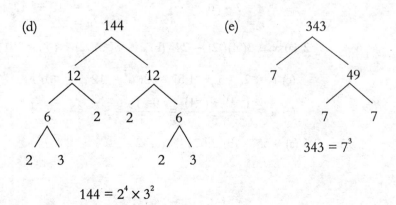

(f) e.g. $1977 = 3 \times 659$, $1978 = 2 \times 23 \times 43$, 1979 is prime,
$1980 = 2^2 \times 3^2 \times 5 \times 11$

4 2, 3, 5, 7, 11, 13, 17, 19, 23, 29, 31, 37, 41, 43, 47, 53, 59, 61, 67, 71, 73, 79, 83, 89, 97

2.8a

1 (a) 5^4 (b) 3^7 (c) $\left(\frac{1}{2}\right)^3$ or $\frac{1}{2^3}$ (d) 6^1 (e) $\left(\frac{1}{7}\right)^4$ or $\frac{1}{7^4}$ (f) 0.21^2

2 (a) 525·22 (to 2 d.p.)   (b) 296·61 (to 2 d.p.)   (c) 0·015625

3 16 777 216

4 (a) $\frac{1}{9}$ (b) $\frac{1}{16}$ (c) $\frac{1}{32}$ (d) $\frac{1}{25}$

5 (a) 27, 9, 3, 1, $0 \cdot \dot{3}$ or $\frac{1}{3}$, $0 \cdot \dot{1}$ or $\frac{1}{9}$, $0 \cdot 0\dot{3}\dot{7}$ or $\frac{1}{27}$
   (b) 125, 25, 5, 1, $0 \cdot 2$ or $\frac{1}{5}$, $0 \cdot 04$ or $\frac{1}{25}$, $0 \cdot 008$ or $\frac{1}{125}$
   (c) 64, 16, 4, 1, $0 \cdot 25$ or $\frac{1}{4}$, $0 \cdot 0625$ or $\frac{1}{16}$, $0 \cdot 015625$ or $\frac{1}{64}$

6 (a) 1   (b) 1   (c) 1   (d) 1   (e) 1

7 (a) 23   (b) 24   (c) 16   (d) 4   (e) 0·024

8 (a) $9^{\frac{1}{2}}$ (b) $64^{\frac{1}{3}}$ (c) $10^{\frac{1}{5}}$ (d) $487 \cdot 49^{\frac{1}{16}}$

9 (a) 17   (b) 2·5   (c) 36   (d) 2

2.8b

1 (a) $2 \cdot 42 \times 10^6$ m   (b) $6 \cdot 085 \times 10^6$ m   (c) $7 \cdot 14 \times 10^7$ m

2 (a) 3 000 000 m   (b) 149 600 000 000 m

3 (a) 3×10^{-3} (b) $5 \cdot 2 \times 10^{-2}$ (c) $8 \cdot 61 \times 10^{-6}$ (d) $7 \cdot 03 \times 10^{-3}$

4 (a) 0·00005   (b) 0·8   (c) 0·00093   (d) 0·0632

5 (a) $3 \cdot 5 \times 10^{12}$ (b) 4×10^4 (c) $3 \cdot 354 \times 10^{15}$
   (d) $2 \cdot 84 \times 10^5$ (to 3 s.f.)

6 $5 \cdot 1084 \times 10^{18}$ m

7 $1 \cdot 429 \times 10^3 \, \text{kg/m}^3$ (to 4 s.f.)

8 3×10^5

9 (a) 6×10^{-3} m   (b) 2000 or 2×10^3 ($1 \, \text{mm} = 1 \times 10^{-3}$ m)

2.8c

1 (a) $r = p - 2q$ (b) $a = 2b + 3c$ (c) $t = 4r - s$
      $r = 7 - 2(^-3)$ $a = 2(^-5) + 3(^-4)$ $t = 4(^-\frac{1}{2}) - (^-5)$
      $r = 7 - {^-6}$ $a = {^-10} + {^-12}$ $t = {^-2} + 5$
      $r = 13$ $a = {^-22}$ $t = 3$

2 (a) $x = 3(^-4)(^-2) = 24$ (b) $a = 5(^-3)(^-2) - (^-2) = 30 + 2 = 32$

   (c) $t = {^-2}(^-4 \cdot 5 + {^-1} \cdot 5) = {^-2}(^-6) = 12$ (d) $p = \frac{12}{^-3} - 2 = {^-4} + 2 = {^-2}$

   (e) $a = \dfrac{\left(^-3\right)^2 + \left(^-4\right)^2}{5} = \dfrac{9 + 16}{5} = 5$

3 (a) 9·5   (b) 2·625   (c) $^-2$

2.8d

1 (a) $3\frac{1}{4} + 2\frac{1}{2} = \frac{13}{4} + \frac{5}{2} = \frac{13}{4} + \frac{10}{4} = \frac{23}{4} = 5\frac{3}{4}$

 (b) $2\frac{1}{2} - 1\frac{1}{8} = (2-1) + \frac{1}{2} - \frac{1}{8} = 1 + \frac{4}{8} - \frac{1}{8} = 1\frac{3}{8}$

 (c) $4 + \frac{1}{4} + \frac{3}{8} = 4 + \frac{2}{8} + \frac{3}{8} = 4\frac{5}{8}$

 (d) $4\frac{3}{7} - 2\frac{8}{9} = \frac{31}{7} - \frac{26}{9} = \frac{279}{63} - \frac{182}{63} = \frac{97}{63} = 1\frac{34}{63}$

2 (a) $\frac{1}{6}$ (b) $\frac{1}{3}$ (c) $\frac{9}{20}$ (d) $\frac{7}{20}$

3 (a) $\frac{5}{2} \times \frac{3}{2} = \frac{15}{4} = 3\frac{3}{4}$

 (b) $\frac{27}{8} \times \frac{11}{4} = \frac{297}{32} = 9\frac{9}{32}$

 (c) $\frac{16}{13} \times \frac{5}{2} = \frac{40}{13} = 3\frac{1}{13}$

4 (a) $\frac{{}^1\cancel{5}}{\cancel{2}_1} \times \frac{\cancel{8}^4}{\cancel{5}_1} = 4$

 (b) $\frac{{}^3\cancel{15}}{\cancel{4}_1} \times \frac{\cancel{12}^3}{\cancel{5}_1} = 9$

5 (a) $\frac{3}{4} \div \frac{1}{8} = \frac{3}{4} \times \frac{8}{1} = 6$

 (b) $\frac{2}{5} \div \frac{1}{2} = \frac{2}{5} \times \frac{2}{1} = \frac{4}{5}$

 (c) $\frac{7}{4} \div \frac{1}{2} = \frac{7}{4} \times \frac{2}{1} = \frac{7}{2} = 3\frac{1}{2}$

2.8e

1 (a) $\frac{3 \times 40}{4 \times 3} = 10$ (b) $\frac{17}{2} = 8\cdot5$ (c) $3 \times 100 \times 50 = 15\,000$

2 (a) $15\cdot8775$ m² (b) £256 (c) £253·88

3 (a) $\frac{3500}{25 \times 20}$ or $\frac{4000}{25 \times 20} = 7$ or 8

 (b) $\frac{200 + 450}{15} = \frac{130}{3} = 40$ or 50

 (c) $\frac{290 - 130}{140} = \frac{16}{14} \approx 1\cdot1$

 (d) $120 \times (380 - 180) = 24\,000$

4 (a) $8\cdot1929825$ (b) $49\cdot538462$ (c) $1\cdot177305$ (d) $25\,172$

2.9a

1 Your investigation. You may have found that all fractions with a denominator (bottom number) of 3 or 9 repeat after 1 decimal place, and those with a denominator of 11 repeat after 2 places. It looks like all fractions with a denominator of 7 repeat after 6 decimal places, but on your calculator you can't be sure.

2 (a) $0\cdot1\dot{4}285\dot{7}$ (b) $0\cdot1\dot{5}384\dot{6}$ (c) $0\cdot1\dot{9}047\dot{6}$

2.9b

	Lower bound	Upper bound
1 (a)	£11·50	£12·49
(b)	£55·00	£64·99
(c)	£725·00	£774·99
(d)	£8·85	£8·94
2 (a)	637·5 kg	638·5 kg
(b)	1650 g	1750 g
(c)	9·5 m	10·5 m
(d)	492·5 cm	497·5 cm
3 (a)	3·65 m	3·75 m
(b)	10 500	11 499
(c) (i)	2·605 kg	2·615 kg
(ii)	2·6095 kg	2·6105 kg

2.10a

1 lower bound perimeter $= 2(39\cdot5 + 17\cdot5) = 114$ m

2 (a) upper bound perimeter $= 2(4\cdot25 + 1\cdot85) = 12\cdot2$ m
　　 lower bound perimeter $= 2(4\cdot15 + 1\cdot75) = 11\cdot8$ m

　 (b) upper bound perimeter $= 2(110\cdot5 + 65\cdot5) = 352$ m
　　 lower bound perimeter $= 2(109\cdot5 + 64\cdot5) = 348$ m

3 new upper bound = max fencing – min size of gate = 302·5 m – 2·25 m
　 = 300·25 m
　 new lower bound = min fencing – upper bound size of gate = 297·5 m – 2·35 m
　 = 295·15 m

4 upper bound $a = 4\cdot85 - 1\cdot65 \times 2 = 1\cdot55$
　 lower bound $a = 4\cdot75 - 1\cdot75 \times 2 = 1\cdot25$

5 (a) 477　　(b) 153

6 (a) upper bound area $= 15\cdot5 \times 8\cdot5 = 131\cdot75$ m²
　 (b) lower bound area $= 14\cdot5 \times 7\cdot5 = 108\cdot75$ m²
　 (c) upper bound $= 30\cdot5$ g/m² $\times 131\cdot75$ m² $= 4018\cdot4$ g

7 (a) To calculate the minimum amount of paint needed you divide the minimum
　　 ceiling area by the maximum paint coverage.
　 (b) lower bound of wall area $= 2(2\cdot05 \times 5\cdot15) + 2(2\cdot05 \times 6\cdot55) = 47\cdot97$ m²
　　 $47\cdot97 \div 13\cdot5 = 3\cdot553$ which rounds to 4 litre tins
　 (c) upper bound of wall area $= 2(2\cdot15 \times 5\cdot25) + 2(2\cdot15 \times 6\cdot65) = 51\cdot17$ m²
　　 $51\cdot17 \div 12\cdot5 = 4\cdot0936$ which gives a maximum of 5 litre tins

2.10b

1 12

2 (a) upper bound $= 16\cdot5$ g　　lower bound $= 15\cdot5$ g
　 (b) 16 000 kg or 16 tonnes
　 (c) 16 500 kg or 16·5 tonnes
　 (d) 15 500 kg or 15·5 tonnes
　 The result is a difference of 1 tonne of steel.

Section 3 answers

3.6a

1 (a) 1, 4, 7, 10, 13   (b) 20, 18, 16, 14, 12   (c) 1, 5, 25, 125, 625

   (d) 1, ⁻1, ⁻3, ⁻5, ⁻7

2 (a) 1, 5, 17, 53, 161   (b) 1, 0, ⁻2, ⁻6, ⁻14   (c) 10, 24, 66, 192, 570

3 (a) Starting with 1 add 2 then 3, then 4 and so on (consecutive numbers)

   (b) Starting with 1 and 1, each term is produced by adding together the last two numbers.

4 (a) + 1 starting at 3

   (b) + 3 starting at 3

   (c) × 2 + 1 starting at 1

   (d) × 4 − 1 starting at 1

3.6b

1 (a) $x = 3$ (b) $a = 10$ (c) $x = 3$ (d) $b = 15$

2 (a) $x = 3$ (b) $a = 2$ (c) $b = 5$ (d) $x = 7$ (e) $x = 6$ (f) $x = 5$

3 (a) $x = 2$ (b) $x = ⁻1$

4 $5(n - 6) = 3(n - 4)$

   $5n - 30 = 3n - 12$

   $\quad\quad 2n = 18$

   $\quad\quad\; n = 9$

5 Put Sandra's age $= x$ then Martin's age is $x + 3$ and Abdul's age is $x - 2$.
   $(x + 3) + x + (x - 2) = 43$ so $x = 14$.
   Sandra is 14, Martin is 17 and Abdul is 12.

6 (a) $(w + 14) + w + (w - 6) = 44$ or $3w + 8 = 44$ (b) 12

7 (a) 35°   (b) 72·5°

8 $x = 3$

3.6c

1 $\sqrt{17}$ is between 4 ($4^2 = 16$) and 5 ($5^2 = 25$)

   $4·1^2\quad = 16·81$
   $4·2^2\quad = 17·64$
   $4·15^2 = 17·2225$
   $4·13^2 = 17·0569$
   $4·12^2\quad = 16·9744\quad\quad 4·13^2$ is too large and $4·12^2$ is too small

   By checking $4·125^2$ we can see whether to round up or down.
   $4·125^2 = 17·015625\quad 4·125^2$ is greater than 17 so you should round down.
   $\sqrt{17}\quad = 4·12$ (to 2 d.p.)

2 9·28 cm (to 2 d.p.)

3

Lower value	Upper value	Mean value	(Mean value)²
4	5	4·5	20·25
4	4·5	4·25	18·0625
4	4·25	4·125	17·015625
4	4·125	4·0625	16·503906
4·0625	4·125	4·09375	16·758789
4·09375	4·125	4·109375	16·886963
4·109375	4·125	4·1171875	16·951233
4·1171875	4·125	4·1210938	16·983414
4·1210938	4·125	4·1230469	16·999516
4·1230469	4·125	4·1240235	17·007569
4·1230469	4·1240235		

so $\sqrt{17}$ = 4·12 (to 2 d.p.)

3.6d

1 (a)

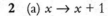

(b)

(c)

1	→	3
2	→	6
3	→	9
4	→	12

1	→	3
2	→	5
3	→	7
4	→	9

1	→	1
2	→	0
3	→	-1
4	→	-2

2 (a) $x \rightarrow x + 1$

(b) & (c)

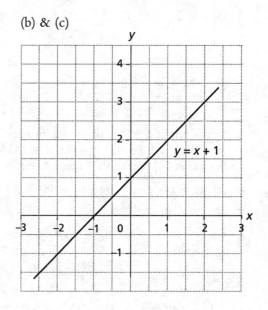

$y = x + 1$

(d) $y = x + 1$

3 (a)

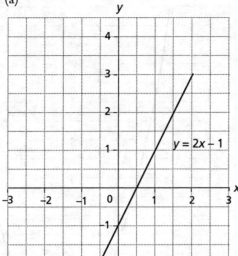

(b)

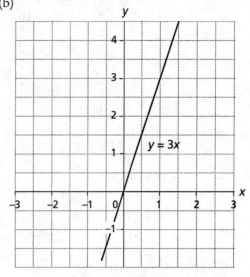

(c)

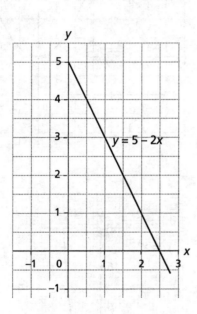

(d)

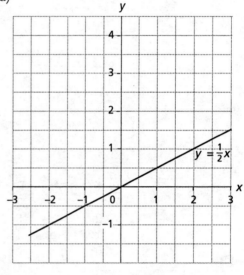

(e)

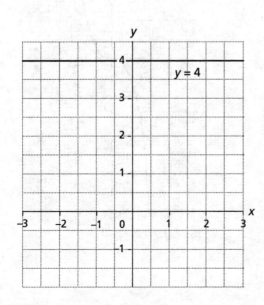

4 (a)

x	$\rightarrow$	$x^2 + 1$
‾3		10
‾2		5
‾1		2
0		1
1		2
2		5
3		10

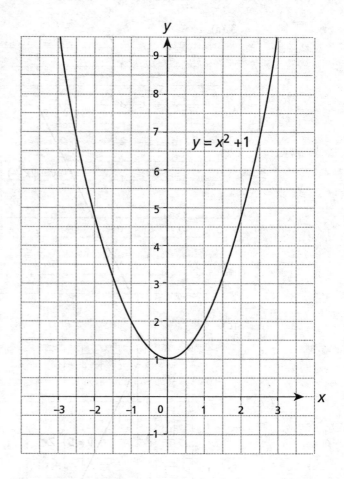

$y = x^2 + 1$

(b)

x	$\rightarrow$	x^3
‾3		‾27
‾2		‾8
‾1		‾1
0		0
1		1
2		8
3		27

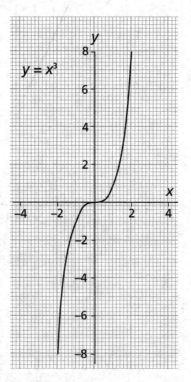

$y = x^3$

3.7a

1 (a) 3, 12, 27, 48, 75   (b) 3, 7, 11, 15, 19

   (c) $\frac{1}{2}$ or 0·5, 2, $\frac{9}{2}$ or 4·5, 8, $\frac{25}{2}$ or 12·5   (d) $\frac{2}{3}$, $\frac{4}{3}$, $\frac{6}{3}$ or 2, $\frac{8}{3}$, $\frac{10}{3}$

2 (a) 20   (b) 160   (c) 2560

3 (a) $3n - 2$ (b) $2n + 1$ (c) $5n - 1$

4 If the bricks are laid out in a single row you get:

bricks	hidden faces
1	1
2	4
3	7

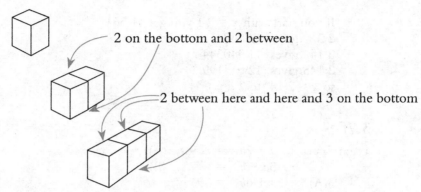

2 on the bottom and 2 between

2 between here and here and 3 on the bottom

The rule is $N = 3n - 2$ where N is the number of hidden faces and n the number of bricks. (Every brick has 3 hidden faces except the two at the ends.)

5 (a) £12 100   (b) £14 800   (c) £18 400   (d) £34 600

6 (a) 3^{n-1} (b) 5^n (c) $4 \times 5^{n-1}$ (d) $7 \times 3^{n-1}$

   (e) $\left(\frac{1}{3}\right)^{n-1}$ or $\dfrac{1}{3^{n-1}}$

7 (a) 2^n (b) 3×2^n

8 (a) $n^2 - 1$ (b) $(n + 1)^2$ (c) $2n^2$

9 (a) $\dfrac{n}{3n - 1}$ (b) $\dfrac{2^n}{2n + 1}$

3.7b

1 (a) $8a^2$ (b) $4(x^3 + x^2)$ (c) $3x^3 + 7y^2$ (d) $4b^5$

2 (a) $8x^7$ (b) $18a^9$ (c) $40y^{11}$ (d) $3x^3y^5$

3 (a) 10^{31} (b) 7^{14} (c) 6×5^{15}

4 (a) a^4 (b) $1·5x^3$ (c) $4x^3$ (d) $2ab$

5 (a) 7^2 (b) 9^3 (c) $5^2 \times 2^2$ (d) 10^{13}

6 (a) a^8 (b) $9x^6$ (c) $256n^{12}$ (d) $a^8b^{12}c^4$

7 (a) $a^{10}b^2$ (b) x^5y^4 (c) $64a^{15}b^3$

3.7c

1 (a) $\frac{1}{10}$ (b) $\frac{1}{7}$ (c) $\frac{1}{3}$ (d) $-\frac{1}{3}$

   (e) $^-4$ (f) 1000   (g) 1

2 (a) 0·0204081   (b) 0·0014224751   (c) 2·3809524   (d) 1408·4507

3 As numbers get close to 0 their reciprocals get very large. As numbers get large (+ or −) their reciprocals get very small (+ or −).

3.7d

1 (a) $^-3, ^-2, ^-1, 0, 1, 2, 3$ (b) 4, 5, 6, 7, 8

3.7e

1 (a) $x^2 - x = 10$ substituting 3 gives $3^2 - 3 = 6$ and substituting 4 gives $4^2 - 4 = 12$

If you start with $x = 3{\cdot}7$ you get $9{\cdot}99$
$3{\cdot}71$ gives $10{\cdot}0541$
$3{\cdot}705$ gives $10{\cdot}022025$
The answer is more than $3{\cdot}7$ and less than $3{\cdot}705$ so $x = 3{\cdot}70$ (to 2 d.p.).

(b) $x^3 + x = 12$ substituting 2 gives $2^3 + 2 = 10$ and substituting 3 gives
$3^3 + 3 = 30$

If you start with $x = 2{\cdot}1$ you get $11{\cdot}361$
$2{\cdot}2$ gives $12{\cdot}848$
$2{\cdot}14$ gives $11{\cdot}940344$
$2{\cdot}145$ gives $12{\cdot}014199$
so $x = 2{\cdot}14$ (to 2 d.p.)

3.7f

1 (a)
$$
\begin{aligned}
a + 2b &= 9 \ \ldots \text{(A)}\\
3a + b &= 7 \ \ldots \text{(B)}
\end{aligned}
$$
$$
\begin{aligned}
3\text{(A)} \quad 3a + 6b &= 27\\
-\text{(B)} \quad 3a + b &= 7\\
5b &= 20\\
b &= 4
\end{aligned}
$$
Substitute $b = 4$ back into (A):
$$
\begin{aligned}
a + 2(4) &= 9\\
a &= 1
\end{aligned}
$$
Check using (B): $3(1) + 4 = 7$

(b)
$$
\begin{aligned}
7x + 3y &= 27 \ \ldots \text{(A)}\\
2x + y &= 8 \ \ldots \text{(B)}
\end{aligned}
$$
$$
\begin{aligned}
\text{(A)} \quad 7x + 3y &= 27\\
-3\text{(B)} \quad 6x + 3y &= 24\\
x &= 3
\end{aligned}
$$
Substituting back into (B):
$$
\begin{aligned}
6 + y &= 8\\
y &= 2
\end{aligned}
$$
Check using (A): $7(3) + 3(2) = 27$

2 (a)
$$
\begin{aligned}
2m + 3n &= 27 \ \ldots \text{(A)}\\
3m + 2n &= 28 \ \ldots \text{(B)}
\end{aligned}
$$
$$
\begin{aligned}
3\text{(A)} \quad 6m + 9n &= 81\\
-2\text{(B)} \quad 6m + 4n &= 56\\
5n &= 25\\
n &= 5
\end{aligned}
$$
Substituting back into (A):
$$
\begin{aligned}
2m + 3(5) &= 27\\
2m &= 12\\
m &= 6
\end{aligned}
$$
Check using (B): $3(6) + 2(5) = 28$

(b)
$$
\begin{aligned}
2a + 5b &= 13 \ \ldots \text{(A)}\\
5a + 3b &= 23 \ \ldots \text{(B)}
\end{aligned}
$$
$$
\begin{aligned}
5\text{(A)} \quad 10a + 25b &= 65\\
-2\text{(B)} \quad 10a + 6b &= 46\\
19b &= 19\\
b &= 1
\end{aligned}
$$

Substituting back into (A):

$$2a + 5(1) = 13$$
$$2a = 8$$
$$a = 4$$

Check using (B): $5(4) + 3(1) = 23$

3 (a)

$$2a + 3b = 16$$
$$3a - b = 13$$
$$2a + 3b = 16$$
$$9a - 3b = 39$$

Adding equations gives

$$11a = 55$$
$$a = 5$$

Substituting back

$$3(5) - b = 13$$
$$^-b = ^-2$$
$$b = 2$$

Check: $2(5) + 3(2) = 16$

(b)

$$7p + 3q = 6$$
$$4p - 2q = 20$$
$$14p + 6q = 122$$
$$12p - 6q = 60$$

Adding equations gives

$$26p = 182$$
$$p = 7$$

Substituting back

$$49 + 3q = 61$$
$$3q = 12$$
$$q = 4$$

Check: $4(7) - 2(4) = 20$

(c)

$$4m + 3n = 93$$
$$3m - 4n = 1$$
$$16m + 12n = 372$$
$$9m - 12n = 3$$
$$25m = 375$$
$$m = 15$$

Substituting back

$$60 + 3n = 93$$
$$n = 11$$

Check: $3(15) - 4(11) = 1$

4

$$2r - 3s = 19 \ldots \text{(A)}$$
$$3r - s = 11 \ldots \text{(B)}$$

From (B) you can get $s = 3r - 11$

Substituting back into (A) gives

$$2r - 3(3r - 11) = 19$$
$$2r - 9r + 33 = 19$$
$$33 - 19 = 9r - 2r$$
$$14 = 7r$$
$$2 = r$$

Substituting $r = 2$ back into (A)

$$2(2) - 3s = 19$$
$$4 - 3s = 19$$
$$4 - 19 = 3s$$
$$^-15 = 3s$$
$$^-5 = s$$

Check: $3(2) - ^-5 = 11$

5 (a) $4h + c = 7 \cdot 35$, $3h + 2c = 7 \cdot 20$

(b) ham rolls cost £1·50 and cheese rolls cost £1·35.

6 (a) $2a + 3c = 1880$, $3a + 2c = 2110$

(b) £514 per adult, £284 per child

7 (a) $x = 3$, $y = 4$ or $(3, 4)$ (b) $x = 2$, $y = 5$ or $(2, 5)$

8 (a)

x	$x - 1$	x	$7 - x$
0	$^-1$	0	7
1	0	1	6
2	1	2	5

$x = 4$, $y = 3$

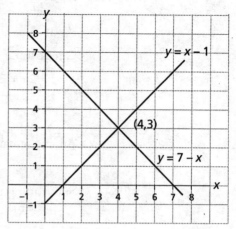

(b) Rearranging equations gives

$y = 3x - 2$

$y = \frac{1}{2}x + 3$

x	$3x - 2$	x	$\frac{1}{2}x + 3$
0	$^-2$	0	3
1	1	1	3·5
2	4	2	4

$x = 2$, $y = 4$

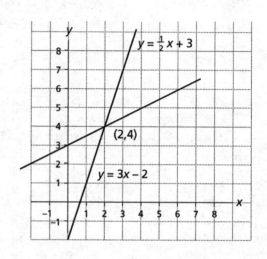

9 (a) $18S + 2G = 610$, $25S + 5G = 925$
(b) $G = {}^-9S + 305$, $G = {}^-5S + 185$
(c) See graph opposite
(d) $G = 35$, $S = 30$

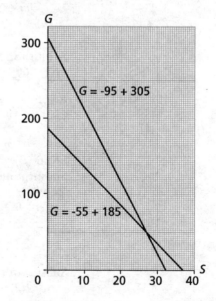

3.7g

1 (a) 85 g   (b) 28 g   (c) 71 g
2 (a) approx. 1·5 oz   (b) approx. 28 oz   (c) approx. 14 oz

3 (a) & (c)

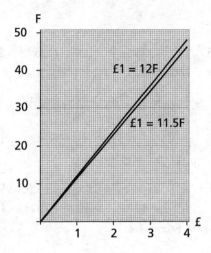

(b) (i) 20F = £1·66   (ii) 35F = £2·92   (iii) £3·50 = 42F   (iv) £35 = 420F

3.7i

1

x	a	b	c	y
-3	9	-6	-15	-12
-2	4	-4	-15	-15
-1	1	-2	-15	-16
0	0	0	-15	-15
1	1	2	-15	-12
2	4	4	-15	-7
3	9	6	-15	0

2 5·5, 7·75, 8·875, 9·4375

3

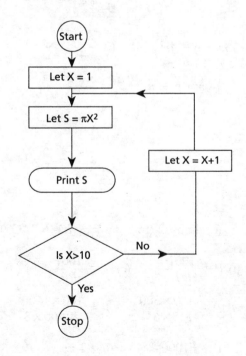

3.8a

1 (a) xy (b) a (c) $3y$ (d) $2a$ (e) b^2 (f) a^2b

2 (a) $x = \sqrt[6]{y}$ (b) $x = y^5$ (c) $x = \sqrt{y^3}$

3.8b

1 (a) $3x + 15$ (b) $^-2x - 10$ (c) $^-3x^2 + 12x$ or $12x - 3x^2$
   (d) $x(12x + 8 - 6x + 12) = x(6x + 20) = 6x^2 + 20x$

2 (a) $x^2 + 2x + 3x + 6 = x^2 + 5x + 6$ (b) $x^2 - 2x + 3x - 6 = x^2 + x - 6$
   (c) $x^2 - 4x - 2x + 8 = x^2 - 6x + 8$

3 (a) $a^2 - ab + ab - b^2 = a^2 - b^2$ (b) $a^2 + ab + ab + b^2 = a^2 + 2ab + b^2$
   (c) $a^2 - ab - ab + b^2 = a^2 - 2ab + b^2$

4 (a) $x^2 + 5x + 5x + 25 = x^2 + 10x + 25$ (b) $x^2 - 2x - 2x + 4 = x^2 - 4x + 4$
   (c) $x^2 - y^2$ (d) $2x^2 + 7x + 6$ (e) $15x^2 + 47x + 28$
   (f) $acx^2 + (ad + bc)x + bd$

5 (a) $2(a + 2b)$ (b) $2a(a - 2)$ (c) $^-2(2a + 3b)$
   (d) $5y(y^2 + 2y - 5)$ (e) $a(x + 2) + 2b(x + 2) = (a + 2b)(x + 2)$

6 (a) $(x + 4)(x + 2)$ (b) $(x + 7)(x - 1)$
   (c) $(x + 5)(x + 3)$ (d) $(x - 4)(x - 5)$
   (e) $(2x + 1)(x + 3)$ (f) $(5x - 1)(x + 2)$

7 (a) $(x + 2)(x - 2)$ (b) $(3x + 1)(3x - 1)$

8 (a) $a(\sqrt{a} + 1)$ (b) $a^3\sqrt{a}\,(a + 1)$ (c) $a^2(\sqrt{a} + 1)$ (d) $\sqrt{2a}\,(2a + 1)$

9 (a) $bx = a - y$ (b) $wx = u - v$ (c) $s = ut + \frac{1}{2}at^2$

   $x = \dfrac{a - y}{b}$ $wx + v = u$ $\frac{1}{2}at^2 = s - ut$

   $at^2 = 2(s - ut)$

   $a = \dfrac{2(s - ut)}{t^2}$

   (d) $byz = ax$ (e) $m + p = 4n^2$ (f) $\dfrac{3}{x+2} = y^2$

   $\dfrac{byz}{a} = x$ $\frac{1}{2}\sqrt{m + p} = n$ $\dfrac{x+2}{3} = \dfrac{1}{y^2}$

   $x + 2 = \dfrac{3}{y^2}$

   $x = \dfrac{3}{y^2} - 2$

3.8c

1 (a) $26\cdot7$ °C (to 1 d.p.)   (b) $43\cdot3$ °C (to 1 d.p.)   (c) $^-6\cdot7$ °C (to 1 d.p.)

2 (a) $I = \dfrac{PRT}{100}$ (b) $P = \dfrac{100I}{RT}$ (c) $T = \dfrac{100I}{PR}$ (d) $R = \dfrac{100I}{PT}$

   $I = \dfrac{2000 \times 6 \times 10}{100}$ $P = \dfrac{100 \times 300}{5 \times 6}$ $T = \dfrac{100 \times 1600}{20\,000 \times 8}$ $R = \dfrac{100 \times 37\,500}{50\,000 \times 10}$

   $I = £1200$ $P = £1000$ $T = 1$ year $R = 7\cdot5\%$

3 (a) $x = \dfrac{y - c}{m}$ (b) (i) $x = 2$ (ii) $x = ^-1$

4 $3\cdot5$ hours

5 $r = \sqrt{\dfrac{V}{\pi h}} = \sqrt{\dfrac{499}{9\pi}} = 4{\cdot}20$ cm (to 2 d.p.)

6 $I = \dfrac{P}{V} = \dfrac{3000}{240} = 12{\cdot}5$ so the minimum size fuse is 13A

3.8d

1 (a) (multiplier rule) $\dfrac{m}{27{\cdot}5} = \dfrac{9}{5{\cdot}5}$ so $m = \dfrac{9 \times 27{\cdot}5}{5{\cdot}5} = 45$

  (b) (constant ratio rule) $\dfrac{t}{43} = \dfrac{5{\cdot}5}{27{\cdot}5}$ so $t = \dfrac{5{\cdot}5 \times 43}{27{\cdot}5} = 8{\cdot}6$

2 £150 = 26 100 Pesetas so £1 = $\dfrac{26\,100}{150}$ = 174 Pesetas (The ratio of Pesetas to £ is 174)

  (a) £250 = 250 × 174 = 43 500 Pesetas

  (b) £60 = 60 × 174 = 10 440 Pesetas

  (c) 10 092 Pesetas = $\dfrac{10\,092}{174}$ = £58

3 (a) The multiplier from 147 Hz to 110 Hz is 110 ÷ 147 = 0·7482993. You divide 65 cm by this number to give the answer.

  65 ÷ 0·7482993 = 86·863636

  The string with a frequency of 110 Hz is 86·9 cm long (to 1 d.p.).

  (Using brackets on calculator: 65 ÷ (110 ÷ 147) = 86·863636.)

  (b) The multiplier from 147 Hz to 196 Hz is 1·3333333.

  65 ÷ 1·3333333 = 48·75

  The string with a frequency of 196 Hz is 48·8 cm (to 1 d.p.).

4 (a) 10 N   (b) 1000 N

3.8e

1 (a) $y = 3x - 1$

x	$3x - 1$
0	⁻1
1	2
2	5

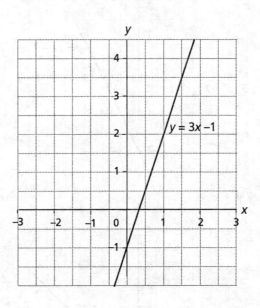

(b) $y = x + 3$

x	$x + 3$
0	3
1	4
2	5

(c) $y = 4x - 2$

x	$4x - 2$
0	$^-2$
1	2
2	6

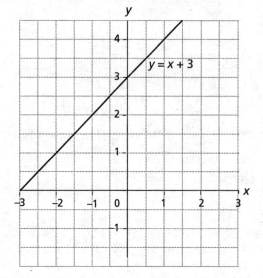

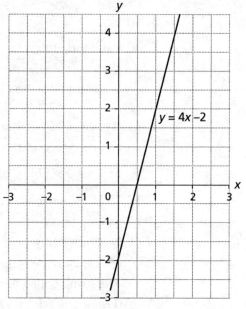

2 (a) $y = 2x - 2$

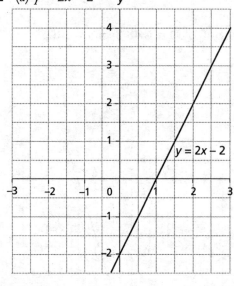

(b) $y = 4x + 1$

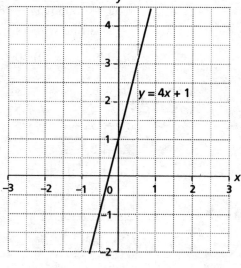

(c) $y = x$

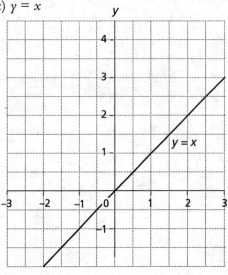

(d) $y = ^-2x$

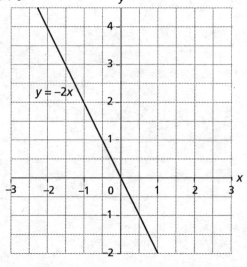

(e) $y = x + 3$

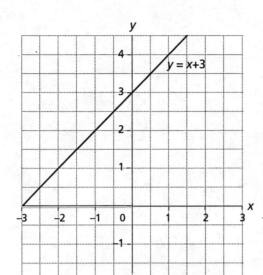

(f) $y = {}^-2x + 3$

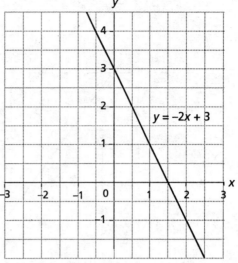

3 (a) $2x + 3y = 12$
$3y = {}^-2x + 12$
$y = {}^-\frac{2}{3}x + 4$

(b) $5x + y = 5$
$y = {}^-5x + 5$

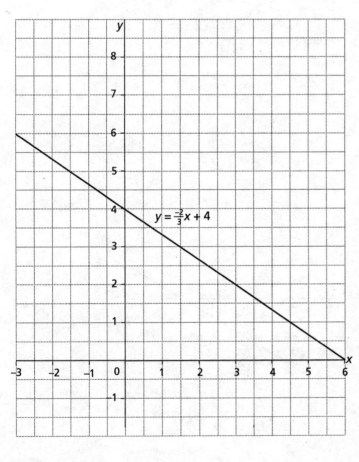

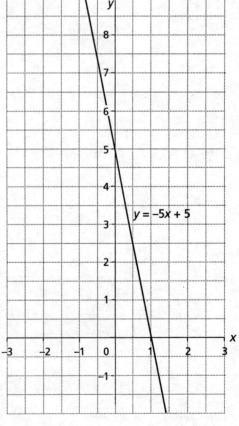

(c) $4x + 3y = 15$

$y = -\frac{4}{3}x + 5$

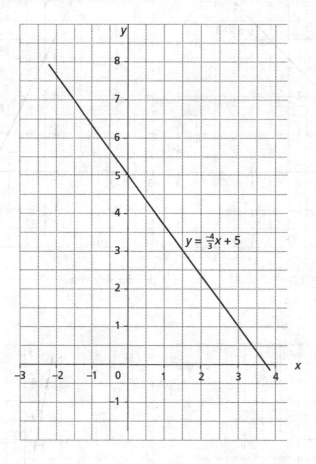

$y = \frac{-4}{3}x + 5$

(d) $3x - 5y = 15$

$y = \frac{3}{5}x - 3$

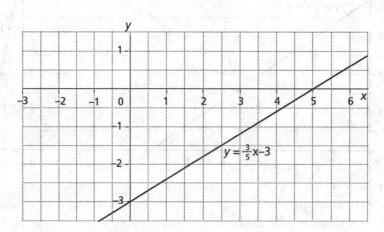

$y = \frac{3}{5}x - 3$

(e) $2x - 3y = 12$
 $y = \frac{2}{3}x - 4$

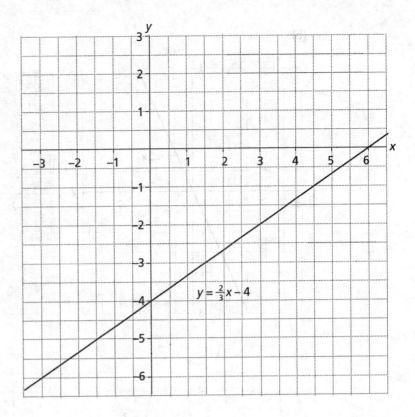

$y = \frac{2}{3}x - 4$

3.8f

1 (a) $6x < 30$
 $x < 5$

(b) $12x + 20 < 32$
 $12x < 12$
 $x < 1$

(c) $2x < {}^-4$
 $x < {}^-2$

(d) $x + 9 > 6$
 $x > {}^-3$

2 (a) $12 - x > 8$
 $12 > 8 + x$
 $4 > x$

(b) $15 - 3x < 2(x - 5)$
 $15 - 3x < 2x - 10$
 $25 < 5x$
 $5 < x$

3 (a) $2x^2 - 1 > 1$
 $2x^2 > 2$
 $x^2 > 1$
 $x > 1$ and $x < {}^-1$

(b) $x(x - 2) < 2(2 - x)$
 $x^2 - 2x < 4 - 2x$
 $x^2 < 4$
 ${}^-2 < x < 2$

3.8g

1 & 2 (a)

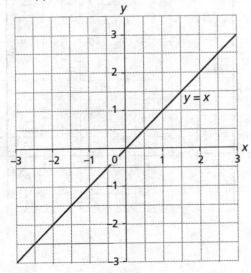

$y = x$

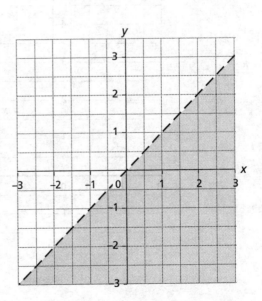

(b)

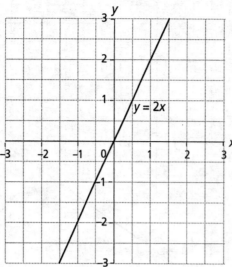
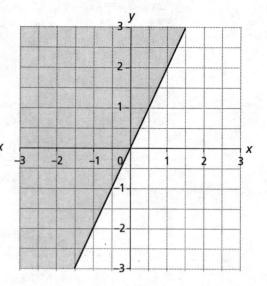

(c)

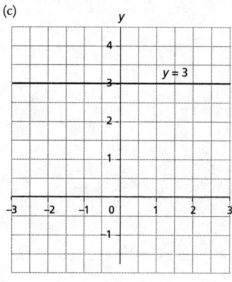
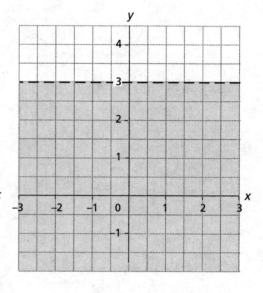

(d)

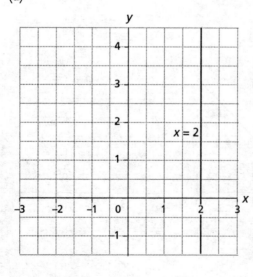
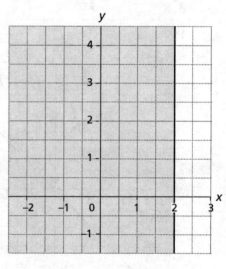

(e)

(f)

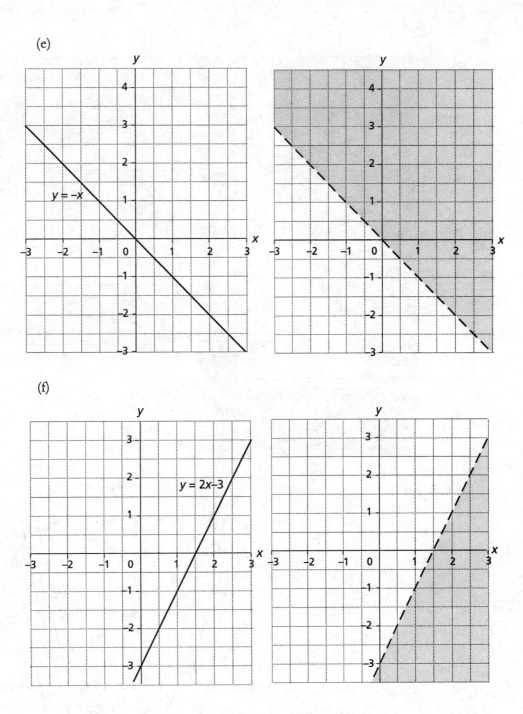

3 (a)

(b)

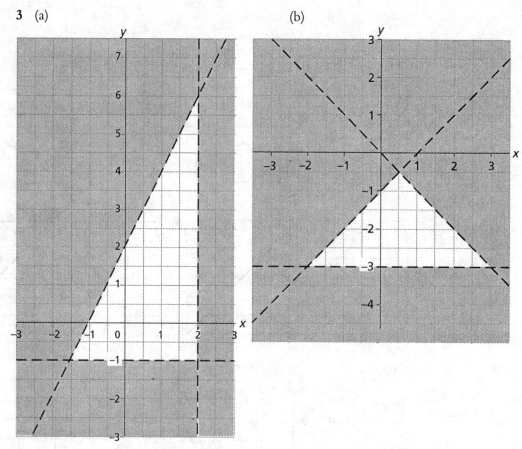

3.8h   **1**

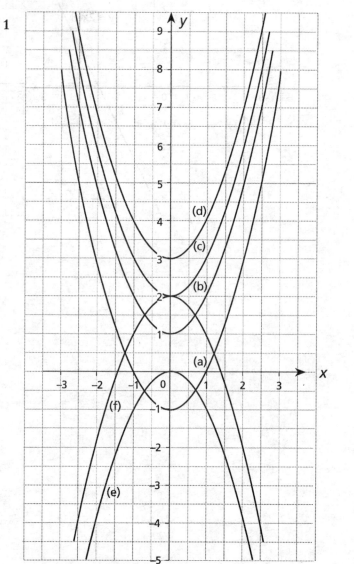

2 (a) Adding n to the x^2 term moves the graph n places up the y–axis.
Subtracting n moves the graph n places down.
(This type of move is called a translation.)

(b) Making x^2 into $^-x^2$ has the effect of turning the graph upside down.

3 (a) $y = 5 - x^2$

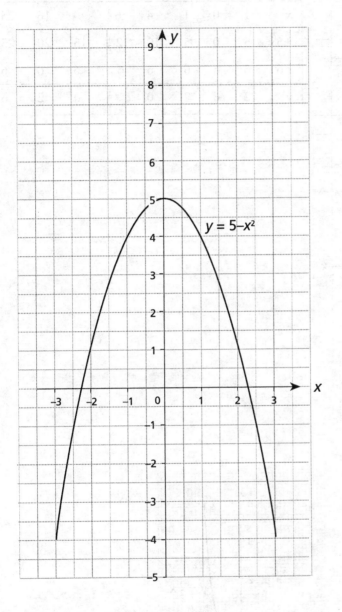

(b) $y = 2x^2 - 3x - 2$

x	3	2	1	$\frac{1}{2}$	0	$-\frac{1}{2}$	$^-1$	$^-2$
$2x^2$	18	8	2	$\frac{1}{2}$	0	$\frac{1}{2}$	2	8
$-3x$	$^-9$	$^-6$	$^-3$	$-\frac{3}{2}$	0	$\frac{3}{2}$	3	6
-2	$^-2$	$^-2$	$^-2$	$^-2$	$^-2$	$^-2$	$^-2$	$^-2$
y	7	0	$^-3$	$^-3$	$^-2$	0	3	12

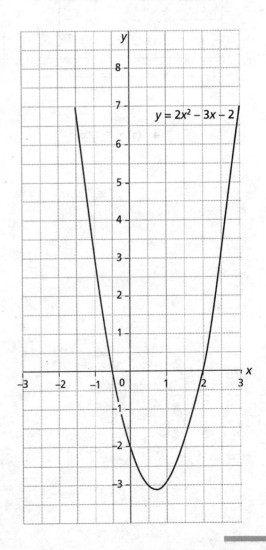

(c) $y = x^2 + 5x + 6$

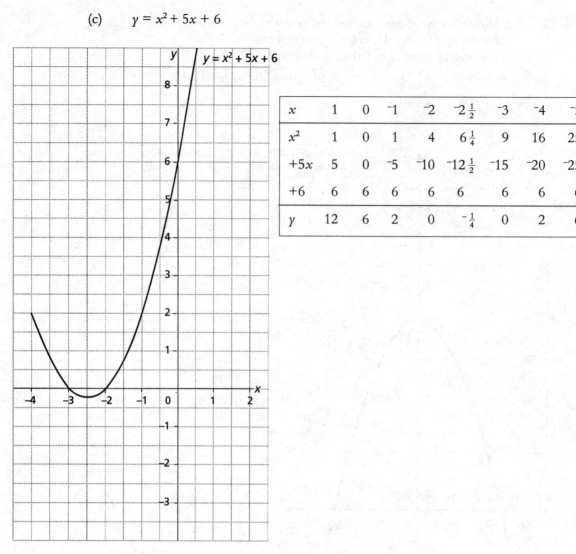

x	1	0	⁻1	⁻2	⁻2$\frac{1}{2}$	⁻3	⁻4	⁻5
x^2	1	0	1	4	6$\frac{1}{4}$	9	16	25
$+5x$	5	0	⁻5	⁻10	⁻12$\frac{1}{2}$	⁻15	⁻20	⁻25
$+6$	6	6	6	6	6	6	6	6
y	12	6	2	0	⁻$\frac{1}{4}$	0	2	6

4   (a) $y = \frac{1}{2}x^3$

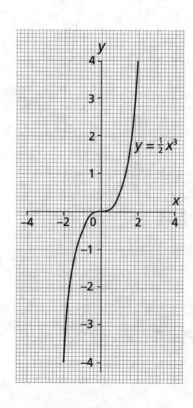

(b) $y = 2 - x^3$

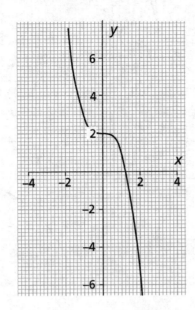

(c) $y = x^3 - 4x^2 + 3x$

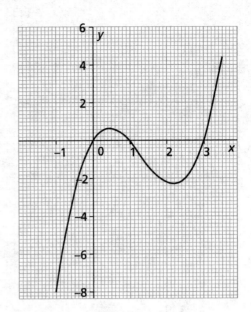

5 (a) $y = \dfrac{2}{x}$

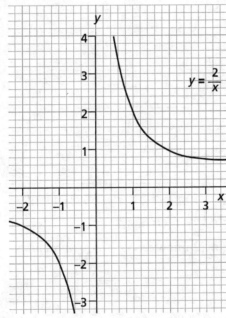

(b) $y = \dfrac{1}{x+2}$

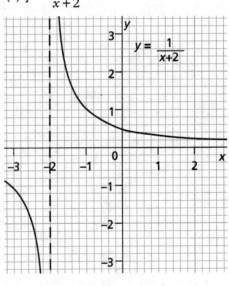

(c) $y = \dfrac{1}{x-2}$

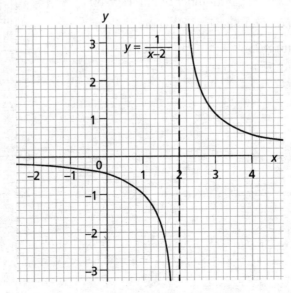

(d) $y = \dfrac{-4}{x}$

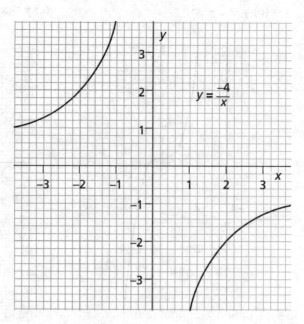

$y = \dfrac{-4}{x}$

3.8i

1 (a) goes with (i)　　(b) goes with (iii)　　(c) goes with (ii)

2 (a) B　　　　　　(b) C　　　　　　(c) D

3 (a)　　　　　　　(b)　　　　　　　(c)

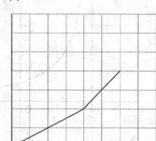 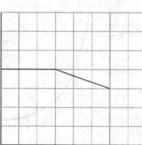 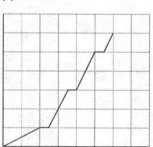

4 (a) 4 hours　　　　(b) 75 miles　　　(c) 30 minutes

5 (a) $\dfrac{75}{1\cdot5} = 50$ mph　(b) $\dfrac{120}{2} = 60$ mph

6 (a) 71 beats per minute　(b) 12 minutes　　(c) 18 minutes

3.9a

1 Cost $= \frac{1}{20} \times$ number of copies $+ 80$

2 (a) & (c) See diagram right

(b) 8·25

(d) $h = 8\cdot25 - (t - 2\cdot5)^2$

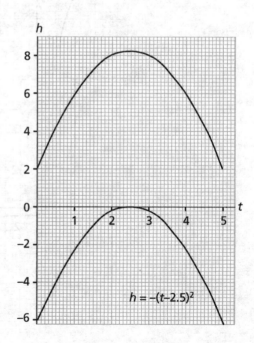

$h = -(t-2.5)^2$

3.9b

1. (a) $x^{-4} \times x^{-3} = x^{-7}$ (b) $6x^{-6}$ (c) $4x^{-3}$ (d) $6a^{-10}$
   (e) $60b^3$ (f) $7x^{-5}y^{-2}$

2. (a) $x^{-6} \div x^{-2} = x^{-4}$ (b) $4x^{-4}$ (c) $7x^{-6}$ (d) $5x^7$
   (e) $7a^{-5}b^3c^9$

3. (a) a^{-21} (b) $\dfrac{b^{-4}}{2}$ (c) $\dfrac{n^{12}}{256}$ (d) $x^{-10}y^{15}z^5$

4. (a) $\sqrt[5]{x^2}$ (b) $\sqrt[7]{x^3}$ (c) $\sqrt[3]{x^2}$ (d) $\sqrt{x^3}$

5. (a) $x^{\frac{5}{6}}$ (b) $x^{\frac{5}{3}}$ (c) $x^{\frac{29}{28}}$

6. (a) $x^{\frac{2}{5}}$ (b) $a^{\frac{7}{6}}$

7. (a) a^2 (b) $x^{\frac{7}{2}}$ or $\sqrt{x^7}$ (c) $x^{\frac{2}{5}}y^{\frac{1}{5}}$ or $\sqrt[5]{x^2y}$

3.9c

1. (a) $x = 1$ or 4 (b) $x = 1$ or 2 (c) $x = {}^-1$ or 2 (d) $x = 2$ (e) no solution

2. (a) The line $y = 4$ crosses the parabola $y = x^2$ at $({}^-2, 4)$ and $(2, 4)$ so $x^2 = 4$ has the solutions $x = {}^-2$ and $x = 2$.
   (b) The line $y = 2x + 3$ crosses the parabola at $({}^-1, 1)$ and $(3, 9)$ so the solutions of $x^2 = 2x + 3$ are $x = {}^-1$ and $x = 3$.
   (c) The line $y = {}^-x$ crosses the parabola at $({}^-1, 1)$ and $(0, 0)$ so the solutions are $x = {}^-1$ and $x = 0$.

3. The curve and the line cross at the points $({}^-3, {}^-1)$ and $(2, 4)$ so the solutions of $x^2 + 2x - 4 = x + 2$ are $x = {}^-3$ and $x = 2$.

4. (a) $x = {}^-1$ (b) $x = 0$ and $x = 3$

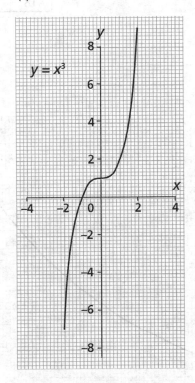 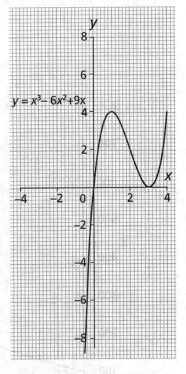

5. (a) The solution of $x^3 = 0$ is given by the point of intersection of $y = x^3$ with the x-axis. The solution is $x = 0$.
   (b) The solution of $x^3 = x^2 - x + 1$ is given by the point of intersection of $y = x^3$ with $y = x^2 - x + 1$. The solution is $x = 1$.
   (c) The solution of $x^3 = 2x - 4$ is given by the point of intersection of $y = x^3$ and $y = 2x - 4$. The solution is $x = {}^-2$.

(d) The solution of $x^3 + x = 0$ is given by the point of intersection of $y = x^3$ and $y = {}^-x$. The solution is $x = 0$.

(e) The solutions of $x^3 - x^2 - 2x = 0$ are given by the points of intersection of $y = x^3$ and $y = x^2 + 2x$. The solutions are $x = {}^-1$, 0 and 2.

3.9d

1

Minutes	Micro-organisms
0	1
1	2
2	4
3	8
4	16
5	32
6	64
7	128
8	256
9	512
10	1024
11	2048
12	4096
13	8192
14	16 384
15	32 768

2 (a)

Year	Money (£)
0	100·00
1	112·00
2	125·44
3	140·49
4	157·35
5	176·23
6	197·38
7	221·07
8	247·60
9	277·31
10	310·58
11	347·86
12	389·60
13	436·35
14	488·71
15	547·36
16	613·04
17	686·60
18	769·00

(b)

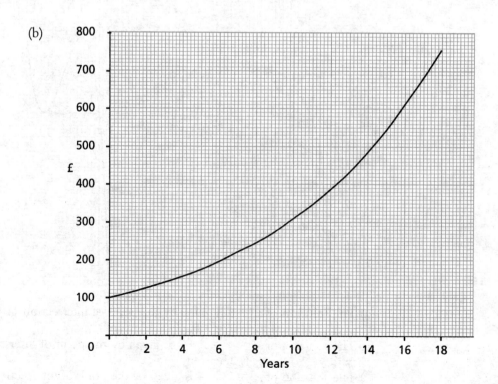

3 (a)

Repeats	Salt in solution (g)
0	25·00
1	17·50
2	12·25
3	8·58
4	6·00
5	4·20
6	2·94
7	2·06
8	1·44
9	0·01
10	0·71

(b)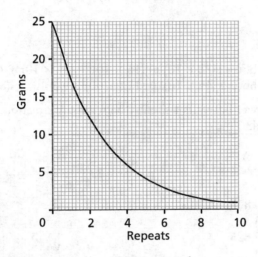

4 (a) 72 seconds   (b) 72 seconds   (c) 72 seconds

3.9e

1 (a) 1   (b) 2

2 (a) approx. 4·5 m/s²   (b) approx. 10·2 m/s²   (c) approx. 20·1 m/s²

3.10a

1 $u_1 = 10$, $u_2 = 25$, $u_3 = 62·5$, $u_4 = 156·25$, $u_5 = 390·625$

2 (a) $u_1 = 5$, $u_2 = 18$, $u_3 = 57$, $u_4 = 174$, $u_5 = 525$
    (b) $u_1 = 10$, $u_2 = 6$, $u_3 = 5·2$, $u_4 = 5·04$, $u_5 = 5·008$

3 (a) $x = 3x - 5$

$5 = 2x$

$x = 2.5$

    (b) $x = \dfrac{15}{x+2}$

$x(x + 2) = 15$

$x^2 + 2x - 15 = 0$

$(x + 5)(x - 3) = 0$

$x = {}^-5$ or $x = 3$

4 (a) $u_1 = 2·49$
$u_2 = 2·47$
$u_3 = 2·41$
$u_4 = 2·23$
$u_5 = 1·69$

    (b) $u_1 = 100$
$u_2 = 0·147$
$u_3 = 6·986$
$u_4 = 1·669$
$u_5 = 4·08$
$u_6 = 2·464$

This sequence does not converge to the fixed point.

This sequence converges to 3 even though u_1 was a long way from that fixed point.

3.10b

1 (a) $x = -\frac{1}{2}$ or $-\frac{3}{2}$ (b) $x = -\frac{4}{3}$ or $-\frac{5}{3}$ (c) $x = -\frac{1}{3}$ or 7

2 (a) $x = 1\cdot19$ or $-4\cdot19$ (to 2 d.p.)   (b) $x = 6\cdot92$ or $-4\cdot92$ (to 2 d.p.)

3 (a) $x = 2\cdot77$ or $-1\cdot27$ (to 2 d.p.)   (b) $x = 1\cdot85$ or $-0\cdot18$ (to 2 d.p.)

4 $-2\cdot79$

5 (a) $1\cdot5$ and $-3\cdot5$ (b) $1\cdot45$ and $-3\cdot45$

3.10c

1 $(x + 1)$

2 (a) $\dfrac{(x-1) + (x+1)}{(x-1)(x+1)} = \dfrac{2x}{x^2-1}$ (b) $\dfrac{6x}{}$ (c) $\dfrac{3-2x}{x^3-x}$

3 (a) $x = 2$ (b) $x = 12$ (c) $x = 3$

3.10d

1 (a) Upper bound $(22 \times 10) + (15 \times 10) + (11 \times 10) + (9 \times 10) = 570$
Lower bound $(15 \times 10) + (11 \times 10) + (9 \times 10) + (8 \times 10) = 430$

(b) The lower bound is a slightly better approximation.

(c) $\dfrac{570 + 430}{2} = 500$

2 $y = x^2(4 - x)$

x	y
0	0
0·5	0·875
1	3
1·5	5·625
2	8
2·5	9·375
3	9
3·5	6·125
4	0

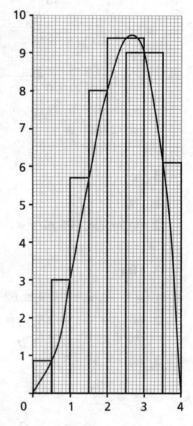

Area under step-graph = $0\cdot5 \times$
$(0\cdot875 + 3 + 5\cdot625 + 8 + 9\cdot375 + 9\cdot375 + 9 + 6\cdot125) = 30\cdot375$

Approximate area under curve is 30 square units.

3 $y = 10 - x^2$

x	-3	-2	-1	0	1	2	3
y	1	6	9	10	9	6	1

$1 \times (\frac{1}{2}(1 + 1) + 6 + 9 + 10 + 9 + 6) = 41$ square units

4 $13\cdot5$ m

5 $2(\dfrac{25+0}{2} + 24 + 21 + 16 + 9) = 165$ m

3.10e

1

x	⁻3	⁻2	⁻1	0	1	2	3
$f(x)$	10	4	0	⁻2	⁻2	0	4

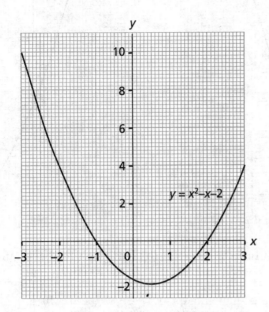

$y = x^2 - x - 2$

2 (a) This graph has been translated up the y-axis 3 places.

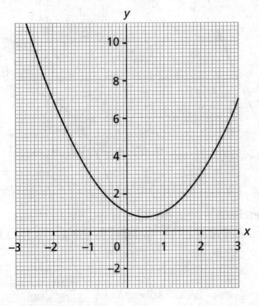

(b) This graph has been translated down the y-axis 1 place.

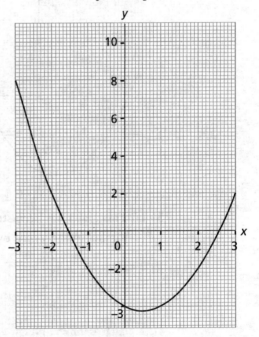

3 (a) This graph has been translated along the *x*-axis 3 places to the left.

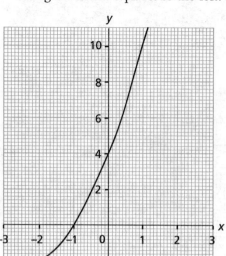

(b) This graph has been translated along the *x*-axis 2 places to the right.

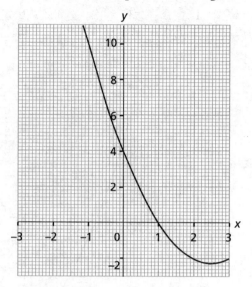

4 (a) This graph has been reflected in the *y*-axis.

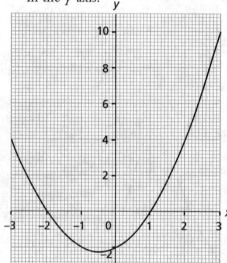

(b) This graph has been reflected in the *x*-axis.

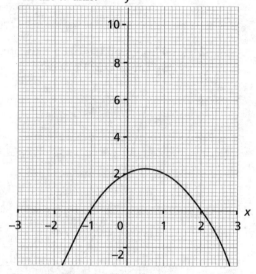

5 (a) This graph has been stretched parallel to the *y*-axis by a factor of 2.

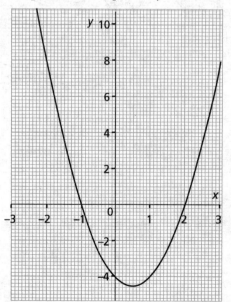

(b) This graph has been stretched parallel to the *x*-axis by a factor of $\frac{1}{2}$.

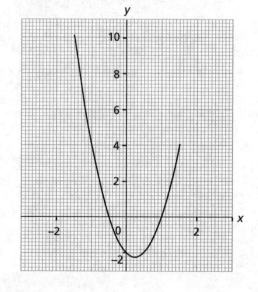

6 This graph has been translated 2 places up and 1 place to the left.

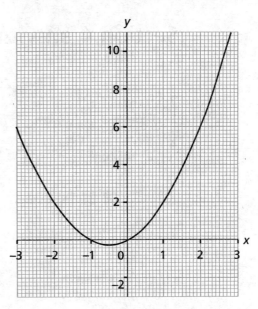

7 (a)

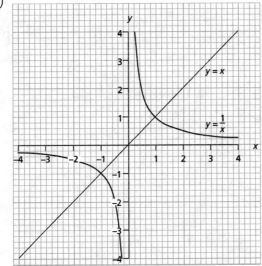

(b)

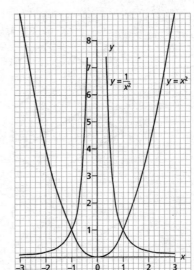

8 (a) When *a* is even the graph is in the 1st and 2nd quadrants. When *a* is odd the graph is in the 1st and 3rd quadrants.

(b) Points where $f(x) = 1$ remain fixed.

(c) $\dfrac{1}{f(x)}$ has lines of discontinuity at points where $f(x) = 0$.

3.10f

1 (a) $y = (x + 4)^2 - 5$

(b) $y = (x - 3)^2 + 4$

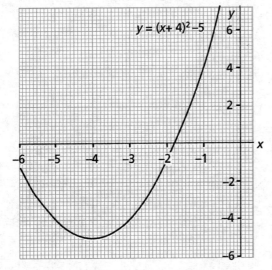

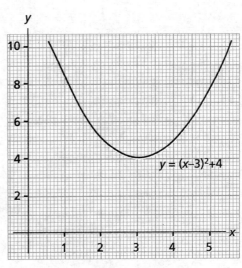

Section 4 answers

4.6a

1 (a) compass   (b) key   (c) whistle   (d) bulldog clip

2   (a)   (b)

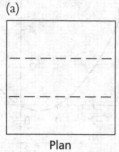

Plan

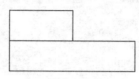

Side view

3

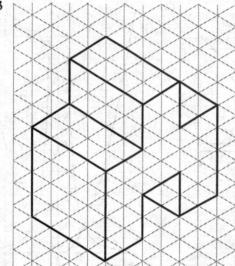

4

Front view

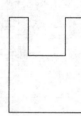

Side view

Plan

4.6b

1

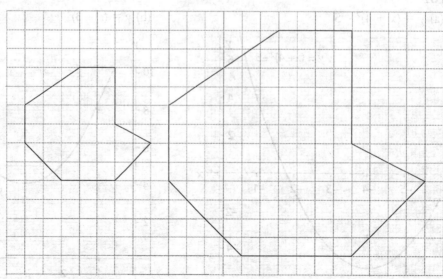

2 (a)

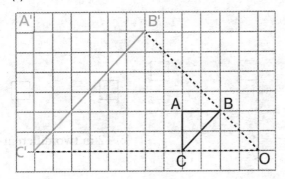

(b)

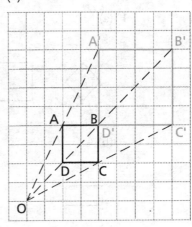

3

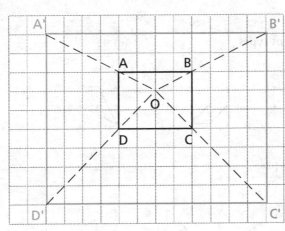

4

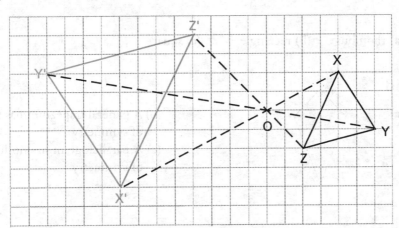

5

(a)

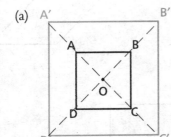

(b)

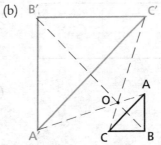

(c) scale factor in (a) is 2, scale factor in (b) is 3

6 (a) 3   (b) 13

4.6c

1 (a)

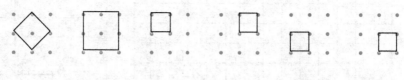

(b) 4

(c) 12 in two different types

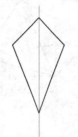

(d) 28 in three different types

(e) 4

(f) 40 in 6 different types

2 (a) rhombus   (b) rectangle   (c) square

4.6d

1 (a)

(b) A general trapezium has no lines of symmetry.

(c) A parallelogram has no lines of symmetry.

(d)

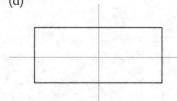

(e)

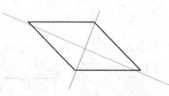

(f)

2 (a) 1   (b) 1   (c) 2   (d) 2   (e) 2   (f) 4

3

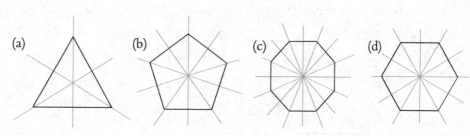

(a)   (b)   (c)   (d)

4 (a) 3   (b) 5   (c) 8   (d) 6

5 (a) angle at the centre $= \dfrac{360°}{6} = 60°$, exterior angle $= 60°$, interior angle $= 120°$

   (b) angle at the centre $= \dfrac{360°}{5} = 72°$, exterior angle $= 72°$, interior angle $= 108°$

6 (a) external angle $=$ angle at the centre $\dfrac{360°}{18°} = 20$ sides

   (b) $180° \times (20 - 2) = 3240°$

7 equilateral triangle and square

8 (a)   (b)   (c)

4.6e

1

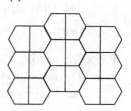
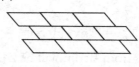

(e) No direction has been given because 180° clockwise and 180° anticlockwise both give a half turn.

2

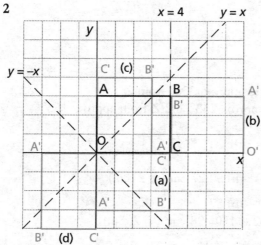

3

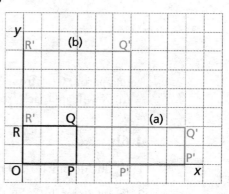

4 The circle has been stretched factor 2 parallel to the y-axis and factor 3 parallel to the x-axis. This gives an enlargement of factor 6. Hence the area of the ellipse will be 6×6 cm^2 = 36 cm^2.

5

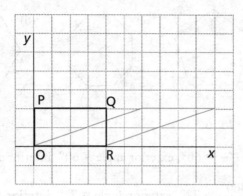

4.6f

1 Repeat 6 [FD 200 LT 60]

4.6g

1 (a) 060°   (b) 115°   (c) 250°

2 (a) 339°   (b) 177°   (c) 24°   (d) 53°   (e) 159°

3 (a) The bearing of Paris from Berlin will be 240°.
  (b) The bearing of Athens from Vienna will be 157°.
  (c) The bearing from Rome to Belgrade will be 068°.

4 (a) & (b)

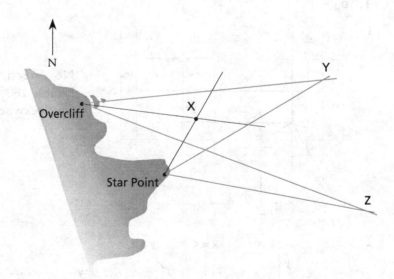

  (c) approx. 073° from X and approx. 336° from Z
  (d) X will approach from approx. 253° and Z from approx. 156°

4.6h

1 (a) 201·06 cm^2 (to 2 d.p.)   (b) 50·27 cm (to 2 d.p.)

2 (a) 9·62 cm^2 (to 2 d.p.)   (b) 571
  (c) 3·5 × 2000 − 571 × 9·62 = 1506·98 cm^2 (to 2 d.p.)

3 (a) 3·77 m (to 2 d.p.)   (b) 78·55 cm

4 (a) 19·6350 m²   (b) 1220

4.7a

1 A (5, 0, 0)   B (5, 0, 3)   C (0, 0, 3)   D (0, 4, 0)   E (5, 4, 0)   F (5, 4, 3)
   G (0, 4, 3)

2 (4, 7, 5) or (5, 4, 7)

3 (a) 8

   (b) (⁻1, ⁻2, 3), (5, ⁻2, 3), (⁻1, 4, 3), (5, 4, 3), (⁻1, ⁻2, ⁻3), (5, ⁻2, ⁻3),
   (⁻1, 4, ⁻3), (5, 4, ⁻3)

4.7b

1 This is a circle with radius 2 cm.

2

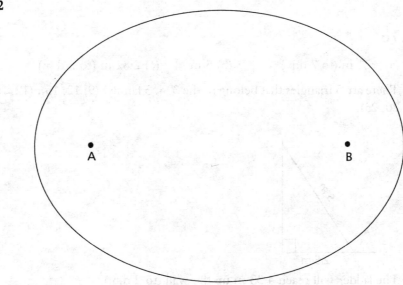

3

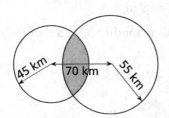

4

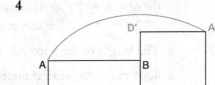

5 The tree must be planted on the dotted line anywhere in the area that is not shaded.

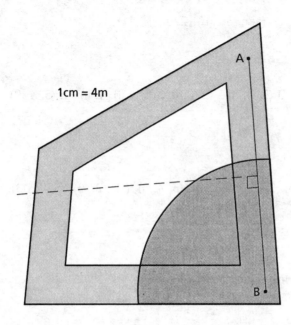

4.7c

1 (a) 7·21 m (to 2 d.p.)   (b) 5 m   (c) 2·82 m (to 2 d.p.)

2 There are 3 triangles that belong to the 3, 4, 5 family: (9, 12, 15), (12, 16, 20) and (15, 20, 25).

3

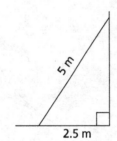

The ladder will reach 4·33 m up the wall (to 2 d.p.).

4 (a) $7^2 + 6^2 \neq 8^2$ so this triangle is not right-angled
   (b) $6^2 + 8^2 = 10^2$ so this triangle is right-angled
   (c) $24^2 + 7^2 = 25^2$ so this triangle is right-angled

5 The length of the vector is 10 units. (This is another 3, 4, 5 triangle!)

6 4061 m (to the nearest metre)

4.7d

1 A $0{\cdot}5 \times 42$ m $\times 26$ m $= 546$ m^2 B $0{\cdot}5 \times 45$ m $\times 26$ m $= 585$ m^2
   C $0{\cdot}5 \times 16$ m $\times 22$ m $= 176$ m^2 D $0{\cdot}5 \times 71$ m $\times 22$ m $= 781$ m^2

   Total $= 2088$ m^2

2 (a) 5·25 m^2
   (b) The banisters form a parallelogram with base 1 m and height 3·5 m giving 3·5 m^2.

3 (a) A 66 m^2 B 126 m^2 C 76 m^2 D 95 m^2
   (b) window in B 20 m^2 window in D 17·5 m^2 doors 12 m^2 each
   (c) 301·5 m^2

4 (a) 156 m²   (b) 156 000 m³

5 962·11 mm³ (to 2 d.p.)

6 (a) 125   (b) 10 × 10 × 12 or 2 × 10 × 60 or 2 × 50 × 12

4.7e

1 (a)   (b)

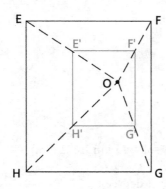
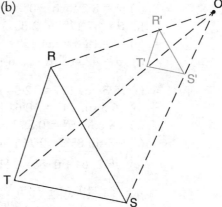

4.8a

1 The angles in each triangle should be the same: 90°, about 53° and about 37°.

2 These angles should also be the same.

3 (a) Two corresponding angles are equal. The angles of a triangle add to 180° so the third must also be equal. Hence ABC and CDE are similar.

(b) $\dfrac{DE}{AB} = \dfrac{CE}{AC}$ therefore DE = $48 \times \dfrac{12}{24} = 24$ units

(c) $\dfrac{BC}{DC} = \dfrac{AC}{EC}$ therefore BC = $\dfrac{18 \times 24}{12} = 36$ units

4 (a) $\dfrac{AB}{AC} = \dfrac{2}{4} = \dfrac{1}{2}$ and $\dfrac{AE}{AD} = \dfrac{5}{10} = \dfrac{1}{2}$ so two corresponding sides are in the same ratio.

The angle between the two sides is angle *A* in each case. Hence the triangles are similar.

(b) Corresponding sides are in the same ratio so $\dfrac{BC}{AB} = \dfrac{DE}{AE}$

therefore BC = $\dfrac{8 \times 2}{5}$ = 3·2 cm

5 IJKL is not similar to the other three quadrilaterals.

4.8b

1 (a) *a* is the hypotenuse   (b) *d* is the side opposite to the angle
      b is the side adjacent to the angle   *e* is the hypotenuse
      c is the side opposite to the angle   *f* is the side adjacent to the angle

(c) *g* is the side adjacent to the angle   (d) *j* is the side opposite to the angle
    h is the hypotenuse   *k* is the side adjacent to the angle
    i is the side opposite to the angle   *l* is the hypotenuse

2 (a) $x = 3 \times \tan 35° = 2{\cdot}10$ m (to 2 d.p.)   (b) $x = 7 \times \sin 40° = 4{\cdot}50$ m (to 2 d.p.)
     (c) $x = 100 \times \cos 18° = 95{\cdot}11$ m (to 2 d.p.)

3 (a) 6·71 m (to 2 d.p.)   (b) 8·20 m (to 2 d.p.)
     (c) 4·04 m (to 2 d.p.)   (d) 14·65 m (to 2 d.p.)

4 (a) $\tan \theta = \dfrac{7\cdot3}{6\cdot8}$ so $\theta = 47\cdot03°$ (b) $\cos \theta = \dfrac{7\cdot2}{16\cdot3}$ so $\theta = 63\cdot79°$

    (c) $\sin \theta = \dfrac{4\cdot2}{5\cdot6}$ so $\theta = 48\cdot59°$ (d) $\sin \theta = \dfrac{3\cdot8}{8\cdot4}$ so $\theta = 26\cdot90°$

5 (a) $\theta = 42\cdot43°$ (to 2 d.p.)

    (b) $x = 7\cdot2 \times \tan 48° = 8\cdot00$ m (to 2 d.p.)
    (c) $x = 8\cdot2 \times \cos 70° = 2\cdot80$ m (to 2 d.p.)
    (d) $\theta = 47\cdot17°$ (to 2 d.p.)
    (e) $x = 18\cdot6 \times \tan 15° = 4\cdot98$ m (to 2 d.p.
    (f) $\theta = 42\cdot40°$ (to 2 d.p.)

6 (a) $16\cdot5 \cos 40° = 12\cdot64$ km (to 2 d.p.)
    (b) $16\cdot5 \sin 40° = 10\cdot61$ km (to 2 d.p.)
    (c) $9\cdot8 \cos 85° = 0\cdot85$ km (to 2 d.p.)
    (d) $9\cdot8 \sin 85° = 9\cdot76$ km (to 2 d.p.)
    (e) $\sqrt{(12\cdot64+0\cdot85)^2 + (10\cdot61+9\cdot76)^2} = 24\cdot43$ km (to 2 d.p.)

    (f) $\tan^{-1}\left(\dfrac{10\cdot61+9\cdot76}{12\cdot64+0\cdot85}\right) = 056°$ (to nearest degree)

7 $17\cdot41$ m² (to 2 d.p.)

4.8c

1 (a) area   (b) length   (c) length   (d) length   (e) volume
    (f) volume   (g) length   (h) volume   (i) length   (j) area

2 (a) m²   (b) m   (c) ml   (d) km   (e) m³

3 (a) volume   (b) volume   (c) length   (d) area   (e) length

4.8d

1 (a) $\begin{pmatrix}1\\2\end{pmatrix}$ (b) $\begin{pmatrix}2\\1\end{pmatrix}$ (c) $\begin{pmatrix}2\\-1\end{pmatrix}$ (d) $\begin{pmatrix}1\\-2\end{pmatrix}$ (e) $\begin{pmatrix}1\\2\end{pmatrix}$

2

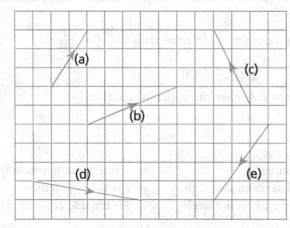

3 (a) $\begin{pmatrix}3\\4\end{pmatrix}$ (b) $\begin{pmatrix}3\\-3\end{pmatrix}$ (c) $\begin{pmatrix}0\\-5\end{pmatrix}$

4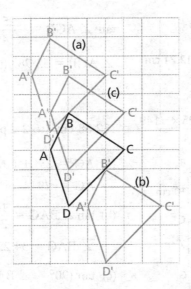

5 (a) $\begin{pmatrix} -2 \\ -3 \end{pmatrix}$ (b) $\begin{pmatrix} -5 \\ 2 \end{pmatrix}$ (c) $\begin{pmatrix} 2 \\ -4 \end{pmatrix}$ (d) $\begin{pmatrix} -6 \\ 1 \end{pmatrix}$ (e) $\begin{pmatrix} 3 \\ 4 \end{pmatrix}$

6 (a) $\mathbf{a} = \begin{pmatrix} 1 \\ 3 \end{pmatrix}$ $\mathbf{b} = \begin{pmatrix} -4 \\ 2 \end{pmatrix}$ $\mathbf{c} = \begin{pmatrix} 4 \\ 4 \end{pmatrix}$ $\mathbf{d} = \begin{pmatrix} 4 \\ 0 \end{pmatrix}$ $\mathbf{e} = \begin{pmatrix} 1 \\ 3 \end{pmatrix}$ $\mathbf{f} = \begin{pmatrix} 3 \\ 4 \end{pmatrix}$

$\mathbf{g} = \begin{pmatrix} 0 \\ -4 \end{pmatrix}$ $\mathbf{h} = \begin{pmatrix} -2 \\ 2 \end{pmatrix}$

(b) $^-\mathbf{a} = \begin{pmatrix} -1 \\ -3 \end{pmatrix}$ $^-\mathbf{b} = \begin{pmatrix} 4 \\ -2 \end{pmatrix}$ $^-\mathbf{c} = \begin{pmatrix} -4 \\ -4 \end{pmatrix}$ $^-\mathbf{d} = \begin{pmatrix} -4 \\ 0 \end{pmatrix}$ $^-\mathbf{e} = \begin{pmatrix} -1 \\ -3 \end{pmatrix}$ $^-\mathbf{f} = \begin{pmatrix} -3 \\ -4 \end{pmatrix}$

$^-\mathbf{g} = \begin{pmatrix} 0 \\ 4 \end{pmatrix}$ $^-\mathbf{h} = \begin{pmatrix} 2 \\ -2 \end{pmatrix}$

(c) $\mathbf{a} = \mathbf{e}$ (d) $|\mathbf{d}| = 4$ $|\mathbf{g}| = 4$ (e) $|\mathbf{c}| = 5 \cdot 66$ (to 2 d.p.) $|\mathbf{f}| = 5$

7 (a) $\begin{pmatrix} 6 \\ 12 \end{pmatrix}$ (b) $\begin{pmatrix} 1 \\ 2 \end{pmatrix}$ (c) $\begin{pmatrix} -4 \\ -8 \end{pmatrix}$ (d) $\begin{pmatrix} -1 \\ -2 \end{pmatrix}$

4.9a

1 (a)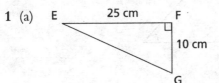

$EG^2 = 25^2 + 10^2 = 725$

$EG = \sqrt{725}$ or $26 \cdot 93$ cm (to 2 d.p.)

(b)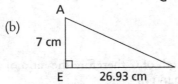

$AG^2 = AE^2 + EG^2 = 7^2 + 725 = 774$

$AG = \sqrt{774}$ or $27 \cdot 82$ cm (to 2 d.p.)

(c) $\tan \angle AGE = \dfrac{7}{\sqrt{725}}$, $\sin \angle AGE = \dfrac{7}{\sqrt{774}}$

$\angle AGE = 14 \cdot 57°$ (to 2 d.p.)

(d)

$BG^2 = 7^2 + 10^2 = 149$

$BG = \sqrt{149}$ or $12 \cdot 21$ cm (to 2 d.p.)

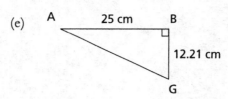

(e)

$\tan \angle AGB = \dfrac{25}{\sqrt{149}}$

$\angle AGB = 63 \cdot 98°$ (to 2 d.p.)

(f) Area of triangle ABG $= \dfrac{25 \times \sqrt{149}}{2} = 152 \cdot 58$ cm^2 (to 2 d.p.)

2

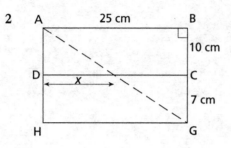

(a) $AG^2 = 25^2 + (10 + 7)^2 = 914$

$AG = \sqrt{914}$ or $30 \cdot 23$ cm (to 2 d.p.)

(b) $\tan \angle BAG = \dfrac{17}{25} = 0 \cdot 68$

$\angle BAG = 34 \cdot 22°$ (to 2 d.p.)

(c) $\tan (90° - \angle BAG) = \dfrac{x}{10}$

$x = 14 \cdot 71$ cm (to 2 d.p.)

3 (a) 7·93 m (to 2 d.p.)   (b) 7·81 m (to 2 d.p.)   (c) 8·13 m (to 2 d.p.)

4.9b

1 ABC is congruent to KLJ because all corresponding angles and all corresponding sides are equal.

ABC and DEF cannot be congruent because they have different angles.

ABC and GHI cannot be congruent because the sides are not in the same ratio.

Since JKL is congruent to ABC and ABC is not congruent to DEF or GHI, the triangle JKL cannot be congruent to DEF or GHI.

DEF and GHI are not congruent because they have different angles.

2 (a) Side, angle, side (SAS)   (b) Not congruent: sides of different length
(c) Angle, angle, side (AAS)   (d) Right angle, hypotenuse, side (RHS)
(e) Side, side, side (SSS)   (f) Not congruent: the sides of length 8 are opposite different angles.

3

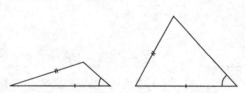

4 Jonathan is right. (AAS)

4.9c

1 The length of D is twice the length of C therefore the ratio of areas is $1^2 : 2^2$ or 1 : 4.
Surface area of D $= 4 \times 600 = 2400$ m^2

2 (a) 1 : 50 (b) $1^2 : 50^2 = 1 : 2500$ (c) $1^3 : 50^3 = 1 : 125\,000$

3 (a) 1 : 10 (b) 200 litres   (c) 15 litres

4.9d

1 (a) $\dfrac{72}{360} \times \pi \times 18 = 11 \cdot 31$ cm   (b) $\dfrac{90}{360} \times \pi \times 12 = 9 \cdot 42$ m

2 radius of outer track = 38 m so length of outside track is $\dfrac{180}{360} \times \pi \times (2 \times 38) = 119\cdot38$ m

3 103° plus overlap

4 (a) $\dfrac{60}{360} \times \pi \times 6 \times 6 = 18\cdot85$ cm²   (b) $\dfrac{120}{360} \times \pi \times 5 \times 5 = 26\cdot18$ m²

   (c) $\dfrac{360-72}{360} \times \pi \times 20 \times 20 = 1005\cdot31$ m²

5 $(\dfrac{110}{360} \times \pi \times 45 \times 45) - (\dfrac{110}{360} \times \pi \times 13 \times 13) = 1781\cdot63$ cm²

6 (a) Sector is $\dfrac{100}{360} \times \pi \times 20 \times 20 = 349\cdot065$

     Area of triangle = 196·961

     Area of segment = 349·065 − 196·961 = 152·10 cm² (to 2 d.p.)

   (b) Volume = 1500 cm × 152·10 cm² = 228 150 cm³ or 228·15 litres

7 (a) $\sin(\tfrac{1}{2} \angle \text{AOB}) = \dfrac{20}{25}$

     $\angle \text{AOB} = 106\cdot26°$ (to 2 d.p.)

   (b) Area of sector = $\dfrac{106\cdot26}{360} \times \pi \times 25^2 = 579\cdot56$ mm² (to 2 d.p.)

   (c) Using Pythagoras gives OX = 15 mm (X is mid-point of AB).

     Area of triangle = $\tfrac{1}{2} \times 40 \times 15 = 300$ mm²

   (d) Area of segment = 579·56 − 300 = 279·56 mm² (to 2 d.p.)

8 (a) $\pi \times 80 \times 100 = 25\ 133$ cm²

   (b) 30 159 cm²

9 $V = \tfrac{1}{3}\pi r^2 h$ $150 = \tfrac{1}{3} \times \pi \times r \times r \times 6$ $r^2 = \dfrac{150 \times 3}{\pi \times 6} = 23\cdot873241$

   so radius = 4·89 cm (to 2 d.p.)

10 $l^2 = 3^2 + 12^2 = 153$

   curved surface area = $\pi r l = \pi \times 3 \times \sqrt{153} = 116\cdot58$ cm² (to 2 d.p.)

11 (a) Volume of Phoebe = $\tfrac{4}{3}\pi r^3 = \tfrac{4}{3} \times \pi \times 110^3 = 5\ 575\ 280$ km³

   (b) Surface area = $4\pi r^2 = 4 \times \pi \times 110^2 = 152\ 053$ km²

12 (a) 15 708 km² (b) 261 799 km³

13 169·65 ml (to 2 d.p.)

4.9e

1
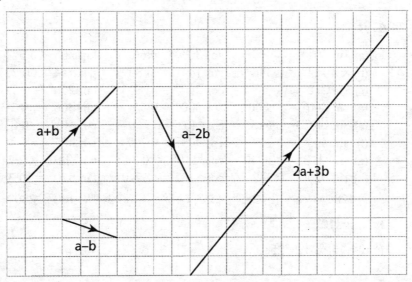

2 (a) $\vec{AC}$　(b) $\vec{AD}$　(c) $\vec{DA}$　(d) $\vec{AC}$　(e) $\vec{DE}$　(f) $\vec{CE}$　(g) $\vec{DC}$　(h) **0**

3 (a) $\mathbf{a} - \mathbf{b}$　(b) $\frac{1}{3}(\mathbf{a} - \mathbf{b})$　(c) $^-\mathbf{a} - \mathbf{b}$　(d) $\frac{2}{3}\mathbf{a} + \frac{1}{3}\mathbf{b}$　(e) $\frac{4}{3}\mathbf{a} + \frac{2}{3}\mathbf{b}$

4 (a) $\begin{pmatrix} 5 \\ 5 \end{pmatrix}$　(b) $\begin{pmatrix} 4 \\ 3 \end{pmatrix}$　(c) $\begin{pmatrix} 3 \\ 7 \end{pmatrix}$

　　(d) $\begin{pmatrix} 4 \\ 2 \end{pmatrix}$　(e) $\begin{pmatrix} 4 \\ 3 \end{pmatrix}$　(f) $\begin{pmatrix} 2 \\ 8 \end{pmatrix}$

5 (a) $\begin{pmatrix} ^-1 \\ 1 \end{pmatrix}$　(b) $\begin{pmatrix} 1 \\ ^-1 \end{pmatrix}$　(c) $\begin{pmatrix} ^-2 \\ 5 \end{pmatrix}$

　　(d) $\begin{pmatrix} 5 \\ 3 \end{pmatrix}$　(e) $\begin{pmatrix} ^-1 \\ 3 \end{pmatrix}$　(f) $\begin{pmatrix} 5 \\ 8 \end{pmatrix}$

6 (a) $\begin{pmatrix} 4 \\ 1 \end{pmatrix} + \begin{pmatrix} ^-2 \\ 3 \end{pmatrix} = \begin{pmatrix} 2 \\ 4 \end{pmatrix}$　(b) $\begin{pmatrix} 4 \\ 1 \end{pmatrix} - \begin{pmatrix} ^-2 \\ 3 \end{pmatrix} = \begin{pmatrix} 6 \\ ^-2 \end{pmatrix}$　(c) $^-2\begin{pmatrix} ^-2 \\ 3 \end{pmatrix} = \begin{pmatrix} 4 \\ ^-6 \end{pmatrix}$

　　(d) $2\begin{pmatrix} 4 \\ 1 \end{pmatrix} + 3\begin{pmatrix} ^-2 \\ 3 \end{pmatrix} = \begin{pmatrix} 8 \\ 2 \end{pmatrix} + \begin{pmatrix} ^-6 \\ 9 \end{pmatrix} = \begin{pmatrix} 2 \\ 11 \end{pmatrix}$

7 $\vec{WX} = \frac{1}{2}\vec{AB} + \frac{1}{2}\vec{BC} = \frac{1}{2}\vec{AC}$, $\vec{ZY} = \frac{1}{2}\vec{AD} + \frac{1}{2}\vec{DC} = \frac{1}{2}\vec{AC} = \vec{WX}$
　　$\vec{XY} = \frac{1}{2}\vec{BC} + \frac{1}{2}\vec{CD} = \frac{1}{2}\vec{BD}$, $\vec{WZ} = \frac{1}{2}\vec{BA} + \frac{1}{2}\vec{AD} = \frac{1}{2}\vec{BD} = \vec{XY}$

8

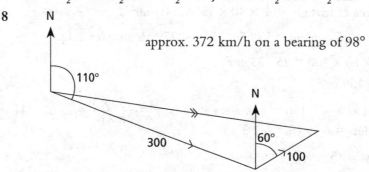

approx. 372 km/h on a bearing of 98°

9 (a) Speed $= \sqrt{3^2 + 8^2} = 8.5$ knots (to 1 d.p.)

　　(b) Bearing $= 60° - \theta$ and $\tan\theta = \dfrac{3}{8}$ so bearing $= 039°$ (to nearest degree)

10 (a) 18·43°　　　　(b) 126·49 N

11 (a) 3·54 mph　　(b) 128·54 mph　　(c) 1·29 mph　　(d) 4·83 mph
　　(e) 128·58 mph　　(f) bearing 031·58°

4.9f

1 (a) $\sin 30° = 0.5$　　　$\cos 30° = 0.866$　　　$\tan 30° = 0.577$
　　(b) $\sin 144° = 0.588$　　$\cos 144° = ^-0.809$　　$\tan 144° - ^-0.727$
　　(c) $\sin 210° = ^-0.5$　　$\cos 210° = ^-0.866$　　$\tan 210° = 0.577$
　　(d) $\sin 300° = ^-0.866$　$\cos 300° = 0.5$　　　$\tan 300° = ^-1.732$
　　(e) $\sin ^-40° = ^-0.643$　$\cos ^-40° = 0.766$　　$\tan ^-40° = ^-0.839$
　　(f) $\sin 405° = 0.707$　　$\cos 405° = 0.707$　　$\tan 405° = 1$
　　(g) $\sin ^-110° = ^-0.940$　$\cos ^-110° = ^-0.342$　$\tan ^-110° = 2.747$
　　(h) $\sin 520° = 0.342$　　$\cos 520° = ^-0.940$　　$\tan 520° = ^-0.364$

2 (a) 128°　　　(b) 285°, 435°, 645°　　　(c) 260°, $^-100°$, $^-280°$

3 (a) $\sin 12°$　　(b) $\cos 1°$　　　　　(c) $\tan ^-53°$

4 30°, 150°, 390°, 510°

5 30°, 330°, ⁻30°, ⁻330°

6 $\theta = 20·56°$ or $200·56°$

4.9g

1 (a)

$x°$	$\sin x$
0	0
10	0.17
20	0.34
30	0.50
40	0.64
50	0.77
60	0.87
70	0.94
80	0.98
90	1.00
100	0.98
110	0.94
120	0.87
130	0.77
140	0.64
150	0.50
160	0.34
170	0.17
180	0

(b)

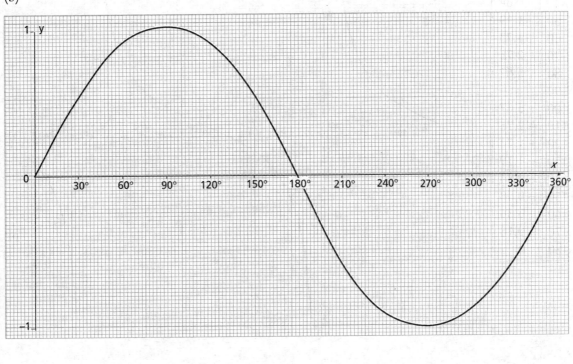

2

$x°$	$\cos x$
0	1.00
10	0.98
20	0.94
30	0.87
40	0.77
50	0.64
60	0.50
70	0.34
80	0.17
90	0
100	− 0.17
110	− 0.34
120	− 0.50
130	− 0.64
140	− 0.77
150	− 0.87
160	− 0.94
170	− 0.98
180	− 1.00

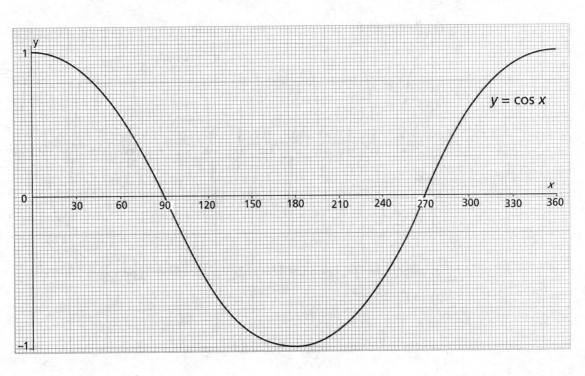

3

$x°$	$\tan x$
0	0
10	0.18
20	0.36
30	0.58
40	0.84
50	1.19
60	1.73
70	2.75
80	5.67
90	–
100	– 5.67
110	– 2.75
120	– 1.73
130	– 1.19
140	– 0.84
150	– 0.58
160	– 0.36
170	– 0.18
180	0

4

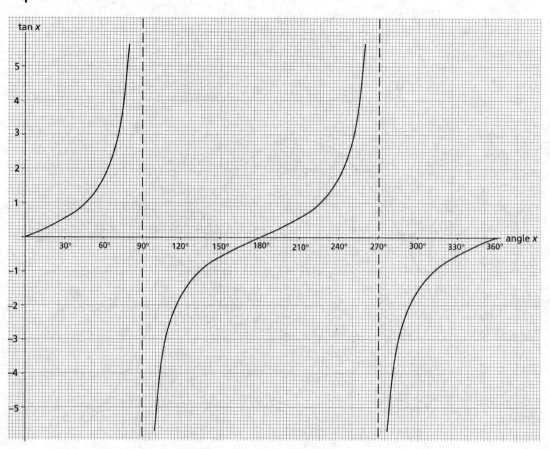

5 (a) 3

(b) $\theta \rightarrow 3 \sin \theta$

6

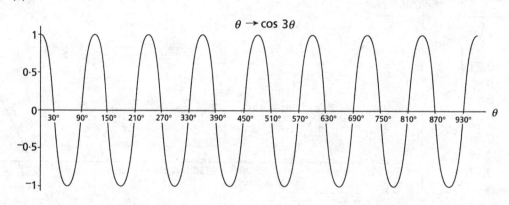

7 (a) amplitude = 4, period = 180° (b) amplitude = 5, period = 120°

8 (a) 180° (b) 90°

9 approx. 15° and 165°

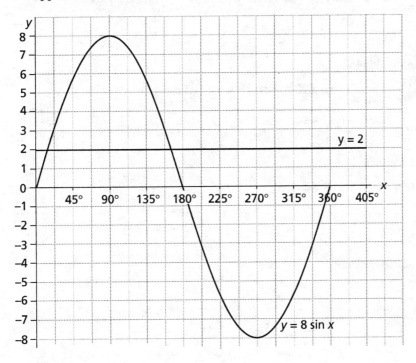

4.10a

1 (a) $a = 50°$ because a and 50° are drawn from the same arc
$b = 60°$ because b and 60° are drawn from the same arc
(b) $c = 70°$ because opposite angles of a cyclic quadrilateral = 180°
$d = 95°$ because opposite angles of a cyclic quadrilateral = 180°
(c) $e = 55°$ because the angle at the circumference is half the angle at the centre
(d) $f = 110°$ The angle at the circumference is half the angle at the centre, which in this case is 360° − 140°

2 $(\frac{1}{2}\text{CD})^2 = 5^2 - 3^2 = 4^2$ so CD = 8 = AB

3 Tangents to a circle are always the same length so ABC is an isosceles triangle.
Therefore $x = \frac{1}{2}(180° - 50°) = 65°$

∠BCA = $x = 65°$ and ∠BCO = 90° so $y = 90° - 65° = 25°$

4 OCA = 30° hence
(a) OAC = 30° because triangle OAC is isosceles
(b) AOC = 120° because angles in triangle add up to 180°
(c) ADC = 60° because this angle is at the circumference and is therefore half of AOC (the angle at the centre)
(d) AEC = 60° because it is drawn from the same chord as ADC
(e) ABC = 120° because it is the opposite angle in the cyclic quadrilateral to the angle AEC
(f) AXC = 60° because XAO = 90°, XCO = 90°, and AOC = 120° and angles in a quadrilateral add up to 360°

4.10b

1 $\dfrac{b}{\sin 85°} = \dfrac{1000}{\sin 70°}$ so $b = 1060·1$ m (to 1 d.p.)

2 Angle $B = 50·3°$ (180° − other two angles)

3 $\dfrac{x}{\sin 50°} = \dfrac{50}{\sin 45°}$ so $x = 54{\cdot}17$ m (to 2 d.p.)

$y = 180° - 50° - 45° = 85°$

$\dfrac{z}{\sin 85°} = \dfrac{50}{\sin 45°}$ so $z = 70{\cdot}44$ m (to 2 d.p.)

4 $\dfrac{143}{\sin 10°} = \dfrac{AX}{\sin 87°}$ so $AX = 822{\cdot}38$ km (to 2 d.p.)

5 $\cos B = \dfrac{15^2 + 18^2 - 17^2}{2 \times 15 \times 18}$ so $B = 61{\cdot}2°$ (to 1 d.p.) and $C = 68{\cdot}1°$ (to 1 d.p.)

6 $10{\cdot}18$ km (to 2 d.p.)

7 (a) $059°$ (b) $130{\cdot}5°$

4.10c

1

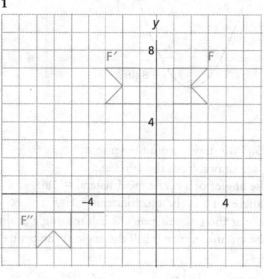

2 (a) & (b)

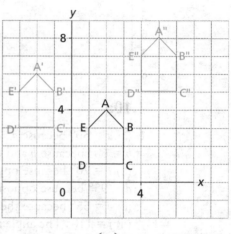

(c) $\begin{pmatrix} 3 \\ 4 \end{pmatrix}$ (d) $\begin{pmatrix} ^-3 \\ ^-4 \end{pmatrix}$

3 (a) & (b)

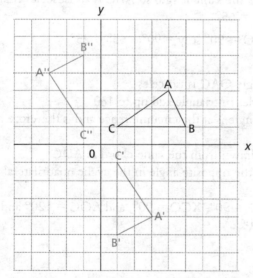

(c) $90°$ rotation about $(0, 0)$

(d) $270°$ or $^-90°$ rotation about $(0, 0)$

4 (a) & (b)

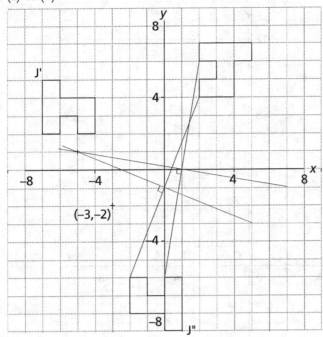

(c) ⁻90° rotation about (⁻5, 1)   (d) 90° rotation about (⁻5, 1)

5 translation $\begin{pmatrix} 2 \\ {}^{-}8 \end{pmatrix}$

6 (a) & (b)

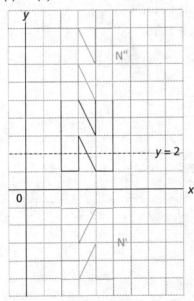

(c) translation $\begin{pmatrix} 4 \\ 0 \end{pmatrix}$

(d) translation $\begin{pmatrix} {}^{-}4 \\ 0 \end{pmatrix}$

7 (a) & (b)

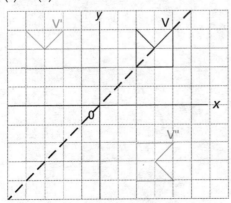

(c) rotation ⁻90° about (0, 0)

(d) rotation 90° about (0, 0)

8 (a) & (b)

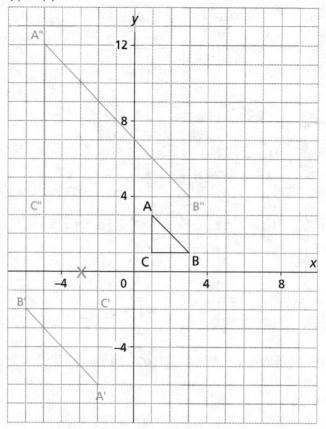

(c) enlargement centre (3, 0) scale factor 4

(d) enlargement centre (3, 0) scale factor $\frac{1}{4}$

9 (a) & (b)

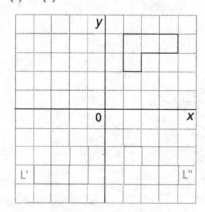

(c) reflection in the *x*-axis (*y* = 0)

10(a) & (b)   (c) rotation 180° about (⁻1, ⁻5)

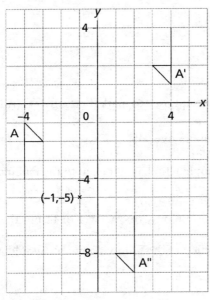

4.10d

1 (a) $\begin{pmatrix} 7 & 1 \\ 8 & 0 \end{pmatrix}$ (b) $\begin{pmatrix} 13 & 3 \\ 24 & 4 \end{pmatrix}$ (c) $\begin{pmatrix} 7 & 0 \\ 14 & ⁻7 \end{pmatrix}$

2 (a) stretch factor 3 parallel to the y-axis   (b) reflection in the x-axis

3 (a) rotation ⁻90° about (0, 0)
   (b) reflection in $y = x$ followed by a stretch factor 3 parallel to the x-axis

4 (a)

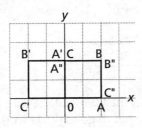

   (b) $\begin{pmatrix} 0 & 1 \\ 1 & 0 \end{pmatrix}$ (c) reflection in $y = x$

5 enlargement factor 16 centre (0, 0)

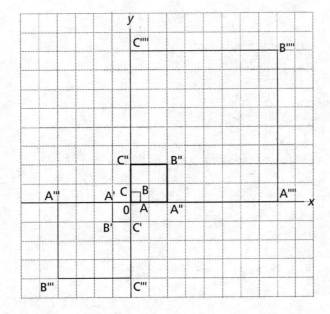

Section 5 answers

5.6a

1 All questions – how are respondents supposed to mark their answer? (ringing/crossing out/…?)

Q1 – There is no category for people over 45.

Q3 – What about divorced people?

Q4 – There is no category for people who haven't been to the cinema in the last 12 months.
  – The categories 11-20 and 20+ overlap.

Q5 – It doesn't say whether to choose only one answer or to put them in order of preference.

Q6 – This question should ask which of the following people would MOST like to see.

2 (a) The age of people surveyed.

(b) Ask people their age.

(c) Whether people surveyed have children or older relatives, how far away from the Community Centre they live (people may expect a youth club to be too noisy), what other facilities are available for the two groups, reports in the press.

3 (a)

Response	Tally	Frequency
A	HHT HHT |||	13
B	HHT HHT		11
C	HHT HHT HHT ||	17
D	HHT ||||	9
	Total	50

(b) Of the four destinations, the most popular is the USA and the least popular is the UK. Almost twice as many people would prefer to go to the USA than to holiday in this country. Spain and Greece are almost equally popular.

About one third of the people surveyed would prefer to go to the USA.

5.6b

1

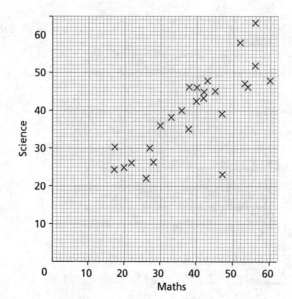

2 (a)

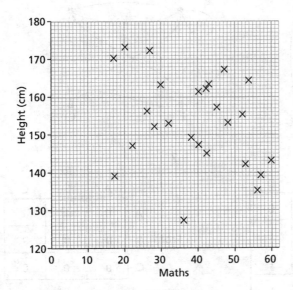

(b) The points are spread all over the graph. You can say that there appears to be no correlation.

5.6c

1 (a) £101·24   (b) £15 517·44

2 (a) £37·93 + £18·97 = £56·90   (b) £100 (over a year)

3

	Bs	Oc	Tcr	Gp	Pc	Ls	Cc
Bs		1	0	1	0	0	0
Oc	1		1	1	1	0	0
Tcr	0	1		0	0	1	0
Gp	1	1	0		1	0	1
Pc	0	1	0	1		1	1
Ls	0	0	1	0	1		1
Cc	0	0	0	1	1	1	

4 (a)

	P	Q	R	S
P	0	1	1	1
Q	1	0	1	1
R	1	1	0	0
S	1	1	0	0

(b)

	A	B	C	D
A	0	1	0	1
B	1	0	2	1
C	0	2	0	1
D	1	1	1	0

5 (a)   (b)

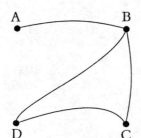
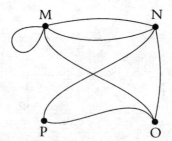

6

	A	B	C	D
A	3	1	1	0
B	1	2	1	1
C	1	1	2	1
D	0	1	1	1

7

		To		
		A	B	C
	A	0	1	1
From	B	0	0	2
	C	0	0	0

8 (a)   (b)

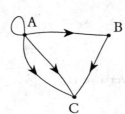

		To		
		A	B	C
	A	1	1	3
From	B	0	0	0
	C	0	0	0

5.6d

1 (a) $6 \times 6 = 36$ (b)

		first die					
		1	2	3	4	5	6
	1	1,1	2,1	3,1	4,1	5,1	6,1
	2	1,2	2,2	3,2	4,2	5,2	6,2
second	3	1,3	2,3	3,3	4,3	5,3	6,3
die	4	1,4	2,4	3,4	4,4	5,4	6,4
	5	1,5	2,5	3,5	4,5	5,5	6,5
	6	1,6	2,6	3,6	4,6	5,6	6,6

2 (a) AA, AB, AC, BA, BB, BC, CA, CB, CC

(b)   (c)

	2nd		
	A	B	C
1st A	AA	AB	AC
B	BA	BB	BC
C	CA	CB	CC

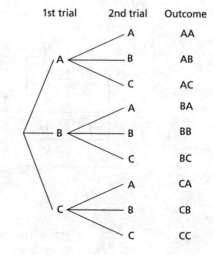

3

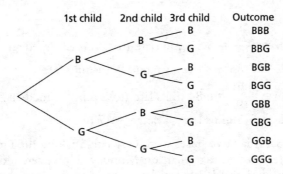

5.6e

1 (a) $\frac{1}{20}$ (b) $\frac{19}{20}$

2 $\frac{9}{13}$

3 $\frac{4}{5}$

4 $\frac{3}{8}$

5.7a

1 (a) girls and boys
  (b) what gender they are and how good at Maths they are
  (c) The girls' results are better so Ian's hypothesis is wrong.
  (d) The sample is very small. It only shows that in this particular class the girls got better Maths results than the boys.

2 (a) Survey motorists. Ask them who pays for their petrol and if they would pay more for unleaded petrol.
  (b) Survey pupils, parents, teachers and anyone else who works in the school. Ask for their opinions on this timetable.

5.7b

1 (a) & (b) Range = 53 – 16 = 37

A reasonable class interval is 5 cars, which gives 8 classes.

Cars	Tally	Frequency
15–19	|||	3
20–24	ЖЖТ	5
25–29	ЖЖТ ||	7
30–34	||||	4
35–39	ЖЖТ	5
40–44	|||	3
45–49	||	2
50–54			1
		Total 30

2 (a)

Class interval	Class mid-value
26–30	28
31–35	33
36–40	38
41–45	43
46–50	48
51–55	53

(b) $28 \times 1 + 33 \times 5 + 38 \times 3 + 43 \times 6 + 48 \times 6 + 53 \times 3 = 1012$

Mean $= \dfrac{1012}{24} = 42\cdot17$ kg (to 2 d.p.)

3 $\dfrac{935}{30} = 31\cdot17$ cars (to 2 d.p.)

5.7c

1 (a) mean = $\frac{124}{19}$ = 6·53 mins late (to 2 d.p.)   median = 6-8 mins late

   mode = 6-8 mins late   range = 14 mins late

(b) mean = $\frac{130}{19}$ = 6·84 mins late (to 2 d.p.)   median = 3-5 mins late

   mode = 3-5 mins late   range = 17 mins late

(c) On Saturday two buses were very late, making the mean number of minutes late greater on Saturday than on Monday. However, most buses on Saturday were between 3 and 5 minutes late. On Monday more buses were between 6 and 8 minutes late: most buses were between 3 and 8 minutes late.

5.7d

1 (a)

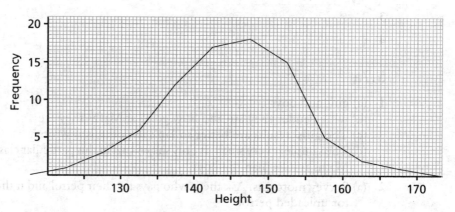

(b)

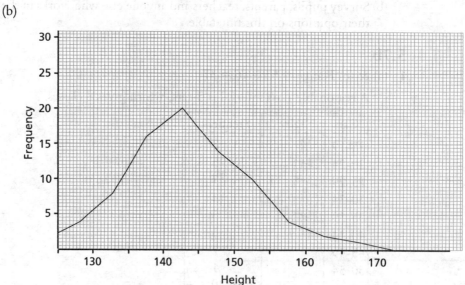

2 The highest point for the boys is behind (to the left of) the highest point for the girls. This means the boys are generally shorter. The polygon for the boys has a higher, narrower peak, which suggests their heights are more concentrated than the heights of the girls.

3 (a)

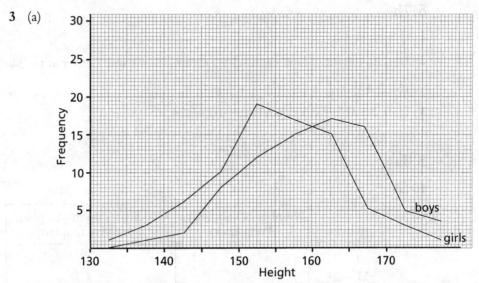

(b) By Year 10 the boys have generally become taller than the girls.

5.7e

1

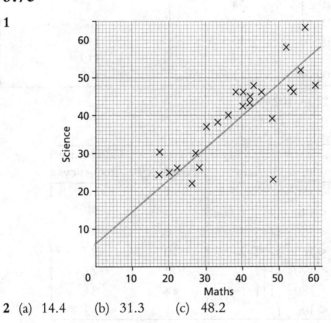

2 (a) 14.4   (b) 31.3   (c) 48.2

5.7f

1 Your experiment

2 (a) 10   (b) 3   (c) 3

3 $\frac{1}{8}$

5.7g

1 (a) Your estimate based on what you expect your next train journey to be and your experience of how late the train is likely to be on that route or at that time of day …

(b) If you know that your parents' car is outside the house and when you go outside that's the next car you'll see, then the probability is 1 if the car is a Ford and 0 if the car is not a Ford. If you are at school you could make an estimate based on what makes of car the teachers drive. Otherwise you can make an estimate based on the cars you generally see in your area. (About 20% of all cars sold in Britain are Fords.)

(c) Your estimate based on the time of year, recent weather patterns …

5.7h

1 $\frac{1}{6} + \frac{1}{6} = \frac{1}{3}$

2 (a) The biscuit chosen cannot be a cream biscuit and a wafer at the same time.

   (b) $\frac{4}{10} + \frac{2}{10} = \frac{6}{10} = \frac{3}{5}$ (c) $\frac{3}{10} + \frac{4}{10} = \frac{7}{10}$

3 (a) $0 \cdot 2 + 0 \cdot 3 = 0 \cdot 5$ (b) $0 \cdot 1 + 0 \cdot 3 = 0 \cdot 4$

5.8a

1 (a)

Marks	Number of candidates (Frequency)	Candidates up to this point (Cumulative frequency)
1 – 10	1	1
11 – 20	3	4
21 – 30	7	11
31 – 40	11	22
41 – 50	21	43
51 – 60	34	77
61 – 70	25	102
71 – 80	13	115
81 – 90	4	119
91 – 100	1	120

   (b) 11   (c) $120 - 102 = 18$

2 (a)

Height (cm)	Tally	Frequency	Cumulative frequency
$120 \leqslant h < 130$			1	1
$130 \leqslant h < 140$	|||	3	4
$140 \leqslant h < 150$	⊞		6	10
$150 \leqslant h < 160$	⊞ ⊞	10	20
$160 \leqslant h < 170$	⊞ ||	7	27
$170 \leqslant h < 180$	||||	4	31
$180 \leqslant h < 190$			1	32

   (b) 20   (c) $32 - 20 = 12$

3 (a) Range $= 4515 - 2150 = 2365$

   Class intervals of 500 g starting from 2 kg gives 6 classes.

Weight (kg)	Tally	Frequency	Cumulative frequency
$2 \leqslant w < 2.5$			1	1
$2.5 \leqslant w < 3$	||	2	3
$3 \leqslant w < 3.5$	⊞		6	9
$3.5 \leqslant w < 4$	⊞ ||	7	16
$4 \leqslant w < 4.5$	|||	3	19
$4.5 \leqslant w < 5$			1	20

   (b) 8

5.8b

1 (a)

Hours watched	Number of people	Cumulative frequency
< 15	1	1
< 20	2	3
< 25	7	10
< 30	11	21
< 35	25	46
< 40	23	69
< 45	17	86
< 50	10	96
< 55	3	99
< 60	1	100

(b)

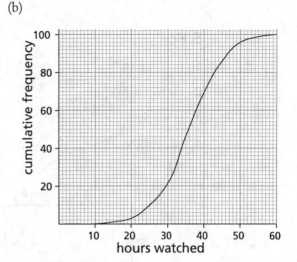

(c) 21

(d)

(e)

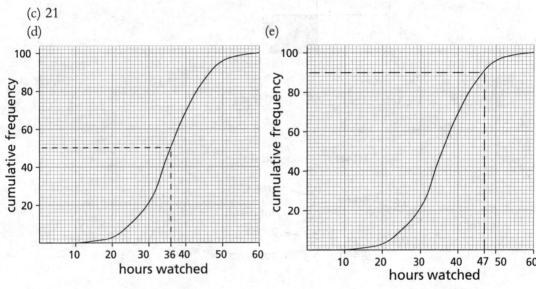

2 (a)

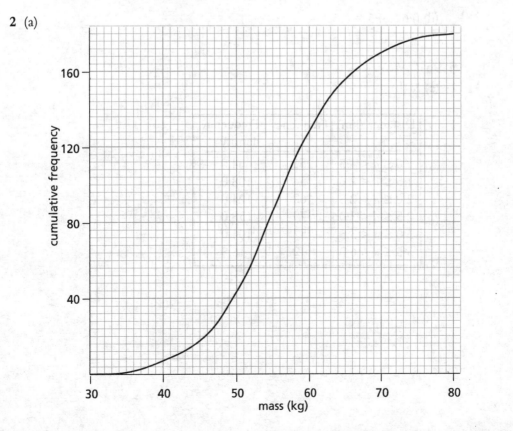

(b) (i) 7   (ii) 52   (iii) 56 kg   (iv) 59 kg   (v) 61 kg   (vi) 11 kg

(c) Half the people weigh between 50 kg and 61 kg.

5.8c

1 0

2 (a) (ii)   (b) (iii)

3 $\frac{1}{6} \times \frac{1}{2} = \frac{1}{12}$

4 (a) $\frac{1}{3} \times \frac{1}{3} = \frac{1}{9}$

(b)

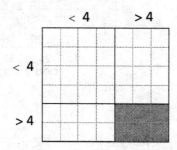

5 (a) $1 - 0.6 = 0.4$ (b) $1 - 0.5 = 0.5$

(c)

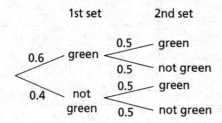

(d) $0.6 \times 0.5 = 0.3$

5.9a

1 (a) & (b)

Distance (km)	Frequency	Frequency density
$0 \le d < 1.5$	51	34.0
$1.5 \le d < 2.0$	54	108.0
$2.0 \le d < 2.5$	62	124.0
$2.5 \le d < 3.0$	79	158.0
$3.0 \le d < 3.5$	52	104.0
$3.5 \le d < 6.0$	42	16.8

(c)

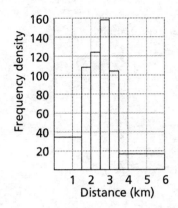

(d) The most commonly travelled distance is 2·5 to 3 km. Most people travel between 1·5 and 3·5 km. Very few people live more than 3·5 km from school.

5.9b

1 (a)

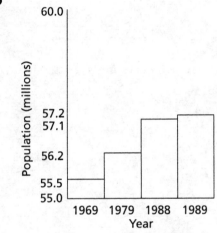

(b)

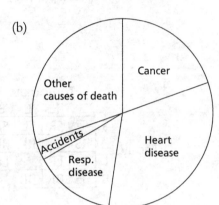

(c)

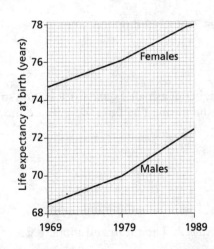

5.9c

1 (a) Test by sampling. Take into account shift, production line, etc.

(b) Test by sampling. Age, breed of cat

(c) Test by sampling. Various shops in a variety of areas, taking into account the age of customers, how much money they have, whether the shop is a specialist shop, etc.

(d) This cannot be tested by sampling. All cables must be tested as all must be safe.

2 Your experiment

5.9d

1

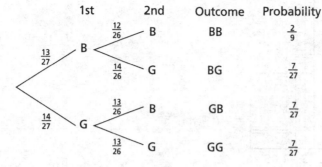

	1st	2nd	Outcome	Probability

$\frac{13}{27}$ B — $\frac{12}{26}$ B — BB — $\frac{2}{9}$

$\frac{14}{26}$ G — BG — $\frac{7}{27}$

$\frac{14}{27}$ G — $\frac{13}{26}$ B — GB — $\frac{7}{27}$

$\frac{13}{26}$ G — GG — $\frac{7}{27}$

2 (a) p(B) = $\frac{3}{9}$ and p(B/B) = $\frac{2}{8}$

  p(B and B) = $\frac{\cancel{3}^{1}}{\cancel{9}_{3}} \times \frac{\cancel{12}}{\cancel{8}_{4}} = \frac{1}{12}$

  (b) p(W) = $\frac{2}{9}$ and p(R/W) = $\frac{4}{8}$

  p(W then R) = $\frac{1}{9}$

3

Tomorrow

		S	R	L	B
	S		SR	SL	SB
Today	R	RS		RL	RB
	L	LS	LR		LB
	B	BS	BR	BL	

5.10a

1 mean = 5   standard deviation = 2·14 (to 2 d.p.)

2 (a) 8·66 (to 2 d.p.)

  (b) 8·76 (to 2 d.p.)

  (c) The girls have a greater mean height but a smaller standard deviation so their heights are more concentrated around the mean. The boys' heights are more spread.

3 507·5 ml

4 14%

5.10b

1 Histogram (a) is concentrated in 1 and 2. The mean and mode is 2.

Histogram (b) is symmetrical so the mean and median are equal to the middle value, 3. This is also the mode.

Histogram (c) represents a distribution in which all values occur with the same frequency. Hence the mean is again the middle value, 3.

2 (a) (i)   (b) (ii)

5.10c

1

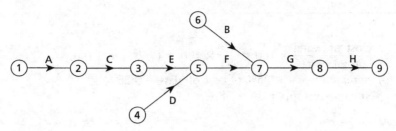

2 (a)

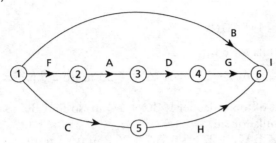

(b) $4\frac{1}{2}$ hours   (c) 3 pm

3 (a) Let x be the number of 24p stamps and y be the number of 32p stamps.

$x > y$

$x + y \geq 20$

$24x + 32y \leq 960$ or $3x + 4y \leq 120$

(b) 16

4 (a) 12   (b) 8

5.10d

1 (a) $\frac{4}{13} \times \frac{4}{13} = \frac{16}{169}$ (b) $\frac{9}{13} \times \frac{9}{13} = \frac{81}{169}$ (c) $1 - \frac{81}{169} = \frac{88}{169}$

2 (a)

1st car	2nd car	Outcome	Probability
R	R	RR	$\frac{5}{26}$
	B	RB	$\frac{5}{26}$
	W	RW	$\frac{1}{13}$
B	R	BR	$\frac{5}{26}$
	B	BB	$\frac{5}{39}$
	W	BW	$\frac{5}{78}$
W	R	WR	$\frac{1}{13}$
	B	WB	$\frac{5}{78}$
	W	WW	$\frac{1}{78}$

R branch: $\frac{6}{13}$; R $\frac{5}{12}$, B $\frac{5}{12}$, W $\frac{2}{12}$

B branch: $\frac{5}{13}$; R $\frac{6}{12}$, B $\frac{4}{12}$, W $\frac{2}{12}$

W branch: $\frac{2}{13}$; R $\frac{6}{12}$, B $\frac{5}{12}$, W $\frac{1}{12}$

(b) (i) $\frac{5}{39}$ (ii) $\frac{1}{3}$

(iii) p(first car blue) + p(first car not blue and second car blue) $= \frac{5}{13} + \frac{8}{13} \times \frac{5}{12} = \frac{25}{39}$

3 (a) $\dfrac{22 + 63}{120} = \dfrac{17}{24}$ (b) $\dfrac{63}{63 + 29} = \dfrac{63}{92}$

(c) $\frac{22}{120} \times \frac{29}{119} + \frac{29}{120} \times \frac{22}{119} = \frac{319}{3570}$

Answers to exam questions

1 (a) $\dfrac{\text{Cost of water}}{\text{total cost}} \times 100 = \dfrac{7}{55} \times 100 = 12\cdot7\%$ (to 1 d.p.)

(b) Increase in cost = 25% of cost of glass = $0\cdot25 \times 12\text{p} = 3\text{p}$
New cost = 55p + 3p = 58p

2 (a) $x(x - 3)$

(b) $pq(2p + q)$

3 (i) $\angle\,\text{BAC} = 90° - 14° = 76°$

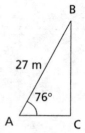

Using the formula for cos,

$\text{AC} = \text{AB} \cos \angle\,\text{BAC} = 27 \times \cos 76° = 6\cdot53$ m (to 2 d.p.)

(ii) Vertical height of top of ladder is BC + 2·3 m, so find BC to 1 d.p.
Using the formula for sin,
$\text{BC} = \text{AB} \sin \angle\,\text{BAC} = 27 \times \sin 76° = 26\cdot2$ m (to 1 d.p.)
Height of top of ladder = 26·2 m + 2·3 m = 28·5 m (to 1 d.p.)

4 Volume of buoy = volume of cone + volume of hemisphere
$= \frac{1}{3}\pi r^2 h + \frac{2}{3}\pi r^3$
$= \frac{1}{3}\pi(0\cdot95^2 \times 1\cdot2 + 2 \times 0\cdot95^3) = \frac{1}{3}\pi \times 2\cdot79775 = 2\cdot93$ m³ (to 2 d.p.)

5 (a) 66 kg
(b) Total number of parts in ratio = 33 + 5 + 7 = 45

Method 1: Divide 900 kg by number of parts
$\frac{900}{45} = 20$
7 parts charcoal = 7×20 kg = 140 kg

Method 2: Amount of charcoal = $\frac{7}{45} \times 900$ kg = 140 kg

(c) % sulphur = $\frac{5}{45} \times 100 = 11\cdot11\%$ (to 2 d.p.)

6 (a) Draw a horizontal line joining C to AB, meeting AB at X.
AD and CX are parallel so angles BAD and BXC are equal (corresponding angles).
Length of BX = AB − CD = 55·9 − 54·8 = 1·1 m
$\angle\,\text{CBX} = 90°$

$\tan \angle\,\text{BXC} = \dfrac{\text{BC}}{\text{BX}} = \dfrac{13\cdot2}{1\cdot1}$

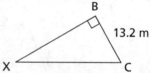

$\angle\,\text{BAD} = 85\cdot24°$ (to 2 d.p.)
(b) By Pythagoras, $\text{CX}^2 = \text{BC}^2 + \text{BX}^2$

$\text{AD} = \text{CX} = \sqrt{13\cdot2^2 + 1\cdot1^2} = \sqrt{175\cdot45} = 13\cdot25$ m (to 2 d.p.)

7 (a) 56
(b) The difference between the terms increases by 2 each time.
(c) Because the sequence starts with an even number and all the values added on are even.
(d) (i) 1, 3, 6, 10, 15, 21
(ii) Each term of the first sequence is twice the corresponding term of this sequence. Hence the formula is $s = n(n + 1)$.

8 (a) $(4 \times 10^{10}) \times (2 \times 10^{-3}) = 8 \times 10^7 = 80\ 000\ 000$ kg

(b) $(8 \times 10^7) \div 10^3 = 8 \times 10^4 = 80\ 000$ acres

9 (a) 1 litre = 1000 ml so 2 litres = 2000 ml
2000 ml ÷ 125 ml = 16 seconds
(b) (i) and (ii)

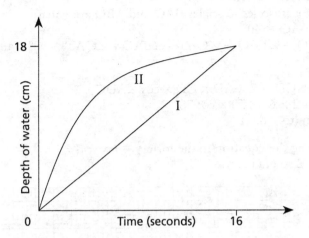

10

(a)

t	0	1	2	3	4	5	6	7	8	9
d	10	9.46	8	6	4	2.54	2	2.54	4	6

(b)

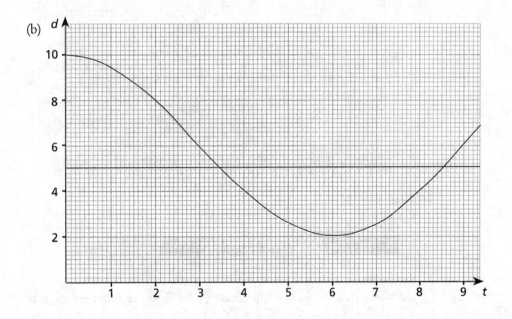

(c) Between 3·30 p.m. and 8·30 p.m.

11 Substituting in 2 gives 2 × 3 = 6
Substituting in 3 gives 3 × 4 = 12
The solution must be nearer 3 than 2 so try 2·7.
2·7 × 3·7 = 9·99 which is very close so try 2·71
2·71 × 3·71 = 10·05 which is just too big
Try 2·705 to check whether to round up or down.
2·705 × 3·705 = 10·02 so round down
$x = 2·70$ (to 2 d.p.)

12 (i) Tangent to a circle makes a right angle with the radius
so ∠OAT = ∠OBT = 90°
Angle sum of a quadrilateral = 360°
Applying to AOBT, ∠ATB = 360° − 90° − 90° − 100° = 80°

(ii) Angles subtended by same chord are equal

so $\angle BPQ = \angle BAQ$

Angle sum of triangle $= 180°$ and $\angle AOB = 100°$

so $\angle BAO + \angle ABO = 80°$

ABO is isosceles so angles BAO and ABO are equal

so $\angle BAO = 40°$

$\angle BPQ = \angle BAQ = \angle OAT - \angle BAO - \angle QAT = 90° - 40° - 30° = 20°$

13 Using cosine rule,

$AC^2 = AD^2 + CD^2 - 2 \times AD \times CD \times \cos \angle ADC$

$= 60^2 + 50^2 - 2 \times 60 \times 50 \times \cos 78°$

$AC = 69{\cdot}7$ m (to 1 d.p.)

14 (a) Rearranging the equation in the form $y = mx + c$,

$y = \frac{1}{2}x + 2$ so gradient is $\frac{1}{2}$

(b)

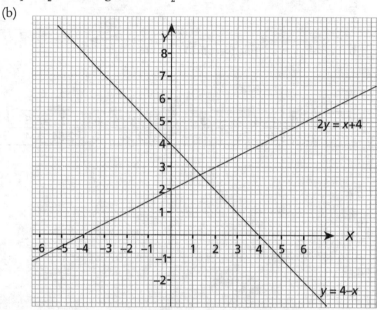

(c) Solutions are given by the point of intersection of the lines,

$x = 1{\cdot}3$ and $y = 2{\cdot}7$. (Check: $4 - 1{\cdot}3 = 2{\cdot}7$)

15 $7 \tan x° = 4$

$\tan x° = \frac{4}{7}$

$$\boxed{4} \; \boxed{\div} \; \boxed{7} \; \boxed{=} \; \boxed{0.5714285} \; \boxed{\text{INV}} \; \boxed{\text{tan}} \; \boxed{29.744881}$$

So one solution is $x = 29{\cdot}7°$ (to 1 d.p.)

tan is also positive in third quadrant (CAST) so the other solution is

$x = 180° + 29{\cdot}7° = 209{\cdot}7°$ (to 1 d.p.)

16 (a) P(both yellow) = P(yellow) $\times$ P(yellow) = $\frac{1}{3} \times \frac{1}{3} = \frac{1}{9}$

(b) (i)

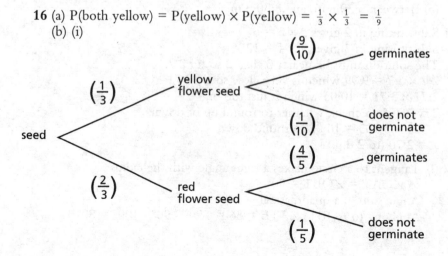

(ii) P(seed is yellow and germinates) = $\frac{1}{3} \times \frac{9}{10} = \frac{9}{30}$

P(seed is red and germinates) = $\frac{2}{3} \times \frac{8}{10} = \frac{16}{30}$

P(seed germinates) = $\frac{9}{30} + \frac{16}{30} = \frac{25}{30} = \frac{5}{6}$

17 (a) Each term is double the previous term. $u_n = 2u_{n-1}$

(b) Dividing through by 3 gives 1, 2, 4, 8, ...

These are all powers of 2,

$2^0, 2^1, 2^2, 2^3, ...$

The power of 2 is 1 less than the number of the term so

$u_n = 3 \times 2^{n-1}$

18 (a) Horizontal surface area = 5 × width of surface

For safety, surface area ≥ 2 m

5 × width ≥ 2 m

width ≥ $\frac{2}{5}$ = 0·4 m

(b) This depth of liquid can be safely stored if the width (w) of the horizontal surface of the liquid is greater than or equal to 0·4 m.

Using Pythagoras,

$(\frac{1}{2}w)^2 + 0.8^2 = 1^2$

$w^2 = 4 \times 0.36 = 1.44$

$w = 1.2$ m so the liquid can be safely stored

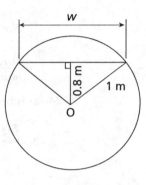

19 (a) (i) $\frac{1}{6}\pi d^3 + \frac{1}{4}\pi d^2 h$

(ii) Both parts of the expression must involve volume. Hence in each part the power of d and the power of h must add to 3.

(b) $\pi d^2 + \pi dh$

20 (a) and (b)

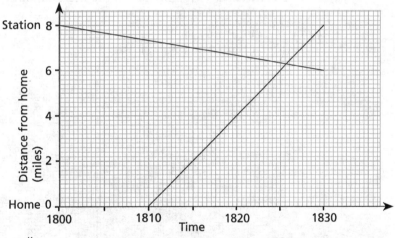

21 (a)

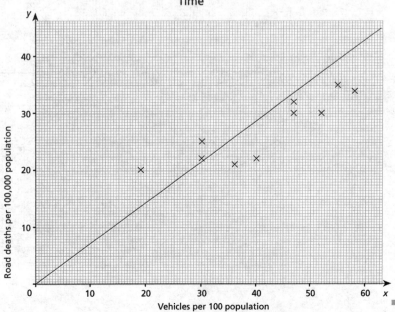

(b) approximately $y = \frac{30}{42} x$ or $y = \frac{5}{6} x$

22 (a) Area of whole disc $= \pi r^2$, $r = \frac{13}{2} = 6 \cdot 5$ cm

$$\boxed{\pi} \boxed{\times} \boxed{6} \boxed{\cdot} \boxed{5} \boxed{x^2} \boxed{=} \quad \boxed{132.73229}$$

Area $= 132 \cdot 73$ cm² (to 2 d.p.)

(b) Area of centre $= \pi r^2$, $r = \frac{6 \cdot 6}{2} = 3 \cdot 3$ cm

Shaded area = whole disc − centre

$$\boxed{\pi} \boxed{\times} \boxed{6} \boxed{\cdot} \boxed{5} \boxed{x^2} \boxed{-} \boxed{\pi} \boxed{\times} \boxed{3} \boxed{\cdot} \boxed{3} \boxed{x^2} \boxed{=} \quad \boxed{98.520346}$$

Shaded area $= 98 \cdot 52$ cm² (to 2 d.p.)

(c) $\dfrac{\text{Shaded area}}{\text{total area}} \times 100 = \dfrac{98 \cdot 520}{132 \cdot 732} \times 100 = 74 \cdot 22\%$ (to 2 d.p.)

23 (a) Ratio is $2 \cdot 87 \times 10^9 : 5 \cdot 97 \times 10^7$

$$\boxed{2} \boxed{\cdot} \boxed{8} \boxed{7} \boxed{\text{EXP}} \boxed{9} \boxed{\div} \boxed{5} \boxed{\cdot} \boxed{9} \boxed{7} \boxed{\text{EXP}} \boxed{7} \boxed{=} \quad \boxed{48.073702}$$

So the ratio is 48 : 1

(b) Time taken = distance ÷ speed $= (7 \cdot 78 \times 10^8) \div (3 \times 10^5)$

$$\boxed{7} \boxed{\cdot} \boxed{7} \boxed{8} \boxed{\text{EXP}} \boxed{8} \boxed{\div} \boxed{3} \boxed{\text{EXP}} \boxed{5} \boxed{=} \boxed{\div} \boxed{6} \boxed{0} \boxed{=} \quad \boxed{43.222222}$$

Time taken = 43 minutes (to the nearest minute)

24 (a) $\begin{pmatrix} 1 & 1 \\ {}^-1 & 1 \end{pmatrix} \begin{pmatrix} 5 & 0 \\ 0 & 3 \end{pmatrix} = \begin{pmatrix} 5 & 3 \\ {}^-5 & 3 \end{pmatrix}$

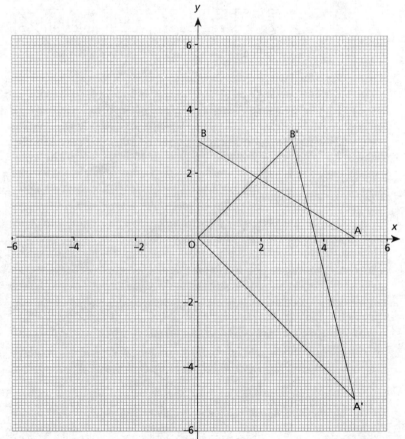

(b) (i) 45°

(ii) By Pythagoras, $OB'^2 = 3^2 + 3^2 = 2 \times 3^2$

$OB' = 3\sqrt{2}$

Scale factor $= \dfrac{OB'}{OB} = \dfrac{3\sqrt{2}}{3} = \sqrt{2}$

(c) Since $\begin{pmatrix} 1 & 0 \\ 0 & 1 \end{pmatrix}$ is the identity, OAB has to be rotated back to its original position.

Since the rotation caused by **M** is 45° it will require 8 applications of **M** to return the triangle to its original position. Hence $n = 8$.

At the same time the triangle will be enlarged by a factor of $\sqrt{2}$ to the power 8.

$(\sqrt{2})^8 = 16$. Hence $k = 16$.

25 Multiply 2 m by 0·7 for each bounce.

| 2 | × | . | 7 | x^y | 3 | = | | 0.686 |

On the third bounce the ball reaches a height of 69 cm (to 2 s.f.).

26 (a) To find a divide the coefficient of x (the number in front of the x term) by 2.
$(x + \frac{5}{2})^2 = (x + 2·5)^2 = x^2 + 5x + 6·25$

Hence $x^2 + 5x - 7 = (x + 2·5)^2 - 6·25 - 7 = (x + 2·5)^2 - 13·25$

(b) $(x + 2·5)^2 = 13·25$

$x + 2·5 = \pm\sqrt{13·25}$

$x = {}^-2·5 \pm \sqrt{13·25}$

| 2 | . | 5 | +/− | + | 1 | 3 | . | 2 | 5 | √ | Min | = | | 1.1400549 |

| 2 | . | 5 | +/− | − | MR | = | | −6.140059 |

$x = 1·14$ or $^-6·14$ (to 2 d.p.)

27 (a) The solutions occur where the line $y = 10$ cuts the curve. Correct to the nearest integer, the solutions are $x = {}^-3$, $x = 0$ and $x = 3$.

(b) (i)

| 1 | 0 | + | 1 | ÷ | 3 | = | √ | | 3.2145503 |

| 3.2145503 | 1/x | + | 1 | 0 | = | √ | | 3.2110879 |

$u_2 = 3·2145503$
$u_3 = 3·2110879$

(ii) 3·21

(c) (i) $x^2 - \dfrac{1}{x} = 10$

$x^2 = 10 + \dfrac{1}{x}$

$x^2 - 10 = \dfrac{1}{x}$

$x(x^2 - 10) = 1$

$x = \dfrac{1}{x^2 - 10}$

(ii) Let $u_1 = 0$
$u_2 = -0.1$

$\boxed{\cdot}\ \boxed{1}\ \boxed{x^2}\ \boxed{-}\ \boxed{1}\ \boxed{0}\ \boxed{=}\ \boxed{1/x}\ \boxed{-0.1001001}$

$u_3 = -0.1001001$
Solution is -0.10 (to 2 d.p.)

(d) $u_{n+1} = \sqrt{10 + \dfrac{1}{u_n}}$

Let $u_1 = -3$

$\boxed{1}\ \boxed{0}\ \boxed{-}\ \boxed{1}\ \boxed{\div}\ \boxed{3}\ \boxed{=}\ \boxed{\sqrt{}}\ \boxed{+/-}\ \boxed{-3.1091264}$

$\boxed{-3.1091264}\ \boxed{1/x}\ \boxed{+}\ \boxed{1}\ \boxed{0}\ \boxed{=}\ \boxed{\sqrt{}}\ \boxed{+/-}\ \boxed{-3.1110073}$

$u_2 = -3.1091264$
$u_3 = -3.1110073$
Solution is -3.11 (to 2 d.p.)